ACTIVITY-BASED COSTING

Making It Work for Small and Mid-Sized Companies

SECOND EDITION

ACTIVITY-BASED COSTING

Making It Work for Small and Mid-Sized Companies

SECOND EDITION

Douglas T. Hicks

JOHN WILEY & SONS, INC.

New York • Chichester • Weinheim • Brisbane • Singapore • Toronto

This book is printed on acid-free paper.

Published simultaneously in Canada.

Library of Congress Cataloging-in-Publication Data:

Hicks, Douglas T.
Activity-based costing : making it work for small and mid-sized companies / Douglas T. Hicks—2nd ed.
p. cm.
Includes bibliographic references and index.
ISBN 0-471-24959-9 (cloth : alk. paper)
1. Activity-based costing. 2. Small business—Accounting. I. Title.
HF5686.C8H49 1998
657'.42—DC21 98-24486
CIP

Printed in the United States of America

10 9 8 7 6 5 4 3 2

First edition of this work was entitled Activity-Based Costing: An Implementation Guide.

To Judi,
my bride of 29 years,
and the four greatest kids on earth,
Jonathan, Meredith, Marcella, and Melanie

Contents

Preface

A fellow consultant recently asked me, "What would you do if, all of a sudden, you couldn't sell activity-based costing any more?" His question was obviously intended to find out what TLA (three-letter acronym) or "non-acronym" management concept I would pursue instead of activity-based costing (ABC). The implication was that an ABC consultant in a world without ABC is analogous to a tax consultant in a world without taxes or an ISO 9000 consultant without ISO 9000. Obviously, if there are no taxes, there is no need for a tax consultant. Similarly, if there is no ISO 9000, there is no need for an ISO 9000 consultant. It would seem logical, then, that if there is no ABC, there is no need for an ABC consultant. Although his question was well intended, his logic was faulty.

Many consultants—tax consultants, ISO 9000 consultants, government contracting consultants, and others—become expert in a man-made body of rules, regulations, and procedures. They then help clients comply with, work around, or exploit these rules, regulations, and procedures to their greatest advantage. If the man-made body of knowledge is made obsolete, there will be no more work for the consultant until he or she finds a new area in which to gain expertise. This is nothing like the situation with ABC.

Although many consultants seem to treat it as such, activity-based costing is not a man-made body of rules, regulations, and procedures. Instead, it is a form of language that has been developed to describe certain laws of nature: the laws of nature that relate to cost behavior. If the language becomes obsolete, the laws of nature will not change. Costs will continue to behave in the same manner as they did when the language of ABC existed. Another language will be developed to describe the very same laws.

In answer to the consultant's question, I indicated that I would continue to do the same type of work I do now, I would just call it something different, as I did in the years before the phrase *activity-based costing* became popular. The name is not important, but the concepts are. Whether called activity-based costing, KapCooplian accounting, or Fido, the concepts underlying cost behavior remain the same.

In this book, I have attempted to keep my description of the nature and use of "activity-based" cost information in terms understandable to accountant and nonaccountant alike. I am simply describing the "activity-based" laws of nature that relate to the behavior of costs in small to mid-sized businesses as I see them and how the small to mid-sized business can exploit these laws to make better business decisions. I have deliberately attempted to avoid as much "ABC jargon" as possible in this book. To some, the jargon enhances the credibility of the concept and makes it seem like a more legitimate "body of knowledge." To me, the jargon simply turns a robust, living concept into a mechanical, inflexible system.

There are no footnotes in this book. The major reason for this is that I seldom read anything about activity-based costing. Yes, I have cost and management accounting books and periodicals on my bookshelves and lying about the office, but they are there for show. Someone in my business is expected to have those things around. I do not read them. One reason is that they are somewhat boring. Unlike Sherlock Holmes, who complained that Dr. Watson "degraded what should have been a course of lectures into a series of tales" (*The Copper Beeches*), my complaint is that ABC writers degrade what should be a series of tales that promote the understanding of cost behavior into a course of lectures that emphasize computational virtuosity. One of the objectives of this book is to express activity-based concepts in a way that will enable the reader to see costs through the "lens" of activity-based costing, not to see every cost as the result of a series of complex computations.

Another reason for my avoidance of most ABC literature is its lack of perspective. It assumes that all companies are large and that all things that can be calculated should be calculated. It relates experiences or examples from Fortune 1000 or similar-sized companies and then uses them to arrive at "universal" truths. Some of those truths may apply to the universe of Fortune 1000 companies, but Fortune 1000 companies make up only a small fraction of the universe itself. Another objective of this book is to stick to the universal truths about ABC—truths that apply to any organization of any size.

As you will find in this book, there are three things that are required for cost information to be used effectively: (1) the business must start with costs that are defined and measured properly; (2) costs, activities, and products or services must be connected by true cause/effect relationships; and

(3) the resulting cost information must be used in appropriate ways. Activity-based costing literature tends to overkill the second item while ignoring the first and third. Another of this book's objectives is to emphasize the importance of the "total package" of cost information, not just the computational purity.

This does not mean that the ideas presented in this book were developed in isolation from mainstream ABC. My clients, friends, and associates see to that. They attend conferences and seminars (other than mine) and read a lot of ABC literature. Their questions, comments, and challenges keep me abreast of the good, the bad, and the ugly in the ABC industry. Especially helpful in recent years have been Ravi Nayar of BDO Seidman, Steve Martin of Geo. S. Olive & Company, Jill Gumpf of Otterbein Homes (especially regarding ABC in the health care industry), and Gary Cokins of ABC Technologies.

One thing that readers of my first book will notice is that I have used the more conventional capitalized three-letter acronym ABC instead of insisting on the lowercase abc. There are several reasons for this change, but the most important reason is that three lowercase letters that do not make up a real word look silly in the middle of a sentence. What I describe in this book is still activity-based costing, the concept to adopt, not Activity-Based Costing, the system to install. The form of the acronym is not really relevant. I have, however, avoided any of the other "ABs" such as ABM (activity-based management) or ABB (activity-based budgeting). In my view, ABC encompasses them all. ABM and ABB are simply things one does with activity-based costing's concepts. The power is in the concept. No additional three letter acronyms are needed to describe using the concept.

This book can be divided into five sections. The first section addresses some general issues regarding ABC. The text begins with a discussion of the first decade of ABC and how it has fallen short of the acceptance levels that the soundness of the concept should have led it to attain (Chapter 1). I then present the "Strange Case of Ace Manufacturing," a composite of the experiences of several companies when they attempted to improve their cost systems by making piecemeal corrections to their traditional costing practices (Chapter 2).

The second section covers the theory of ABC, from defining and measuring costs, to developing an activity-based cost structure, to using activity-based cost information in the support of management decisions. A definition of activity-based costing is provided, which clearly shows its relevance for small and mid-sized organizations (Chapter 3). I then describe the importance of determining true economic costs (Chapter 4) instead of simply using general ledger costs calculated using generally accepted accounting principles (GAAP). In Chapter 5, the framework that can be used to establish an accurate cost flow-down structure for any business is described. To reinforce this "logic of activity-based costing," Chapter 6 walks the reader through the application of that logic to a small distribution company. Chapter 7 describes the appropriate use of activity-based cost information in a wide variety of decision situations. After providing a package of practical activity-based cost modeling tools (Chapter 8), I proceed to reinforce both the development of a business' ABC structure and the use of activity-based modeling tools through two case studies of out-of-the-ordinary businesses based on two of my "real life" clients (Chapter 9).

In the third section, I describe how all this theory can be used to develop a spreadsheet-based cost accumulation and distribution model of a company. After explaining the general structure for building such a model (Chapter 10), I describe the situation at Small Time Manufacturing, a small contract manufacturer that will serve as an example for both building and using a model to support management's decision-making processes (Chapter 11). In Chapters 12 and 13, step-by-step instructions are provided for building a cost accumulation and distribution model that will enable Small Time Manufacturing to develop both the fully absorbed and incremental costs its management will need to make sound, fact-based decisions.

The fourth section shows how the concept of ABC, supported by an activity-based cost accumulation and distribution model, can be used to provide management with accurate and relevant decision costing information. Continuing the Small Time Manufacturing example, I explain how ABC can be used to support product pricing decisions and product/ product line drop/add decisions (Chapter 14), how the model can be used in its "what if?" mode to support capital expenditure decisions, direct continuous improvement efforts, and to evaluate "special order" opportunities (Chapter 15), and how the model can be used to support multiyear pricing decisions (Chapter 16).

The final section discusses impediments to the adoption of ABC by small and mid-sized organizations (Chapter 17) and summarizes the need for an approach to activity-based cost information at small and mid-sized businesses (Chapter 18).

An activity-based approach to cost information is not an option for businesses hoping to succeed in the next millennium—it is a requirement. That does not mean, however, that every company has to implement a complicated ABC system. It means that every company must have a means of determining its true economic costs, an understanding of the behavior of those costs and how they relate to its products and services, and the ability to use its knowledge of product and process costs to make sound, fact-based business decisions. The theories and methods described in this book will enable small and mid-sized businesses to benefit from the new management concept today, thereby strengthening the probability of their continued success tomorrow.

I have become indebted to many in the preparation of this work. D. T. Hicks & Co.'s "regulars" have helped to develop and prove the book's concepts for more than a hundred clients during the past 13 years. These include Gordon Nelson, Dan Popa, Bill Mooney, Rand Urbin, Jill Gumpf, and Monica Fox. Gordon was able to "hold down the fort" while I sequestered myself to work on the manuscript, and he continued to remind me that I am neither Charles Horngren nor Charles Dickens, just a simple consultant. I will always be indebted to both Jerry D. Pierick and Alex Jackson III, whose guidance and encouragement in the early 1980s led to many of the unconventional views presented in this book. Finally, I am indebted to my son, Jonathan D. Hicks, whose computer graphic skills made possible the methods used to visualize the ABC concepts and techniques presented in this book.

Douglas T. Hicks

Farmington Hills, Michigan
October 30, 1998

ACTIVITY-BASED COSTING

Making It Work for Small and Mid-Sized Companies

SECOND EDITION

1

Activity-Based Costing: The First Decade

The basic concepts and mechanics of activity-based costing (ABC) have been around for decades. For a variety of reasons, however, they were seldom used. Although cost accounting and transaction recording were the two key driving forces in the development of accounting ideas prior to the twentieth century, several key events during this century placed cost accounting squarely in the "back seat" of accounting theory and practice.

PRE-ABC ERA

As the century began, specialized branches of accounting were not necessary. When the first decade introduced a federal income tax, a new specialized area began—tax accounting. In the 1930s, when the Security and Exchange Acts placed a greater emphasis on financial accounting, cost accounting was split off as a separate discipline, with financial accounting surviving as the mainstream of accounting. Because tax and financial accounting practices are mandated by law or regulation, compliance with them is not optional. As a result, organizations spent most of their accounting resources on these two areas. Cost accounting was made a stepchild and relegated to a role of supporting its two law- and regulation-backed siblings.

As the century continued, events such as the compilation of the Internal Revenue Code (IRC) in 1954 and the creation of the Financial Accounting Standards Board (FASB) in the early 1970s, placed even greater emphasis on the compliance aspects of accounting, aspects served by financial and tax accounting. Cost accounting developed somewhat during this period but, in keeping with its second-class citizen status, was severely limited in its ability to keep up with changing times.

Perhaps the complacency of a United States growing into an industrial giant while other countries' economies were being decimated by two world wars also suppressed any interest in the development of cost accounting. U.S. companies did not need to know their costs very well because the United States was the only nation that still had companies capable of mass-producing quality products for use within the country as well as worldwide. Fortunately, as the country's grip on industrial supremacy began to slip in the 1970s and early 1980s, knowledgeable individuals began to question the relevance of traditional cost accounting practices. They noted that, unlike financial and tax accounting, which serve to keep an organization in compliance with laws and regulations, *an organization's cost accounting information can actually make or break an otherwise sound business.*

PRIMARY PURPOSE OF COST INFORMATION

The reason faulty cost information can have such a devastating impact on an organization can be seen from a listing of uses and users of cost accounting information:

Use	*User*
Overall inventory valuation	Outsiders
Overall cost of goods sold	Outsiders
Strategic planning	Management
Capital budgeting	Management
Operational planning	Management
Operational budgeting	Management
Product cost control	Management
Process cost control	Management
Product costing/pricing	Management
Decision modeling	Management
Financial analysis	Management

It is easy to see from this listing who ranks as the major user of cost information. Management uses cost information regularly in its strategic and tactical decision making. Outsiders care only that the organization's overall cost of goods sold and inventory valuation are correct.

Why was it, then, that most cost accounting systems were (and in most cases still are) based on laws, regulations, and pronouncements of tax and financial accounting authorities? A major reason was that many accountants in industry came from financial or public accounting backgrounds. They carried the outside reporting orientation of their prior positions with them to their roles in industry. The possibility that something may be wrong with using financial reporting-oriented cost data in making management decisions simply never occurred to them.

Another reason was the misconception that maintaining two cost systems is too expensive and the benefits of having the second system cannot outweigh its additional expense. Because the tax and financial rules carry the weight of law, there is no option but to have a system that keeps the organization in compliance. A cost system that reflects reality is optional. The decision on a second system was easy if management believed such a system would be too costly.

A third reason was that the simple, extremely generalized costing practices, such as those allowed to comply with financial and tax requirements, were within the computational limitations of manual and pre-1980 computer systems. It was difficult enough to install a system that could simply track direct labor or machine hours. Developing one any more complex was out of the question.

For these and other reasons, day-to-day cost accounting systems were developed to support financial and tax accounting. Throughout the development of accounting during the first eight decades of this century, this practice held until it evolved into an accepted law of nature: An organization's cost accounting system exists to support its financial and tax accounting systems. This was the "first philosophical error" in the establishment of most cost systems. Some rudimentary system must exist that will enable a company to comply with financial and tax requirements, but an organization's cost system should be designed to provide management with the cost information it needs to make sound business decisions.

DAWN OF THE ABC ERA

In the early 1980s, challenges began to the ways in which cost information was calculated and used. Individuals such as Robert Kaplan, Robin Cooper, H. Thomas Johnson, Peter Turney, and Eli Goldratt began challenging the relevance of traditional costing practices in articles, books, and speeches. Goldratt's now famous statement that "cost accounting is the number one enemy of productivity" was a particularly effective "call to arms." As a result, academics, practitioners, and associations began to develop new approaches to cost information. These included Drs. Kaplan, Cooper, Johnson, and

Turney, as well as organizations like the Consortium for Advanced Manufacturing International (CAM-I), Institute of Management Accountants (IMA), and the Society of Management Accountants of Canada (SMAC). The efforts of these and many other individuals and groups developed a body of knowledge that came to be known as *Activity-Based Costing*, or simply *ABC*, in the late 1980s.

As often happens, the development of a catchy title that can be represented by a TLA (three-letter acronym) kicked off the establishment of a new industry: "The ABC Industry." Software packages were developed to assist in the implementation of ABC. Expensive seminars were offered to educate potential users in the theory and use of ABC. Academics sought to "outdo" each other with new and better ways to describe, define, and design ABC systems. Large accounting and consulting firms established their own "ABC Consulting Groups" to perform six-figure consulting projects. Smaller firms sent their accountants and industrial engineers to seminars to become instant "ABC Experts" and begin their ABC practices. To add more prestige to the subject, some began calling it activity-based management (ABM) or activity-based budgeting (ABB), both of which can basically be defined as using activity-based costing information to better manage the business. Some consultants in related areas began calling their services ABC to attract more clients. Like many other concepts, proponents of ABC/ABM/ABB began placing its position at the center of the universe with all other disciplines revolving around it.

As all this activity has taken place, the complexity of ABC has grown. It has begun to develop its own nomenclature. Instead of being a concept to adopt, it has become a system to implement. To many, the software, not the concept, has become activity-based costing. The perception that ABC is a complex set of mechanics that must be integrated into an organization's day-to-day reporting systems has become widespread. Attempts have been made to codify the procedures for implementing ABC, almost as if they were a tax code or body of financial pronouncements. Activity-based costing has begun to become an end in itself, not a means to an end. So much focus has been placed on the various implementation tools that have been developed to accommodate ABC's growing complexity that the tools themselves have become mistaken for the concept.

ABC AT SMALL AND MID-SIZED BUSINESSES

It is suggested that the high cost and complexity of ABC has discouraged most small and mid-sized organizations from improving their cost information. In both its 1996 and 1997 Activity-Based Costing Surveys, the Cost Management Group of the IMA found that size was a significant factor in whether an organization adopted ABC. Whereas sales of firms adopting ABC averaged $101 to $500 million, nonadopters' sales were in the $11 to $100 million range. No mention was made of organizations with sales below $11 million, which would lead to the conclusion that adoption in that group was almost nil. The report stated that "several companies cited the lack of resources (people and dollars) as a reason for not adopting ABC," and "this issue is probably most prevalent in smaller companies."

As will be discussed in Chapter 17, it is not the lack of resources that keeps small firms from adopting ABC, it is the *perceived* lack of resources that does so. Word gets around about six-figure consulting fees, hundreds of person-days of work, massive data collection efforts, new software, and expensive system conversions. No wonder smaller organizations believe they do not have the resources to undertake a project to adopt ABC! Fortunately, this perception is incorrect. Activity-based costing is a beautifully simple concept that can be adopted in a wide variety of ways. The complex, integrated systems devised by consultants and software companies are not usually required. The goal of ABC is to develop usable cost information that accurately reflects the cause-and-effect relationships between costs, activities, and products or services. Sometimes, all that is required is that managers change the way they think. At other times, modifications must be made in how an existing cost system works. Personal computer spreadsheets often can be developed to provide accurate and relevant cost information "offline."

To be universally useful, particularly to be useful to small and mid-sized organizations, ABC must be understood at its basic conceptual level. Systems and software are secondary issues that present only one approach to adopting the concept. Trying to adopt ABC by applying detailed, step-by-step instructions for its implementation or by trying to "fill in the blanks" of a software package is like trying to paint a self-portrait using someone else as a model. Although the resulting painting will probably qualify as a portrait, it will come out looking a lot more like the other person than it will looking like you.

After a decade of development and promotion, ABC seems to have fallen far short of the acceptance levels that the soundness of the concept should have led it to attain. It has probably done more to improve the profitability of software developers, conference coordinators, and consulting firms than it has the profitability of users. The responses I receive to a question I ask whenever I address a group of nonaccountants reinforces this view. When presenting the concept of ABC to such groups, I begin with the question, "How many people here have heard about activity-based costing?" Usually, 60 to 70% of the individuals in the audience will raise their hands. When I ask the follow-up question, "How many people here have heard anything good about activity-based costing?," only about half of those hands are raised. Obviously, something is preventing the message from getting through.

The biggest obstacle to the universal acceptance and use of ABC has been, in my view, the emphasis placed on its "computational virtuosity" instead of its "business utility" by the industrial engineers, software developers, and accountants who promote and implement the concept. The backgrounds from which these individuals come are detail oriented, so it is only natural that they are impressed with the theoretical correctness and precision of ABC's calculations. The tendency of such practitioners is to develop solutions that are more detailed and complex than the problem deserves or requires. Owners and managers of businesses, however, do not care about "computational virtuosity." They are impressed with ideas that have "business utility," the ability to help them make more money and earn a better return on their (or their owner's) investment. They want practical solutions to the problems at hand, not "overengineered" solutions that seem more complicated than the problems they are designed to solve.

If ABC is to gain the universal acceptance it deserves, it needs to be understood as the simple, yet valuable, business tool it really is. The chapters that follow describe this simple concept and how it can be used to create a powerful business tool that can improve the financial performance of any business, regardless of its industry, size, or complexity.

2

Strange Case of Ace Manufacturing

Over the years, financial executives at many companies have told me that, instead of performing the type of activity-based analysis of their business described in this book, they would correct the major flaws in their current system and then "fine tune" the cost information as needed. This usually happens after one of the company's employees picks up one or two "tidbits" at an activity-based costing (ABC) conference or seminar and then returns to implement the "tidbits" without considering the company's overall cost and operating structure.

Ace Manufacturing is an example of one such company. It recognized that its cost information was inaccurate and decided to take action. Its approach was to identify and correct its system's deficiencies "one step at a time," without the benefit of a wall-to-wall, activity-based analysis of its operations. Before venturing into a discussion of ABC, it might be useful to review the "Strange Case of Ace Manufacturing."

ACE MANUFACTURING

Ace Manufacturing, Inc., is a $10 million manufacturer of machined and assembled products. Its products can be divided into two product lines: Product Line A and Product Line B. The company's management is very interested in the relative profitability of the two product lines. Ace Manufacturing has a simple, traditional approach to product costing in which direct material and direct labor are charged directly to each job with overhead then being added as a plant-wide percentage of direct labor cost. For pricing and profitability decisions, general and administrative expenses are added as a percentage of total cost input. The company's basic cost and rate structure are detailed at the top of Exhibit 2.1.

The company's $10 million sales are divided evenly between Product Lines A and B. Both products require $1,250,000 of direct material and $500,000 of direct labor costs. After applying the overhead and general and administrative (G&A) rates, both Product Lines appear to generate a $500,000 profit contribution as shown in Scenario 1 detailed at the bottom of Exhibit 2.1. Ace Manufacturing's certified public accountant (CPA) told

Exhibit 2.1 Ace Manufacturing, Inc.: Selected Financial Information, Scenario 1

Sales	$10,000,000
Direct material cost	$2,500,000
Direct labor cost	$1,000,000
Manufacturing overhead cost	$4,000,000
G&A costs	$1,500,000
Total costs and expenses	$9,000,000
Profit contribution	$1,000,000
Overhead rate (% of direct labor)	400%
G&A rate (% of total cost input)	20%

***** Scenario 1 *****

		Product Line A	Product Line B	Total
Sales		$5,000,000	$5,000,000	$10,000,000
Direct material cost		$1,250,000	$1,250,000	$2,500,000
Direct labor cost		$500,000	$500,000	$1,000,000
Overhead @	400%	$2,000,000	$2,000,000	$4,000,000
Total manufactured cost		$3,750,000	$3,750,000	$7,500,000
G&A @	20%	$750,000	$750,000	$1,500,000
Total costs and expenses		$4,500,000	$4,500,000	$9,000,000
Profit contribution		$500,000	$500,000	$1,000,000

them this method of costing was just fine because it complied with generally accepted accounting principles (GAAP).

CHANGING TO MULTIPLE OVERHEAD RATES

Realizing that they had two totally different production activities, machining and assembly, whose cost structures were different, the company's management decided that they would separate the two production activities for costing purposes. To do this, they determined how much of the $1 million in direct labor and how much of the $4 million in overhead related to machining and how much related to assembly. The results are shown in the top portion of Exhibit 2.2. The new overhead application rates for these

Exhibit 2.2 Ace Manufacturing, Inc.: Selected Financial Information, Scenario 2

	Machine	Assembly	Total
Direct labor cost	$250,000	$750,000	$1,000,000
Manufacturing overhead cost	$1,750,000	$2,250,000	$4,000,000
Overhead application rate	700%	300%	400%

***** Scenario 2 *****

		Product Line A	Product Line B	Total
Sales		$5,000,000	$5,000,000	$10,000,000
Direct material cost		$1,250,000	$1,250,000	$2,500,000
Direct labor cost/machine		$50,000	$200,000	$250,000
Overhead @	700%	$350,000	$1,400,000	$1,750,000
Direct labor cost/assembly		$450,000	$300,000	$750,000
Overhead @	300%	$1,350,000	$900,000	$2,250,000
Total manufactured cost		$3,450,000	$4,050,000	$7,500,000
G&A @	20%	$690,000	$810,000	$1,500,000
Total costs and expenses		$4,140,000	$4,860,000	$9,000,000
Profit contribution		$860,000	$140,000	$1,000,000

manufacturing operations were 700% of direct labor cost for machining and 300% of direct labor cost for assembly.

Using these revised rates to cost the two products resulted in a completely different view of product profitability. Because only 10% of Product Line A's direct labor related to the high-overhead machining work, its total cost dropped from $4,500,000 to $4,140,000, and its profit contribution increased by $360,000 to $860,000. Forty percent of Product Line B's direct labor, however, took place in the high-overhead machining operations, which raised its cost from $4,500,000 to $4,860,000 and dropped its profitability by $360,000 to only $140,000. These calculations are detailed in Scenario 2, Exhibit 2.2. Again, Ace Manufacturing's CPA told them this method of costing was fine because it complied with GAAP.

CHANGING TO MULTIPLE OVERHEAD BASES

A second look at machining, however, made it apparent that direct labor is not the major force driving the cost of machining operations. Although about $250,000 of the $1,750,000 overhead can be attributed to the laborer (fringe benefits, human resource support, plant management, payroll costs, etc.), the balance of $1,500,000 relates to the operation of the equipment (supplies, lubricants, utilities, maintenance, depreciation, etc.). As a result, it was decided that machining costs should be split into two parts—those related to the operator's labor and those related to the 15,000 hours during which the machinery is in operation annually. The calculation of these new rates is shown at the top of Exhibit 2.3. Overhead would be added for the machining operations at 100% of direct labor cost plus $100 for every hour of machine operating time.

In applying these new rates to the two product lines, Ace found that those parts machined for Product Line A require much longer cycle times than those machined for Product Line B. In other words, when the operators load a Product Line A part on the machine and begin machining operations, it runs much longer before it has to be removed and the next part started than is the case with parts relating to Product Line B. Specifically, the 9,000 hours during which machines worked on Product Line A parts demanded only $50,000 of direct labor involvement, whereas the 6,000 hours spent on Product Line B parts required $200,000 of direct labor support.

As shown in Scenario 3 at the bottom of Exhibit 2.3, this resulted in an increase of costs related to Product Line A to $4,860,000, dropping its profit contribution to $140,000, and a decrease of Product Line B costs to $4,140,000, raising its profit contribution to $860,000. This is a complete

Exhibit 2.3 Ace Manufacturing, Inc.: Selected Financial Information, Scenario 3

	Machine	Assembly	Total
Direct labor cost	$250,000	$750,000	$1,000,000
Machine-driven overhead	$1,500,000		$1,500,000
Labor-driven overhead	$250,000	$2,250,000	$2,500,000
Manufacturing overhead cost	$1,750,000	$2,250,000	$4,000,000
Machine operating hours	15,000		
Direct labor overhead	100%	300%	250%
Machine hour overhead	$100.00		

***** Scenario 3 *****

		Product Line A	Product Line B	Total
Sales		$5,000,000	$5,000,000	$10,000,000
Direct material cost		$1,250,000	$1,250,000	$2,500,000
Direct labor cost/machine		$50,000	$200,000	$250,000
Overhead @	100%	$50,000	$200,000	$250,000
Direct labor cost/assembly		$450,000	$300,000	$750,000
Overhead @	300%	$1,350,000	$900,000	$2,250,000
Machine operating hours		9,000	6,000	15,000
Overhead @	$100.00	$900,000	$600,000	$1,500,000
Total manufactured cost		$4,050,000	$3,450,000	$7,500,000
G&A @	20%	$810,000	$690,000	$1,500,000
Total costs and expenses		$4,860,000	$4,140,000	$9,000,000
Profit contribution		$140,000	$860,000	$1,000,000

reversal of Scenario 2's profitability figures. Ace Manufacturing's CPA again told them this method of costing was just fine because it complied with GAAP.

SEGREGATING "THROUGHPUT"-DRIVEN COSTS

There are certain costs included in machining overhead, however, that really do not vary with machine operating time. Instead, these costs vary with the number and type of parts produced. It can be said that these vary with "throughput," not the amount of time it takes to generate that "throughput." For example, one of the reasons cycle times are longer for Product Line A parts is that the metals from which they are machined are much harder than those from which Product Line B's parts are machined. Consequently, very expensive, diamond-tipped, perishable tools are required for Product Line A's parts, while much cheaper carbide tools can be used for parts destined for Product Line B. Each tool is good for a finite number of parts based on how many "chips it cuts," not how long it takes to cut them. As a result, it is possible to establish a "direct" cost of perishable tooling for each part and then exclude perishable tooling costs from the overhead pool.

After removing these throughput-driven costs from machining overhead and treating them as direct, the overhead cost per machine hour dropped from $100 to $80, as shown at the top of Exhibit 2.4. Costing the two products using these new rates further increased the cost of Product Line A to $4,944,000, dropping its profit contribution to only $56,000. Product Line B's cost, however, dropped to $4,056,000, and its profit contribution rose to $944,000, as shown in Scenario 4 detailed in Exhibit 2.4. Once again, Ace Manufacturing's CPA told them this method of costing was just fine because it complied with GAAP.

IDENTIFYING PRODUCT LINE COSTS

Not yet addressed were the $1,500,000 of G&A expenses that were still being charged to products as if they were caused (or driven) by "cumulative dollars of cost." A cursory review revealed that $287,000 of these administrative costs were directly attributable to developing and supporting Product Line A and $106,500 did the same for Product Line B.

As a result, Ace further modified its product costing practices to charge these product support and development costs to Product Lines A and B through separate percentage rates based on cumulative conversion costs. This resulted in a reduction in the G&A rate from 20 to 14%. These

Exhibit 2.4 Ace Manufacturing, Inc.: Selected Financial Information, Scenario 4

		Machine
Original machine-driven overhead		$1,500,000
Throughput-driven overhead—Product Line A	$250,000	
Throughput-driven overhead—Product Line B	$50,000	$300,000
Revised machine-driven overhead		$1,200,000
Machine operating hours		15,000
Machine hour overhead		$80.00

***** Scenario 4 *****

		Product Line A	Product Line B	Total
Sales		$5,000,000	$5,000,000	$10,000,000
Direct material costs		$1,250,000	$1,250,000	$2,500,000
Throughput costs		$250,000	$50,000	$300,000
Machine labor/overhead		$100,000	$400,000	$500,000
Assembly labor/overhead		$1,800,000	$1,200,000	$3,000,000
Machine hours		9,000	6,000	15,000
Overhead @	$80.00	$720,000	$480,000	$1,200,000
Total manufactured cost		$4,120,000	$3,380,000	$7,500,000
G&A @	20%	$824,000	$676,000	$1,500,000
Total costs and expenses		$4,944,000	$4,056,000	$9,000,000
Profit contribution		$56,000	$944,000	$1,000,000

changes are shown at the top of Exhibit 2.5. As shown in Scenario 5 at the bottom of Exhibit 2.5, profit contribution for Product Line A now appears to be a negative $24,767, whereas Product Line B now contributes $1,024,767 of profit, more than 100% of the company's total. As was the case with all earlier costing methods, Ace Manufacturing's CPA told them this method of costing was fine because it complied with GAAP.

Exhibit 2.5 Ace Manufacturing, Inc.: Selected Financial Information, Scenario 5

Product support and development		
Product Line A		$287,000
Product Line B		$106,500
Other general and administrative costs		$1,106,500
Total general and administrative costs		$1,500,000
Product support and development cost as a percentage of conversion costs		
Product Line A	Base = $2,870,000	10.0%
Product Line B	Base = $2,130,000	5.0%
Revised G&A rate	Base = $7,893,500	14.0%

***** Scenario 5 *****

		Product Line A	Product Line B	Total
Sales		$5,000,000	$5,000,000	$10,000,000
Direct material costs		$1,250,000	$1,250,000	$2,500,000
Conversion costs		$2,870,000	$2,130,000	$5,000,000
Product support and development				
Product Line A	10.0%	$287,000		$287,000
Product Line B	5.0%		$106,500	$106,500
G&A @	14.0%	$617,767	$488,733	$1,106,500
Total costs and expenses		$5,027,767	$3,975,233	$9,000,000
Profit contribution		($24,767)	$1,024,767	$1,000,000

SUMMARY

As can be seen in the summary in Exhibit 2.6, the same set of facts (remember, the facts did not change—Ace just incorporated more of them into its cost calculations) resulted in five very different calculations of profit contribution. As a matter of fact, Ace's first step in improving cost information, separating manufacturing into two separate overhead centers, actually made the cost information worse, not better. Not only that, but all five methods are acceptable under GAAP.

Exhibit 2.6 Ace Manufacturing, Inc.: Selected Financial Information, Overview of Scenarios 1 through 5

	Product Line A	Product Line B	Total
Profit Contribution:			
Scenario 1	$500,000	$500,000	$1,000,000
Scenario 2	$860,000	$140,000	$1,000,000
Scenario 3	$140,000	$860,000	$1,000,000
Scenario 4	$56,000	$944,000	$1,000,000
Scenario 5	($24,767)	($1,024,767)	$1,000,000

All of the scenarios in the "Strange Case of Ace Manufacturing" represent costing structures actually used by many of my manufacturing clients in their "pre-ABC" days. In every case, management had been perfectly content to rely on the cost information generated by these costing structures in supporting critical management decisions. Ignorance was bliss. Unfortunately, ignorance also led to inappropriate decisions, causing financial damage that was too great to repair for one client and that required years to repair for several others.

Suppose that management relied on the cost information generated in Scenario 1. What actions do you believe it would take? Would those actions be the same if it relied on the cost information in Scenario 2? What if it believed and relied on the information generated in Scenario 3? Would the information in Scenarios 4 and 5 have changed their actions? It is critical that management have accurate and relevant cost information at its fingertips if it is to make sound decisions.

It is obvious, however, that Ace Manufacturing's management did not have anything near accurate and relevant cost information on which to base its decisions. As a matter of fact, there is no assurance that the cost information under Scenario 5 is accurate. There may still be major costing issues that have not been addressed. Without a comprehensive wall-to-wall, activity-based analysis of the company's operations, Ace cannot be assured that a "time bomb" is not still hidden somewhere in its cost information that will lead it to make a critical, if not fatal, decision in the future.

As you read the rest of this book, keep Ace Manufacturing's situation in mind and see how an activity-based analysis of its activities and costs would have enabled it to determine and begin using the most appropriate cost structure from the start.

3

What Is Activity-Based Costing?

"How do you modify the complex and detailed methods that large organizations use to implement activity-based costing (ABC) so that they can also be used by small and mid-sized businesses?" As one who has helped scores of small and mid-sized companies realize the benefits of ABC over the past decade, I am asked this question, or one like it, quite often. My answer is, "It cannot be done. But that's okay, because it should not be done." As one might guess, my answer usually disappoints and often confuses the inquirer.

The blitz of propaganda by ABC entrepreneurs and theorists during the past decade has, unfortunately, given too many decision makers the impression that ABC always requires the purchase and installation of specialized software, a minutely detailed analysis of activities and costs, and the development of an extensive data collection system to maintain all of the ABC data. Although this might be the case at very large organizations, it is seldom the case at small or mid-sized businesses or at "jobs shops" of any type or size.

Too many "experts" treat ABC as a set of sophisticated mechanics and complex computations. Once learned, the mechanics and computations become these experts' proverbial hammer, and, once they have this hammer, every organization they see looks like a nail. This emphasis on mechanics and computations has proven to be a major obstacle in the acceptance of ABC as a practical management tool at most small and mid-sized companies.

A much more appropriate question would be, "How can small and mid-sized organizations incorporate the concepts that comprise ABC into their decision-making process in a cost-effective way?" This question deserves a thoughtful answer, because ABC is a powerful management concept that can be adopted and used by *any* organization to gain a competitive advantage through greater understanding of product or service costs, process costs, and the organization's overall cost behavior.

It is important, however, to clearly understand one fact before we venture any further: Small and mid-sized businesses *are not* just little big businesses! There are important differences between small and large firms other than simple differences in scale. The language, theories, and concepts of management may be universal, but the methods used to put those theories and concepts into practice cannot be the same for organizations that are vastly different in size. In other words, the mechanics used to implement management concepts at large companies cannot simply be scaled down and then used to implement the same concepts at a smaller company.

Smaller businesses have organizational structures that are much more compressed than those of larger businesses. In addition, small business managers' spans of authority tend to be wider. Combine these characteristics of being both "close to the action" and responsible for a wide variety of activities and you find that small business managers can effectively accumulate much of the information they need through informal systems and interpersonal communications.

The challenge for the small and mid-sized business is first to identify the critical management information that cannot be handled effectively through either informal systems or interpersonal communications, and then to develop practical, cost-effective methods for formally accumulating and processing that information.

When some sort of formalization is required, the successful small or mid-sized business takes advantage of Pareto's law and gains 80% of the concept's benefits while investing only 20% of the time, effort, and resources that would be required to implement a scaled-down version of a formal, big-company system that implements the same concept. This does not mean, however, that the company must do without the remaining 20% of the concept's benefits. The balance of the benefits are realized when the "brainware" involved in the concept is incorporated into the existing informal, interpersonal system. In other words, the 20% of the concept not adopted through a formal system is adopted as management changes its emphasis, its philosophy, or the way it looks at the information it is already receiving.

Fortunately for us, Pareto was just as right regarding the adoption of ABC as he was for any other application of his law.

ABC AT SMALL AND MID-SIZED BUSINESSES

A step-by-step description of the methodology for incorporating activity-based cost information into the decision-making process of small and mid-sized businesses is covered in the remaining chapters of this book. At this point, however, an accurate description of what ABC actually is should go far in clearing away the misconceptions that have kept many companies from realizing its benefits.

In order to be effective at a small or mid-sized business, ABC should not simply be defined as a method of accurately assigning (or allocating) accounting costs to the company's products or services. Although the company will be able to use ABC to obtain a more accurate assignment of costs to products or services, that is only one thing the concept can be used for—it is not the concept itself.

Activity-based costing should not be defined as a new management philosophy that dictates how to best run the business. Although properly developed ABC information can be used to highlight areas for reducing costs, increasing throughput, and improving productivity, those are still things the concept can be used for—they are not the concept itself. At times, going through the ABC process causes a major "paradigm shift" in the way the organization views itself, resulting in a significant change in the company's philosophy and strategy. Again, this is only one thing the concept can be used for—it is not the concept itself.

Neither is ABC a complex, "Rube Goldberg"-type system, that must be integrated into the company's day-to-day accounting and reporting routines. It can, and in some cases should, be incorporated into the day-to-day routines of a business, but in most cases it does not need to be a "system" at all. It can, instead, function effectively in the form of an "offline" decision support tool.

How, then, should a small or mid-sized business view ABC? To such an organization, ABC should be viewed as a concept around which it can construct an economic model of its business that will provide the accurate and relevant cost information necessary to support sound business decisions of all types. This definition contains five critical points that must be understood if ABC is to have "business utility" at all types and sizes of organizations. These five points are:

1. Activity-based costing is a concept.
2. It serves as a basis for an economic model.
3. Cost information must be accurate.
4. Cost information must be relevant.
5. Cost information must support all types of management decisions.

ABC Is a Concept

Activity-based costing's basic premise is that a company's outputs (its products and services) give rise to the need for operating, management, and administrative activities, which, in turn, necessitate that costs be incurred in providing those activities. In one direction, these operating, management, and administrative costs can be assigned to the outputs that caused them to be incurred by routing them first to the activities that made them necessary and then to the outputs that made the activities necessary. In the other direction, the volume and mix of outputs can be used to project the demand for the various operating, management, and administrative activities. This demand, in turn, can be used to project the costs of providing those activities.

The concept of ABC is as simple as that. More elaborate definitions simply narrow the concept into subsets with limited, not universal, applicability. By keeping this definition in mind, the business can move on to the next critical point; namely, the concept of ABC is the basis for constructing an economic model of the business.

Basis for an Economic Model

Models are simplified versions of a more complex reality. Their purpose is to illuminate real-life phenomena. Of course, some degree of simplification is required if the model is to be easily understood and used, but good models always include the main elements of reality and their relationships. Simplification occurs by omitting or generalizing the nonessentials.

Models are intellectual tools that assist in the thought process and can take on many forms. They can be a simple drawing on a cocktail napkin or a complete, life-sized prototype. They can be a simple linear equation ($A + Bx = C$), or comprehensive computer simulations such as those that enabled the National Aeronautics and Space Administration (NASA) to land men on the moon and return them to Earth safely.

Economic models are simplifications of the economic activity that will take place under real-life conditions. Economic models of an organization's cost behavior are simplifications of what will take place under the company's real-life conditions. Like all models, economic models can take on many forms. At one extreme, the model might be nothing more than the abstract understanding ("brainware") of cost behavior. At the other extreme might be an expensive, complex, and computerized ABC system. It is very important to understand that models can be expressed in a wide variety of ways and that what may be appropriate for one company might be totally inappropriate for another.

Cost Information Must Be Accurate

Activity-based costing must provide accurate cost information. Cost information is "accurate" when it is close enough to reflecting reality that it will not direct management into making a bad decision. Accuracy is not the same as precision. Accuracy implies that the information is free from mistake or error—the information is not wrong. Precision, however, implies exactness—the information is correct in all of its minute details. Auto companies have long demanded that their suppliers be precise, requiring that unit costs be carried out to four and five decimal places. Unfortunately, these costs were most often based on cost systems that in no way reflected the actual manufacturing operations being performed. As a result, these always precise costs are usually totally inaccurate.

Any quest for precision in cost information is a hopeless one, because the nature of cost measurement and behavior makes precision impossible. The quest for accurate cost information, however, is a very attainable goal and one that all businesses, regardless of size, must pursue if they are to thrive and grow into the next century.

Cost Information Must Be Relevant

Accuracy by itself, however, is still not enough. Cost information must also be relevant. A decision maker needs different cost information for different purposes. Perfectly allocated and fully absorbed unit costs based on general ledger accounting information may be an impressive show of computational virtuosity, but as management information, they are practically useless. Costs must be identified, defined, and calculated in ways that are relevant to the decision at hand. Some decisions require fully absorbed costs and some incremental costs. Some should be based on historical accounting costs and some on future accounting or cash costs.

Cost Information Must Support All Types of Management Decisions

Activity-based costing must support sound business decisions of all types. Too many businesses focus their costing efforts on calculating the "fully absorbed" unit costs of their products or services. Although this is an important use of cost information, there are many other decisions that require different types of cost information. Activity-based costing must address these other decision situations as well. The cost impact of special orders, long-term contracts, capital equipment additions, new programs, cost reduction activities, outsourcing, changes in volume and mix, overtime/new hire alternatives, and a myriad of other decision alternatives or volume and mix scenarios must all be supported by activity-based cost information if it is to be an effective tool for the small or mid-sized business.

AN ACTIVITY-BASED MODEL

As this description of ABC implies, it is very unlikely that a small or mid-sized business needs a comprehensive, fully integrated ABC system. It is, however, imperative that small and mid-sized businesses have cost information that reflects reality if they are to be successful in the future. This information can be obtained by using the concept of ABC to develop an economic model of the business, in whatever form of model is most appropriate for the specific company, that accurately reflects the cost behavior of the organization. This economic model can then be used to calculate the relevant cost information needed to support the wide range of decisions for which cost information is an important factor.

THREE KEYS TO EFFECTIVE ABC

To be effective, a small or mid-sized company's activity-based economic model must:

- Begin with costs that are accurately defined and measured
- Properly reflect the cause and effect relationships between the company's product/services, activities, and costs
- Be used in appropriate ways

No matter how well designed an activity-based model of an organization is, if the cost information it is processing is improperly defined and measured, the model's output will not reflect reality. This point is usually overlooked by those implementing ABC. They begin with the general ledger, one place that accurate and relevant cost information definitely will not be found. The failure of the general ledger to accurately measure costs is discussed in detail in Chapter 4. Once costs are properly defined and measured, the activity-based model must accurately represent the causal relationships between an organization's products and/or services, the activities they make necessary, and the costs caused by those activities. A structure for developing and evaluating those relationships is described in Chapter 5. Finally, no matter how accurate cost information is, if it is not used in appropriate ways, the entire effort of developing the information will be for naught. Decision costing, the appropriate use of cost information, is discussed in detail in Chapter 7.

WHICH SMALL AND MID-SIZED BUSINESSES ARE MOST AT RISK?

It is difficult, if not impossible, to generalize on the degree to which inaccurate or irrelevant cost information might be putting an organization's continued success, or even its survival, at risk. Each company's circumstances are unique. There are, however, certain characteristics that are frequently found to exist at organizations whose actions are continually being misdirected due to inaccurate and irrelevant information. Eight of those characteristics that are likely to put a small or mid-sized business at considerable risk are identified next.

1. *The company does not assign indirect costs to products or services at all, but marks up prime costs (direct material and direct labor) by an amount that it believes is adequate to cover all indirect costs and provide for the desired profit.*

   This is the ultimate example of "flying blind." By not applying indirect costs at all, these costs are, in effect, being assigned as a percentage of direct costs. They are just part of the markup (which is a percentage of direct costs).

   Many small and mid-sized distributors fall into this category. These distributors do not assign operating and administrative costs to products or customers. Instead, they add a mark up percentage to the cost of products distributed that, it is hoped, will cover all of the company's costs plus the desired profit. Even more surprisingly, there are still manufacturing companies that continue to trace material (a significant cost) and direct labor (an insignificant cost in most cases) in great detail while ignoring the assignment of indirect costs (which, in most cases, is a much greater element of cost than the direct labor). One company we visited did not even trace direct labor costs. Material cost was traced to a job and then "marked up" by a percentage to cover all conversion costs, administrative costs, and profit.

   Unless the direct labor or the total of direct material and labor costs are relevant indicators of what causes indirect costs to be incurred, these methods of cost assignment (or lack of cost assignment) can lead to a multitude of inappropriate management decisions.

2. *The organization has only a single, organization-wide rate or multiple rates applied on only one type of base for assigning indirect costs to products and services.*

   If a business sells more than one product or service or if it sells products or services to more than one market or customer, it is highly unlikely that a single, organization-wide indirect costing rate, or even several departmental rates with a common base (e.g., direct labor dollars, direct labor hours, or machine hours), will adequately assign costs to the appropriate products, services, customers, product lines, or markets. Remember Ace Manufacturing (Chapter 2)?

   All of a business' operations are not created equal. Each has different cost behavior and different factors influencing that behavior.

The various levels of cost involved in an organization's multitude of activities makes organization-wide rates too general to be accurate. The variety of "measurables" that cause costs (e.g., orders, shipments, set ups, admissions, acuity levels, labor hours, quotation "hit rates," machine hours) makes a single basis for all indirect costing rates too general as well. The more varied the products or services, or the more different the customers or markets, the more distortion will result from using a single base for indirect cost assignment.

3. *The organization has been incorporating new, technologically advanced operating processes into its operation without making corresponding changes in the way it costs its products, services, and processes.*

The incorporation of new operating processes usually causes major changes in the way work is performed. It is the cost of that work that the company's cost accounting practices attempt to measure. If the work changes significantly, the "metrics" used to measure it must also change if the costs are to fairly represent the resources required to perform the work.

A simple example is a case of a company that adds new controls to a piece of equipment that makes it possible for one operator to run more than one piece of equipment at a time. Depending on the cycle times required for the products being produced, an operator can now operate up to three machines at once. In the past, each piece of equipment needed a full-time operator whenever it was in use. The company's cost accounting practices were structured so that the cost of owning, maintaining, and operating the equipment followed the operator as a percentage of the operator's labor cost. As long as there was a one-operator, one-machine relationship, this practice worked. With the introduction of the new controls, however, the practice no longer provides a realistic picture of the cost of machining. The cost of one hour of operator labor could be accompanied by the cost of operating one, two, or three machines. Without revising costing practices to reflect this new situation, significant cost distortions will lead to poor decisions.

4. *The business finds itself competitive on one end of its product or service line, but not on the other end.*

All costing practices, even activity-based practices, calculate the cost of approximately one half of a business' products or services at levels higher than actual and the other half at levels that are lower than actual. With activity-based methods, the variance from actual is reduced to levels that do not seriously impact decision making. The more general the costing practices, however, the greater the amount by which costs will vary from actual. As a result, a company with overgeneralized costing practices will believe that certain families of products or services cost substantially more than is actually the case, and other families of products or services cost less.

Because the market determines the price, a company with over-generalized costing practices will often find that it either cannot be profitable at the market price or must accept very low margins on certain products while, at the same time, it is extremely competitive and can, perhaps, even charge a premium for other products. Often, the sole reason for these apparent differences in competitiveness is the inaccuracy inherent in the way the company costs its products and services.

In manufacturing, this often takes the form of being more competitive on short runs than long runs, on large parts than small parts, or on machine operations than assembly or other manual operations. In distribution, this sometimes takes the form of being more competitive on slow-turning products than fast-turning products, on repackaged products than those that are not repackaged, or on sales to smaller customers than those to larger customers. In long-term care, this might show that the facility is more competitive on high-acuity residents than those with lower acuity levels or on those with special needs versus those without them.

5. *The business has costing principles and mechanics that have been influenced by outside reporting requirements.*

Cost recovery is a phrase that may have done more to distort product and service costs than any other. Two arenas in which this occurs frequently are in government contracting and health care. In recent years, similar methods have begun to develop in other customer-dominated markets, as in the dealings between an automotive industry supplier and an automobile manufacturer (or more correctly, a company that designs, assembles, and markets automobiles). In these arenas, the desire to limit a supplier's or provider's profit has resulted in the creation of "one size fits none" costing rules that may have once been intended to fairly reflect costs but have since evolved into ways for the supplier or provider to generate revenues (or recover costs). At these businesses, costing decisions are often based on which cost treatment will result in the highest amount of revenue, not the most accurate representation of cost.

Unfortunately, many of these organizations continue to believe that the complex systems created for cost recovery purposes are theoretically sound and generate cost information that reflects reality. Many government contractors have operated with totally inappropriate costing systems for decades simply because they are afraid of the impact of a change in accounting method on the revenues they receive under their contracts. Health care providers actually use the same information used to generate revenues in the "Medicare Reports" when making management decisions.

One frequently occurring situation encountered at auto suppliers is sad but humorous. During a plant tour, I stand with a plant manager or controller and watch a relatively complex setup taking place. I ask, "Does this setup get charged directly to the job or product, or is it just part of your overhead?" Too often the answer is, "We have to charge it to overhead; the customer would never pay us for it if we charged it directly to the job." According to this logic, if a customer will not reimburse a supplier for a cost, then the cost is not directly related to the work done for them. This does not seem like a rational basis for developing sound cost information for supporting decisions.

6. *The industry in which the business operates has begun to require long-term pricing commitments.*

Multiyear pricing agreements require the ability to estimate an organization's cost structure several years into the future if well-informed decisions are to be made. This is particularly true if the business is growing, if its product/service mix is changing, or if it is making changes in the way it produces its products or provides its services. To be successful, it must understand its cost structure during those years in which the long-term contract will be executed. It needs to know if additional volume without corresponding increases in support costs will help reduce future costs. It needs to know whether planned improvements will provide the type of cost decreases necessary to make the contract profitable over its life. It needs to know if the price needs to be "front loaded" if it is to prove profitable.

A detailed discussion of long-term pricing appears in Chapter 16. The point here is that a company that must make long-term pricing commitments must have a tool that will enable it to look into the future in a rational way if it is to make rational pricing decisions. Without such a tool, pricing decisions may be made today that will inevitably lead to the failure of the company several years down the road.

7. *The company must now provide a wider variety of products and services and/or must serve a greater number of customers or markets.*

Now, more than ever, customers want customized products and services. Very few companies still have the luxury of providing standardized products or services that are produced or provided in the ways they find most advantageous. Each new option, each new process, and each new customer puts demands on the development of cost information that are not adequately handled by simple, traditional costing techniques.

Consider the example of an injection molder that had always used black material in molding its products. By simply adding additional colors to the material used, the molder adds a significant amount of complexity to its operation. Different colors make changeovers more frequent and more complex. Some colors require greater quality control efforts than others. Some colors cannot be reground and reused. Additional colors demand more storage areas and inventory management efforts. All of these need to be taken into account if the molder is to gain an accurate understanding of the cost of the ever-widening variety of products being produced in those colors. Overgeneralized costing practices will simply hide those cost differentials.

8. *The company has certain customers or markets that require a disproportionate amount of selling, scheduling, service, or other support activity.*

   An organization that accepts both government and commercial contracts performs some activities that relate exclusively to government contracts and others that relate only to commercial jobs. A health care provider performs certain activities in order to be paid by Medicare and others to be paid by a private insurance carrier. An advertising agency has certain clients for whom its creative and development work is much more at risk than it is for other clients. A distributor has some markets requiring a much greater marketing effort than is required in others. A manufacturer has one customer whose behavior causes more last-minute scheduling changes than its other customers. If any of these differences are significant, costing practices must be able to incorporate those differences into the way it determines costs.

IS ABC WORTH THE REQUIRED INVESTMENT?

Stories of ABC implementations requiring many person-months of effort, six-figure consulting fees, and painful system conversions have scared off many companies who had been considering the concept. Fortunately, such investments in time and money are not needed to develop a relevant and accurate economic model of a small or mid-sized business.

Our experience has shown that incorporating ABC concepts into the decision-making apparatus of an autonomous small or mid-sized organization has required an investment of as low as .1% of sales for a company on the high end of the range (close to 500+ employees) to .3% of sales for a company on the low end of the range (less than 50 employees). Compared to the benefits to be gained, the investment is insignificant.

For example, suppose that the only benefit to be gained from adopting ABC will be an improvement in the profitability of contracts awarded. By not being awarded a few of the contracts that would have been inadvertently underquoted using old cost information and, instead, being awarded a few other contracts that would have been inadvertently overquoted, the company should have no difficulty in realizing at least a 1% improvement in margin. Compared to an investment that amounted to between .1% and .3% of sales, the result is a payback of 1 to 4 months for an investment that will continue to generate benefits indefinitely. Chapter 14 contains an example of the tremendous impact this can have on a company's profitability.

SUMMARY

Activity-based costing is a high-powered decision support tool that is well within the means of small and mid-sized organizations. With ABC, a company can gain the accurate and relevant cost information it needs to support the myriad of decisions it makes that require cost information. The key to its effective use is to understand that it is a concept, not a system. Although large businesses may need complex and costly systems to benefit from the concept due to the disadvantages of largeness, the small and mid-sized business can gain the same benefits by exploiting the advantages of smallness and using ABC to create an economic model of the organization that will provide the accurate and relevant cost information it needs to support critical management decisions of all types.

4

Deadly Virus of Generally Accepted Accounting Principles

Determining True Economic Costs

This first prerequisite of accurate, activity-based cost information is the accurate measurement of costs. No matter how closely the activity-based distribution of costs to activities, products, or services reflects actual cause and effect relationships, the final answers will be wrong if the process starts with inaccurate or irrelevant cost information. As a result, this issue of cost measurement will be addressed before we venture any further.

ACCOUNTING AND ASTRONOMY

One evening, I arrived at my hotel in a small, out-of-the-way town where I was to start a project with a new client on the following day. After unpacking, I decided that I would stop by the lounge for a nightcap before turning in. As I entered the lounge, I saw a strange assortment of individuals engaging in debates at almost every table.

At the first table I passed, an argument was taking place between a fellow with a complexion so pale that it appeared he never saw the sun and another individual whose complexion was so red that it appeared he had spent days in the sun without the benefit of a sunscreen. The reddish individual was pressing the point that it was absolutely necessary to close a company's books every 88 days. No shorter period of time was of any use, but any wait longer than 88 days jeopardized management's ability to get timely information. His pale companion thought that such frequent closings were just a way to ensure job security. The pale fellow's contention was that books need be closed no more frequently than every 248 years. Any shorter time frame was just a waste of time and effort.

The second table I passed yielded a different, though similar, argument. The two individuals at that table, both of whom had very green complexions, agreed that a company should close its books up "nice and tight" every 1.9 years. They also agreed, however, that 1.9 years was too long to wait to find out operating results, and, as a result, interim "soft closes" were necessary to provide management with more timely information. Their disagreement was over the length of these interim periods. One of the debaters insisted that these "soft closes" take place every 34 hours. The other was just as insistent that 34 hours was much too long a period to wait for operating results and that "soft closes" must take place every 7 hours.

After reaching the bar, I asked the bartender if he knew who these individuals were who were having such unusual arguments. He told me that they were all members of a group holding a convention at the hotel. After checking with one of the wait staff, he indicated that the group was the Institute of Solar System Accountants. With his answer, all became clear.

The two debaters at the first table were from Mercury (the red-complected one) and Pluto (the one with the pale complexion). Because the Mercurian lives on a planet that orbits the sun once every 88 days, it is obvious to him that a company's books should be closed and its results measured every 88 days. The laws of physics dictate it. His old friend from Pluto, however, had a different perspective altogether. The planet on which he resides orbits the sun only once every 248 years. As a result, it is obvious to him that 248 years is the only proper period for measuring operating results. As far as he was concerned, the laws of physics made it obvious.

At the second table were two residents from our neighbor, Mars. It should have been obvious from their green complexions. Because they both reside on the same planet, which orbits the sun every 1.9 years, they could agree on the proper period for "hard closing" the books. The two were, however, from two different schools of Martian accounting thought; one was from the Phobosian school and the other from the Deimosian school. The Phobosians think that Mars' moon Phobos, which orbits the planet every 7 hours, is the appropriate indicator of accounting periods. The Deimosians, however, believe that the 34-hour orbit of Mars' other moon, Deimos, provides a more correct period for measuring accounting results. It appears that Martians may never be able to agree on which moon has greater financial significance.

As I sat back to enjoy my nightcap I thought to myself that here on Earth, we would never permit such irrelevant astronomical events to influence the measurement of our financial results—or would we?

ACCOUNTING AND BASEBALL

One of the first things a beginning accounting student is told is, "Accounting is the scorecard of business." Although this analogy is partially true when the "entire package" of accounting (income statement, balance sheet, changes in working capital, footnotes, etc.) is included, when used to describe the most frequently referenced accounting statement—the income statement—the analogy begins to break down.

Suppose a new expansion baseball team begins its first game. In the first inning, its opponent loads the bases before the third out is made. When the next inning starts, the bases will be empty. In business, the next inning starts with the bases still loaded. Unfortunately, the new team loses its first game 10 to 0. The second game will start with the score 0 to 0. In business, the second game will start with the team still behind 10 to 0. The team's first season ends with a disappointing 40 win, 122 loss record. Fortunately, next season will begin with a record of no wins and no losses. In business, the second season starts with the 40 win, 122 loss record carried forward.

The scorecards in both business and baseball record only things that happen. Neither record things that should happen but do not. The new team has only three good starting pitchers. As a result they go with a three-man rotation, which helps out in the short run but jeopardizes those pitchers' health in the long term. The team might also fail to adequately invest in a farm system to provide quality players for the future. Neither of these things shows up in its current scorecards. In business, failure to adequately maintain equipment or invest in research and development generates favorable, not unfavorable, results in its current scorecards. In neither case does such critical information show up when current results are examined.

ACCOUNTING PERIODS AND GENERALLY ACCEPTED ACCOUNTING PRINCIPLES

A business operates on a continuum, not in discrete periods of time. It does not have innings, games, or seasons. Moving from the last day of one month to the first day of the next month has no more significance than moving from the 8th to the 9th of the month, or from the 22nd to the 23rd. Unfortunately, if we are to be able to measure performance, we must either find a way to do it continuously or arbitrarily select time periods within which we will perform our measurements. Comprehensive continuous reporting would be too costly for the benefit to be obtained, so we elect to create reporting periods.

We could have selected a primary reporting period of 1,000 days with interim periods of 10, 20, 40, or 50 days. We could have selected a primary reporting period of 1 million minutes with interim periods of 50,000 minutes. We could have selected a primary reporting period of 365 days, with 10 interim periods, five of 36 days and five of 37 days. All of these would have been just as valid as the scheme we have chosen; a primary period that coincides with one Earth orbit around the sun and twelve interim periods that roughly coincide with moon orbits around the Earth.

To provide rules for "keeping score" during these arbitrary reporting periods, accountants have developed an ever growing body of generally accepted accounting principles (GAAP). Building on a base of what might be viewed as accounting's *common law* (the basic rules for transaction recording, matching revenues and expenses, capitalization rules, depreciation methods, etc.), authoritative bodies have generated scores of promulgations, statements, and pronouncements to cover specific areas in which questions arise or new kinds of transactions require accounting clarification.

During seminars on this topic, I make a point of asking accountants in the audience whether they can identify any authoritative accounting pronouncement, or any GAAP for that matter, that sacrifices the accuracy of an organization's balance sheet so that the income statement can be properly stated. In five years, no one has been able to identify one. When I reverse the question, however, and ask if they can identify any authoritative accounting pronouncement (or other GAAP) that sacrifices the accuracy of an organization's income statement so that the balance sheet can be properly stated, dozens have been identified. The one most often cited is Financial Accounting Standard (FAS) 106, which required that estimated retiree health care benefits, which had been recorded on a pay-as-you-go basis, be accrued as of a single balance sheet date. The resulting charge, which was large at many organizations, was made to the income statement, distorting the results for the period ending on the balance sheet date.

The point here is that the primary focus of GAAP is on assuring nice, conservative balance sheets, not accurate measures of operating performance. Any income statement distortions caused by GAAP can be explained away in footnotes. Unfortunately, footnotes do not show up in the general ledger. As a result, "the books" themselves are distorted when kept in compliance with GAAP.

IMPACT OF ASTRONOMY AND BASEBALL ON GAAP

The following summarizes the discussion thus far with relation to cost information. Although businesses operate on a continuum, it is necessary for accountants to break that continuum into accounting periods so that results of operations can be measured and financial position determined periodically. Of the myriad of legitimate ways available for breaking the continuum into accounting periods, we have decided to structure ours around the orbits of astronomical bodies. After years of using months and years for reporting results, we have begun to apply the "scorecard" analogy too literally and use accounting information as if each month and year is an independent time period that starts with a "clean slate," like each inning, game, or season in baseball.

The rules we developed to quantify accounting results in our general ledgers (i.e., GAAP) have not been designed to provide accurate income statement (including cost) information, but to provide nice, conservative balance sheets at the end of each period. In addition, accounting records only those things that have happened or that are highly likely to happen, not things that should have happened but did not. As a result, if we use the cost information recorded in our general ledgers, we will not be using cost information that was designed to reflect reality. Instead, we will be using cost information that represents a "plug" between two balance sheets. This situation describes one of the greatest obstacles to developing accurate and relevant cost information; namely, the Deadly Virus of GAAP.

RETROACTIVE/PROSPECTIVE BALANCE SHEET MODIFICATIONS

There are several "strains" of the Deadly Virus of GAAP. The first one can be described as retroactive/prospective balance sheet modifications. This strain comes in a variety of forms. One has already been mentioned: the introduction of new accounting pronouncements.

Every once in a while, accounting authorities either clarify the acceptable way to account for certain transactions or change their mind. When this occurs, an authoritative pronouncement is made. Often, these require that companies make either "big bang"-to-date (or creation-to-date if you prefer) or "from now until the end of time" adjustments. Financial Accounting Standard 106 was such a pronouncement. It required that all future health care benefit costs for currently retired employees be estimated and booked as a liability all at once. This was done to accurately reflect the liability for these benefits on the balance sheet, not to properly record the cost in the period to which it applied. These benefits were earned by the employees during their years of employment, prior to the date of the entry, but would be paid out in the future, after the date of the entry. The general ledger would show all of the cost in the year the entry was made, probably a year in which little or none of the cost belongs. If a company making such an adjustment begins to calculate its product or process costs using general ledger cost information, it will be distorted by this retroactive/prospective balance sheet modification.

Another example of this strain of the virus occurs at businesses with self-insurance reserves. Earlier in my career, I was controller for a group of divisions at a large New York Stock Exchange (NYSE) listed corporation. One of the "rituals" my division controllers were required to perform each year was to calculate a set of costing rates for the current year that were based on the prior year's actual results. Once they performed their calculations, they forwarded the results to me for my review and approval.

One year, the proposed rates received from one of my largest divisions included an unusually large increase in the fringe benefit rate. On my next visit to the division, I reviewed the rate with the controller. As he had done in each of the previous 20 years he had been division controller, he had taken the previous year's actual costs and labor hours and used them to establish the new "actual" rates. The problem seemed to stem from the fact that, instead of a normal workers' compensation cost of $100,000, the previous year's cost had been $700,000.

At this division, the first $200,000 of each workers' compensation claim was funded by the company, only the excess was insured. Unfortunately, this division experienced three substantial claims during the prior year. As a result, it was required to book $600,000 in additional reserves at year end. The charge, of course, was made to workers' compensation expense. Because the rates developed by my division controller were going to be used to quote new work during the current year, I objected to the inclusion of the entire $600,000, which was going to be paid out over six or seven years, in the division's rate structure. I thought it unwise to charge jobs with costs that we would not actually be incurring during the year.

My division controller could not see my point. He had calculated the rates using the same mechanics that had worked for 20 years and no one had objected to them before. Finally, I said something that caused him to bolt out the door and grab the keys to the company truck. I knew then that he finally understood. What I had said was, "You realize, don't you, that if these three poor souls get run over by a truck on their way to therapy, we'll have a negative $600,000 workers' compensation charge this year?" The truth of the matter was that the three claims did make our workers' compensation cost go up. They did not, however, make it go up by $600,000 for only one year, to return to its former level in future years. They actually made the general level of our workers' compensation costs increase by a smaller amount over the next several years. Including the general ledger cost impact of this retroactive/prospective balance sheet modification in the costs used to develop cost information would have caused considerable distortions in our understanding of the division's product and process costs.

Another example of a retroactive/prospective balance sheet modification also comes from my days as a group controller. Most of my divisions had defined-benefit pension plans. Under such plans, covered employees would receive specific pension benefits on retirement based on their years of service, wage levels during employment, and so forth. The company was required to fund the plan in an actuarially sound manner. Each year, a pension expense was determined, in accordance with GAAP, through a complex set of calculations that included the pension fund's value as of the balance sheet date.

One of my divisions had approximately 500 employees. It had maintained this employment level for a number of years and would continue to maintain that level for a decade after the date of this example. During all of these years, the employees worked full time, earning, among other things, the right to receive their pension benefits on retirement. In the late 1970s, when interest rates were at extremely high levels, we were able to stock the fund with many high-quality, high-return investments. As interest rates fell, the market value of these investments grew to the point that, as of one balance sheet date, the increased fund value made it unnecessary to book any pension expense during the year ending on that date. As a result, the division's general ledger recorded no pension expense during that one Earth orbit.

Did we not actually incur pension expense during that year? Workers earned pension benefits during that Earth orbit the same way they did during orbits that required the division to record several hundred thousand dollars of expense in the General Ledger. If we included the general ledger cost impact of this retroactive/prospective balance sheet modification in the costs used to develop cost information, we would have again caused considerable distortions in our understanding of the division's product and process costs.

The distortions in measuring costs over the "continuum of operations" caused by these and other retroactive/prospective balance sheet modifications must be taken into account if a business is to develop the accurate and relevant cost information required for management to make sound business decisions.

EXPENSES THAT ARE INVESTMENTS

Accountants are conservative by nature. They will always take the most pessimistic view when devising accounting rules. When a business spends money, it must be able to prove, beyond a doubt, that there is future value in the expenditure to be allowed to treat it as an investment in the company's general ledger. If it cannot be so proved, the expenditure is recorded as an expense. This is probably as it should be when creating financial statements for outside parties who do not have management's intimate knowledge of a business, its products, and its markets. Another benefit accrues to those businesses that expense as much as possible; it reduces their income and, as a result, their income tax bill. This is another sound reason for expensing as much as possible in the general ledger.

This conservative view of expense versus investment does not, however, result in accurate measures of performance or in cost information that leads management to make sound decisions. A simple example of the distortion caused by accounting's conservative definition of investment occurred at a company in the printing industry. For years, this printer's annual sales were in the $20 million range. This level of business was maintained through the efforts of three salespeople. The owner of the business decided that, after years of stagnation, it was time to grow. To begin building volume, he hired three more salespeople at a cost of $160,000 annually. Needless to say, business did not jump to $40 million overnight. After one year, business had expanded by 20% to $24 million. When the time came to calculate cost rates for use is quoting new work, the printer's accountant included the cost of all six salespeople in the selling, general, and administrative (SG&A) rate. This, of course, raised the SG&A rate considerably, as a 100% increase in selling cost was spread over a volume increase of only 20%.

Was the $160,000 annual cost of the three additional salespeople actually an expense that should be included in the SG&A rate applied to the printer's new $24 million level of business? They are not all needed to support that volume of business, so why should all of their cost be associated with that business? In reality, despite what the general ledger says, most of the $160,000 was a market building investment. The owner of the printing company took $160,000 of the company's profits and invested it in doubling the size of the business over a number of years. In concept, this expenditure was no different than purchasing a new press on which a future increase in business could be run. That expenditure would have been treated as an investment, so why not the cost of the three salespeople, or at least part of their cost.

Accountants will point out that, unlike a new press, the amount paid to these salespeople cannot be recovered, at least in part, by selling the asset. As a result, it would not be appropriate to capitalize the cost and treat it as an asset on the balance sheet. That may be true, but so what? Are we to always let the balance sheet determine the proper means of measuring operating performance? Assuming that the new salespeople were expected to double the printer's volume over five years, the business' operating performance was at least $128,000 better than shown in the general ledger. They reached 20% of the goal in the first year, so 20% of their cost, or

$32,000, would be a legitimate cost to apply to the $24 million new base of business. The balance of $128,000 is an investment.

With a goal of increasing volume by $4 million each year over five years, the printer will be investing $320,000: $128,000 in the first year, $96,000 in the second, $64,000 in the third, and $32,000 in the fourth. In year five, when the business attains the $40 million level, all of the salespeople's costs will be properly considered an expense. "Bottom line" performance measurement should not be contaminated by treating these investments as expenses. More important, costing rates should not be inflated by including the cost of all salespeople when quoting new jobs. This artificially inflated rate could, in and of itself, prove an obstacle to attaining the hoped for level of business.

Another example of an investment treated as an expense occurred at a company that manufactured low-volume, "customized standard" components for special machine tools. The items produced by this manufacturer were all based on only a few standardized models. The complexity of the business was due to the fact that almost every contract required that the component they manufactured fit into spaces that were different sizes and shapes. As a result, almost every job was a custom job. This also meant that every time a new contract was won, a new set of prints had to be prepared so manufacturing would know what to produce. Preparation of a set of these prints took up to two weeks.

As a way to reduce print preparation time, make the company more competitive on smaller jobs, and improve profitability on all jobs, the company decided to invest in a computer-aided design (CAD) system. The company estimated that, once the CAD system was up and running, they could complete a set of prints in two to three hours. After the hardware and software were purchased and the engineers trained, they began using the new system. The first time the new system was used to prepare a set of prints, it took three weeks. The second set took over two weeks. Approximately one year after the system was installed, the company could complete a set of prints in the projected two or three hours.

Two important activities were taking place during the CAD system's first year of operation. First, engineers were moving down "the learning curve" and becoming more expert in the system's use. Second, the company was building a "print library" that made it possible for engineers to locate the prints of a job with dimensions close to the one at hand, make the required changes, and quickly generate prints for the new job. Both of these activities had to take place before the system could produce prints in two to three hours.

Were the costs of these two activities expenses that should be included in the company's "engineering overhead" rate? Were they "direct labor" costs that should have been charged to the individual jobs? Or were they additional investments required to make the original investment work? What difference is there between these start-up costs for the CAD system and the internal construction costs for a new manufacturing line? If key components and subsystems for the new line are purchased for $200,000 and the company spends another $200,000 having its engineering and maintenance personnel install the line, all $400,000 would be capitalized. How is that different from buying a CAD system for $200,000 and then spending another $200,000 having engineering learn the required skills and create the print library necessary for the system to perform to its capabilities?

An unconventional view, but perhaps one that would have given the company the greatest strategic advantage, would have been to (1) view the CAD system as a $400,000 investment that required a $200,000 down payment with the balance paid in regularly declining installments over one year and (2) start assuming that print preparation takes only two to three hours immediately. The justification of the expenditure would have been based on the benefits to be realized from a $400,000 investment. All print preparation in excess of the two- or three-hour target would be considered deferred payments on the original $400,000 investment. This way the company would have improved its competitiveness on small jobs and its overall performance immediately—not because of an accounting trick, but because it realized that the cost of making a purchased asset operate is just as much an investment as the cost of the asset itself.

As discussed, this view is unconventional and many accountants will be uncomfortable with it. But how much more appropriate is it to charge the cost of making the CAD system operate to the jobs on which it is used before it is fully operative, either as a direct charge or through an artificially inflated engineering overhead rate?

The final example of investments that are treated as expenses covers two situations: program or project up-front engineering and development expenses and experience curve inefficiencies early in a program or project. More companies than ever are becoming involved in multiyear contracts. Health care organizations contract with health maintenance organizations (HMOs) on a multiyear basis just as auto suppliers must agree to long-term contracts with auto makers. Both must usually promise annual price reductions (an example of using activity-based costing [ABC] in support of a multiyear contract pricing decision is included in Chapter 16). The cost measurement problems inherent in multiyear programs or projects is caused by the fact that more than one Earth orbit around the sun takes place during their life.

The objective of a multiyear contract should be to earn the required profit margin and return during the contract's life, not during each individual year of its existence. A manufacturer, for example, should view it more as a contract for constructing a bridge than one to sell products in individual months and years. For example, one manufacturer has an opportunity to bid on a three-year, fixed price program that requires the shipment of 10,000 parts each year. The company estimates that it will cost $10 to make each part during the first year. By moving down the experience curve and implementing improvements developed under their total quality management (TQM) program, they estimate that the cost per unit will fall to $9 in year two and $8 in year three. This means a total cost of $270,000 during the life of the contract. To meet its target of a 10% profit margin, the contract will need to generate $300,000 in revenue. As a result, it quotes a price of $10 per unit.

During the first year of the contract, the actual cost per unit matches the original $10 per unit estimate. How much profit will the manufacturer earn on the contract during this period? The general ledger will indicate that it broke even. Because the company was dead "on the cost curve" that was the basis for a price that would earn a 10% profit margin during the life of the contract, however, it actually earned a $1-per-unit profit. If the average cost during the first year was $9.80, it would have earned $1.20 per unit. If the actual unit cost was $10.20, it would have earned only $.80 per unit. Similarly, if it produces the product at the originally estimated cost each year, it would earn $1 per unit each year. The general ledger, however, would have shown a profit of $1 per unit in year two and $2 per unit in year three.

Which set of measurements is more indicative of the company's actual performance on the contract? Did it not invest some of those expense items early in the contract in order to win the contract in the first place and then earn its target profit during the contract's life?

The distortions in measuring costs over the "continuum of operations" caused by these and other investments that are recorded as expenses must also be taken into account if a business is to develop the accurate and relevant cost information required for management to make sound business decisions.

DEPRECIATION

Although the concept of depreciation has some theoretical basis in financial accounting, it is probably the most irrelevant and irrational number in the general ledger when cost information is needed for performance measurement or decision making. One of the first things my professor said when I began Cost Accounting 101 in college was, "Sunk costs are irrelevant." Unfortunately, no one pointed out that, from a decision-making perspective, a company's capital investment is its biggest "sunk cost." As a result, a "depreciation expense" is calculated using any one of several allowable lives and any one of several allowable methods. If any one of three lives and any one of four depreciation methods can be selected, 12 different, equally acceptable depreciation expenses can be calculated. A bookkeeping entry that charges irrelevant sunk cost to future operations is then made to make cost measurements not just irrelevant, but misleading.

Once purchased, the cost of a capital asset is irrelevant. Up to the point of purchase, the cost is very relevant. The benefits to be gained from its purchase should be sufficient to provide an adequate return on the funds to be invested in the capital. However, once the money is spent, it becomes a sunk cost and is, therefore, irrelevant. Assume a company has an opportunity to purchase a capital asset for $250,000. By incorporating that asset into its business operations, it believes it will be able to reduce cash operating costs by $100,000 per year. In deciding whether it should purchase the asset, the company can use this 40% return on investment and 2.5-year payback period to compare it to other investment options. Once the asset is purchased, however, it does not matter whether it paid $500,000 for it or got it for free. What does matter is that it now has the capability to generate more cash in the future.

Once a company purchases a capital asset, there are two things it can do with it to benefit the organization. It can sell it or use it. For example, the company in the previous paragraph purchased the capital asset for $250,000. The day after it was purchased, it learned that the equipment will not actually save the company $100,000 per year—it will save only $50,000 annually. At the same time, another company offers to buy the equipment for $200,000. The company has two options: (1) It can sell the equipment for $200,000, or (2) it can use it to save $50,000 per year. If the company could invest the $200,000 proceeds from selling the equipment in another asset that would save more than $50,000 annually, it would be better off doing so. If, however, no other use of the funds is available that would generate a savings of more than $50,000 annually, it should use the equipment to generate the lower-than-anticipated amount of savings. Note that the original cost of the equipment has no impact on the choice between the two available options. The reason is simple: Once an asset is purchased, its cost is irrelevant.

Consider the cases of two identical manufacturers. Each operated a fully depreciated piece of equipment in a cost center with the cost structure and cost application rate shown below:

Fixed cash costs	$ 30,000
Variable cash costs	70,000
Depreciation expense	0
Total annual cost	$100,000
Total machine hours	4,000
Cost per machine hour	$ 25.00

In order to reduce future maintenance costs and improve productivity, both organizations purchase identical machines. Company A was able to purchase its machine for $200,000, but Company B paid $300,000. Both machines were acquired for cash, and both organizations elected to depreciate the equipment for financial reporting purposes over a 10-year life using the straight-line method. The benefits of the new equipment were the same for both organizations. They were both able to reduce variable operating costs by $30,000 and the machine time required to meet current production levels by 25%. After the machines' installation, the two organizations' revised cost structures and cost application rates were as shown below:

	Company A	*Company B*
Fixed cash costs	$ 30,000	$ 30,000
Variable cash costs	40,000	40,000
Depreciation expense	20,000	30,000
Total annual costs	$ 90,000	$100,000
Annual machine hours	3,000	3,000
Cost per machine hour	$ 30.00	$ 33.33

Both Company A and Company B were then invited to bid on a new product that would have required 1.33 hours of machine time on their old equipment. Prior to purchasing the new machines, both organizations would have estimated the cost of machining as $33.33 (1.33 hours × $25 per hour). With the productivity improvement, each organization estimated the need for only one hour of machine time, with Company A estimating its cost at $30.00 and Company B estimating its cost at $33.33.

Because all other factors were equal, Company A obtained the order based on the lower quoted price that resulted from its lower cost estimates. Unfortunately for Company B, it will remain at a competitive disadvantage to Company A on any products requiring the use of the new equipment for the foreseeable future. This condition exists only because Company A was able to negotiate a lower purchase price for a type of machine that both organizations now own and operate with equal effectiveness. This lack of competitiveness at Company B is, however, only illusory, created by the mistaken idea that the original cost of its equipment is relevant to decisions that are made after the equipment is purchased.

The starting point for each organization's decisions should be based on its position at the time those decisions are being made. Past decisions cannot be changed. Company B paid too much for its equipment. So what? As it looks into the future, it has exactly the same capabilities and will incur the same costs as Company A, so why should it compound its earlier mistake by estimating that its cost of producing the product will be more than 10% higher? The actual hourly cost of producing the product at either organization will be $23.33 ($70,000/3,000 hours). Both organizations should estimate manufacturing costs accordingly.

The obvious next question becomes, "If an organization does not include depreciation expense in its product cost, how is it going to generate the funds for future capital spending? Will it all have to come out of the slim profit margins a competitive marketplace allows?." Of course, an organization needs to generate the capital funds necessary to maintain its current level of business and technological position through the sale of its products, but what benefit is there to looking through the rear-view mirror to determine what the amount should be?

Capital funds are needed for two purposes: (1) to provide funds for future capital acquisitions (including payments for leasing capital equipment) and (2) to pay the debt incurred in making past acquisitions. Both of these needs are future cash flow oriented. They have nothing to do with past expenditures. As a result, the capital funds that need to be generated through operations must be based on the cash required by the organization to pay for unfunded past acquisitions (not the debt service, just the principal) as well as future acquisitions, keeping in mind that some of the future acquisitions also may be made with borrowed funds.

Suppose an individual took $10 million out of savings and paid cash for all the capital assets necessary to start a new manufacturing operation. Further suppose that, with minor exceptions, these assets would be the only capital assets needed to operate the facility for the next 10 years. The new operation's competitors, on the other hand, have been in business for years. Not only do they have older, highly depreciated assets, they also will have substantial capital needs during the next 10 years just to maintain their current level of manufacturing capability.

From a future cash flow standpoint, the new facility has a considerable advantage over its competitors. It will have a need for only nominal funds beyond those required for operating expenses. As previously noted, its competitors will have much greater capital needs. By including historical, financial depreciation in cost estimates for pricing purposes, however, the new organization will artificially inflate its understanding of product cost and throw away this competitive advantage. It will be attempting to collect capital funds it does not need as part of the price of its products.

The competition, however, will be including very little depreciation expense in its cost estimates (remember, they have older, highly depreciated assets) and, as a result, will be calculating artificially low product costs, causing them to fail to accumulate the funds necessary to meet their future capital spending requirements. Their lower prices will win many orders, but when the day comes for maintaining their production capabilities, the funds will not be there.

By excluding historical, financial depreciation from its costs for pricing purposes and substituting a lower, more forward looking capital requirement, the new manufacturer can gain the advantage over the older firm and, perhaps, even drive them out of business. Does this scenario sound at all familiar? Substitute Japan or Germany for the new manufacturer and the United States for the older firm. Now does it sound familiar?

Another question arises with regard to the inclusion of depreciation expense (or any other capital accumulation device for that matter) in product cost for pricing purposes. Should we burden the individual activities in which we have made capital investments in the past, or plan on making them in the future, with the task of generating funds for making future capital acquisitions?

With a few exceptions, companies are not made up of a variety of independent operations that are "sold" to customers separately. The more normal case is for a company's capital assets to form a system, or several systems, that are used to provide a line or "portfolio" of products and services. For example, one company manufactures a line of lawn carts—nonmotorized, two-wheeled trailers that are pulled by garden tractors. To manufacture these products, the company needs a variety of manufacturing capabilities. It must be able to saw, slit, punch, stamp, paint, assemble, and package products. In the normal course of business, it does not just saw, slit, punch, stamp, paint, assemble, or package a product; it performs almost all of these operations on every product. It has, in effect, a system for manufacturing lawn carts.

If the lawn cart manufacturer finds that it can make the system more productive by making a major capital investment in a new stamping press, is the expenditure benefiting just the stamping operation, or is it providing benefits to the system? Similarly, if the addition of the new stamping press improves the system to the point that the paint system cannot keep up with production, does the cost of additional painting capability benefit only painting operations, or is it making the system more productive? In almost all cases, capital equipment is purchased to enhance the system. Under such circumstances, is it logical for individual operations, such as stamping or painting, to bear the capital cost of expenditures that are made for the strategic benefit of the system as a whole? Perhaps companies should begin to look at themselves as systems for adding value, not individual work centers, when it comes to accumulating the capital funds necessary to maintain their current volume of business and technological position.

The phrase "maintain their current volume of business and technological position" was used several times in this discussion. The capital necessary to expand a business comes from profits. It is not a cost that should be attributed to current operations. As a consequence, such capital requirements should not be included in any capital costs being attributed to current business. Current business should, however, provide the capital funds necessary for a company to maintain its current position. The two key requirements for a company to maintain its position are that it keep its current volume of business, as well as its technological position relative to its competitors.

There is an approach to including capital expenditures in product costs for pricing purposes that takes care of both of these problems. noted above. The first step is to eliminate depreciation totally as a cost in estimating product cost. Instead, a cost element called a *capital accumulation allowance* (CAA) should be created. A company would develop a CAA for each of the "systems" into which it divides itself. The amount of the CAA would be determined by taking a long-term look at the funds required to support the system. For example, the lawn cart manufacturer looks at itself as a system for manufacturing lawn carts. It estimates the capital expenditures needed to maintain its current position during the next five years and the funds needed to retire the debt incurred in making earlier capital expenditures and comes up with the spending estimate shown below:

	($000)				
	Year 1	Year 2	Year 3	Year 4	Year 5
Debt retirement	$200	$100	$ 50	$ 50	$ 100
New expenditures	120	200	330	300	325
New financing			(100)	(100)	(100)
Net expenditures	$320	$300	$280	$ 250	$ 325

According to this summary, the average annual funds required to support capital spending during the five-year period will be $295,000 (the average of the *net expenditure* amounts). As a result, product costing estimates should be designed to accumulate this $295,000 annually. If a need for accelerated capital spending in the future becomes apparent, this need will gradually work its way into the CAA and not cause any sudden change in the company's cost structure. This does, of course, require that the organization do some serious long-term planning—a process that is already required for any firm that hopes to survive and prosper.

The next step is to attach the CAA to individual products. One logical and simple method, although not the only possible one, is to calculate the CAA as a percentage of the organization's conversion costs and apply it to individual product cost estimates using that percentage. For example, if a manufacturer incurs $1,900,000 in direct labor and $4,000,000 in nondepreciation indirect manufacturing cost, the percentage would be 5% [$295,000/($1,900,000 + $4,000,000)]. A product with conversion costs of $1 would then have $.05 added for the CAA.

In this manner, the entire system would be funding the capital program, regardless of where the funds need to be spent. The more value added to the product (to the extent that conversion costs mirror value added), the more burden it will bear for future capital spending.

Using a CAA instead of historical, financial depreciation expense also has other benefits. Suppose a manufacturer was competitive using historical depreciation, but the 5% CAA makes it noncompetitive. This would give the company an early warning that it will not be able to meet its long-term goals, or perhaps even survive, unless it finds ways to further improve its profitability or less expensive ways to maintain its manufacturing capability. The annual $295,000 is necessary to meet those goals. If it is not generated, the company will appear to be competitive right up to the time it either goes deeply into debt or out of business.

Suppose this company had a great deal of highly depreciated equipment. As a result, its annual depreciation provision in Year 1 was only $100,000, and in the following years it increased to $110,000, $120,000, $143,000, and $163,000, respectively. During this period the operation was very competitive, was able to turn an acceptable profit, and had collected $636,000 (its depreciation cost) in excess of its cash expenses for funding capital expenditures. Unfortunately, that amount was $839,000 short of the capital funding needs outlined in the earlier summary. As a result, it would be necessary to either cut capital spending back to less than half of the level deemed necessary to meet the company's objectives, use $839,000 of profit to fund these "nongrowth" expenditures, go $839,000 further into debt than planned, or a combination of all these actions. The following summary shows the year-by-year build-up of the capital funding shortfall:

	($000)				
	Year 1	Year 2	Year 3	Year 4	Year 5
Net expenditure plan	$320	$300	$280	$250	$325
Depreciation expense	100	110	120	143	163
Annual shortfall	220	190	160	107	162
Cumulative shortfall	$220	$410	$570	$677	$839

By knowing early that the planned results cannot be obtained without significant improvements in productivity, management can take the actions necessary to effect those improvements. If the opportunities for improvement prove to be insufficient, management can then make the strategic decisions most beneficial to the company's future. Whether the decision is to abandon or sell the business, milk it as a cash cow until it disappears. By looking for a new market, adopting totally new manufacturing technologies, or any other action, the use of the CAA and a base for charging the CAA to products as they use the entire system will help the organization gain control of its own destiny before events overtake it and drive it out of business or deep into debt.

The distortions in measuring costs over the "continuum of operations" caused by the depreciation expense must be taken into account if a business is to develop the accurate and relevant cost information needed to make sound business decisions.

NONANNUAL COST CYCLES

Not all cost or business cycles pay attention to the Earth orbiting around the sun. For example, a major piece of equipment at one company must undergo extensive preventive maintenance after every 12,000 hours of operation. During a normal year, the equipment will operate approximately 5,000 hours. As a result, the cost of performing preventive maintenance will appear in the company's general ledger every two or three years. The annual cost to operate this equipment, excluding preventive maintenance, is approximately $500,000. Each time preventive maintenance procedures are performed, the cost is $60,000. Is the cost to operate this piece of equipment $100 per hour ($500,000/5,000 hours) during those years in which preventive maintenance does not take place and $112 per hour ($560,000/5,000 hours) during those years in which it does? Or is the cost better determined by adding a preventive maintenance cost of $5 per hour ($60,000/12,000 hours) to a base operating rate of $100 per hour regardless of when the preventive maintenance actually occurs? The latter would seem to be the more accurate choice.

The same situation presents itself in other areas, such as the development of new marketing materials or a new advertising campaign. At times, an attempt is made to match the cost with the periods receiving the benefits. Smaller organizations, however, particularly privately held ones, will prefer to record the entire cost in the general ledger as an expense and improve cash flow by taking the tax deduction immediately. Management must be alert for situations in which cost cycles and Earth orbits do not coincide and make the appropriate adjustments before using cost information in any ABC calculation.

Similar problems also occur in many organizations whose business includes an occasional product line. An occasional product line is one in which contracts are won on an irregular basis. In some years, there may be no revenue-generating activity at all coming from the product line, whereas in other years, it will provide a significant boost in sales. Although revenues are not generated every year, costs relating to the product line are incurred every year.

One example of this situation occurs in the trade show exhibit industry. Firms in this industry create, construct, and manage trade show exhibits for their customers. They handle a large number of exhibits that might generate from a few thousand dollars to several hundred thousand dollars in revenue annually. In the day-to-day operation of their businesses, they must have a great deal of creativity, artistic ability, construction and project management skills, and the ability to manage events at remote locations. The same skills required to be successful working with trade show exhibits year after year are also necessary in a product area with much less regularity—museum exhibits. A firm might be fortunate to win two or three of these contracts every decade. When a museum contract is won, however, revenues can run into the millions of dollars.

These museum contracts are not won by serendipity or luck. They must be actively and continuously pursued. A successful firm will incur significant marketing and development costs every year, even those in which no museum-related revenues are generated. For example, a firm with $20 million in annual revenue from trade show exhibits might spend $200,000 annually in pursuit of museum contracts. Those efforts might result in a $6 to $8 million job every four years. How should the $200,000 be handled during those years with no museum business? Should it be assigned to the trade show contracts? Should it not be assigned to anything? How about those years in which museum contracts do exist? Should only $200,000 be assigned to those contracts? Whatever the solution, it should be obvious that the museum exhibit product line pays no attention at all to the Earth orbiting around the sun. In order to properly determine product or product-line profitability, adjustments must be made to general ledger expense information before it can be effectively used in ABC.

The distortions in measuring costs over the continuum of operations caused by nonannual cycle costs must be taken into account if a business is to develop the accurate and relevant cost information needed to make sound business decisions.

EXPENSES THAT ARE NOT INCURRED

There are many situations in which a company postpones certain costs in order to improve earnings for a particular period. Maintenance is deferred, research and development (R&D) curtailed, or marketing cut back during a particular Earth orbit. On the continuum of operations, these costs must still be incurred if the business is to maintain its existing level of business. If the expenditures are not made, equipment will break down, new products or services will not be developed to replace old ones, or competitors will begin to take away market share. Such costs cannot be overlooked if an organization is to understand its product or service cost or the true cost of its operating processes.

To maintain its current production capability over the continuum of operations, one manufacturer of wheels for agricultural equipment must spend approximately $250,000 per year for equipment maintenance. The operation's manager, who had decided that this was his last year in that position, made the decision to improve his last year's earnings by deferring as much maintenance as possible. This way, his track record would be improved and his bonus would be higher. As a result, maintenance costs during the last year were only $50,000; just enough so that no major equipment would break down and impact current operations. Should the $200,000 reduction in maintenance cost be reflected in lower product costs? If general ledger amounts are used to calculate product costs, it will.

There are many similarities between the treatment of these types of costs and the treatment that was suggested for accumulating capital funds earlier in this chapter. There are certain levels of maintenance, R&D, marketing, and other costs that must be maintained over the continuum of operations if the organization is to keep its current volume of business. The pharmaceutical company that does not spend enough on R&D will show improved profits in the short run, its product costs will appear lower and its competitiveness will appear to be improved. Unfortunately, it will be slowly liquidating itself in the process. For a pharmaceutical company, R&D is at least as important as, and probably more important than, capital spending. Similarly, the consumer products company that cuts its marketing costs below necessary levels can improve short-term earnings and make its product costs appear lower. For a consumer products company, marketing expenditures are at least as important as, and probably more important than, capital spending. A consumer products company that cuts marketing costs below the required level will be liquidating itself.

Establishing the appropriate amount of costs such as these requires more effort and a greater understanding of the business than does simply using the general ledger amounts, but they must be established to keep these costs from distorting cost measurements over the continuum of operations.

DEATH SPIRAL

An error made in a majority of the small and mid-sized companies we have worked with over the past decade can lead to what is often called the "death spiral." That error is the calculation of product costing rates based on last year's costs and volume of business or on the upcoming year's budgeted costs and volume of business.

Consider the case of one $10 million contract manufacturer. This company receives contracts to manufacture unique products to customer specifications. All products are unique, so there is no market price it can use when bidding on these contracts. Instead, it has to "fish" for the market price by estimating the cost of manufacturing the products under each contract and adding a target margin that would generate an acceptable profit should the contract be awarded. To develop these cost estimates, it calculates annual costing rates based on the prior year's actual activity.

During one year, a strike at its major customer caused its sales to fall to $9 million. Knowing that the drop in sales was only temporary, the company maintained its normal management and support structure throughout the strike period. When it developed its costing rates for the following year, it did as it always did: It took the previous year's actual costs and bases and calculated new rates. As you might have guessed, the rates were higher than in previous years. As a result, the company bid prices that were somewhat higher in order to meet their gross margin objective. Not surprisingly, the higher prices made the manufacturer less competitive, causing sales to drop to $8 million. When it came time to develop costing rates for the next year, the company again took the previous year's actual costs and bases and calculated new rates. You can probably guess what happened to sales in the subsequent year.

This contract manufacturer had fallen into the "death spiral." While maintaining the support structure of a $10 million business, it based its rates on lower and lower levels of activity, causing the rates to rise. Even after making some staff cutbacks, rates continued to rise. The reason for its decline in sales stemmed from a misunderstanding of the term *actual.* According to the dictionary, *actual* means "existing as a fact; real." In accounting, however, *actual* is the financial measurement of a set of aberrations that will never be repeated. Instead of using rates based on the most recently experienced set of aberrations (or on an assumed future set of aberrations), the company should have used its *real* costing rates.

Real costing rates are those that exist at the volume and mix of business for which the company has structured itself. Some refer to this volume and mix of business as the company's *practical capacity.* This $10 million manufacturer has structured itself to be a $10 million manufacturer. When sales fell to $9 million, it was still a $10 million manufacturer and should, therefore, have used rates that reflected that volume and mix of business when estimating the cost of core business even if that volume and mix was not attained. Costing contracts at the lower level of operations ensures only that the company will become less competitive and have difficulty returning to the $10 million level. Developing rates at the $8 million level makes the problem even worse. Rates should be maintained at the $10 million level until the company consciously restructures itself for another volume and mix of business.

Although the *downward* death spiral described above is the one most commonly encountered, there is an *upward* death spiral that can also lead a company into trouble if it is not careful. The upward death spiral occurs when a company experiences a significant, but temporary, increase in business. Suppose the $10 million manufacturer received a one-time order for $8 million that would be shipped over a two-year period. As a result, sales would increase to $14 million for two years before returning to the $10 million level supported by the company's core business.

Knowing that the increase is only temporary, management makes maximum use of its existing resources by working extra shifts and weekends, outsourcing many processes, using contract production and administrative personnel, leasing a trailer to provide additional office space, and so forth. Unfortunately, accounting personnel calculate costing rates in the same manner as always, using actual costs and bases. As a result, costing rates decline during the years in which the one-time order was being manufactured. The numbers showed a definite reduction in the cost of the company's $10 million core business as the lower rates were applied. When new business was quoted, the company was able to maintain its target margin at more competitive prices.

Once the one-time order was completed, the profitability of the company's $10 million core business dropped significantly. This was due, of course, to the company's passing "phantom" cost reductions, caused only by the extra volume generated by the one-time order, through to their customers. As a result, the year after completing the one-time order, the company had a portfolio of unprofitable or marginally profitable contracts. Years might pass before the portfolio returns to acceptable levels of profitability. As was the case when volume began to decline, the company should have never looked at itself as anything other than a $10 million manufacturer when costing core business. From a costing standpoint, the one-time order was a layer of business laid on top of the core business, it should never have been blended in with it.

SUMMARY

Generally accepted accounting principles are not designed to provide cost information that represents economic reality. They serve a very valuable purpose, but that purpose is not to provide cost information that is useful in helping management make its day-to-day and strategic decisions. Before it is used in developing any kind of decision costing information, general ledger cost data must be purged of any viruses that would cause a material impact on the accuracy or relevance of the information provided to management for use in supporting its decisions.

5

Logic of Activity-Based Costing

As discussed earlier, activity-based costing (ABC) is a simple concept that is used to develop the accurate and relevant cost information needed to support business decisions of all types. This concept links costs with the activities that make them necessary and the accumulated cost of activities with the products or services that make them necessary. By incorporating the concept of ABC into the way they develop cost information, owners and managers of all types of organizations can provide themselves with the accurate and relevant cost information necessary to attract more profitable contracts, use capital funds more effectively, make better make/buy decisions, focus continuous improvements on areas with the greatest return, and generally make more informed and, as a result, more effective business decisions.

The fundamental concept underlying ABC can be summarized as follows:

- The jobs, products, and services an organization provides require it to perform activities, and those activities cause it to incur costs.
- Costs that cannot be directly attributable to a job, product, or service are associated with the activities that make them necessary.
- Each activity's accumulated cost is then associated with the jobs, products, or services that make the activity necessary.

The concept is as simple as that. Costs are either assigned directly to a job, product, or service, or they are assigned to the various activities performed by the organization. Those costs assigned to the organization's activities are eventually assigned to its jobs, products, or services as the cost of the various activities are associated with the jobs, products, or services that made them necessary.

The implementation of ABC requires the development of an economic model that reflects the actual cause-and-effect relationships between the organization's costs, activities, and products or services. This chapter describes the fundamental steps necessary to develop the conceptual design of such a model.

DESIGNING THE ACTIVITY-BASED COST FLOW

One of the easiest ways to visualize an activity-based flow of costs from their incurrence to their assignment to jobs, products, and services is through a series of "ABC Cost Flow-Down" diagrams. Exhibit 5.1 provides the starting point for our discussion. At the top of Exhibit 5.1 is a shaded area labeled "Variety Corporation Costs." The shading in this area indicates that all costs incurred by Variety Corporation are contained there. They have not been classified. They have not been assigned to any activity. The area simply represents all of the costs that the corporation has incurred. At the bottom of the exhibit is an area labeled "Variety Corporation Cost Objectives" (i.e., the company's various jobs, products, or services). The absence of shading indicates that no costs are included in that area. Our objective in going through the series of diagrams that follow is to find the cause-and-effect pathways that will enable the costs in the "Variety Corporation Costs" area to flow to those "Variety Corporation Cost Objectives" that make them necessary.

THROUGHPUT OR DIRECT COSTS

As previously noted, the starting point of ABC is to associate costs that are not directly attributable to a job, product, or service with the activities that make them necessary. As a first step, we will define those costs that *are* directly attributable to a job and therefore not subject to ABC's cause-and-effect analysis. These costs we will categorize as *throughput or direct costs.*

With one major exception, throughput or direct costs are those amounts paid to organizations or individuals outside of the company that are both directly related to and easily traceable to a specific job, product, or service. They include such traditional direct costs as merchandise purchased for resale, raw materials, purchased components, supplies bought for a specific program or project, purchased subassemblies, and outsourced value-adding services (e.g., heat treating, plating, machining, assembling).

Exhibit 5.1 Variety Corporation Costs and Cost Objectives

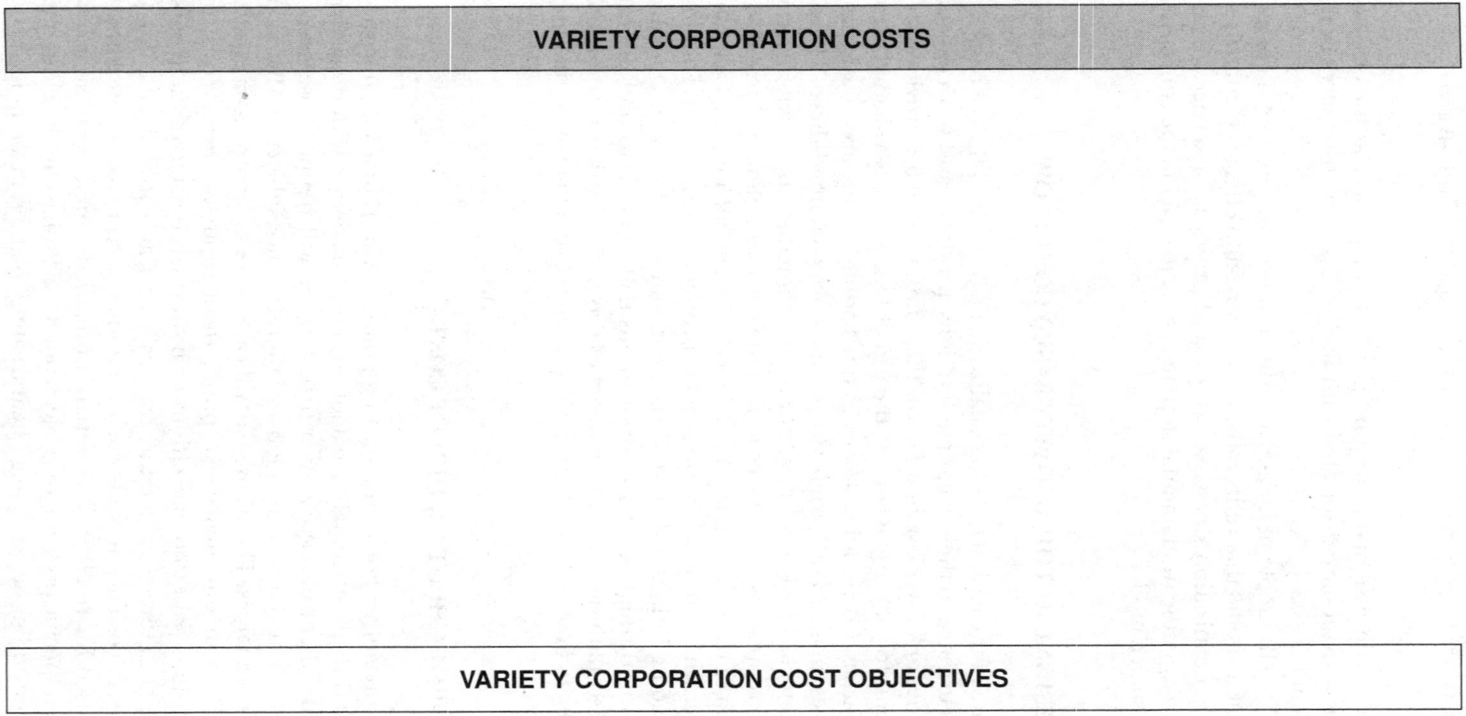

VARIETY CORPORATION COSTS

VARIETY CORPORATION COST OBJECTIVES

In cases in which the cost is significant and a practical means of assigning the cost to specific cost objectives is developed, costs treated as *indirect materials* in traditional cost systems, such as perishable tooling or coating materials, can also be included in this category.

The one major exception to this definition is contract labor. Labor that is purchased from an outside vendor in lieu of its being performed by an employee should not be considered a throughput or direct cost. This should not be confused with "contracting out" an entire process which is a throughput or direct cost. Similarly, the traditional direct cost of *direct labor* is also excluded from this category. All labor activities internal to the company, whether performed by employees or contract labor, are not considered direct in the traditional sense. Instead, they are assigned to the activities that made them necessary.

Once we have identified these throughput or direct costs have been identified, the process of associating the balance of a company's costs with the activities that make them necessary can begin. Although specific activities will vary considerably from company to company, categories of activities will not. As a result, activity categories will be used in this discussion.

SERVICE AND OPERATIONS SUPPORT ACTIVITIES

The first activity category is service and operations support activities. These are activities that generally do not exist to act directly on an organization's cost objectives. Instead, they exist primarily to support other activities within the organization. The following activities are commonly included in this category:

- *Building and grounds*—provides and maintains the physical facilities in which other activities can take place.
- *Human resources*—provides the administrative services necessary to support the employees performing other activities.
- *Information systems or data processing*—provides information systems support for the performance of other activities.
- *Maintenance*—maintains the equipment necessary for other activities to operate.
- *Supervision*—provides the required supervision for other activities.
- *Education or training*—provides the training required for employees to effectively perform the organization's various activities.
- *Engineering*—can, at times, be associated with a specific cost objective, but may also provide research and development (R&D) services, support for sales and marketing efforts, assistance in improving other

activities, or technical support in the procurement of certain throughput or direct items.

- *Accounting*—supports the procurement of supplies and throughput or direct items in its accounts payable/cash disbursement work, the firm's employees in its timekeeping and payroll work, and the general administration of the business in its bookkeeping, cash management, budgeting, and tax work.
- *Production control or scheduling*—plans and schedules activities that can be associated with specific cost objectives.
- *Purchasing*—provides the procurement services needed to ensure that the appropriate throughput or direct items, as well as indirect supply items, are available when needed by other activities.
- *Sales and marketing*—provides services to ensure that there are jobs, products, or services that make all of the other activities necessary.
- *Quality control*—provides services to ensure that throughput or direct items, operating processes, and completed jobs meet the company's and the customers' quality requirements.
- *Receiving/material handling*—provides services to ensure that the correct throughput or direct items are received in the proper quantities and that items are moved through the facility from activity to activity as needed.
- *General and administration*—provides general support for the organization as a whole, such as strategic planning, dealing with investors, bank relations, closing the books, and general management.

Large companies may create activity centers to accumulate the costs of these and many more service and operations support activities. In smaller organizations, in which all of these activities are performed by a handful of individuals, these activities might be combined into a few more generalized activity centers.

The key requirement of a service and operations support activity is that it exist, in whole or in part, to support other activities within the organization.

THROUGHPUT OR MATERIAL SUPPORT ACTIVITIES

Throughput or material support activities are those activities that exist to ensure that the appropriate throughput or direct items are available when needed by the organization. A sufficient number of activity centers should be created in this category to account for the different levels of effort needed to support different categories of throughput or direct items. In analyzing these activities, it is often useful to first divide them into two subcategories: (1) those activities that ensure the appropriate items arrive and are paid for and (2) those activities that occur between the time the items arrive and the time they are consumed or used by the business' operating processes.

For example, a company may have a few high-volume, raw material items that require only a small amount of purchasing activity even though they represent a high percentage of the raw material dollars spent. At the same time, there may be many low-volume items that require a great deal of purchasing activity even though they represent only a small percentage of the raw material dollars spent. Under such circumstances, it would be advisable to have separate activity centers for high-volume raw materials and low-volume raw materials. In this way, the higher procurement cost per dollar or per unit of low-volume raw materials will follow those materials to the jobs or products on which they are used. Likewise, the lower procurement cost per dollar or per unit of high-volume raw materials will follow them to the jobs or products on which they are used.

Similarly, some purchased components may be "off-the-shelf" items that require very little testing when received by the company. Other purchased items may be highly customized or have other characteristics that make a considerable amount of inspection and testing necessary when received. In this situation, it would be advisable to have separate activity centers for receiving "low-inspection" purchased components and "high-inspection" components. By doing so, the higher inspection cost of high-inspection components will follow them to the jobs or products on which they are used, and the lower inspection cost of low-inspection components will follow them to their jobs or products.

The amount of effort required to warehouse or handle different throughput or direct items until they are used can also be the basis for creating activity centers. One company uses both high-cost, quality-sensitive fabric and lower-cost covering with less quality sensitivity in producing its products. The storage area for the high-cost, quality-sensitive fabric is tightly secured, and precise perpetual records are maintained to ensure that a minimum amount of fabric is wasted and that it is ordered only when absolutely necessary. As a matter of fact, three individuals are assigned full time to the area where this fabric is stored. The lower-cost, less quality-sensitive coverings, on the other hand, are kept in a general storage area and receive the same amount of security and record-keeping support as any ordinary purchased materials in the facility. In such a situation, it is advisable for the company to create a separate activity center to accumulate the cost of supporting the high-cost, quality-sensitive fabrics so that the cost of supporting this category of throughput or direct cost will follow the fabric to the jobs or products on which it is used.

Sometimes, an activity center might be needed to support items purchased from a specific vendor. Such was the case with a company that negotiated a contract with a single vendor to supply all of its off-the-shelf component parts. An order point and order quantity was established for each of the items included in the contract. Each week, a representative of the vendor would visit and review the inventory status of all items covered by the contract. The vendor representative would then send releases to his company, via computer modem, for all items that had fallen below their order point. The next day, another representative of the vendor would deliver the released items to their assigned areas within the company's component warehouse and provide a delivery document to the company's accounts payable department. Once a month, the vendor would send an invoice to cover the entire month's transactions. The only company activities required to support these off-the-shelf items were to provide storage space within its facility, negotiate the contract annually, perform periodic spot checks, and pay the bill once each month.

It should be apparent that very little support is required for the procurement and handling of these off-the-shelf items. As a result, the company created a throughput or material support activity center for accumulating the cost of supporting this one vendor.

One often overlooked throughput or material support activity involves those activities that support outsourced value-adding services. A great deal of effort often goes into activities such as locating and qualifying the vendor, scheduling and transporting materials to and from the vendor's location, maintaining inventory and other records regarding parts moving back and forth, and vouchering and paying the vendor's invoices. Despite these efforts, the cost of these activities seldom follows the throughput or direct cost of the outsourced value-adding services to the jobs or products on which they are performed. By having one or more activity centers to accumulate the cost of these activities, such an oversight can be avoided.

The following are important steps to remember in developing an appropriate group of throughput or material support activity centers:

- First, identify all activities involved in the procurement, receipt, and storage of raw materials, purchased components, outside manufacturing services, and other "direct" items
- Once segregated, these activities must then be divided into activity centers that reflect the different amount of effort required to support the different categories of throughput or direct costs.

MARKET OR CUSTOMER SUPPORT ACTIVITIES

Not all markets or customers require the same level of support. For example, one market that represents half of a company's sales might require three times as much marketing and support work as the market in which it sells the other half of its products. A variety of conditions can cause these differences. It could simply be that standard operating procedures in one market are more cumbersome and involved than in another. Such would be the case with a company that has both government and commercial contracts. Where the company's government contracts demand knowledge of government contracting law, compliance with a myriad of regulations, and maintenance of specific, detailed accounting records, its commercial contracts may require only timely delivery of the appropriate product or service at the agreed to price.

In other cases, it could be the nature of the customers within the market. The original equipment manufacturing (OEM) market, for example, may require long, protracted negotiations, but result in large, multiyear orders. Once orders are received, market support consists of crossing the "t's" and dotting the "i's" necessary to make the big customers' bureaucracy work effectively. The aftermarket, on the other hand, may require a great deal more support. Sales efforts are more continuous and intense as sales representatives visit a large number of small customers spread over a wide geographic area. Credit and collections efforts are greater as many small amounts are collected from a great number of customers, each with its own internal system and level of creditworthiness.

Various other factors might also cause market differences. A company may have one market or customer for whom it must prepare 20 or more proposals for each contract it receives, whereas other markets or customers generate contracts on a much higher percentage of proposals. One market might require a high level of involvement in trade shows, marketing materials, and sales calls, whereas another market requires only the annual distribution of a catalog. In most cases, the amount of effort required in dealing with domestic versus international markets will be quite different.

Sometimes, it is not the market that makes a difference as much as specific customers (or groups of customers) within the market. In other words, some customers can be "sweethearts" while others are "jerks." The behavior of jerks causes the organization to incur extra costs that should not be distributed in a way that results in their being assigned to work performed for sweethearts. This behavior can take on many forms, such as constant schedule changes, excessive returns, particularly cumbersome business practices, regular specification or engineering changes, excessive red tape, or unnecessary site visits.

One company had a jerk customer that represented approximately 10% of its annual volume. The problems with this customer were a result of its constant schedule changes. The customer would often provide only four weeks' notice for adding a product to the schedule whose key component had a minimum five-week lead time. The vendor for that key component was specified by the customer, who was well aware of the vendor's five-week lead time requirement, and it would not approve any alternative source. Schedules would fluctuate widely on a daily basis to such an extent that the company would receive calls at 7:15 A.M. and be told to stop producing the product they had setup for a four-hour run at 7:00 A.M. (as required by the customer's schedule) and run another product instead.

The behavior of this customer had several effects on the company. Inventory had to be purchased on speculation, tying up floor space and working capital as well as adding the risk of obsolescence, shrinkage, and damage. Overall plant scheduling efforts were so complicated that the production control manager estimated that four of her seven employees would not be necessary if the jerk customer did not exist. Finally, the chaos caused by this customer had an impact on other customers' jobs, causing a two- to three-percentage-point drop in efficiency when producing the sweethearts' products. It was obvious that this company needed to establish an activity center to accumulate the excess costs attributable to this one jerk customer and, ultimately, to associate the costs with that customer's products.

The jerk concept can also exist in reverse. A business can have one or more super sweethearts, whose behavior makes them much easier to work with than the average customer. These customers enable the business to avoid activities (and therefore costs) that are required for other customers. Often, these are customers with which the business has a special relationship. This relationship may reduce the amount of marketing effort required when dealing with super sweethearts or may reduce the amount of coordination and support when executing contracts received from them.

For example, one $20 million manufacturer of low-cost ($300 to $500 each), customized products had a customer that represented about 30% of its total sales volume. No other customer accounted for over 5% of its sales. All of the manufacturer's customers required it to submit a bid for each job. Because individual orders were relatively small, this required that the manufacturer employ a group of six estimators. Overall, the manufacturer was awarded one third of the jobs on which it submitted bids (including bids to its major customer). To streamline its bidding process, the manufacturer created a product pricing template, which made it possible to develop a price quotation by "pricing out" selected physical characteristics of the final product. This new template enabled the manufacturer to reduce the number of estimators from six to four.

As a means of reducing costs for both itself and its major customer, the manufacturer provided that customer with a copy of the template and taught them how to use it. This enabled the customer to create a quotation from the manufacturer without having to contact them at all. As long as the correct physical characteristics were loaded into the template, the manufacturer would live with the calculated price. The reduction in incoming quotations that resulted from this move enabled the manufacturer to further reduce the number of estimators from four to three. The remaining three estimators worked only on the 70% of the business that did not come from the one major customer. As a result, an activity center to accumulate bid and proposal costs was established and the accumulated cost distributed only to the many smaller customers. The major customer's jobs were no longer charged with any bid and proposal costs because that customer did not require any bid and proposal activity.

If the cost to support different market or customer categories is not determined and then assigned to the jobs, products, or services sold in those categories, product cost and profitability will not be fully understood and used to the company's advantage. Activity centers should be established to accumulate these varying market or customer costs and assign them appropriately to each market's jobs and products.

The following are important points to remember in developing an appropriate group of *market or customer support* activity centers:

- First, identify all activities involved in marketing the company's products and services or in postaward indirect customer support.
- Once segregated, these activities must then be divided into activity centers that reflect the different amount of effort required to support the different market or customer categories.

PRODUCT OR PRODUCT-LINE SUPPORT ACTIVITIES

Just as different markets or customers can require different support levels, not all products or product lines require the same level of support. For example, a technical product line that represents one third of a company's sales might require two thirds of its engineering and quality effort, whereas a nontechnical product line requires only one third of its effort. Similarly, products made from exotic materials might require a significantly higher level of engineering support than those made from standard types of steel.

A machine tool company manufactures and sells two lines of equipment. One line consists of standard base units to which minor modifications can be made to customize them before delivery. The other line consists of machine tools built "from scratch" to meet customer requirements. In order to have an appropriate mix of base units that will be able to meet the demands of a wide variety of customers with little modification, the company has a group of engineers who work to develop new types of base units and to improve existing base units to keep them up-to-date with the latest technology and make them usable in a wider range of applications. None of their work has anything to do with custom-built machine tools.

The custom-built machine tool line, however, requires a great deal more technical support in marketing and developing proposals for prospective customers. This additional support is not required because of the market in which the equipment is sold. Both lines are sold to the same universe of customers. The added support is due to the nature of the product line. As a result, this machine tool builder needs to create activity centers to separately accumulate the cost of supporting the two product lines and ensure that the accumulated support costs are attributed to the correct line of products.

Similarly, a manufacturer and distributor of industrial chemicals sells approximately half of its products under its own brand name (the house brand) and sells the other half to smaller distributors in packages that bear the customer's brand identification (private labels). In order to support the private label line of products, it maintains an art department that develops attractive labeling for its customers and creates the silk screens that are used to apply the customer's private label onto its containers before shipment. Less than 5% of this activity's work supports the house brand. Over 95% of its work supports the 50% of its volume sold under private labels. As a result, this company created activity centers to accumulate the cost of "house art" and "private label art" separately and associate the accumulated cost of each activity center with the appropriate product line.

Often, each of a company's product lines are sold to a different marketplace. Product Line A is sold in Market 1 and Product Line B is sold in Market 2. Does the company have two different product lines, or is it serving two different markets? When the correlation is so close, it does not really matter. The objective is to get the activity costs to the right jobs, products, or services and classifying them either way will get the job done.

If the cost to support different products or product lines is not determined and then assigned to the jobs, products, or services sold in those categories, product or service cost and profitability will not be fully understood and used to the company's advantage. Activity centers should be established to accumulate these varying product or product-line costs and assign them appropriately to each category's jobs, products, and services.

The following are important points to remember in developing an appropriate group of *product or product-line support* activity centers:

- First, segregate all activities that are incurred to support the company's products and services.
- Once segregated, these activities must then be divided into activity centers that reflect the different amount of effort required to support the different product or product-line categories.

VALUE-ADDING OR DIRECT ACTIVITIES

In traditional costing systems, many of the non–throughput or direct costs are charged to cost objectives through the *value-adding or direct activities.* These are activities taking place that turn the things a company buys (or has consigned to it) into the things it sells or that are directly attributable to the service being provided. In a manufacturing business, direct labor dollars or hours have been the most popular bases for charging these costs to products, although machine hours, cycle time, cell hours, and line hours have been in use as well. In the printing industry, press hours have been the primary means of assigning costs to jobs. In service industries, costs have generally followed the cost of the direct service providers as a cost per labor hour.

As should be apparent from the discussion of activity categories, many of the activity costs that have historically been included in these rates have had little or no relationship to the performance of value-adding or direct activities. We have already discussed costs that are caused by the types of throughput or direct items the company uses, by the types of markets or customers it serves, and by the types of products or product lines it provides. In later sections, costs caused by certain transactions or events and costs that are legitimately categorized as general and administrative expenses will be discussed. Under an activity-based approach, costs relating to other activity categories no longer blindly follow value-adding or direct activities to job orders. Instead, they are accumulated in appropriate activity centers and directed to the job, products, or services that require those centers' activities.

Despite their diminished role under ABC, value-adding or direct activities still carry a large portion of many companies' costs to cost objectives. The costs carried, however, are limited to those that actually have something to do with the performance of the activity itself. As is already acknowledged at those companies that do not use a single, facility-wide overhead rate, not all value-adding or direct activities cost the same for each unit of activity performed. As a result, activity centers should be established within this category to take into account the varying levels of cost and support required by different value-adding or direct activities within the facility as well as the different methods that are appropriate for assigning activity center costs to the organization's cost objectives.

In health care, for example, the cost of activities performed by registered nurses (RNs) do not require the same level of cost and support as those performed by nurses' aides. This difference is not limited to the different pay levels of RNs and aides. The higher turnover among aides makes the educational support for this activity much higher than for RNs. As a result, the educational cost per hour of aide activity is usually higher than for RN activity. This, and other support differences, make it advisable to have different activity centers for accumulating the cost of RNs and aides.

A walk through a manufacturing facility should make it obvious that all of the value-adding or direct activities do not require the same level of cost and support, nor would the same method of assigning their cost to cost objectives be appropriate. An activity in which a worker operates an expensive piece of equipment that consumes a significant amount of utilities in its operation would obviously not cost the same as an activity in which a worker stands at a table manually assembling a product. Similarly, an activity in which a worker performs "hands-on" value-adding work (e.g., assembly or manual machining) could not use the same method of assigning its cost to a cost objective as one in which a worker is not directly involved at all (e.g., heat treating or plating).

There are many criteria for establishing an appropriate set of activity centers for value-adding or direct activities. They not only include the similarities or differences between the various individual activities, but the organization's view toward depreciation, whether the activities are independent or part of a series of dependent activities, whether the same size crew always attends the activity, whether the same type of worker always performs the activity, the degree of accuracy desired by the organization's management, and many more. Many of these criteria are discussed in other sections of this book, so they will not be discussed here. The point that must be kept in mind is that activity centers should be established to take into account both the varying levels of cost and support required by different value-adding or direct activities and the different methods that are appropriate for assigning activity center costs to the organization's cost objectives.

The following are important points to remember in developing an appropriate group of value-adding or direct activity centers:

- First, segregate all activities that are incurred in performing the company's value-adding or direct work.
- Once segregated, these activities must then be divided into activity centers that reflect the different amount of cost and support effort involved in performing each of the activities and the different methods that are needed for assigning each activity center's cost to the appropriate cost objectives.

EVENT OR TRANSACTION ACTIVITIES

The occurrence of certain events or transactions sets off "chains of administrative activities" that cause a company to incur costs. For example, the receipt of a customer order is an event that sets off a chain of administrative activities that starts with entering the order into the system and culminates with the deposit of a check. In between, various types of standard administrative activities can take place: A work order is created, material requirements are determined, production is scheduled, shipping documentation is completed, transportation is arranged, and an invoice is prepared. Some companies will have many other identifiable activities in the chain.

In many cases, the amount of activity will not vary significantly from event to event. For example, the receipt of an order for a $100,000 job may not generate significantly more activity along the chain than the receipt of a $10,000 job. Actually performing the work required to complete the job may vary considerably (purchasing, engineering, manufacturing, etc.), but the administrative cost caused by the event may not. In other cases, the amount of effort required for certain sizes or types of events or transactions may be different enough to warrant dividing them into two or more categories. If both technical and nontechnical products or services are sold and the amount of effort required along the chain of administrative activities is significantly different, separate technical order and nontechnical order transactions might be necessary. Similarly, orders received manually may require a different amount of effort than those received over the electronic data interchange (EDI). In such cases, manual order and EDI order activity centers may be appropriate.

These types of events can be viewed as "administrative setups"—a front office parallel to manufacturing process setups. Most companies understand that the profit contribution of a job, product, or service must be large enough to cover the "fixed" investment in its setup if the business is to be profitable. Fewer realize that the fixed investment in a job, product, or service also includes one or more of these "event or transaction" activities and that they must also be covered by the job's contribution if it is to be profitable.

Sometimes, events can be created that serve as surrogates for certain value-adding, direct, or other types of activities. For example, a manufacturing company used to include setup costs as part of manufacturing overhead. If the time required for setups varies by plus/minus 20%, the effort required to measure the exact time for every setup may not be a cost-effective endeavor. Including the fact that there is a setup, however, might still be critical for understanding the cost of manufacturing jobs or products of different volumes. As a result, an activity center for the value-adding or direct event of a setup can be established and the average cost per setup used in job or product costing. Similarly, the cost of preparing a shipment might not vary enough to justify keeping track of the time required for each individual shipment, while including the fact that a shipment, which does have a cost, must be prepared is important for understanding the cost of a job. This is another case in which it might be valuable to create an activity center to accumulate the cost of shipments and a cost determined for the value-adding or direct event of a shipment established for use in costing the job or product.

Finally, *event or transaction activity* centers are useful for measuring the cost of some activities whose nature makes them impractical or impossible to calculate otherwise. A prime example is the cost related to "picking" an order at a distributor. It should be intuitively obvious that a $10,000 order received by a distributor that has a $3,000 margin will be more profitable if it is for 10 of 1 item than if it is for 1 each of 10 items. If it is for 1 of 10 different items, workers have to go to 10 different locations in the warehouse to pick the order. If it is for 10 of 1 item, they need only go to one location. This difference can be measured if an activity center is created to collect order-picking costs and an average cost "per line item ordered" calculated to charge those costs to the cost objective. This is another use of event or transaction activities as a surrogate for value-adding or direct activities.

Event or transaction activities are useful devices for a making accurate measurements of important cost items when more precise measurements are either impossible, impractical, or not worth the cost of more elaborate calculation. The following are important points to remember in developing an appropriate group of event or transaction activities:

- First, segregate all activities that are required due to specified events or transactions.
- Once segregated, these activities must then be divided into activity centers that reflect the different amount of cost and effort involved in performing the various events or processing the various transactions.

GENERAL AND ADMINISTRATIVE ACTIVITIES

After identifying and placing activities into the categories already discussed, there will remain certain costs and activities that exist for the general management and administration of the company. These include strategic planning; certain R&D efforts; closing the books; preparing annual budgets; dealing with the board, investors, or the bank; and a few others. As mentioned in Chapter 4, there are also certain costs and activities, often categorized as *general and administrative,* (G&A) that have absolutely nothing to do with the company's existing volume and mix of business. These include market-building expenditures, R&D for products intended to expand business volume, and other expenses that are, in effect, investments in the future growth of the business. As investments, these costs are not expenses that should be associated with jobs, products, or services included in the company's current business. They represent a reinvestment of the company's profits. As such, they should be excluded from determining any costing rates used to calculate the cost of any of the organization's current jobs, products, or services.

Activity centers should be established to accumulate the costs of current G&A activities and those that actually represent a reinvestment of company profits. The following are important points to remember in developing an appropriate group of G&A activity centers:

- First, assign activities that are attributable to throughput or material support, market or customer support, product or product line support, value-adding or direct activities, and events or transactions to those activities categories. The remaining activities can then be considered for the G&A activity category.
- Once identified, these activities must then be separated into two activity centers—one that reflects the amount of effort required to administratively support the company's current volume and mix of business and one that reflects the administrative effort being invested in the company's growth.

Using these activity categories and the resulting activity centers, we can begin to develop the pathways for directing costs to the jobs, products, and services that caused them to be incurred.

COST FLOW-DOWN STEP 1: ASSIGNING COSTS TO ACTIVITIES

Exhibit 5.2 shows the first step in an activity-based cost flow-down process. All costs are assigned to either the cost objectives themselves (if they are throughput or direct costs) or to the appropriate activity centers (all other costs). Costs that flow directly into the individual activity centers included in the diagram's activity center categories include the wages and fringes of individuals working exclusively within the activity center, the depreciation or lease cost of equipment used exclusively within the activity center (unless one chooses to use another device, such as a capital accumulation allowance, in lieu of these costs), supplies and utilities consumed within the activity center, and any other cost directly attributable to the activity center. The wages and fringes of individuals whose work can be attributed to more than one activity center and the depreciation or lease cost of equipment that can be attributed to more than one activity center must first be directed into a service or support activity center. It can then be divided among the various activity centers that receive the benefit in the flow-down process' second step.

Exhibit 5.2 Activity-Based Cost Flow-Down Process: Step 1

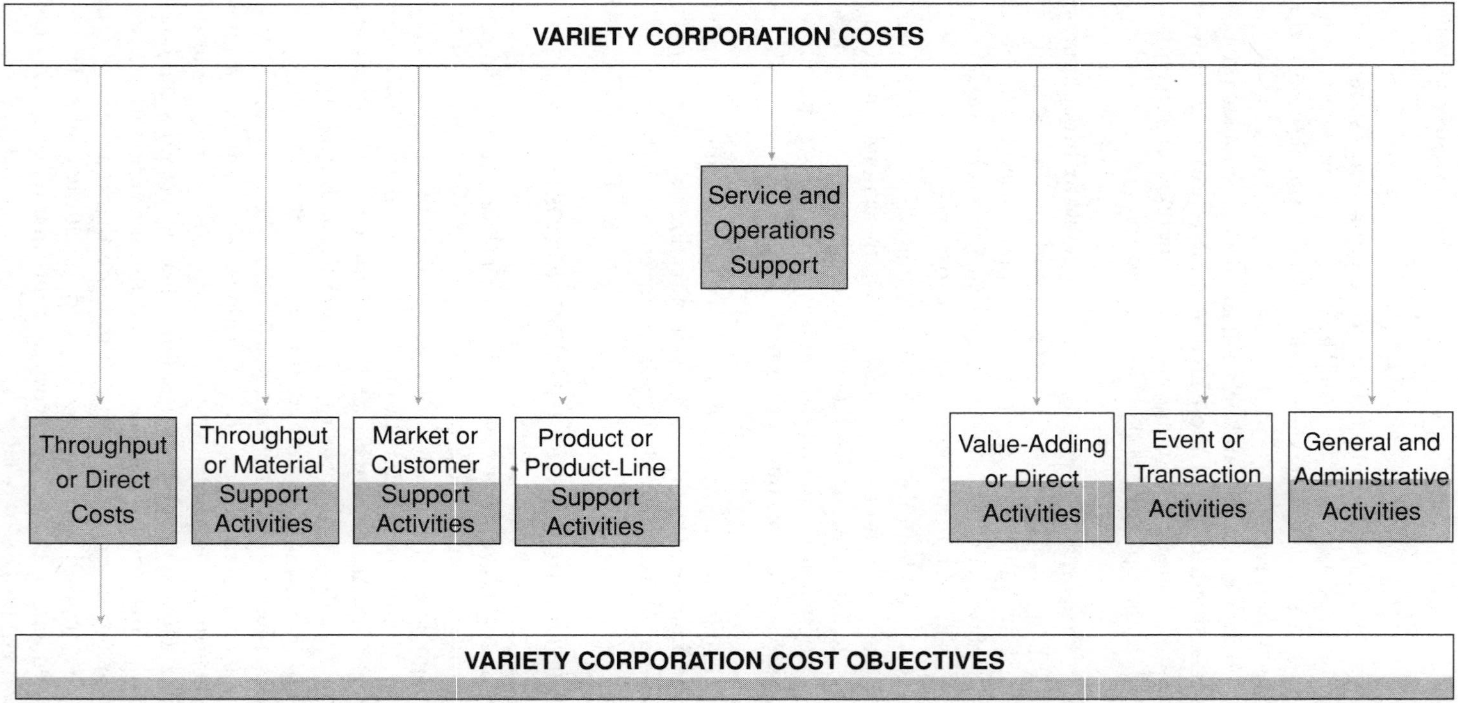

VARIETY CORPORATION COSTS

Service and Operations Support

Throughput or Direct Costs

Throughput or Material Support Activities

Market or Customer Support Activities

Product or Product-Line Support Activities

Value-Adding or Direct Activities

Event or Transaction Activities

General and Administrative Activities

VARIETY CORPORATION COST OBJECTIVES

At the conclusion of the first step, those costs that can be directly attributable to cost objectives, and the total cost of the various service and operations support activity centers will be known. (Distributions among service and support activity centers do take place, but these *internal* distributions will not be discussed here to keep the focus on the general flow-down concept.) The full cost of activities within the other activity center categories, however, are not yet known. To determine the cost of those activity centers, we must distribute the costs accumulated in the service and operations support activity centers to those activity centers that they support. This is done in Cost Flow-Down Step 2 shown in Exhibit 5.3.

COST FLOW-DOWN STEP 2: ASSIGNING COSTS AMONG ACTIVITIES

In the flow-down process' second step, the cost of service and operations support activity centers are distributed to the other activity centers that made them necessary. Exhibit 5.3 shows the distribution of these activity center costs to other activity center categories, but distributions also take place within the service and operations support activity center category. These distributions are made using either a relevant statistical base (e.g., square footage, operating hours, headcounts) or an analysis of the activities performed by the service or operations support activity.

For example, a support activity that has accumulated the cost of owning, operating, and maintaining the physical facility (building and grounds) might distribute its cost based on the square footage occupied by each of the other activity centers. Similarly, a support activity that has accumulated the cost of performing the company's human resource and payroll processing activities (human resources) might distribute its cost based on employee headcount.

Many support activity centers have no convenient and relevant statistical basis for distributing their cost. Those distributions must be made on the basis of an *activity analysis* that estimates the percentage of each activity's effort that is performed in support of each of the other activity centers.

One company, for example, has a support activity that includes two individuals who purchase all materials and outside manufacturing services, arrange transportation for outgoing shipments, manage the activities of the outside manufacturers, create work orders for jobs released to the plant floor, and deal with inquiries from the company's most difficult customers regarding the status of their orders. The distribution of this support activity's accumulated cost might be determined as follows:

- The percentage of time spent purchasing materials would be distributed to a material support activity center (a throughput or material support activity).

Exhibit 5.3 Activity-Based Cost Flow-Down Process: Step 2

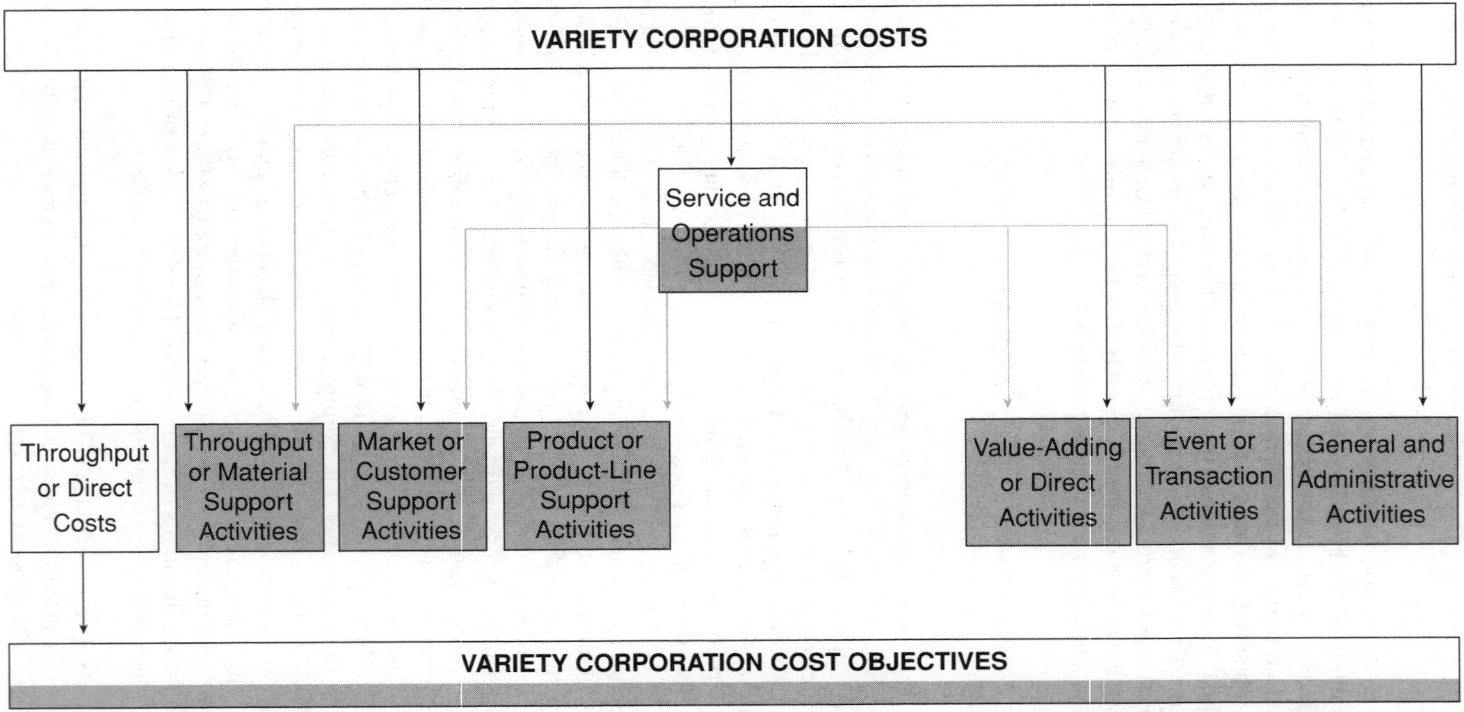

VARIETY CORPORATION COSTS

Service and Operations Support

Throughput or Direct Costs

Throughput or Material Support Activities

Market or Customer Support Activities

Product or Product-Line Support Activities

Value-Adding or Direct Activities

Event or Transaction Activities

General and Administrative Activities

VARIETY CORPORATION COST OBJECTIVES

- The percentage of time spent purchasing the services and managing the activities of outside manufacturers would be distributed to an outside manufacturing services support activity center (another throughput or material support activity).
- The percentage of time spent creating work orders for jobs released to the plant floor and arranging transportation for outgoing shipments would be distributed to an order support activity center (an event or transaction activity).
- The percentage of time spent dealing with inquiries from the company's more difficult customers would be distributed to a difficult customer support activity center (a market or customer support activity).

In this manner, the cost of this support activity would be distributed to the activity centers that made it necessary.

It should always be kept in mind that the goal of ABC is accuracy, not precision. As a general rule, it is usually safe to ignore any distribution from a service or support activity center that represents less than 5% of the activity center's total cost. If, for example, activity analysis of an activity center shows that 45% of its effort is in support of one activity center, 30% is in support of another, and the remaining 25% split between a dozen other activity centers (none of which requires as much as 5%), it is probably safe to distribute the 25% to G&A. Some precision may be lost, but there will be very little impact on accuracy. After all, something split in such small proportions among so many activity centers is pretty general in nature.

Each support activity that does not have a convenient and relevant statistical distribution basis would be distributed in this manner. Once the distributions are complete, the total cost of each throughput or material support activity center, market or customer support activity center, product or product-line support activity center, value-adding or direct activity center, event or transaction activity center, and G&A activity center would be known.

In some cases, a certain amount of cost will remain in a service or support activity. This will occur when the service activity can charge some of its time directly to a cost objective. The major example of this is engineering. Although a significant portion of engineering's effort may be in support of procurement, marketing, R&D, and other activities, some of its efforts are often chargeable directly to job orders on which engineers are working. Treatment of these remaining costs is included in the discussion of Cost Flow-Down Step 3.

One possible complication arises when costs are distributed from one service and operations support activity to another; namely, the activity centers involved might support each other. The earlier examples of building and grounds and human resources activities are typical of this complication.

If there are employees involved in building and grounds activities and human resources activities take up space, the two activity centers should, theoretically, "cross-charge" each other. Allowing this to take place, however, will add more mathematical complexity (solving simultaneous equations) than is warranted by the amount of accuracy that will be gained. When the objective of accuracy, not precision, is kept in mind, the need for any such cross-charging disappears. The lesser of the two distributions can be ignored without losing any accuracy.

In cases in which two or more service and operations support activity centers are heavily dependent on each other, it is usually because they are not really separate activity centers. For example, if it is determined that 30% of engineering supports quality control and 40% of quality control supports engineering, it is usually best to combine them into a quality control/engineering activity center. In a dozen years of designing activity-based cost flows at over 100 organizations, we have never found it necessary to cross-charge activity centers, and only twice have we combined two or more heavily interdependent activity centers.

"CAFETERIA LINE" OF ACTIVITY CENTER COSTS

After Step 2, the company knows the cost of the various types of activities it performs. For example, it may now know the cost of purchasing and handling various categories of material and purchased components as well as the costs involved in supporting those manufacturing services provided by outside contractors. It may know the extra costs involved in dealing with one or two particularly difficult customers as well as the costs incurred in performing a number of very different value-adding or direct operations. It may know the costs involved in processing orders and in picking orders in the warehouse. It may know the cost of providing RN services to various wings of a long-term care facility. In short, it now knows the total cost of the activities included in each of its activity centers.

The situation is analogous to a cafeteria line that has been set up to provide all of the different food items that will be required by the cafeteria's customers. The cafeteria knows the total cost of providing the demanded quantity of each food item included in the line. What it needs to do next is find a way to determine the cost of the volume and mix of food items selected by each customer as they go through the cafeteria line. Not all customers will take the same items, nor will they always take the same quantity of any particular item. In the activity-based flow-down scheme, the various activity centers are analogous to the various food items available on the cafeteria line, and jobs, products, and services (the cost objectives) are the line's customers.

From an ABC perspective, all organizations are service organizations, and the cost objectives are its customers. In a manufacturing firm, each job or product is a customer, and as it "goes through the line," it should pick up the appropriate amount of each service it requires to become the final product. In a long-term care facility, each resident is a customer, and as the resident "goes through the line," he or she should pick up the appropriate amount of each service required. In a distribution business, each customer is a cost objective, and as the customer "goes through the line," it should pick up the amount of each service it requires the distributor to perform to be able to complete its orders. Exhibit 5.4 represents this process of measuring the cost of all services being provided to each cost objective as it "goes through the line."

COST FLOW-DOWN STEP 3: ASSIGNING ACTIVITY COSTS TO JOBS/PRODUCTS

An appropriate statistical basis must be identified to associate the accumulated cost of each activity center to the cost objectives that made the activities included in the activity center necessary. Once the basis is determined, a rate can be established to attach the activity center costs to individual cost objectives.

While determining the bases for attaching activity costs to cost objectives it is again important to keep in mind that the goal of ABC is accuracy, not precision. The cost flow-down steps discussed thus far have been designed so that costs incurred by the organization are charged to the appropriate cost objectives. By creating the appropriate activity centers and accumulating the appropriate amount of activity costs within them, the organization has gained information such as the cost of supporting outside processors, the extra costs of dealing with "jerk" customers, and the costs required to support particular product lines. Obviously, for the process to be complete, it is imperative that the cost of supporting outside processors be assigned only to those cost objectives that require outside processors, the extra costs of dealing with jerk customers be assigned only to those cost objectives relating to jerk customers, and the costs of supporting particular product lines assigned only to cost objectives within those product lines.

The question that must be answered for each activity center before deciding on the base for assigning its costs to cost objectives is, "Now that we will be assigning this activity center's cost to the correct cost objectives, how important is the precision with which we assign them among those correct cost objectives?." For example, 4% of an organization's total activity cost is associated with supporting its outside processors. Only 30% of its products include the use of outside processors. The organization will now

Exhibit 5.4 Activity-Based Cost Flow-Down Process: Step 3

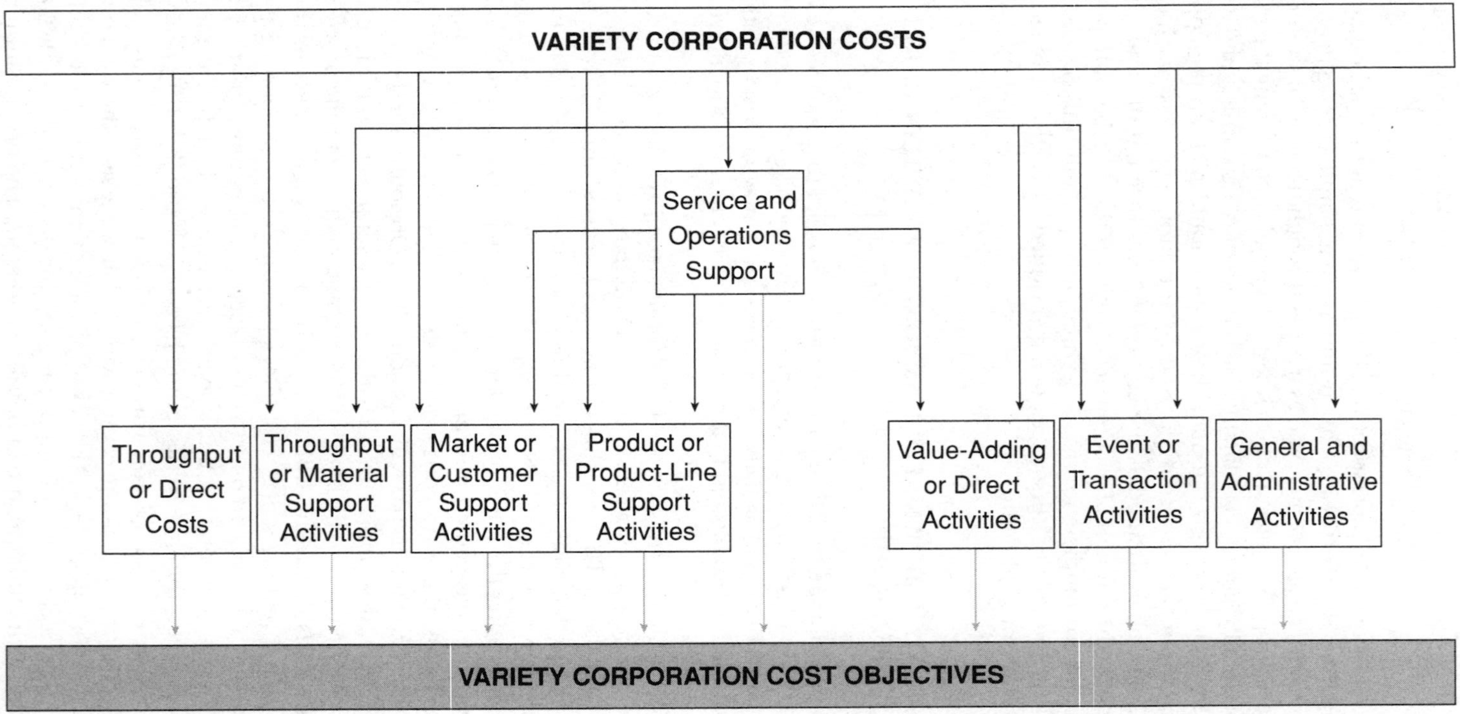

VARIETY CORPORATION COSTS

Service and Operations Support

Throughput or Direct Costs

Throughput or Material Support Activities

Market or Customer Support Activities

Product or Product-Line Support Activities

Value-Adding or Direct Activities

Event or Transaction Activities

General and Administrative Activities

VARIETY CORPORATION COST OBJECTIVES

be assigning the cost of supporting outside processors only to the 30% of its products that require them. How important is the precision with which it assigns those costs among those products? If it is important, then a theoretically correct basis must be used. If it is not, a simple surrogate base, such as assigning the support cost as a percentage of outside processing cost, will be more than adequate for accurately assigning support costs among the appropriate products.

If 3% of the organization's activity costs are caused by one jerk customer that represents 10% of its sales, can it simply add the activity center's costs to the jerk customer's products as a percentage of manufacturing cost (or some similar cost base), or is it important to more precisely direct those costs to particular products through some more theoretically sound basis? Similarly, if 2% of the organization's total activity costs supports one product line representing 60% of its volume, and 4% of its total activity cost supports its other product line which represents 40% of its volume, is it enough to simply add the support activity center costs as a percentage add-on or is greater precision important?

If enough thought is put into the creation of activity centers, fairly simple bases are more than adequate for assigning the costs of most throughput or material support, market or customer support, product or product-line support, and G&A activity centers. More complex and theoretically sound methods can be reserved for the value-adding or direct and event or transaction activity centers.

Common methods for assigning throughput or material support activity center costs to cost objectives are as a percentage of material or outside processing cost, a cost per pound, or a cost per some other relevant quantity unit. In job shop settings, where items are purchased for specific jobs, support costs are often assigned as a cost per material/throughput item required for the job.

Adding support costs as a percentage of direct or value-adding cost is usually adequate for market or customer support and product or product-line support activity centers. In some situations, however, a cost per unit of sales (such as a cost per sales order received) or a percentage of merchandise cost (particularly for distributors) may be more appropriate.

Value-adding or direct activity center costs usually require the highest degree of precision and have the most variability. Bases such as a cost per labor hour; machine hour; cycle hour; pound, foot, or other unit of measure processed; resident day; and square foot day occupied are frequently used. Event or transaction activity center costs are often assigned as a cost per order, order line item, delivery, meal served, engineering change, job, setup, shipment, admission, or discharge. (A variety of concepts for assigning these types of activity costs to cost objectives are discussed in Chapter 8.)

Finally, the most appropriate method for assigning the cost of G&A activity centers is usually as a percentage of cumulative activity cost. This method is based on the assumption that G&A activities support the other activities that take place within the organization. They do not support throughput or direct costs (although some of the other activities whose costs are included in the "activity cost" bases were in support of those costs). For example, two cost objectives accumulated $100 of cost before the assignment of G&A. The cost of one cost objective consisted of $20 of material and $80 of activity cost; the other consisted of $80 of material and $20 of activity cost. The business needed to operate at a level that added four times more cost to one cost objective than the other. As a result, it seems appropriate that the one demanding four times the activity be assigned four times the cost of administering that activity.

There are times when other bases may be appropriate. If an effective job has been done in creating all of the organization's other activity centers, however, very little cost should remain for G&A activities and a simple percentage of accumulated activity cost will suffice.

COMPLETION OF COST FLOW-DOWN STEP 3

Once Step 3 of the flow-down process is completed, costs have been assigned to the jobs, products, or services that caused them to be incurred. This was accomplished by first associating costs with the activities that made the costs necessary and then associating the cumulative costs of activities to the jobs, products, or services that made the activities necessary—the simple concept underlying ABC. This is not, however, the end of the process. All we have done to this point is taken a given amount of cost and developed the "plumbing" for those costs to flow down through the activities that caused them to the jobs, products, or services that caused the activities.

This *fully absorbed* cost information is important and, by itself, can help an organization make more informed decisions and become more successful. Among these benefits can be better core business pricing decisions and more focused cost reduction and continuous improvement efforts. If it stops at this point, however, the organization will never experience many of ABC's benefits. To receive those benefits, it must be able to use ABC to accumulate costs, not just to distribute costs. This is done by taking what was learned in developing the cost flow-down and reversing the process. Begin with the organization's jobs, products, and services; determine what activities are required to produce or provide them; and accumulate the cost of providing all of those activities. This process is summarized in Exhibit 5.5.

Exhibit 5.5 Summarization of Activities Needed for Products or Services and the Cost of Providing Them

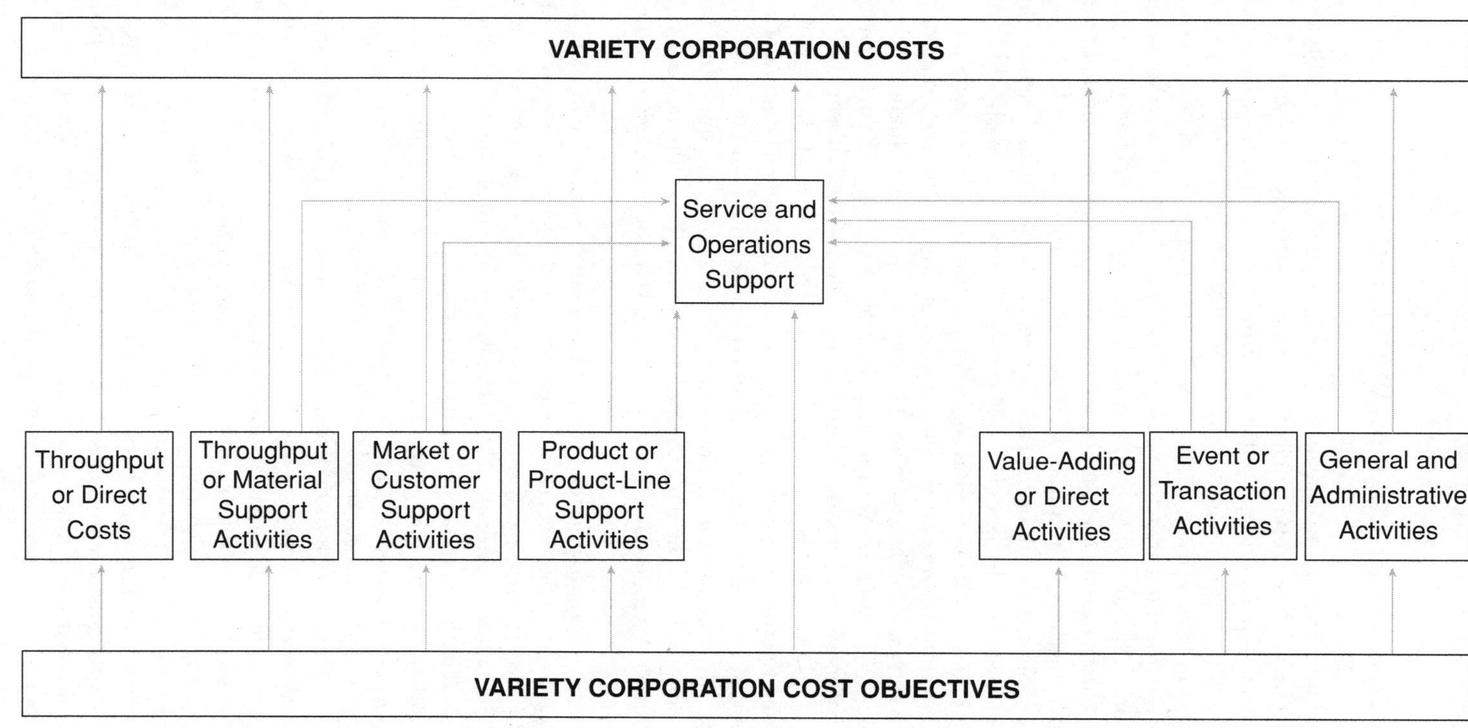

ACTIVITY-BASED COST ACCUMULATION

Should we accept this special order despite the fact that our ABC rates show that we will lose money on it? Would it cost less if we outsourced this process instead of performing it ourselves? Should we make this component part or purchase it from someone else? At what price can we sell our excess capacity to another market and improve our profits? What will be the savings if we invest in capital that will reduce cycle time by 20%? Should we drop the product line that offsets 40% of the profit we are making on our other two product lines? These are just a few of the questions a manufacturer might ask whose answer requires accurate cost information.

Similar questions exist in other industries. A health care provider might ask: "Based on the services I am likely to have to perform, should I accept this capitated contract? Should we hire a contractor to provide dietary services? What would be the bottom-line impact of closing down our maternity unit?" A distributor might ask: "Should I add this low-margin, high-volume product line? Will our profits improve if we stop servicing this particular market?" Answers to these questions also require accurate cost information.

Unfortunately, the cost information developed during the activity-based flow-down process is useless for these decisions. The flow-down process took a given amount of cost, assigned it to activities, and then assigned activity costs to cost objectives. Answers to each of these questions involves a change in the activities required to operate the business. As a result, the costs will change. The change, however, will not be reflected by the activity-based cost rates.

For example, outsourcing a component will not eliminate all of the costs assigned to that component, nor will the increase in cost be limited to the invoice price paid to the component's supplier. Similarly, dropping a product line will not eliminate the amount of cost attributed to that product line. It might eliminate less cost, or it might eliminate even more costs. In the same way, adding a low-margin, high-volume product line might add almost no cost to the operation of the distribution business, or it might add more cost than the margin provided by the additional sales.

These questions do not need *fully absorbed* cost information; they need *incremental* cost information. Only by reversing the flow-down process, so that the outputs of the organization (the sum of its cost objectives) determine the activities that will be required and those activities, in turn, determine the costs that will be incurred, will ABC information provide answers for these questions. Viewing ABC as a concept for developing a model that both accumulates and distributes costs makes it a much more comprehensive tool for supporting almost any decision that requires accurate and relevant cost as an input. (A more detailed discussion of how such a cost accumulation and distribution model can be developed is presented in Chapter 10.)

SUMMARY

Activity-based costing is not a complex concept. In its simplest form, it takes costs, associates them with the activities that made them necessary, and then takes the accumulated cost of the various activities and associates them with the jobs, products, or services that made the activities necessary. Almost any organization can develop an effective flow-down of costs using the activity categories and cost flow patterns outlined in this chapter. To be effective, however, an organization must not be satisfied with an ABC model that simply distributes a given amount of cost. It must use ABC's concept in reverse and accumulate the cost required to provide a given quantity and mix of its jobs, products, or services. Only in this way will it be able to support the myriad of decisions that require incremental cost information.

6

Case Study: Acme Distributors

Before going further into the topic, let us take a look at how the logic of activity-based costing (ABC) can be used to develop an accurate flow of costs in a simple example. Acme Distributors distributes a variety of merchandise to both big retail chains (big chains) and small individual retailers (little retailers). Its current operating information can be summarized as follows:

Revenue	$10,000,000
Costs and expenses:	
Purchased merchandise cost	7,500,000
Operating expenses	1,500,000
Total costs and expenses	$ 9,000,000
Profit contribution	$ 1,000,000
Profit % to revenue	10.0%
Operation cost % of merchandise cost	20.0%

Acme marks up all of its merchandise by 33.3% to provide a 25% gross profit on everything it sells. In determining customer or product profitability, it uses the 20.0% "operating cost as a percentage of merchandise cost" rate calculated above as a means of applying operating costs to those customers or products. For example, if a customer purchases $1,000 of merchandise, $200 of operating costs are added to determine the *fully absorbed* cost of the transaction.

Acme's management believed that this simple method of applying costs was more than adequate for a distributor of its size until they had their accounting personnel prepare a customer profitability analysis. The results of this analysis were quite surprising. All customers showed the same profitability; 10% profit as a percentage of revenue. For example, the results for one big chain and one little retailer were as follows:

	Big Chain	*Little Retailer*
Revenue	$400,000	$50,000
Merchandise cost	300,000	37,500
Operating cost @ 20% of merchandise cost	60,000	7,500
Total costs and expenses	360,000	45,000
Profit contribution	$ 40,000	$ 5,000
Profit % to revenue	10.0%	10.0%

The reason all customers ended up with the same level of profitability should be obvious: Acme spread operating costs across all products and customers like peanut butter, using merchandise cost as a knife. This costing practice was too general and, even worse, it had no theoretical foundation. Costs were allocated in this manner because it was easy, not because it was correct.

DEVELOPING AN ABC STRUCTURE—SERVICE AND SUPPORT ACTIVITIES

To gain a greater understanding of customer profitability, Acme decided to take an activity-based view of its operations, using the methodology outlined in Chapter 5. After a brainstorming session involving the company's key management personnel, the company decided that its operations could be divided into seven major activities: procurement, receiving/put-away, warehousing, order fulfillment, order picking, marketing, and general and administrative (G&A). All of these activities would have to be further analyzed before they could be directed toward specific customers or products, so they were all classified as *service and operations support* activities. Merchandise cost was considered *throughput or direct* cost. With these activities identified, Acme began to develop an ABC cost flow-down diagram as shown in Exhibit 6.1.

Exhibit 6.1 Acme Distributors' ABC Cost Flow-Down Diagram: Starting Point

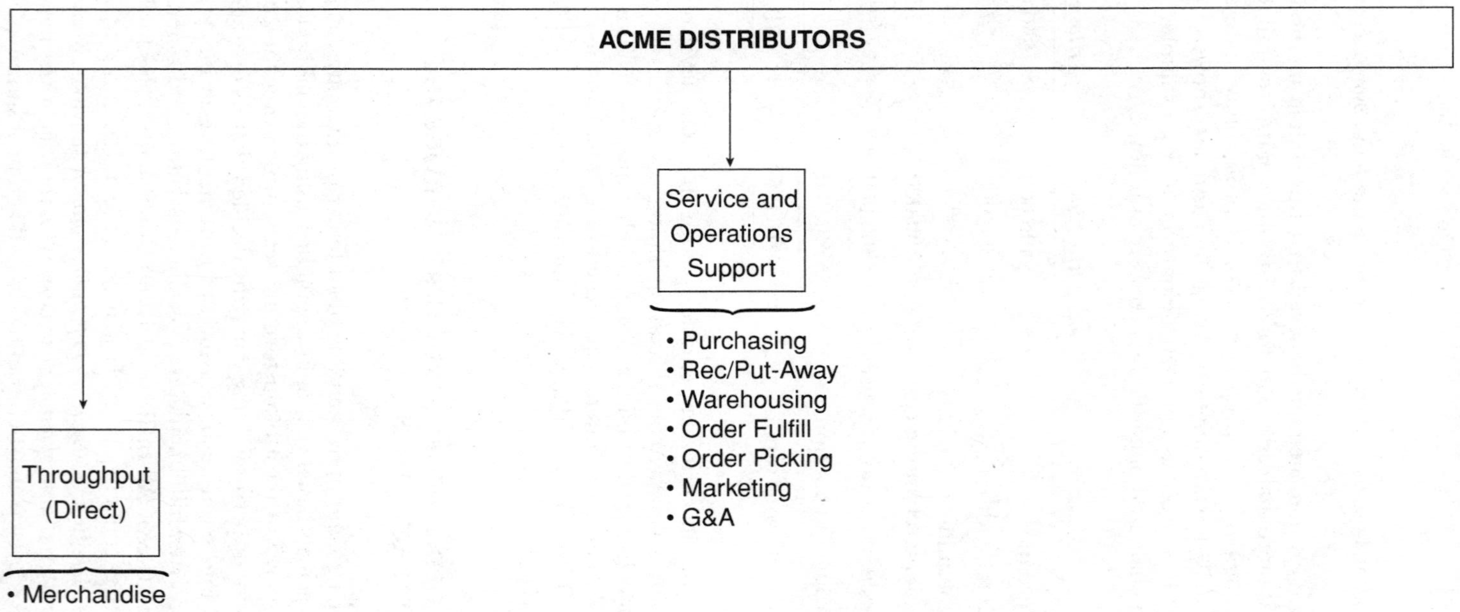

Having reached this point, Acme's management gave its accounting personnel the assignment of determining how the company's $9 million of costs should be assigned to the activities that caused them to be incurred. The results of this analysis are summarized as follows:

Purchased merchandise	$7,500,000
Procurement	125,000
Receiving/put-away	75,000
Warehousing	300,000
Order fulfillment	200,000
Order picking	300,000
Marketing	200,000
G&A	300,000
Total costs	$9,000,000

DEVELOPING AN ABC STRUCTURE—OPERATING ACTIVITIES

After completing the initial assignment of costs to activities, management then addressed the problem of establishing relevant activity centers or cost pools that would enable them to assign these activity costs to products and customers in a relevant way. They could see no logical way to divide its products into product lines, but they thought that it might be informative if they divided marketing efforts into those that supported big chains and those that supported little retailers. They also determined that no value-adding activities (e.g., repackaging, special labeling, etc.) took place but that a great deal of value might be gained if they better understood the cost related to their slow-turning merchandise versus their quick-turning merchandise.

There was no significant difference in the amount of effort required to process different types or sizes of orders, so they established an event/transaction activity to accumulate the cost of order fulfillment that could be charged to cost objectives as a *cost per order.* The effort required to pick the items ordered, however, varied considerably from order to order. The more different products included on an order, the longer it took to pick the order. This suggested that the number of different products, or *line items,* on an order was a good representation of the level of effort. Accordingly, management established an event/transaction activity to accumulate the cost of order picking that could be charged to cost objectives as a *cost per line item.* A final activity was established to accumulate those costs that were truly G&A in nature.

Exhibit 6.2 shows Acme Distributors' cost flow-down structure as it existed after these decisions. Before venturing further, Acme's management decided that they needed to identify those products defined as quick turning and those defined as slow turning. They also needed to classify all of their customers into the two categories: big chains and little retailers. Finally, they needed to measure the volume of activity falling into each of these categories. The volume would be measured in terms of dollars of merchandise sold. After these categorizations and measurements, the following matrix was prepared:

	Big Chains	***Little Retailers***	***Totals***
Quick turns	$1,875,000	$1,875,000	$3,750,000
Slow turns	1,875,000	1,875,000	3,750,000
Totals	$3,750,000	$3,750,000	$7,500,000

As the matrix shows, half of the merchandise sold to both customer categories is quick turning and half is slow turning. In addition, Acme's volume of business is the same in each customer category.

At this point, Acme is ready to distribute the accumulated cost in each of its service and support activities to those downstream activities that can be associated with customers and products. As can be seen in Exhibit 6.2, there are seven activities to which these activity costs can be distributed. These activities are:

- Throughput/material support activities
  1. Quick-turning merchandise support
  2. Slow-turning merchandise support
- Market/customer support activities
  3. Big chain market support
  4. Little retailer market support
- Product/product line support activities
  No activities identified in this category
- Direct/value-adding activities
  No activities identified in this category
- Event/transaction activities
  5. Orders
  6. Line items
- G&A activities
  7. G&A

Exhibit 6.2 Acme Distributors' ABC Cost Flow-Down Diagram: Assigning Costs to Activities

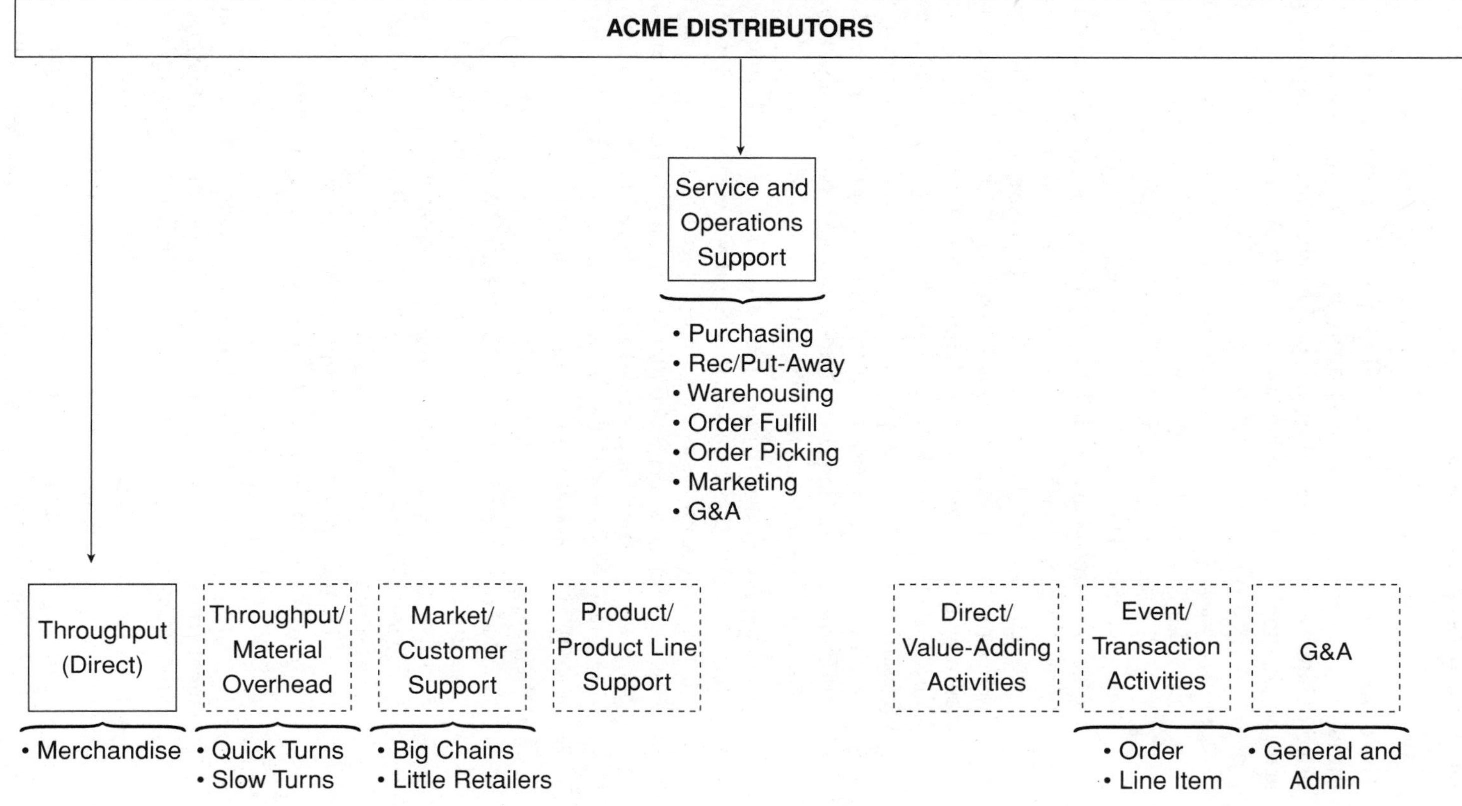

The distributions from the service and support activities were determined through an activity analysis of each activity. In some cases, the analysis consisted of interviews with the individuals performing the service and support activities; in others, it was based on available statistical measures.

- *Procurement.* Interviews with procurement personnel indicated that the effort required to purchase each dollar of quick-turning merchandise was only about half that required to purchase slow-turning merchandise. There were two major reasons for this situation. First, quick-turning items tended to be purchased in higher volumes; thus, each purchasing transaction involved more dollars of merchandise. Second, because they were purchased more frequently, quick-turning items were usually covered by blanket orders. Slow-turning items tended to be purchased with *spot buys.* The interviews also indicated that about 10% of the procurement effort went toward buying office supplies and other administrative items. As a result of the interviews, the distribution of procurement was set at 30% to quick-turning merchandise support, 60% to slow-turning merchandise support, and 10% to G&A.
- *Receiving/put-away:* Because sales of quick- and slow-turning merchandise were equal, material receipts were the same for quick-turning merchandise as they were for slow-turning merchandise. Consequently, it was assumed that the amount of receiving/put-away effort was the same for each category. As a result, the distribution of this activity was set at 50% to quick-turning merchandise support and 50% to slow-turning merchandise support.
- *Warehousing.* Although the same amount of quick- and slow-turning merchandise is received during the year, the slow-turning merchandise sits around about three times longer than the quick-turning items. Measurements indicate that three-quarters of the warehousing space is filled with slow-turning merchandise. Only one quarter is used to store quick-turning items. Using these square footage statistics, the distribution of this activity was set at 25% to quick-turning merchandise support and 75% to slow-turning merchandise support.
- *Order fulfillment.* All activities in this area relate to the processing of incoming orders. As a result, the distribution of this activity was set at 100% to orders.
- *Order picking:* All activities in this area relate to picking orders. As a result, the distribution of this activity was set at 100% to line items.
- *Marketing:* Although each big chain requires a great deal more marketing effort than a little retailer, there are many more little

retailers. The interviews with marketing personnel indicated that 55% of their effort went toward marketing to little retailers, whereas only 40% was directed toward big chains. The balance represented *institutional marketing* efforts that marketed the organization as a whole. As a result of the interviews, the distribution of this activity was set at 55% to little retailer market support, 40% to big chain market support, and 5% to G&A.

- *G&A*. Interviews with G&A personnel indicated that, although the majority of the work performed in this area was truly general and administrative, 5% of the effort related to the consolidation of products ordered to provide for efficient order picking and another 5% related to the processing of incoming orders. As a result, the distribution of this activity was set at 5% to orders, 5% to line items, and 90% to G&A.

In summary, Acme Distributions' service and support activity distributions were as follows:

Procurement:	
Quick-turning merchandise support	30%
Slow-turning merchandise support	60%
G&A	10%
Receiving/put-away:	
Quick-turning merchandise support	50%
Slow-turning merchandise support	50%
Warehousing:	
Quick-turning merchandise support	25%
Slow-turning merchandise support	75%
Order fulfillment:	
Orders	100%
Order picking:	
Line items	100%
Marketing:	
Big chain market support	40%
Little retailer market support	55%
G&A	5%
G&A:	
Orders	5%
Line items	5%
G&A	90%

With this distribution information, Acme is ready to perform the distribution of Service and Support activities, which will complete the distribution of all activity costs to those activities or cost pools that can be assigned to cost objectives. This step in the cost flow-down process is shown in Exhibit 6.3.

The actual distribution mechanics, which are simple enough to be performed manually, are documented in Exhibit 6.4. As can be seen at the bottom of the exhibit, the $9 million of Acme Distributors' costs were distributed to merchandise or to activities that can be attributed to cost objectives as follows:

Throughput/direct costs:	
Quick-turning merchandise	$3,750,000
Slow-turning merchandise	3,750,000
Throughput/material support activities:	
Quick-turning merchandise support	150,000
Slow-turning merchandise support	337,500
Market/customer support activities:	
Big chain market support	80,000
Little retailer market support	110,000
Event/transaction activities:	
Orders	215,000
Line items	315,000
G&A activities:	
G&A	292,500
Total costs	$9,000,000

DEVELOPING AN ABC STRUCTURE—ASSIGNING COSTS TO COST OBJECTIVES

What remained to be done at this point was to develop rates that could be used by Acme to attach these activity costs to its cost objectives—its products and customers. All the information required to perform these calculations was already known except for two items: the number of orders processed and the number of line items picked. After reviewing their records, Acme determined that 25,000 orders had been processed and 157,500 line items had been picked.

This last step in the cost flow-down development is shown in Exhibit 6.5. The actual rate calculations, which are again simple enough to be performed

Exhibit 6.3 Acme Distributors' ABC Cost Flow-Down Diagram: Assigning Cost Among Activities

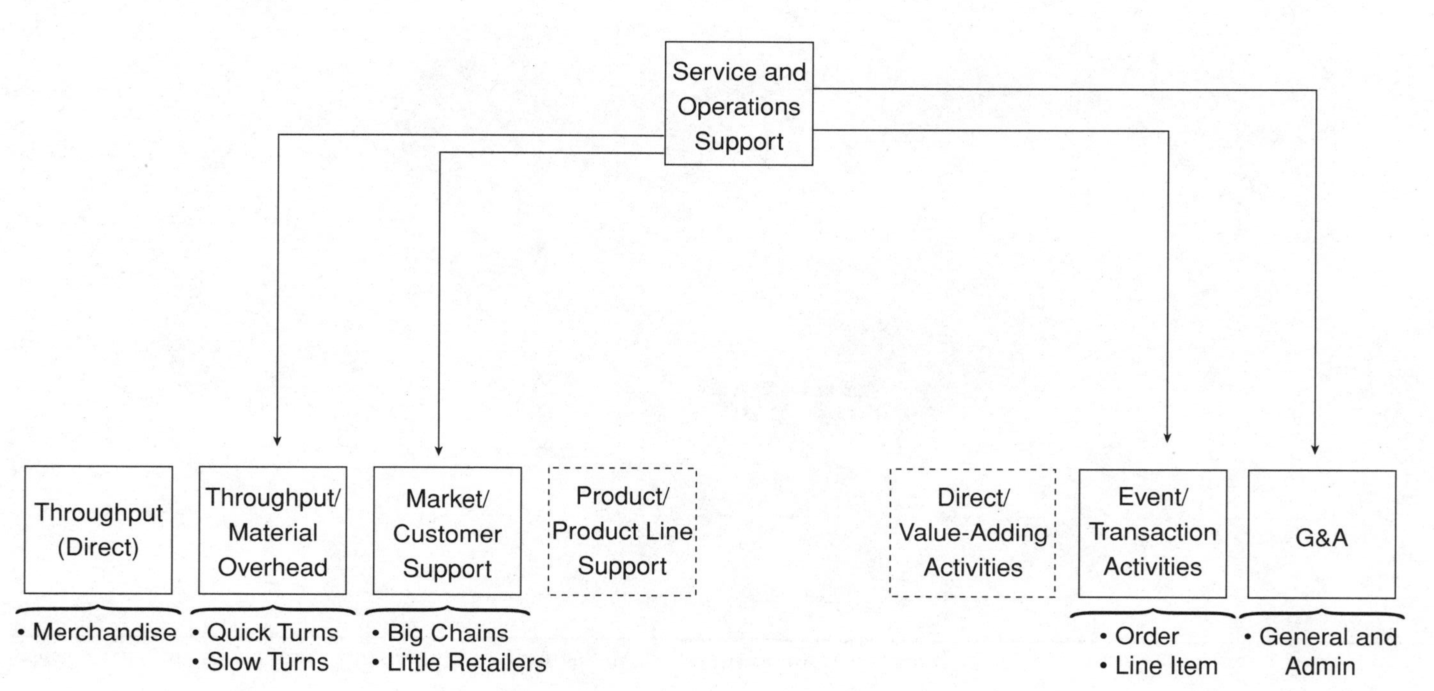

Exhibit 6.4 Acme Distributors' Distributing Cost Among Activities: Distribution Mechanics ($000)

			Merchandise		Merchandise Support		Market Support				
		Total	Quick Turns	Slow Turns	Quick Turns	Slow Turns	Big Chains	Little Retailers	Orders	Line Items	G&A
Merchandise	%	100%	50%	50%							
	$	$7,500.0	$3,750.0	$3,750.0							
Procurement	%	100%			30%	60%					10%
	$	$125.0			$37.5	$75.0					$12.5
Receive/Put-Away	%	100%			50%	50%					
	$	$75.0			$37.5	$37.5					
Warehousing	%	100%			25%	75%					
	$	$300.0			$75.0	$225.0					
Order Fulfillment	%	100%							100%		
	$	$200.0							$200.0		
Order Picking	%	100%								100%	
	$	$300.0								$300.0	
Marketing	%	100%					40%	55%			5%
	$	$200.0					$80.0	$110.0			$10.0
G&A	%	100%							5%	5%	90%
	$	$300.0							$15.0	$15.0	$270.0
Total Costs		$9,000.0	$3,750.0	$3,750.0	$150.0	$337.5	$80.0	$110.0	$215.0	$315.0	$292.5

Exhibit 6.5 Acme Distributors' ABC Cost Flow-Down Diagram: Rate Calculations

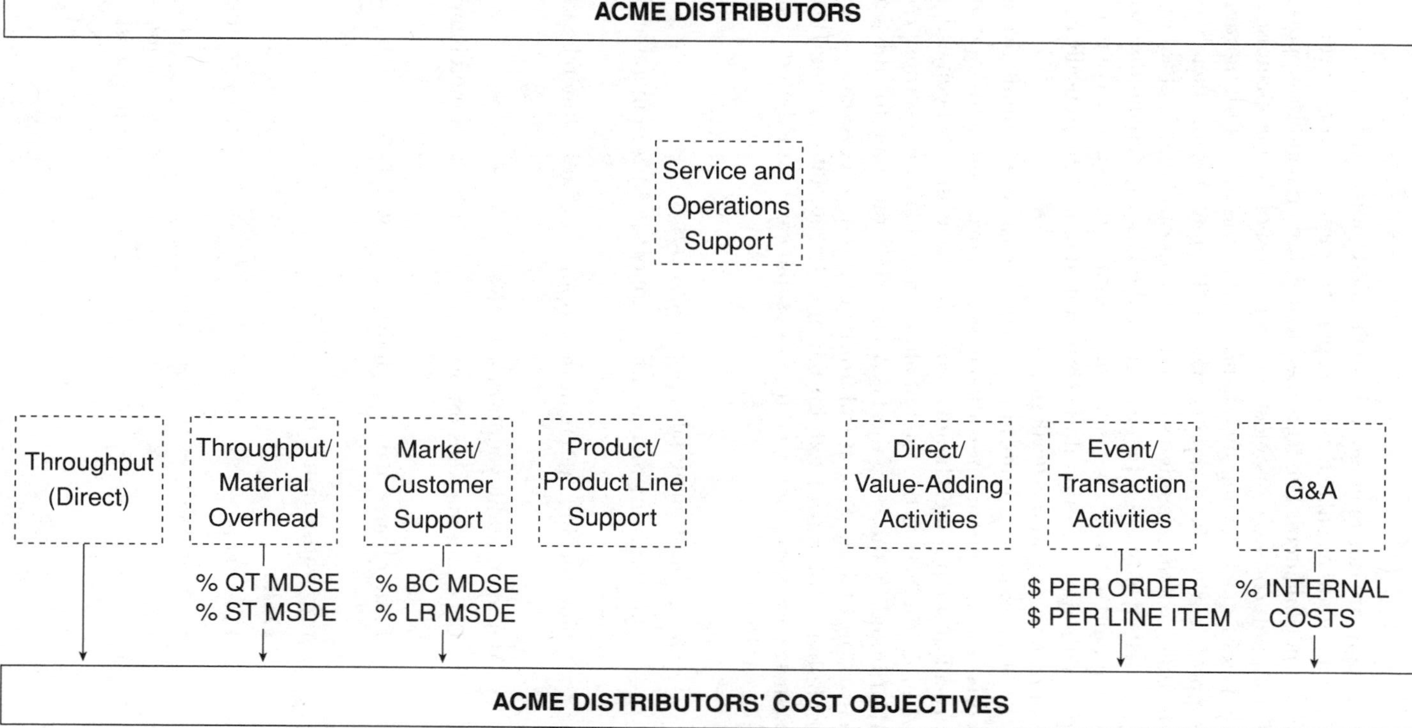

manually, are documented in Exhibit 6.6. As noted earlier, the cost of order fulfillment was calculated as a cost per order and the cost of order picking as a cost per line item. The basis used to assign merchandise support and market support costs to cost objectives was the cost of the merchandise itself. The dollars of quick-turning merchandise carry the quick-turning merchandise support activity costs as a percentage of the quick-turning merchandise cost; the dollars of merchandise sold to big chains carry the big chain market support activity costs as a percentage of the cost of merchandise sold to big chains; and so forth. The use of merchandise cost as a base is a practical, simple method of assigning these costs, not the most theoretically correct. For our example, however, it will suffice.

General and administrative activity costs used cumulative operating costs as a base. For an individual cost objective, cumulative operating costs are all of the nonmerchandise costs that have already been assigned to it. Overall, the base is the total of all nonmerchandise less those costs being distributed by the rate, the G&A cost. The rationale for this base is discussed in Chapter 8, so it will not be covered here. As can be seen in the right-hand column of Exhibit 6.6, the $1,500,000 of Acme Distributors' activity costs were converted into rates that can be attributed to cost objectives as follows:

Throughput/material support activities:	
Quick-turning merchandise support	@ 4.0% of merchandise cost
Slow-turning merchandise support	@ 9.0% of merchandise cost
Market/customer support activities:	
Big chain market support	@ 2.1% of merchandise cost
Little retailer market support	@ 2.9% of merchandise cost
Event/transaction activities:	
Orders	@ $8.60 per order
Line items	@ $2.00 per line item
G&A activities:	
G&A	@ 24.2% of cumulative operating costs

Exhibit 6.6 Acme Distributors' ABC Cost Flow-Down: Rate Calculations Mechanics

Activity Centers/ Cost Pools	Activity / Pool Costs ($000)	Rate Basis Amount ($000)	Rate Basis Description	Rate
Merchandise support:				
Quick turns	$150.0	$3,750.0	Merchandise dollars	4.0%
Slow turns	$337.5	$3,750.0	Merchandise dollars	9.0%
Market support:				
Big chains	$80.0	$3,750.0	Merchandise dollars	2.1%
Little retailers	$110.0	$3,750.0	Merchandise dollars	2.9%
Order fulfillment	$215.0	25,000	Number of orders	$8.60
Order picking	$315.0	157,500	Number of Line Items	$2.00
G&A	$292.5	$1,207.5	Cumulative operating costs	24.2%
Total cost	$1,500.0			

DETERMINING CUSTOMER PROFITABILITY

With this rate information, Acme's management can now revisit the customer profitability analysis they attempted earlier in this chapter. At that time, their "peanut butter" approach to assigning operating costs to customers and products resulted in inaccurate and useless information that showed all customers generating the company's average profit to revenues percentage. With the new activity-based rate structure, the costs will be assigned to customers and the products they buy using a much more rational basis. Using the earlier examples of the big chain and the little retailer, some of the differences can be seen.

Additional information regarding our two example customers is needed before customer profitability can be determined. Based on the cost assignment bases for applying the activity costing rates, Acme needs to determine, for both customers, what percentage of their purchases were quick-turning merchandise and what percentage were slow-turning items, in which customer category they are classified, how many orders they placed, and how many line items were included in those orders. In the case of Big Chain, 50% of its purchases were quick-turning items, 50% were slow-turning items, it is classified as a big chain, and it placed 1,040 orders that included 8,320 line items. Little Retailer, however, had an 80%/20% mix of quick-turning/slow-turning merchandise, is classified as a little retailer, and placed 26 orders that included 312 line items.

Exhibit 6.7 details the use of this information and the activity-based rates to calculate Big Chain's profitability. As noted in the earlier analysis, sales to Big Chain were $400,000 and merchandise cost was $300,000. To determine the appropriate amount of merchandise support cost attributable to Big Chain, the $300,000 of merchandise cost must be split between quick turning and slow turning. The 50%/50% split previously noted results in $150,000 of merchandise in both categories. By applying the 4.0% and 9.0% rates for quick-turning merchandise support and slow-turning merchandise support, respectively, Acme calculates costs of $6,000 to support the quick-moving items and $13,500 to support the slow-moving items. All of Big Chain's sales fall into the big chain category, so the base for applying market support costs is $300,000. Using the big chain market support rate of 2.1%, the company calculates costs of $6,300 to support the big chain marketing effort.

Applying the $8.60 per order and $2.00 per line item rates to Big Chain's order and line item totals results in support costs of $8,944 and $16,640 respectively. At this point, $51,384 in operating costs have been attributed to Big Chain. This represents the sum of the merchandise support, market support, order, and line item costs and serves as the base for

Exhibit 6.7 Customer Profitability Analysis: Big Chain

		Base	Rate	Revenue or Cost
Revenue				$400,000
Merchandise cost				$300,000
Merchandise support:				
Quick turning	50%	$150,000	4.0%	$6,000
Slow turning	50%	$150,000	9.0%	$13,500
Market support:				
Big chains	100%	$300,000	2.1%	$6,300
Little retailers	0%	$0	2.9%	$0
Order fulfillment:				
Annual orders		1,040	$8.60	$8,944
Order picking:				
Annual line items		8,320	$2.00	$16,640
General and administration:				
cumulative operating cost		$51,384	24.2%	$12,435
Total annual cost				$363,819
Annual profit contribution				$36,181
Profit contribution % to sales				9.0%

applying G&A costs at its 24.2% rate. The resulting $12,435 brings the total operating cost attributable to Big Chain to $63,819 and the total cost relating to the customer's $400,000 revenue to $363,819. This results in a profit to revenue percentage of 9.0%, slightly below Acme Distributors' 10.0% average.

The profitability of Little Retailer is detailed in Exhibit 6.8. As reported earlier, sales to the little retailer were $50,000 and the cost of the merchandise sold was $37,500. The 80%/20% quick-turn/slow-turn split in Little Retailer's merchandise purchases established bases of $30,000 for applying the quick-turn merchandise support rate of 4.0% and $7,500 for applying the slow-turn merchandise support rate of 9.0% to this customer's business. The result is a total of $1,875 attributable to Little Retailer for merchandise support activity costs. Little Retailer is included in Acme's little retailer customer category. As a consequence, all $37,500 of its merchandise purchases provides a base for applying the 2.9% rate for marketing activities relating to little retailers. This adds another $1,088 to the costs attributable to this customer.

Little Retailer ordered only 26 times during the year. Included on those orders were 312 line items. Using the appropriate rates, these facts add $224 in order costs and $624 in line item costs to Little Retailer's total. At this point, the sum of the operating costs attributable to Little Retailer total $3,811. Using this as the G&A activity base adds another $922, using its 24.2% rate. This brings the grand total of operating costs that relate to Little Retailer to $4,733 and total costs relating to its $50,000 revenue to $42,233. This leaves a profit contribution of $7,767 or 15.5% of revenues—a profit far greater than Acme's average.

Try a little common sense to see if the results obtained using Acme's new activity-based rates and bases can be explained. Big Chain turned out to be less profitable than the average customer. Had it attained the average 10.0% profit as a percentage of revenues, it would have shown a profit of $40,000 instead of the $36,181 determined by the activity-based rates. Several characteristics of Big Chain and its buying habits can account for the difference.

Half of the merchandise purchased by the average customer is quick-turning stock and half is slow-turning. This same relationship holds true for Big Chain, so merchandise support is not an area of difference. Market support, however, is 2.53% for the average customer. This can be determined by taking the $190,000 marketing cost attributed to the two customer categories (remember $10,000 was included in G&A) and dividing by the total merchandise cost base of $7,500,000. Since the big chain market support rate is only 2.1%, marketing costs related to Big Chain would actually be $1,300 less than the average customer (2.53% average rate less 2.1% big chain rate times Big Chain's $300,000 merchandise base).

Exhibit 6.8 Customer Profitability Analysis: Little Retailer

		Base	Rate	Revenue or Cost
Revenue				$50,000
Merchandise cost				$37,500
Merchandise support:				
Quick turning	80%	$30,000	4.0%	$1,200
Slow turning	20%	$7,500	9.0%	$675
Market support:				
Big chains	0%	$0	2.1%	$0
Little retailers	100%	$37,500	2.9%	$1,088
Order fulfillment:				
Annual orders		26	$8.60	$224
Order picking:				
Annual line items		312	$2.00	$624
General and administration:				
cumulative operating cost		$3,811	24.2%	$922
Total annual cost				$42,233
Annual profit contribution				$7,767
Profit contribution % to sales				15.5%

Big Chain's ordering characteristics, however, more than offset this cost advantage. The average customer buys $300 worth of merchandise on each order ($7,500,000 merchandise divided by 25,000 orders). In addition, the average line item represents $46.62 worth of merchandise ($7,500,000 divided by 157,500 line items). If Big Chain's ordering habits were average, it would have sent 1,000 orders ($300,000 merchandise divided by $300 per order) that would have included 6,300 line items ($300,000 merchandise divided by $46.62 per line item). Instead, it placed 1,040 orders that contained 8,320 line items. This means that 40 more orders and 2,020 more line items had to be handled by Acme's personnel than would have been required for an average customer ordering the same amount of merchandise as Big Chain. At $8.60 per order and $2.00 per line item, this increased the costs attributed to Big Chain by $4,383 ($344 for order handling and $4,040 for order picking). The 24.2% G&A needs to be added to the net of these cost differences to see if they explain Big Chain's less than average profitability. The cost variances from average for Big Chain can be summarized as follows:

Market support	$1,300	favorable
Order	344	unfavorable
Line items	4,040	unfavorable
Subtotal	$3,084	unfavorable
G&A	746	unfavorable
Total variance	$3,830	unfavorable

Adding the $3,830 back to Big Chain's activity-based profit of $36,181 results in a profit of $40,011, approximately 10% of revenues.

Big Chain's lower-than-average profitability makes sense, based on its ordering habits. The fact that its orders are smaller and contain more line items than the average order makes it necessary for Acme to perform more work for each dollar of merchandise sold to it. As a result, Acme gets to keep less of the 25% gross profit on Big Chain's business than it does the average customer's business.

Unlike Big Chain, the activity-based approach indicated that Little Retailer was much more profitable than the average customer. Perhaps common sense can help explain their level of profitability. Had Little Retailer achieved only the average 10.0% profit as a percentage of revenue, it would have shown a profit of $5,000 instead of the $7,767 profit determined by activity-based rates. Little Retailer's buying habits and the type of merchandise it buys can account for this difference.

A noted earlier, half of the merchandise purchased by the average customer is quick turning and half is slow turning. This results in an average merchandise support rate of 6.5% ($487,500 support cost divided by $7,500,000 of merchandise). Of the merchandise purchased by Little Retailer, however, 80% was quick turning and only 20% slow turning. This resulted in merchandise support costs of only $1,875 attributable to Little Retailer, $562 less than the $2,437 cost (6.5% times the $37,500 merchandise cost) that would have been attributable to it had its merchandise mix been average. Because Little Retailer is a little retailer, market support costs cause it a market disadvantage. Earlier, the average market support rate was calculated at 2.53% of merchandise cost. This would make Little Retailer's market support cost, calculated at a 2.9% rate, $139 higher than average (2.9% Little Retailer rate less 2.53% average rate times Little Retailer's $37,500 merchandise base).

Little Retailer's ordering characteristics, however, provide the majority of its cost advantage. If it were an average customer, Little Retailer would have sent Acme 125 orders ($37,500 merchandise divided by $300 per order), which would have included 787 line items ($37,500 merchandise divided by $47.62 per order). Instead, it placed only 26 orders that contained just 312 line items. At $8.60 per order and $2.00 per line item, this decreased the costs attributable to Little Retailer by $1,801 ($851 for order handling and $950 for order picking). Again, the 24.2% G&A needs to be added to the net of these cost differences to see if they explain Little Retailer's higher-than-average profitability. The cost variances from average for Little Retailer can be summarized as follows:

Merchandise support	$ 562	favorable
Market support	139	unfavorable
Order	851	favorable
Line items	950	favorable
Subtotal	$2,224	favorable
G&A	538	favorable
Total variance	$2,762	favorable

Subtracting the $2,762 from Little Retailer's $7,767 profit results in a profit of $5,005, approximately 10% of revenues.

Little Retailer's higher-than-average profitability makes sense, based on the type of merchandise it orders and its ordering habits. The fact that it orders mostly quick-moving merchandise and that its orders are larger and contain fewer line items than average makes the work Acme must perform for each dollar of merchandise sold to it much less than average. As a result, Acme gets to keep a great deal more of the 25% gross profit on Little Retailer's business than it does the average customer's business.

In the Acme Distribution case study, we have developed the "plumbing" to flow costs from their incurrence, through Acme's activities, to its cost objectives. This represents the *cost distribution* function of ABC. We have not attempted to use this structure to develop a model to perform its cost accumulation function. That will be saved for another case covered in Chapters 11 through 16. What should be apparent from the case, however, is how a well-thought-out cost flow-down structure can be used to make giant strides in providing management with more accurate and relevant information. In Acme Distribution's case, it was all done manually. No special software or even computerized spreadsheet was required. With some well-structured intellectual effort and a small amount of physical effort, Acme Distributors was able to begin realizing the benefits of ABC.

THE STRUCTURE VS. THE NUMBERS

There is another important lesson, however, to be learned from the Acme Distribution case study. It is a lesson that many individuals, especially accountants and engineers, have often found difficult to accept: *The activity-based cost flow-down structure is much more critical to accurate cost information than the numbers that flow through that structure.*

In other words, the design of the activity-based cost flow (the structure of the model) is more critical to the accuracy, efficiency, and usefulness of ABC than is the precision of the numbers (costs, distribution percentages, activity measures, etc.) that flow through the structure (or model). Acme Distribution can be used to illustrate this point.

Using the cost, activity measure, and distribution data that was used to calculate rates using the activity-based cost flow, we found that Big Chain generated a 9.0% profit for Acme Distributors and Little Retailer generated a 15.5% profit. Let us now run two other sets of data through the activity-based cost flow and see how different these customers' profit pictures look. The details of the calculations using these two alternate data sets will not be discussed, but you can follow Alternate Case 1's calculations in Exhibits 6.9 through 6.12 and Alternate Case 2's calculations in Exhibits 6.13 through 6.16.

Exhibit 6.9 Alternate Case 1: Distributing Costs Among Activities ($000)

			Merchandise		Merchandise Support		Market Support				
		Total	Quick Turns	Slow Turns	Quick Turns	Slow Turns	Big Chains	Little Retails	Orders	Line Items	Gen & Admin
Merchandise	%	100%	50%	50%							
	$	$7,500.0	$3,750.0	$3,750.0							
Procurement	%	100%			45%	50%					5%
	$	$100.0			$45.0	$50.0					$5.0
Receive/ put-away	%	100%			60%	40%					
	$	$100.0			$60.0	$40.0					
Warehousing	%	100%			35%	65%					
	$	$250.0			$87.5	$162.5					
Order fulfillment	%	100%							100%		
	$	$250.0							$250.0		
Order picking	%	100%								100%	
	$	$250.0								$250.0	
Marketing	%	100%					40%	50%			10%
	$	$250.0					$100.0	$125.0			$25.0
G&A	%	100%							10%	10%	80%
	$	$300.0							$30.0	$30.0	$240.0
Total costs		$9,000.0	$3,750.0	$3,750.0	$192.5	$252.5	$100.0	$125.0	$280.0	$280.0	$270.0

Exhibit 6.10 Alternate Case 1: Activity-Based Cost Flow Data

Activity Centers/ Cost Pools	Activity/ Pool Costs ($000)	Rate Basis Amount ($000)	Rate Basis Description	Rate
Merchandise support:				
Quick turns	$192.5	$3,750.0	Merchandise dollars	5.1%
Slow turns	$252.5	$3,750.0	Merchandise dollars	6.7%
Market support:				
Big chains	$100.0	$3,750.0	Merchandise dollars	2.7%
Little retailers	$125.0	$3,750.0	Merchandise dollars	3.3%
Order fulfillment	$280.0	23,000	Number of orders	$12.17
Order picking	$280.0	160,000	Number of line items	$1.75
G&A	$270.0	$1,230.0	Cumulative operating costs	22.0%
Total cost	$1,500.0			

Exhibit 6.11 Alternate Case 1: Customer Profitability Analysis, Big Chain

		Base	Rate	Revenue or Cost
Revenue				$400,000
Merchandise cost				$300,000
Merchandise support:				
Quick turning	50%	$150,000	5.1%	$7,650
Slow turning	50%	$150,000	6.7%	$10,050
Market support:				
Big chains	100%	$300,000	2.7%	$8,100
Little retailers	0%	$0	3.3%	$0
Order fulfillment:				
Annual orders		1,040	$12.17	$12,661
Order Picking:				
Annual line items		8,320	$1.75	$14,560
General and administration:				
cumulative operating cost		$53,021	22.0%	$11,665
Total annual cost				$364,686
Annual profit contribution				$35,314
Profit contribution % to sales				8.8%

Exhibit 6.12 Alternate Case 1: Customer Profitability Analysis: Little Retailer

		Base	Rate	Revenue or Cost
Revenue				$50,000
Merchandise cost				$37,500
Merchandise support:				
Quick turning	80%	$30,000	5.1%	$1,530
Slow turning	20%	$7,500	6.7%	$503
Market support:				
Big chains	0%	$0	2.7%	$0
Little retailers	100%	$37,500	3.3%	$1,238
Order fulfillment:				
Annual orders		26	$12.17	$317
Order picking:				
Annual line items		312	$1.75	$546
General and administration:				
cumulative operating cost		$4,134	22.0%	$909
Total annual cost				$42,543
Annual profit contribution				$7,457
Profit contribution % to sales				14.9%

Exhibit 6.13 Alternate Case 2: Distributing Costs Among Activities ($000)

			Merchandise		Merchandise Support		Market Support				
		Total	Quick Turns	Slow Turns	Quick Turns	Slow Turns	Big Chains	Little Retails	Orders	Line Items	Gen & Admin
Merchandise	%	100%	50%	50%							
	$	$7,500.0	$3,750.0	$3,750.0							
Procurement	%	100%			25%	70%					5%
	$	$75.0			$18.7	$52.5					$3.8
Receive/put-away	%	100%			40%	60%					
	$	$125.0			$50.0	$75.0					
Warehousing	%	100%			30%	70%					
	$	$200.0			$60.0	$140.0					
Order fulfillment	%	100%							100%		
	$	$300.0							$300.0		
Order picking	%	100%								100%	
	$	$300.0								$300.0	
Marketing	%	100%					45%	50%			5%
	$	$200.0					$90.0	$100.0			$10.0
G&A	%	100%							0%	0%	100%
	$	$300.0							$0.0	$0.0	$300.0
Total costs		$9,000.0	$3,750.0	$3,750.0	$128.7	$267.5	$90.0	$100.0	$300.0	$300.0	$313.8

Exhibit 6.14 Alternate Case 2: Activity-Based Cost Flow Data

Activity Centers/ Cost Pools	Activity / Pool Costs ($000)	Rate Basis		Rate
		Amount ($000)	Description	
Merchandise Support:				
Quick turns	$128.7	$3,750.0	Merchandise dollars	3.4%
Slow turns	$267.5	$3,750.0	Merchandise dollars	7.1%
Market support:				
Big chains	$90.0	$3,750.0	Merchandise dollars	2.4%
Little retailers	$100.0	$3,750.0	Merchandise dollars	2.7%
Order fulfillment	$300.0	28,000	Number of orders	$10.71
Order picking	$300.0	150,000	Number of line items	$2.00
G&A	$313.8	$1,186.2	Cumulative operating costs	26.5%
Total cost	$1,500.0			

Exhibit 6.15 Alternate Case 2: Customer Profitability Analysis, Big Chain

		Base	Rate	Revenue or Cost
Revenue				$400,000
Merchandise cost				$300,000
Merchandise support:				
Quick Turning	50%	$150,000	3.4%	$5,100
Slow Turning	50%	$150,000	7.1%	$10,650
Market support:				
Big chains	100%	$300,000	2.4%	$7,200
Little retailers	0%	$0	2.7%	$0
Order fulfillment:				
Annual orders		1,040	$10.71	$11,143
Order picking:				
Annual line items		8,320	$2.00	$16,640
General and administration:				
cumulative operating cost		$50,733	26.5%	$13,444
Total annual cost				$364,177
Annual profit contribution				$35,823
Profit contribution % to sales				9.0%

Exhibit 6.16 Alternate Case 2: Customer Profitability Analysis: Little Retailer

		Base	Rate	Revenue or Cost
Revenue				$50,000
Merchandise cost				$37,500
Merchandise support:				
Quick turning	80%	$30,000	3.4%	$1,020
Slow turning	20%	$7,500	7.1%	$533
Market Support:				
Big chains	0%	$0	2.4%	$0
Little retailers	100%	$37,500	2.7%	$1,013
Order fulfillment:				
Annual orders		26	$10.71	$279
Order picking:				
Annual line items		312	$2.00	$624
General and administration:				
cumulative operating cost		$3,469	26.5%	$919
Total annual cost				$41,888
Annual profit contribution				$8,112
Profit contribution % to sales				16.2%

The data used in the Acme Distributors example (Base Case) and the two alternative sets of input data are detailed below:

	Base Case	*Alt Case 1*	*Alt Case 2*
Costs and expenses:			
Purchased merchandise	$7,500,000	$7,500,000	$7,500,000
Procurement	125,000	100,000	75,000
Receiving/put-away	75,000	100,000	125,000
Warehousing	300,000	250,000	200,000
Order fulfillment	200,000	250,000	300,000
Order picking	300,000	250,000	300,000
Marketing	200,000	250,000	200,000
G&A	300,000	300,000	300,000
Total	$9,000,000	$9,000,000	$9,000,000
Merchandise support:			
Quick turn	$3,750,000	$3,750,000	$3,750,000
Slow turn	$3,750,000	$3,750,000	$3,750,000
Market Support:			
Big chains	$3,750,000	$3,750,000	$3,750,000
Little retailers	$3,750,000	$3,750,000	$3,750,000
Distributions:			
Procurement			
—Quick-turning merchandise	30%	45%	25%
—Slow-turning merchandise	60%	50%	70%
—G&A	10%	5%	5%
Receiving/put-away			
—Quick-turning merchandise	50%	60%	40%
—Slow-turning merchandise	50%	40%	60%
Warehousing			
—Quick-turning merchandise	25%	35%	30%
—Slow-turning merchandise	75%	65%	70%
Order fulfillment			
—Orders	100%	100%	100%

Order picking			
—Line items	100%	100%	100%
Marketing			
—Big chain market	40%	40%	45%
—Little retailer market	55%	50%	50%
—G&A	5%	10%	5%
G&A			
—Orders	5%	10%	0%
—Line Items	5%	10%	0%
—G&A	90%	80%	100%
Activity measures			
Orders	25,000	23,000	28,000
Line items	157,500	160,000	150,000

Note that in all cases, total costs are $9 million. The company knows what its total costs were, so they should not be different. They are not usually difficult to ascertain once the categories have been defined, so the split of merchandise between quick and slow moving and the split of merchandise sales between big chains and little retailers remained the same in all cases. The distributions of "service and operations support activity centers, however, vary considerably, sometimes by 10 to 20 percentage points. Finally, the total tally of order and lines items also varies between cases.

After "crunching" each case's data through the activity-based cost flow structure, the comparative profitability of the big chain and the little retailer are as follows:

	Base Case	***Alt Case 1***	***Alt Case 2***
Big chain	9.0%	8.8%	9.0%
Little retailer	15.5%	14.9%	16.2%

Not much of a difference. Why would such different data result in such similar results? The reason is that the activity-based cost structure is the primary determinant as to what the results will be. If the cost structure is faulty, the most accurate data obtainable will not make the results accurate. If the cost structure is sound, even "soft" data will result in reasonably accurate costs. Of course, wild guesses or random data will not result in accurate costs either way. If, however, the cost, activity measure, and distribution data are based on the best estimates available from the individuals most qualified to make those estimates, accurate activity-based cost data will be obtained.

This fact cannot be emphasized enough. Approximately 80% of the accuracy from an ABC implementation comes from the design of the cost flow structure. Only 20% comes from the data. Some of my more respected colleagues in the ABC community think I might even be a little light on the importance of the structure. One has even suggested that it represents 90% of the improved accuracy of activity-based cost data.

Every ineffective ABC implementation I have seen has been due to a poorly designed cost flow structure. None have been due to bad input data. In almost all of these cases, a vast majority of the work involved in adopting ABC was spent in collecting data and building a computer model that parallels an inappropriate cost flow structure. Unfortunately, most accountants and engineers like to calculate numbers and play with the computer more than they like to conceptualize cost flow structures. The result is a lot of unsatisfactory ABC implementations.

SUMMARY

Only by developing a conceptually sound activity-based cost flow-down structure can an ABC implementation succeed. Acme Distributors was able to make giant strides in its understanding of customer profitability as well as the costs involved in some of its more critical processes through a great deal of intellectual energy and a little bit of physical energy. To make ABC effective, the impulse to act must be suppressed until a disciplined, structured thought process has been completed. Only then will the impulse to act be directed toward a useful end.

7

Decision Costing: The Real Reason for Activity-Based Costs

One of the fears of an activity-based costing (ABC) consultant is that, after the project is done and the consultant goes home, a client will go from using bad cost information inappropriately to using good cost information inappropriately. As a result, we spend a good deal of time on our projects talking about *decision costing*—selecting the relevant cost information and then using it appropriately. A lack of decision costing skills is one of the major reasons we find for the failure of ABC as a management tool at those companies who have adopted it.

Decision costing information can be divided into two categories: fully absorbed cost information and incremental cost information. Fully absorbed cost information requires the distribution of all of an organization's costs to its cost objectives with each cost objective picking up its fair share of the organization's costs. The basic cost distribution mechanics of ABC are a means of developing accurate, fully absorbed cost information. Incremental cost information requires the calculation of the organization-wide cost changes that will be brought about by a specific action. The cost accumulation mechanics of ABC are a means of developing accurate, incremental cost information. A few types of decisions require only fully absorbed costs. Often, fully absorbed costs direct management attention to potential problem areas, but the ultimate decision costs are incremental. Most decision types, however, are straightforward incremental cost decisions.

In the following sections, some of the common errors encountered in the decision costing use of cost information will be discussed, the ways in which using both the cost accumulation and cost distribution modes of ABC can be used to provide accurate and relevant decision costing information in almost any situation will be explored. These sections do not try to cover theories of pricing, capital budgeting, or any other discipline. They are presented to show the importance of accurate and relevant cost information if these theories are to be used to effectively improve an organization's financial performance.

PRICING DECISIONS

In most cases, the first decision that comes to mind when cost information is discussed is the pricing decision. To some, the reaction is negative. They say that cost information is irrelevant in pricing decisions because the market, not cost, determines price. To others, the reaction is positive. They say that accurate product or service costs are essential. Without them, a company cannot know whether it is quoting jobs or pricing products and services at a profit. Still others are somewhere between these two extremes. They know that knowledge of product or service cost is important but are not quite sure how it fits into the complex considerations of a pricing decision.

The first thing that must be understood is that the market, not cost, determines the price of a job, product, or service. A company needs accurate and relevant cost information to determine whether it wants to "play the game" at the market price. The connection is not between cost and price; instead, the connection is between cost and the desirability of selling at the market price.

Some of the cost/price confusion arises because, in many businesses, there is no easily ascertainable market price. The contract manufacturer, for example, sells its manufacturing capabilities to produce unique products on a job-by-job basis. They manufacture to a customer's specifications. There is no catalog or price list to look up the market price of such an item because it is unique. The market price will be determined through the customer's solicitation of quotes from a variety of potential suppliers. Because there is no market price known in advance, each contract manufacturer must determine a price at which it would be willing to accept the contract. To do this, the company estimates the cost of completing the job and adds a desired profit. In this manner, the contract manufacturer "fishes" for the market price and makes sure that, if it "catches the fish," it will earn the profit it decided was acceptable for the job. When this process is repeated hundreds or thousands of times, it begins to appear that cost and price are somehow connected. They are not. The connection is between cost and the desirability of selling at the market price.

CORE BUSINESS PRICING

Another objection sometimes made to the emphasis placed on product cost lies in the fact that "the objective is to optimize the profit and return of the overall organization, not each individual product or service." As was the case with the earlier objection that the market, not cost, determines price, this statement is true, but the conclusion that product cost information is, therefore, unimportant is not. Opportunities for new business do not usually present themselves consecutively. A company does not ordinarily quote one job, wait until a decision is reached, and then quote another job. Most often, it has numerous quotations outstanding at once and does not know for sure which ones will be awarded. It does not know an individual job's impact on the company's overall profit and return because it does not know what the company's specific volume and mix of business will be if the job is awarded. This is particularly true in an organization that publishes periodic price lists or catalogs. For all practical purposes, such an organization has tens of thousands of quotations outstanding at any point in time with no specific knowledge of which ones will result in orders.

Fully absorbed costing rates, set at the company's *real* volume and mix of business, are the relevant cost information for such core business pricing decisions. The real volume and mix of business is that for which the organization has structured itself (as discussed in the "Death Spiral" section of Chapter 4, this should not be confused with the *actual* or even the *budgeted* volume and mix of business). *Core business* can be defined as the products or services normally produced, distributed, or performed by the organization when sold under normal market conditions. Both elements of the definition are important, because if either a product or service not normally handled is involved or the sale is made under abnormal market conditions, fully absorbed cost information ceases to be relevant.

In general, it is an organization's core business that must cover its basic costs of operation. Pricing policies must be structured so that the cost of activities caused by its various products and services are covered by the revenues received in exchange for those products and services. It should be obvious that a company will attract a lot of business when its pricing policies are structured to give away the work it performs for customers, but it will have trouble attracting business when those policies result in charging customers for work the company does not perform. Under normal competitive conditions, failure to take into account the cost of work actually being performed when establishing sales prices will result in an unprofitable mix of orders being awarded.

Consider the case of a company whose overall productivity is better then average for its industry and marketplace. Under normal economic conditions, the market will allow for this company, whose costs are lower than industry average, to charge a price that will enable it to recapture its costs and earn enough of a profit to ensure its continuing ability to supply the marketplace. If our average company accurately calculates its costs and adds a market-supportable profit margin on each of one hundred jobs, it should be competitive on all jobs and will earn the targeted profit margin on any job it is awarded. This situation can be seen graphically in Exhibit 7.1, in which the horizontal axis represents the 100 jobs bid and the vertical axis the percentage accuracy of the cost estimate. The market prices shown are approximately 25% above accurately determined costs. The area between the market price and the 100% accurate job costs represents the potential profit on any contract awarded.

If, however, this company uses an inappropriate, overgeneralized methodology to calculate its costs, it will overestimate the cost on approximately one half of the jobs and underestimate the cost on the other half. As a result, it will establish its *cost plus profit* pricing at levels that will be under the market for those jobs whose costs were underestimated and over the market for those whose costs were overestimated. This situation can be seen graphically in Exhibit 7.2, in which jobs are sequenced from left to right starting with the one whose cost was most underestimated and ending with the one whose cost was most overestimated. Looking at the Quoted Price and Market Price lines, it is obvious that the company will be much more likely to be awarded contracts on the left side of the diagram—those on which it has underestimated its costs. Unfortunately, actual costs do not care whether they have been over- or underestimated, they will be *actuals* either way. As Exhibit 7.3 clearly shows, if the company is awarded those contracts that were inadvertently priced below market, it has little or no chance of financial success. However, it will be missing out on the potential profits that could have been earned at the market price on those jobs its inaccurate costing methodologies caused it to overprice.

Companies in industries that have established market prices often believe that it is not important that they have accurate product or service costing information because they already know market prices. They have no need to fish for them. Actually, product and service costing information is just as important to these organizations as it is to those who must fish for the market. Instead of using cost to determine an acceptable price, these companies need accurate product and service costing information to determine which products or services will earn them the desired profit at the market price.

Most organizations are not equally as good at everything they do. They are more cost effective at making some products or providing some services than they are at others. Exhibit 7.4 graphically illustrates the situation in which these companies find themselves. In this case, the vertical axis represents the company's cost relative to the industry's average cost,

Exhibit 7.1 Market Price/Profit Potential

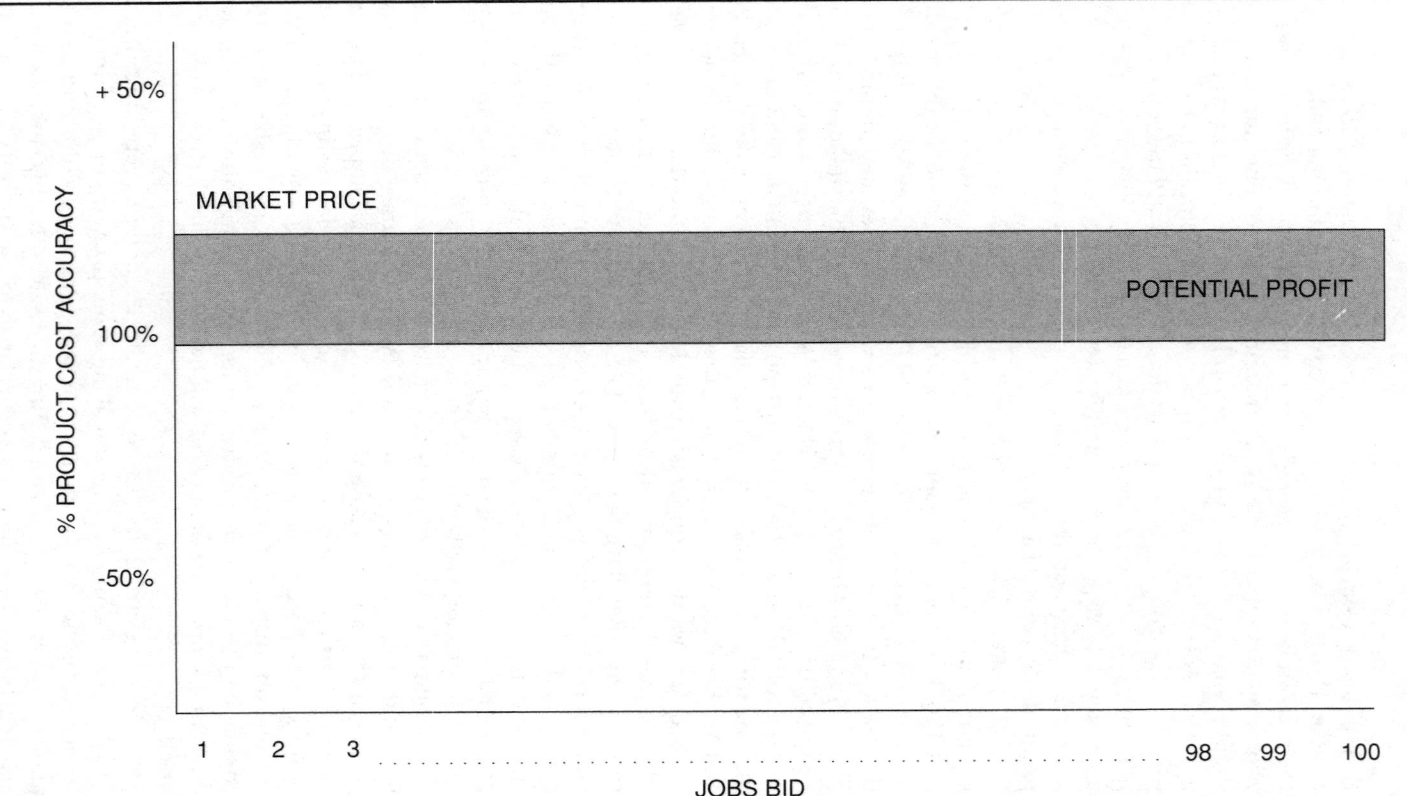

Exhibit 7.2 Pricing Based on Overgeneralized Cost

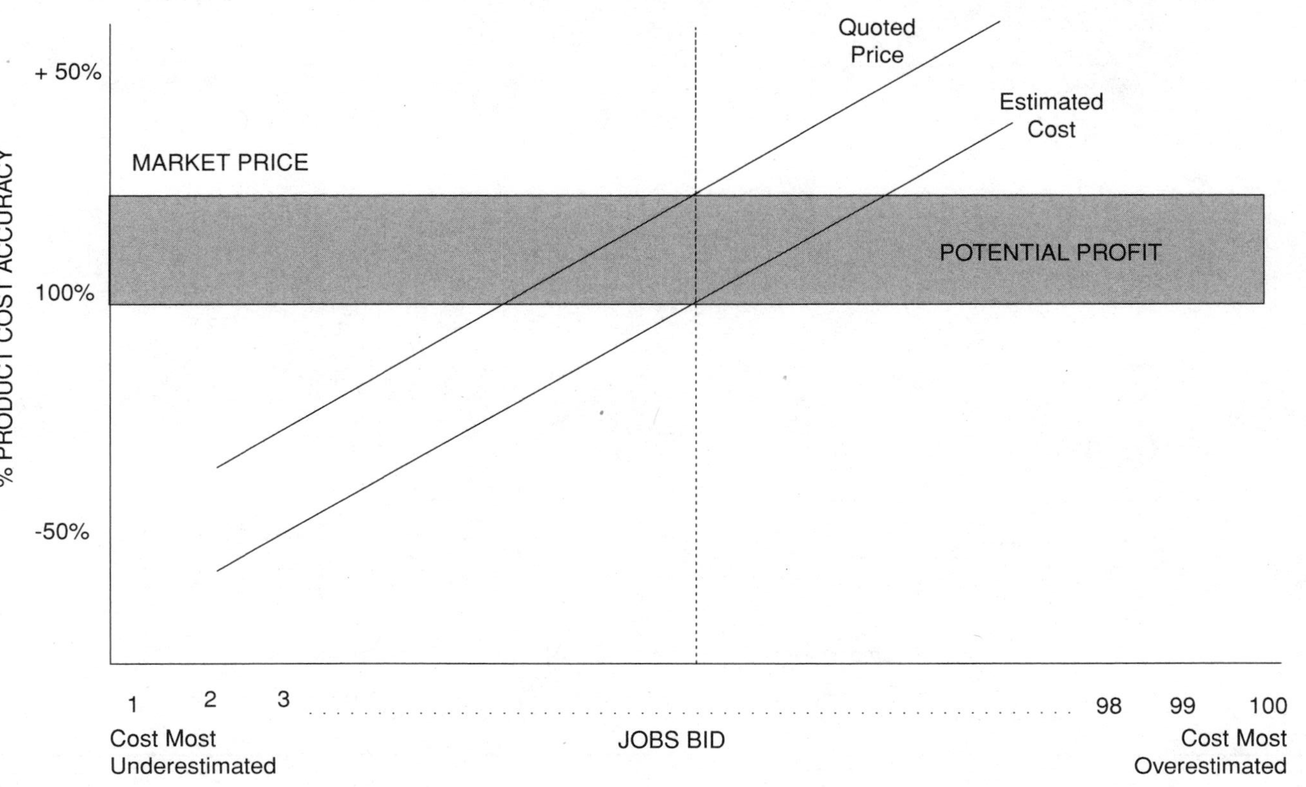

Exhibit 7.3 Profitability Analysis of Jobs Won

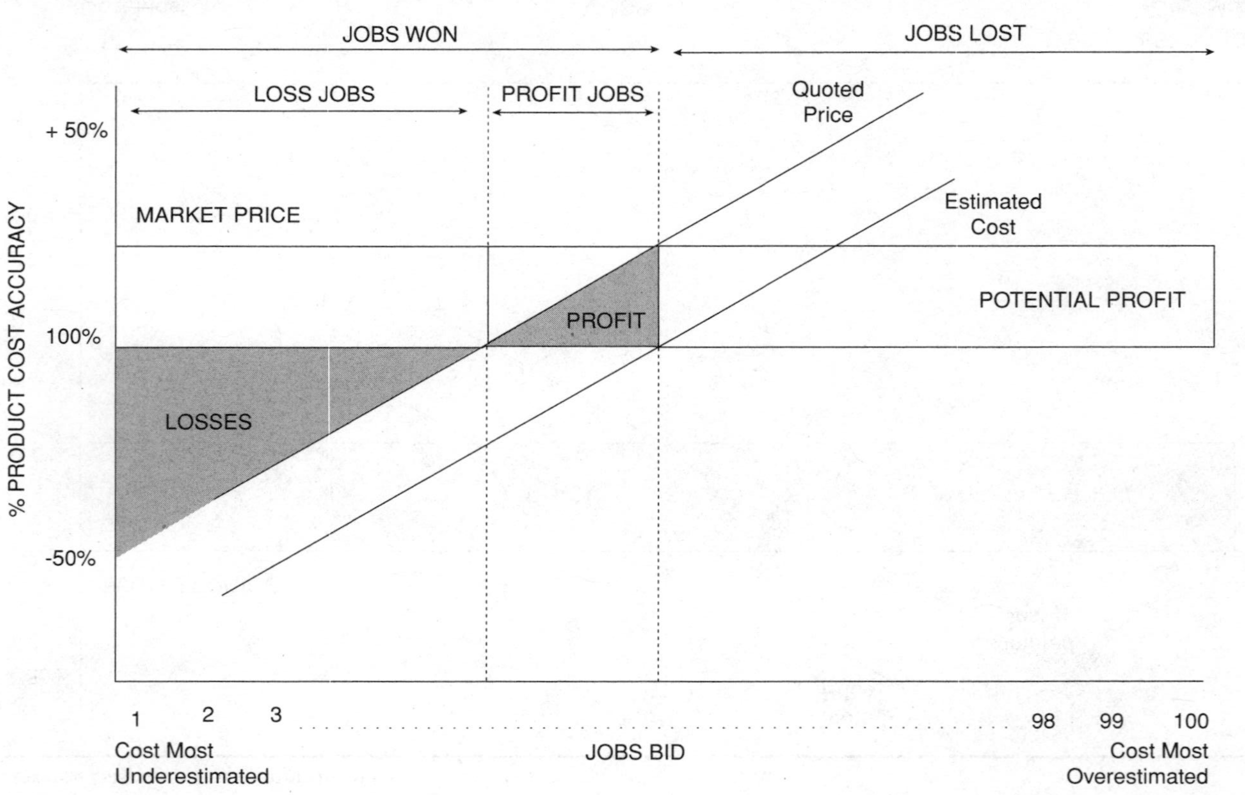

Exhibit 7.4 Profitability Analysis at Market Prices

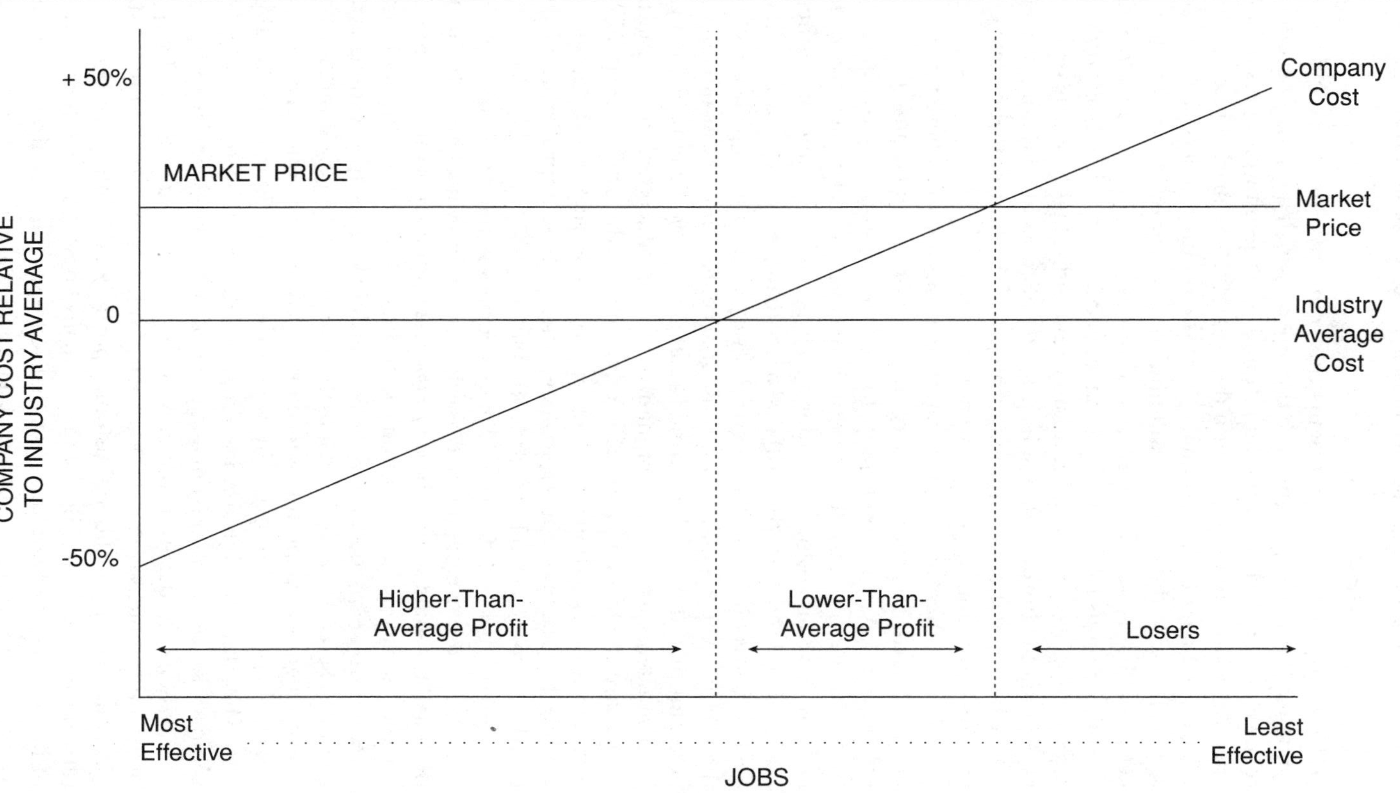

and the horizontal axis represents the company's products and services sequenced from left to right, with the one on which it is most cost effective relative to the market on the far left and the one on which it is least cost effective relative to the market on the far right. The market price is shown relative to the industry's average cost of the product or service.

Obviously, the company will find contracts or orders won at the market price that appear on the left side of the graph much more desirable than those on its right side. Without an accurate knowledge of product or service cost, however, it will not know how individual products or services rank along the horizontal axis. Its pricing policies and marketing strategies will be based on the assumption that all products contribute the same profit margin—an assumption we know not to be true.

Despite these arguments, many organizations still believe that they do not need accurate product or service cost information because they do not believe they have the opportunity to pick and choose the jobs they accept. In their view, they must do whatever is necessary to retain customers, market position, and volume. As long as an adequate volume of business is attracted and retained, they will find a way to make the company profitable. Such a view is much too shortsighted. Every company can pick and choose the jobs it accepts—maybe not those it accepts tomorrow or next week or next month, but through informed strategic actions, a company can evolve its product mix to one that emphasizes those products or services on which it can earn the biggest profit. Similarly, knowing the profit contribution of each of the organization's products or services provides a first step in learning how costs can be reduced to allow some of those unprofitable jobs, customers, or contracts to become profitable.

All this being said, it should always be kept in mind that the objective is to make money overall, not necessarily on each individual job. The focus of profitability should actually be on *portfolios* of business, not on each individual product, service, job, transaction, or contract. One loser contract must be accepted from a particular customer in order to be awarded two big winner contracts. Several development jobs must be undertaken for another in order to win a high-volume production contract. A distributor must service one customer's low-volume branches in order to service its high-volume headquarters. The ultimate objective is to manage the portfolio of portfolios (the company's overall business) in a way that leads it to its financial goals.

When considering a company's core business, regardless of the appropriate unit of measurement, be it each product, job, product line, marketplace, industry portfolio, or customer portfolio, the fully absorbed costing rates developed using ABC let the company know to what extent each unit of measurement covers the costs that it causes the organization to incur. These are the costs that should be taken into account when making core business pricing decisions.

SPECIAL ORDER PRICING

Special orders are often easy to recognize, but sometimes they are not so obvious. The simple rule for identifying a special order is that it is any order that does not fall under the definition of core business. We earlier defined *core business* as the products or services normally produced, distributed, or performed by the organization when sold under normal market conditions. As a result, special orders are products or services that are not normally produced, distributed, or performed by the organization or that are not sold under normal market conditions.

For example, one manufacturer stamps out steel components and welds them together into a product that is sold as a subassembly to another manufacturer. Two years ago, this manufacturer had an opportunity to submit a quote to one of its regular customers for a three-year contract to manufacture a particular subassembly. This fell under the definition of core business (normal product/normal market conditions); therefore, it calculated its fully absorbed cost of manufacturing the product and arrived at a cost of $4 each. It then added its target margin of 15% and submitted a quote of $4.60. Unfortunately, one of its competitors quoted the job at $3.50 each and was awarded the contract. That competitor has now gone out of business (you can probably guess why). As a result, the customer has come to the manufacturer and asked if it would complete the last year of the now defunct company's contract at the $3.50 unit price.

Initially, the manufacturer viewed this as a real Hobson's choice. It could agree to complete the contract and keep a valued customer happy while losing $.50 on each unit shipped, or it could decline and lose some of its goodwill with the customer while avoiding the loss in profits. It viewed this decision as one involving core business. After all, when it originally quoted the job, it was considered core business. It is the same kind of product it usually quotes as core business. What would make the decision costing of this opportunity any different?

The difference is that this decision is not being made under normal market conditions. The price has been established. It is not submitting a competitive quote in an attempt to win the contract. Instead, the customer has given it a "take it or leave it" offer to complete the contract at the other manufacturer's price. The decision costs in this case are not fully absorbed costs, they are incremental costs. Our manufacturer should determine the incremental cost of manufacturing this subassembly for one year and weigh that against the additional revenue that will be received from its sale. The original cost estimate of $4 per unit is irrelevant (even after updating for two years of inflation and process changes).

A common way of determining such an incremental cost is to recost the job using only the company's *variable cost rates.* This approach, however, can also be deceptive. When calculating fully absorbed costing rates, a certain volume and mix of business are assumed. Conventional thinking says that only the fixed element of a company's costing rate is impacted by a change in volume and mix. A change in volume or mix will change the denominator by which the fixed costs are divided and, as a result, the *fixed cost rate* will either increase or decrease. The variable cost portion of the rate is assumed to be linear.

As the thoughtful application of ABC will reveal, there is no nice neat definition of *fixed* and *variable* cost. All costs are fixed over the very short term and all are variable over the very long term. In the manufacturer's current case, will the addition of the new business require the addition of another shift? Will it require that some employees work more overtime? Will the company need to add some equipment? Will it be necessary to add some extra engineering resources? Answers to these types of questions can either make variable costs (which are assumed to be linear in costing rates) nonlinear, or make fixed costs variable.

The oversimplified classification inherent in using variable cost rates to calculate incremental costs overlooks one important rule in decision costing: *The definitions of fixed and variable costs are situation specific.* As a result, decisions, such as the one faced by the manufacturer, must be based on the activity-based cost behavior of the company as it goes from the volume and mix of activities that will exist without the order to the volume and mix of activities that will be required if it accepts this special order. This requires a global "before and after" or "with and without" calculation. The cost accumulation mechanics of ABC are the method appropriate for supporting this decision. The actual mechanics for using ABC to perform this calculation are covered in Chapter 15. The important point here is that accurately determined incremental costs, not fully absorbed costing rates, are the relevant decision costs for making a decision such as this one.

Sometimes, special orders come on a much grander scale. The discussion of the "upward death spiral" in Chapter 4 gave a brief example of such an order. In that chapter was an example of a $10 million manufacturer who received a one-time order for $8 million that would be manufactured and shipped over a period of two years. After that order, business was expected to fall back to the $10 million level. How should the manufacturer have viewed this one-time order when requested to submit a quote. Was it *core business* or was it a *special order*? Although the manufacturer was (as far as we can tell) still manufacturing the same type of products it usually produces, it was certainly not quoting under normal market conditions. The potential contract was not only exceptionally large, it was a one-time deal and would not result in a permanent increase in the company's volume of business. It is a layer of business temporarily set on top of the company's core business. As a result, it was a special order.

This order would again require the determination of incremental costs. A job of this size will surely make variable costs nonlinear and turn fixed costs into variable costs. The profit contribution of this job should be measured by the additional revenue it will generate less the incremental cost that will be incurred. Here again, ABC's cost accumulation mechanics are the method appropriate for supporting this decision.

Let us put one more "spin" on the situation. What if the $4 million in additional annual business ($8 million over two years) was not part of a one-time contract but, instead, represented the addition of a new customer or product line that could be expected to continue indefinitely? Would the decision costing be any different? To decide, we need to go back to the basic question: Is it core business or is it a special order?

In this last case, it appears as though the company is raising its core business to a new and higher level. This is not a layer temporarily set on top of its core business but additional volume that actually changes the measure of the company's core business. As a result, our manufacturer needs to determine what its fully absorbed product costs would be if it was to receive the contract. To do so requires the ability to project the cost structure of the company at a higher volume and different mix of activities. Once that is done, the projected rate structure would then be appropriate for costing the product or products involved in the same manner as any core business product cost would be performed.

It must be kept in mind that these discussions relate to the relevant cost information to use in supporting these various types of pricing decisions. The prices themselves should reflect *cupidity*. Get all that you can get. Do not get lazy and let the cost information make the decision. Relying on cost information as the primary determinant in pricing decisions is just as big a mistake as ignoring cost information in making those decisions.

STRATEGIC/PRODUCT-LINE PRICING

Earlier in this chapter, it was pointed out that the objective of a company's pricing strategy is to optimize the profit and return of the overall organization, not each individual product or service. It was emphasized that the market, not cost, determines a product or service's sales price. For an organization that provides more than one type of product or service or that sells their products or services in two or more distinct markets, these facts raise an interesting question. How should the organization price its various products or services in a way that optimizes its overall performance?

Consider the example of a manufacturer of investment-cast products. Once this company has cast the metal into its basic shape, it must then machine the part into a finished product. Throughout the years, the company had outsourced the majority of its machining requirements. Its expertise was in investment casting the basic shapes. It did not believe it had sufficient volume to make its own machine shop self-sufficient. An analysis showed the company, however, that if it acquired the equipment and skills required to perform its own machining activities, it would reduce the cost of machining even if it used its new capabilities only 40% of the time. As a result, the company went ahead and acquired its own equipment and hired the necessary skilled employees. Costs went down as predicted.

Once it was in place and operating, the investment caster found it disturbing that the machine shop was being used only 40% of the time. The company was already close to capacity in its investment-casting activities, so it could not provide any more volume internally. Additionally, management did not believe there was enough potential business to justify additional investment-casting equipment. Any additional machining activity had to be generated from outside. Therefore, the company decided to sell some of its excess machining capacity on the outside.

Fortunately, the investment caster understood that it was not becoming a provider of machining services; it was simply an investment caster that was selling excess machining capacity on the outside. The difference may be subtle, but it is important. If the company viewed these additional machining services as part of its core business, the costs used in its pricing decisions would be different than they would be by viewing machining activities as a way to "make a little money on the side."

The company began by determining how many more hours of machining activity could be undertaken without requiring the addition of any staff or indirect production personnel or the purchase of any additional capital. It then calculated the increase in total company costs involved in increasing machining activity to this higher volume. By dividing the increase in cost by the additional machining hours, it arrived at an incremental cost per machine hour that could be used as a basis for its pricing decision. This incremental cost per machine hour came to less than half of the market price for machining activities.

Because it was not in the machining business, the investment caster wanted to set a price that would sell itself, thereby eliminating the need to spend money on marketing or other product-line support activities. It also wanted its price to be low enough that it would be in control of the amount of machining business it had at any point in time. This would ensure that this incremental business did not interfere with its core business of manufacturing investment cast products. As a result, it established a price at about 40% above the incremental cost per hour calculated earlier, a price that was only about 70% of the going rate in the market. This strategic price, which no sane company with machining as a core business would dare to match (because it would not support the administrative, support, facility, and technical cost of being in the industry), ensured the company a steady supply of business for its excess machining capacity and an incremental profit that added a significant amount to the company's bottom line without a significant increase in investment. This did not make the company very popular among its former suppliers of machining services, because it put some pricing pressure on their business. This loss of popularity was a small price to pay, however, for the improvement in profit and return on investment.

Somewhat ironically, when the company's monthly sales and margin analysis was generated by its accounting system, it showed all of these outside machining jobs as losers. This was, of course, because the accounting system's cost of sales calculations were all based on fully absorbed costs, which did not reflect the true nature of this incremental business. Had they been priced to earn a fully absorbed profit, they either would never have been awarded in the first place, or the company would have had to incur additional costs of becoming a full-service machining company.

In this case, accurate and relevant cost information was a critical element in the pricing decision, although it was the market, not cost, that determined the price. Cost determined whether the action would be worth taking at the price that would generate the appropriate volume.

Similar situations exist in most organizations that have more than one line of products or services. These organizations have a dynamic that single-product or service organizations do not have. This dynamic involves the impact that each line of business has on the others. The objective is to optimize the operating results of the organization as a whole; therefore, each product or service line cannot be treated as a stand-alone business if effective decisions are to be made.

One highly visible instance of this situation is in the auto industry. The business press often reports how an auto company loses money or, if it is lucky, breaks even on the many subcompact through mid-sized units it produces, but makes obscene profits on the luxury cars and sport utility vehicles it sells. Although the straightforward accounting would indicate that smaller, basic units are bad news and the big, sporty luxury units are good news, the reality of the situation is that the sale of the profitable units would either be impossible or their cost would far exceed the market price if the far less profitable, small, basic units were not sold in sufficient quantity.

When companies have this multiproduct/service dynamic, they need a dynamic costing tool if they are to make effective pricing decisions. For example, suppose one company manufactures and sells two products, Product A and Product B, from a single facility. An analysis by marketing indicates that the impact of various prices on demand for these two products is as follows:

Product A:

Price:	$ 1,000	Demand:	10,000 units
Price:	$ 1,250	Demand:	7,500 units
Price:	$ 1,500	Demand:	6,000 units

Product B:

Price	$ 5,000	Demand:	2,000 units
Price	$ 6,000	Demand:	1,600 units
Price	$ 7,000	Demand:	1,300 units

How should the company price the two products to optimize its financial return? Obviously, prices of $1,000 and $5,000 would generate the most revenue, but would the company even have the capacity to produce that many of both products? What would be the bottom-line impact of pricing products at $1,250 and $5,000? Would that be more profitable than pricing at $1,000 and $6,000?

The only way to know the bottom-line impact of these pricing decisions is to have a dynamic cost model that can pass the activities that would result from the expected demand through capacity screens and then determine the total cost that would be incurred by the organization to meet the demand that would be generated at the selected prices. These are not decisions in which fully absorbed cost information would have any relevance. They require incremental costs. What is the overall cost differential between producing 7,500 Product As and 1,300 Product Bs and producing 6,000 Product As and 1,600 Product Bs? How does that compare to the revenue that would be generated at pricing levels that would generate those levels of demand? The profitability of each product is not important in this decision; it is the combined profitability—the profitability of the entire organization—that is essential.

The cost accumulation capability of an effectively designed ABC model provides the mechanics for developing accurate and relevant cost information to use in supporting these types of strategic or product-line pricing decisions. The different volumes of each product require different levels of the organization's key activities. The measure of those activities drives the cost of providing them. The sum of the cost of all of the activities (plus any direct or throughput costs) provides the cost basis for determining profitability under each possible decision scenario.

LONG-TERM CONTRACTS

In more and more industries, whether it be automotive supply or health care, customers are demanding long-term pricing commitments. When a company is lucky, the requirement is for a fixed price over a number of years. More often than not, however, the long-term commitment is to reduce the price by a certain amount annually during the course of the contract. Capitation pricing in health care is an area in which this concept has been spreading. Auto industry supplies have been suffering from annual reduction pricing for almost a decade. When the pricing decision calls for a long-term commitment, understanding costs and cost behavior becomes an even more important element in the decision making process than usual.

When a company must estimate the cost of a contract in which the service will be provided or the product manufactured in the short-term, it at least has a good idea of what the cost structure of the organization performing the service or manufacturing the product will look like when the contract is completed. However, when it must estimate the cost of a contract whose performance extends over a number of years, it must be able to look out three, four, or even five years to anticipate what the cost structure of the organization will be at the time the work required under the contract takes place.

The future cost structure of the organization working on a long-term contract could look far different from that of the organization at the time it estimates the contract's cost. The volume of business could change significantly. The capital employed to produce the product or provide the service could be radically different. Cost reductions could be realized. Wage rates will have changed. Fringe benefit packages may have been modified. The organization may have moved to a different facility. In short, the cost structure in existence when the contract's cost is estimated will probably bear little resemblance to the cost structure that will exist when the work under the contract is actually performed.

To effectively estimate the cost of long-term contracts, an organization must be able to project the cost structure that will be in existence in future periods. Those cost structures need to take into account changes in the volume and mix of activities that will be performed by the organization, differences in the way those activities will be performed, and differences in the economics of the organization's various elements of costs (wages, fringes, utilities, supplies, taxes, etc.). For example, it currently costs one machining company $60.50 per hour to operate its equipment for 10,000 hours. Over the next three years, it projects that its volume will increase by 2,000 hours per year. If it has an opportunity to quote on a four-year contract, what cost per hour should it use to estimate machining costs for the contract?

Some organizations might add an inflation factor to the current rate to provide for costs increases. Others might hold the rate constant and assume that cost reductions will be found to offset any economic cost increases. Still others might divide the current $60.50 rate into its fixed and variable elements, add an inflation factor to the variable costs, and recalculate annual rates based on each year's increase in the volume of machining activity. Although the final method represents a step in the right direction, all three methods are the kinds of things accountants do in a back room without paying any attention to what management actually plans on doing in the future. It is only by finding out what plans the company has for the future and incorporating those into projected rates for the coming years that the accurate and relevant cost information necessary to make an informed pricing decision will be obtained.

Exhibit 7.5 depicts one means of developing the accurate and relevant cost information needed for this decision. The column headed "Year 1" represents the current cost structure of the company resulting in its $60.50 per machine hour rate. The columns headed Year 2, Year 3, and Year 4 represent the forecasted costs for those "out years" based on management's actual plans and forecasts.

One key element in the company's cost reduction efforts is the development of new controls that will make it possible for its machines to run without the two-person crews that are currently required. The company estimates that over the next three years, it will be able to make these new controls operative to the extent that average crew sizes will be reduced from 2.0 to 1.8, 1.6, and 1.5 in Years 2, 3, and 4, respectively. Economic changes are expected to increase the cost of fringe benefits until Year 3, when some additional, cost-reducing options will be given to the employees in selecting their health care coverage. In addition, wage rates themselves are expected to increase by 3% annually.

The company's engineering and maintenance groups have also just completed modifications to the equipment that will correct long-standing utility usage problems and result in a one-third reduction in the machines' utility usage. In addition, a program is currently underway that, when completed late in Year 3, will enable the company to get 25% more usage out of its perishable tools. Perishable tools themselves are expected to increase in cost approximately 6% annually. Supervision and other overhead costs are also expected to rise due to economics and staff increases, as shown in the exhibit.

After completing the analysis summarized in Exhibit 7.5, the company has a much more rational basis on which to make multiyear pricing commitments. Although the rates are just estimates, they represent a much more realistic picture of the future than simple mathematical gymnastics performed in the back room. They provide an accurate representation of future cost structures based on management's plans and forecasts for the future. Using these rates in supporting long-term pricing decisions will enable management to capitalize today on volume and economic changes as well as operating improvements that will be made in the future and, as a

Exhibit 7.5 Developing Cost per Machine Rates

	Year 1	Year 2	Year 3	Year 4
Machine hours	10,000	12,000	14,000	16,000
Crew size	2.0	1.8	1.6	1.5
Fringe benefit rate	35%	37%	34%	34%
Hourly labor rate/hour	$15.00	$15.60	$16.20	$16.80
Utility cost/hour	$3.00	$2.00	$2.00	$2.00
Tooling cost/hour	$5.00	$5.30	$5.60	$4.70
Supervision costs	$20,000	$21,200	$22,472	$23,820
Other overhead costs	$100,000	$120,000	$140,000	$160,000
Cost summary:				
Operator labor	$300,000	$336,960	$362,880	$403,200
Fringe benefits	$105,000	$124,700	$123,400	$137,100
Utility costs	$30,000	$24,000	$28,000	$32,000
Tooling costs	$50,000	$63,600	$78,400	$75,200
Supervision costs	$20,000	$21,200	$22,472	$23,820
Other overhead costs	$100,000	$120,000	$140,000	$160,000
Total costs	$605,000	$690,460	$755,152	$831,320
Machine hours	10,000	12,000	14,000	16,000
Cost per machine hour	$60.50	$57.54	$53.94	$51.96

result, enable the company to win those contracts on which it has a greater chance of meeting its financial objectives, despite promising fixed or reduced prices during the contract's performance.

A well designed ABC model provides the mechanics to accurately develop projected cost structures for all of an organization's activities into the future. Chapter 16 contains a more comprehensive long-term pricing example that details how a cost accumulation and distribution model can be used to effectively support this fast growing area of decision making.

CAPITAL EXPENDITURE DECISIONS

Another area in which cost plays a major decision support role is capital expenditure decisions. Like many areas of management theory, capital expenditure decisions have a myriad of theoretically sound tools that can be used to evaluate potential uses of an organization's capital investment funds and to compare the relative benefits of various investment opportunities. These include using discounted cash flow, internal rates of return, and *hurdle rates*, as well as the old standbys of return on investment and payback period. Many companies have developed sophisticated methodologies for using these statistical tools in their capital budgeting activities. These tools, however, are much like computer systems. No matter how logical and sophisticated, if you put garbage in, you get garbage out. Unfortunately, the cost information many organizations enter into these tools is garbage, so it is obvious what kind of information results from their use.

A good example comes from my personal experience. A number of years ago, one of the divisions for which I was responsible wanted to submit an appropriation request for $100,000 that proposed adding new controls to a machine center. By adding these new controls, the division believed it could reduce the number of operators necessary to run the machine center from two to one. In keeping with the company's accepted methodologies, we split the division's costing rate into fixed and variable elements. By eliminating the need for the second operator, we were able to eliminate all the variable costs associated with the operator. These included the operator's wages and fringes which amounted to approximately $25,000. They also included variable utility, tooling, and other costs that amounted to another $15,000. As a result, our justification included a $40,000 annual cost saving that would result from this $100,000 expenditure.

The appropriation request was approved, the controls were purchased and installed, and the division was able to operate the machine center with one operator instead of two—a successful investment. Only one problem remained: None of the promised cost savings were real. Eliminating one operator did not provide any reduction in the variable tooling or utility costs.

The machine center ran as many hours as before, consuming the same amount of utilities. It cut just as many chips as before, eating up the same amount of tooling. That was not all. The operator was reassigned to another machine center that had previously had only one operator. No wage or fringe reduction was realized. Not needing an employee does not reduce costs; not having the employee does. The physically observable benefit did materialize, however—one operator versus two—so the expenditure was deemed a success.

This is not to say that the expenditure should not have been made. The new controls improved the machine center's throughput. They reduced the time it took to remove a completed part and start manufacturing another. They reduced the changeover time required to reconfigure and retool the machine center when a different part's manufacture was to begin. This also reduced set-up time, which made smaller quantity jobs more profitable. These improvements made it possible to increase the amount of product the division could produce without purchasing another expensive machine center. Although these benefits may have been sufficient to justify investing in the new controls, we will never know.

If a company is to make rational capital expenditure decisions, it must be able to accurately measure the cost impact of proposed expenditures. Note that the phrase used in the previous sentence is *cost impact*, not *cost reduction*. Sometimes, the cost impact is a cost reduction as would be the case if capital was being purchased to make a specific operation less expensive without any impact on the balance of the organization.

There are many situations, however, in which a capital expenditure impacts areas outside of the activity in which it is placed. For example, one company sells a product that goes through three manufacturing activities. Each unit requires .6 hour in activity center 1, .4 hour in activity center 2, and .8 hour in activity center 3. Currently, it sells 10,000 of these products annually at $210.00 each. The cost to manufacture these 10,000 units is summarized in Exhibit 7.6. Although operating below capacity overall, the company cannot produce any more items because activity center 2 is at capacity. The $2,100,000 revenue less the $1,970,000 cost of manufacturing provides a $130,000 margin.

Engineers at the company have devised a means of improving the productivity in activity center 2 that will allow it to produce the same amount of product in 80% of the time previously required. The cost of incorporating this improvement would be $100,000. This means that, if the improvement is made, only .32 hour of activity center 2's operations will be required for each unit produced. The 800-hour reduction in the time required to manufacture the company's 10,000 units will result in a reduction in the company's operating cost of $32,000 (800 hours × $40 per hour variable cost rate—for simplicity, we are assuming in this case that the variable costing

Exhibit 7.6 Cost Structure Prior to Capital Expenditure

		Activity Center #1	Activity Center #2	Activity Center #3	Total
Capacity (in hours)		10,000	4,000	14,000	
Units produced and sold	10,000				
Actual operating hours		6,000	4,000	8,000	
Material cost per unit	$100.00				$1,000,000
Variable operating cost per hour		$30.00	$40.00	$45.00	
Fixed operating costs		$120,000	$60,000	$90,000	$270,000
Variable operating costs		$180,000	$160,000	$360,000	$700,000
Total operating costs		$300,000	$220,000	$450,000	$1,970,000
Total operating cost per hour		$50.00	$55.00	$56.25	

rate does reflect true cost reductions). This would raise the margin to $162,000 ($130,000 previous margin + $32,000 savings). Using this cost-reduction approach to evaluating this capital expenditure would result in a return on investment of 32% and a payback period of a little over three years.

The engineers have also devised a means of improving the productivity in activity center 3. In this case, a $100,000 investment will allow activity center 3 to produce the 10,000 units annually in 87.5% of the time previously required. The savings in this case would be $45,000 (1,000 hours × $45 per hour variable cost rate). This would raise the margin to $175,000 and provide a return on investment of 45% and a payback period of a little over two years. Using these cost reductions as a means of comparing the two investment alternatives would seem to favor improvements to activity center 3.

Is there more to evaluating these investment alternatives than simply determining the reduction in costs? Will either of these expenditures allow the company to do more than simply ring up an additional profit of $32,000 or $45,000? At $210.00 each, the company could generate sales of 10,000 units, which was all it could sell with the capacity constraint in activity center 2. Making activity center 3 more productive will improve profits, but it will not enable the company to generate any more volume, because the capacity constraint in activity center 2 would still exist. The improvement in activity center 2's productivity, however, provides another benefit: Volume can be increased.

The market has shown that at a price of $210 each, 10,000 units of product can be sold. To increase volume, the price will need to be reduced. Because the improved productivity in activity center 2 will allow it to produce 25% more products, the company's management performed a study to determine at what price it could generate an additional 2,500 units in sales. It found that by reducing the price to $205 each, volume could rise to 12,500 units.

Taking this potential for increased sales into account, the company calculated the total cost to manufacture 12,500 units. As shown in Exhibit 7.7, total cost will increase to $2,355,000. With a revenue increase to $2,562,500, this would generate a margin of $207,500, an increase of $77,500 over the preinvestment margin. Before evaluating this opportunity, however, the company must also consider the additional working capital investment. It estimates that the additional volume will increase working capital by $50,000, resulting in a total investment of $150,000 for this alternative. Even with the working capital increase included, this alternative would provide a return of over 50% and a payback period (which does not include working capital as part of the investment) of 1.3 years.

This more complete analysis indicates that improving activity center 2's productivity can provide a greater return than would be available by

Exhibit 7.7 Cost Structure After Capital Expenditure

		Activity Center #1	Activity Center #2	Activity Center #3	Total
Capacity (in hours)		10,000	4,000	14,000	
Units produced and sold	12,500				
Actual operating hours		7,500	4,000	10,000	
Material cost per unit	$100.00				$1,250,000
Variable operating cost per hour		$30.00	$40.00	$45.00	
Fixed operating costs		$120,000	$60,000	$90,000	$270,000
Variable operating costs		$225,000	$160,000	$450,000	$835,000
Total operating costs		$345,000	$220,000	$540,000	$2,355,000
Total operating cost per hour		$46.00	$55.00	$54.00	

making the investment to improve activity center 3, despite the fact that the cost reduction would be greater in activity center 3.

The purpose of this example is not to provide a guideline for determining incremental costs in supporting capital expenditure decisions. It oversimplifies the process too much to serve as an example for that. Instead, its purpose is to illustrate how important it is to be able to accurately determine incremental costs—the only relevant costs for all capital expenditure decisions—when evaluating possible uses for a company's limited capital funds. Whether being used to calculate cost reductions or the overall cost impact of a new product line, new program, new facility, or new production process, a well-designed ABC model can serve as a tool to provide the critical cost information that is necessary if an organization is to spend its capital funds wisely.

OUTSOURCING (MAKE/BUY) DECISIONS

Outsourcing decisions are another area in which the determination of accurate and relevant costs are critical if a rational decision is to be made. It is also an area in which accurate, but irrelevant, costs are frequently used inappropriately. A frequently encountered situation is one in which a manufacturing company compares its cost of manufacturing a component part with the price it would pay to a supplier for manufacturing that component part for them.

A good example took place at a client of mine several years ago (obviously, the event occurred before they became a client). This client had a component part that it manufactured at a fully absorbed cost of about $5. It manufactured 20,000 of these parts annually. Another company offered to manufacture the same part for them at a unit price of $4. The $20,000 annual savings was too much for them to resist, so they outsourced the manufacture of the part. Unfortunately, eliminating the $5 part did not eliminate all of the costs involved in its manufacture. Over one half of the costs included in the $5 per unit were distributions from support activities whose slight workload reduction would not enable them to reduce their costs. As a result, over $2.50 of each unit's cost remained even after the part was eliminated. Those costs were simply distributed to the other manufactured products that remained. When added to the $4 per unit price from the new supplier, the net impact of the decision was an increase of over $1.50 ($4 purchase cost + $2.50 ongoing cost - $5 former fully absorbed unit cost) per unit, or $30,000 annually.

Too often, when the company discovers that its own manufacturing cost is greater than the price a supplier would charge, the part is outsourced. At times, outsourcing is the right decision, but if fully absorbed manufacturing costs and piece price are the two amounts being compared, the decision is based on irrelevant cost information regardless of how accurate that cost information may be.

Outsourcing, like most management decisions supported by cost information, requires the accurate determination of incremental costs. The amount of cost that would go away if the company no longer manufactured the component and the additional cost that would be incurred if the component were manufactured outside of the organization are the correct decision costs. Would outsourcing reduce more costs than would be added?

The costs that are added are not simply the prices charged by the new vendors. Increasing the supplier base can also increase the internal costs necessary to support and control the suppliers. Additional purchasing, receiving, accounts payable, material control, or quality staff might need to be added. Higher inventories might need to be maintained. Operations might be disrupted due to a less reliable source of supply (or, in some cases, operations might run smoother due to a more reliable source of supply). All of these costs must be considered if an informed decision is to be made.

The time frame and size of the outsourcing effort are also important factors. The cost behavior will be different if an item is outsourced due to a temporary surge in business than if it is a permanent, long-term elimination of an internal process. Similarly, the outsourcing of a few items might not require an increase in support activities, whereas a larger outsourcing program would require a great deal of additional support. An organization must take all of these considerations into account and then determine the incremental impact of the proposed action if it is to make an informed decision.

Outsourcing decisions are not limited to manufacturing situations. Should a health care facility outsource its dietary or billing activities? Should a printer outsource its prepress operations? Should a government unit outsource its trash collection or tax collection activities? Should an insurance company outsource its internal audit function? Should a software company outsource its manufacturing and packaging operations?

In all of these situations, the ability to accurately determine incremental costs, such as can be done with a properly designed ABC model, is a prerequisite if an organization is to make rational outsourcing decisions.

OTHER DECISION SITUATIONS

There are too many decision situations in which accurate and relevant cost information is required to discuss them all in this chapter. Other areas, such as directing continuous improvement efforts, performance measurement, forecasting and planning, product mix management, benchmarking, and product or product-line drop/add decisions also require accurate and relevant cost information if they are to be done effectively. In most cases, incremental costs must be determined. In others, fully absorbed costs are appropriate. In all cases, effective decision making requires that accurate and relevant cost information be provided.

SUMMARY

It is the purpose of ABC to provide an organization's managers with the decision costing information they need. As can be seen by the situations presented in this chapter, the ability to determine the incremental costs resulting from a possible decision are critical to sound decision making. Fully absorbed costs are interesting and useful, but incremental costs are powerful. Any incorporation of ABC concepts that fails to provide a model that will enable management to accurately determine these incremental costs will fall short in achieving the concept's purpose.

8

Activity-Based Costing Model Toolbox

There are a variety of modeling tools available for putting together both the conceptual and physical activity-based costing (ABC) model. By modeling tools, I am not referring to the software used to create an ABC model. Modeling tools are the various internal mechanics that can be used to create a model that comes as close as practical to reality. In both building the model conceptually and turning it into a physical decision support tool, an organization must be aware of as many tools (or design options) as possible if the model is to be effective. This chapter presents a collection of ABC modeling tools that have been proven useful in developing sound, activity-based models.

OPERATING LABOR DEMAND/SUPPLY EQUATION

If a model is to accurately reflect labor costs, especially when used to project labor costs while performing "what if" analyses, it must include mechanics that determine how much operating labor will be required and how the required labor is to be provided. In simply distributing actual costs through an ABC model, this is not important, but in projecting labor costs under different decision scenarios, it is critical. A tool for ensuring that operating labor cost projections provide a realistic look at the future is the operating labor demand/supply equation.

Stated algebraically, the operating labor demand/supply equation is as follows:

$$OH \times CS \times (1 + IA) = HC \times SH \times (1 + OT)$$

where

OH = operating hours
CS = crew size
IA = indirect activity percentage
HC = headcount of operating labor personnel
SH = the annual straight-time hours available from each individual
OT = the average overtime percentage worked by operating labor personnel

The left side of the equation determines the demand for operating labor and the right side indicates how that labor is to be supplied.

Operating hours represent the chronological hours of operating activity required measured in whatever unit of time measure is used for the activity (e.g., labor hours, line hours, cell hours, machine hours, press hours, cycle time). Crew size represents the average number of individuals that are present during each hour of operating time. For example, if five individuals work on a manufacturing line, a crew size of five would be attributed to each line hour. A crew size of one would be attributed to each labor hour, because labor hours are already measures of an individual's time. If one individual can operate two pieces of equipment at the same time, a crew size of .5 would be attributed to each piece of equipment's machine hours. By multiplying operating hours by crew size, the "perfect world" amount of operating labor necessary to support the required number of operating hours can be determined.

Because we do not live in a perfect world, operating labor is sometimes less than 100% efficient. These individuals often perform indirect activities, such as moving material or helping during setup. Once they complete a job, they are not instantaneously reassigned to another. Sometimes, a crew of three individuals performs activities that are supposed to be performed by two workers. These and many other situations make the actual demand for direct labor greater than the simple product of operating hours and crew size. If we are to build effective models, we must include these inefficiencies or *direct working indirect* activities in our projections of labor demand. This is accomplished by "grossing up" operating labor hours by an indirect activity percentage. Once this is accomplished, we have calculated the real world amount of operating labor necessary to support the required number of operating hours.

Now that we have determined how many labor hours will be required, we must decide how they will be provided. There are options for providing the required hours of labor, and each option has a different cost. We can have a certain number of employees who work a moderate amount of overtime, a greater number of employees who work little or no overtime, or a smaller number of employees who work a great deal of overtime. Whatever option we choose, we must supply the required number of labor hours.

Headcount represents the full-time equivalent (FTE) headcount of individuals who are available to fill the demand for operating labor. Annual straight-time hours represents the number of annual hours each FTE is actually available to perform work at straight-time pay. For example, an individual working eight hours per day, five days per week will, in theory, be paid for approximately 2,080 straight-time hours annually (depending on where the weekends fall). They will not, however, be working all the time they are paid and, if they are absent, some of those hours may not be worked or paid during the year. Assume that the average employee has 80 hours of vacation, 88 hours of paid holiday, is absent 24 hours per year, and has 30 minutes of break time each day. The straight-time hours available from this average employee would be 2,080 less the 80 hours of paid vacation, 88 hours of paid holidays, 24 hours of absenteeism, and 118 hours of paid break time (2,080 hours – 192 hours of vacation/holiday/absenteeism = 1,888 hours of time at work of which 1/16th [30 minutes/480 minutes] or 118 hours is break time). The net result is 1,770 straight-time hours available per FTE head/per year.

The product of FTE and annual straight-time hours available per FTE provides the total number of operating labor hours that are available without overtime. The difference, if the supply is less than demand, must be covered by overtime. The difference, if demand is less than the supply, indicates that either there should be less workers or the indirect activity percentage used in calculating the demand was too low.

Why do we need to go through this elaborate balancing act when calculating the cost of operating labor? We must go through this procedure because the cost per hour of labor is a function of all of the variables involved. At a given point in time we may be able to calculate the average cost per hour of operating labor, but once volume or mix changes, or any of the other cost variables change (e.g., number of paid holidays, overtime percentage, cost of health insurance, average vacation days), that cost per hour of operating labor changes. Exhibits 8.1 and 8.2 detail the impact that changes in both demand and supply have on this labor cost per hour.

The top of Exhibit 8.1 shows the build-up of production labor demand for one company. At the volume of business being modeled, the company needs 20,000 operating hours. In this case, operating hours represent the number of cell hours required. Each of this company's cells is structured for a crew of two individuals. As a result, the 20,000 cell hours generates a demand for 40,000 production labor hours. Historically, however, the

Exhibit 8.1 Operating Labor Supply/Demand Equation: Scenarios 1, 2, 3, and 4

THE OPERATING LABOR SUPPLY/DEMAND EQUATION

	Scenario 1	Scenario 2	Scenario 3	Scenario 4
Operating hours	20,000	20,000	20,000	20,000
Crew size	2.0	2.0	2.0	2.0
Net labor demand	40,000	40,000	40,000	40,000
Indirect allowance	20.0%	20.0%	20.0%	20.0%
Gross labor demand	48,000	48,000	48,000	48,000
Headcount	27	24	21	19
Annual straight-time hours/employee	1,750	1,750	1,750	1,750
Hours available without overtime	47,250	42,000	36,750	33,250
Overtime required	1.6%	14.3%	30.6%	44.4%
Gross hours supplied	48,000	48,000	48,000	48,000
Straight-time labor	$480,000	$480,000	$480,000	$480,000
Overtime premium	$3,750	$30,000	$56,250	$73,750
Paid time off benefits	$89,100	$79,200	$69,300	$62,700
Purchased fringes per employee	$81,000	$72,000	$63,000	$57,000
Purchased fringes per dollar paid	$51,557	$53,028	$54,500	$55,481
Total production labor cost	$705,407	$714,228	$723,050	$728,931
Cost per operating hour	$35.27	$35.71	$36.15	$36.45
Cost per operating labor hour	$17.64	$17.86	$18.08	$18.22
Cost per labor hour	$14.70	$14.88	$15.06	$15.19

Memo Information:

Straight-time labor rate/hour	$10.00
Overtime premium percentage	50.0%
Purchased fringes per employee	3,000
Purchased fringes per dollar paid	9.0%

Exhibit 8.2 Operating Labor Supply/Demand Equation: Scenarios 2, 2a, 2b, and 2c

THE OPERATING LABOR SUPPLY/DEMAND EQUATION

	Scenario 2	Scenario 2a	Scenario 2b	Scenario 2c
Operating hours	20,000	20,000	20,000	18,000
Crew size	2.0	1.5	2.0	2.0
Net labor demand	40,000	30,000	40,000	36,000
Indirect allowance	20.0%	20.0%	10.0%	20.0%
Gross labor demand	48,000	36,000	44,000	43,200
Headcount	24	18	22	22
Annual straight-time hours/employee	1,750	1,750	1,750	1,750
Hours available without overtime	42,000	31,500	38,500	38,500
Overtime required	14.3%	14.3%	14.3%	12.2%
Gross hours supplied	48,000	36,000	44,000	43,200
Straight-time labor	$480,000	$360,000	$440,000	$432,000
Overtime premium	$30,000	$22,500	$27,500	$23,500
Paid time off benefits	$79,200	$59,400	$72,600	$72,600
Purchased fringes per employee	$72,000	$54,000	$66,000	$66,000
Purchased fringes per dollar paid	$53,028	$39,771	$48,609	$47,529
Total production labor cost	$714,228	$535,671	$654,709	$641,629
Cost per operating hour	$35.71	$26.78	$32.74	$35.65
Cost per operating labor hour	$17.86	$17.86	$16.37	$17.82
Cost per labor hour	$14.88	$14.88	$14.88	$14.85

Memo Information:

Straight-time labor rate/hour	$10.00
Overtime premium percentage	50.0%
Purchased fringes per employee	$3,000
Purchased fringes per dollar paid	9.0%

company pays for 20% more production labor hours than it theoretically needs. To include this labor in its model, a 20% indirect allowance is added to the 40,000 hours to generate a gross production labor requirement of 48,000 hours. These 48,000 hours represent the amount of production labor that will be required to support the 20,000 operating (cell) hours being modeled.

After backing 330 hours of vacation, holiday, paid break, and other paid time off benefits out of the 2,080 straight-time hours paid to each employee annually, the company is left with only 1,750 straight-time hours that each employee is actually available for work. This means that if the company does not want its employees to work any significant overtime, it will need about 27 employees to provide the required hours (Scenario 1). If, however, the labor force works about 14% (Scenario 2) overtime, only 24 employees will be required. Similarly, if approximately 30% overtime is appropriate (Scenario 3), only 21 employees will be necessary, and if 45% overtime is acceptable (Scenario 4), only 19 employees will be required. Although it will have to pay a premium for overtime hours as overtime increases, it will purchase health, dental, and life insurance coverage for less employees. The resulting cost per hour and total cost of providing production labor for the operating 20,000 hours will be different under each scenario.

In all cases, the 48,000 hours of labor will generate $480,000 of cost at the straight-time rate of $10.00 per hour. Overtime premium will, of course, increase as the overtime hours increase. The number of overtime hours multiplied by an overtime premium of 50% of the $10 hourly rate will determine the overtime premium. Paid time off benefits amount to $3,300 per employee (330 hours multiplied by the $10 hourly rate). The total paid time off benefit cost for each scenario is calculated by multiplying the number of employees by the $3,300. Fringe benefits that are driven by headcount (e.g., health insurance, unemployment taxes, life insurance) amount to $3,000 per employee annually and those fringe benefits that are driven by the amount of compensation paid to the employees (e.g., employer portion of FICA and Medicare) amount to 9.0% of wages paid.

In Exhibit 8.1, the hourly production labor cost required to support the 20,000 operating hours ranges from $35.27 to $36.45. This variation is a result of different combinations of headcount and overtime to provide 48,000 labor hours. If the 48,000 hours changes, however, new decisions must be made on how to provide the revised total of labor hours, and those decisions must make sense if the model is to be effective.

Exhibit 8.2 illustrates the operation of the operating labor demand/supply equation as demand changes. The exhibit begins with Scenario 2 from Exhibit 8.1 and first reduces the required crew size from 2.0 to 1.5

(Scenario 2a). This drops the demand for production labor to 36,000 hours. Assuming that the company desires to keep overtime at about the same level as before, only 18 employees will be necessary to support the 20,000 operating hours (Scenario 2a). The cost will decrease to $26.78 per operating hour. If, however, the crew size remained at 2.0 but the company found a way to cut the indirect allowance by one half, the company could support the 20,000 operating hours with only 22 employees at the same level of overtime (Scenario 2b). This will reduce the cost to $32.74 per operating hour. Finally, if the company finds a way to improve cell throughput so that the same amount of business can be generated in only 18,000 operating hours, 22 employees working a little over 12% overtime would be required and the cost per operating hour would remain about the same at $35.65, but the operating time required for each product would decrease by 10%, effectively lowering the cost by 10% (Scenario 2c). If all three things are accomplished (crew size reduced to 1.5, indirect allowance reduced to 10%, and required operating hours reduced to 18,000), the labor cost per operating hour would be reduced to $24.53 and products would require only 90% of the time to produce as they did before—a net reduction of 37.5% in the operating labor cost of each product being manufactured in the cell.

Balancing the operating labor demand/supply equation is an essential part of any ABC model that is designed to go beyond simple cost distribution and actually simulate cost behavior. By ensuring that projected staffing is in line with the projected demand for labor and that the resulting accumulation of costs reflects the blend of headcount and overtime included in the model, the model builder will be able to create a model that parallels reality in this critical area where modeling reality can prove to be most difficult.

SCREENS

Just as the operating labor demand/supply equation helps to ensure that an ABC model does not violate the laws of physics, the model also needs screens for the same purpose. Screens are included in models as *macro capacity tests* to ensure that when projections of cost under various assumptions are made, they do not hide miraculous activities that, if the miracles do not occur, make the model's projections impossible. For example, a machining company that projects 10,000 machine hours should make sure that 10,000 machine hours are actually available considering the number of machines it owns, the number and length of shifts it is assuming in the model, downtime requirements for maintenance and setup, the built-in excess capacity necessary to accommodate seasonality, and so forth. A machine tool builder should ensure that there are enough "square foot days" available within the facility to construct its machine tools. A distributor should ensure that there is sufficient storage space to warehouse its additional business.

Screens do not need to be complex. They are not intended to be tools for production planning or detailed capacity planning. Their purpose is to make sure that the ABC model does not inadvertently assume things that are impossible. Consider a plastic injection molder who has grouped his presses into three categories: small, mid-sized, and large. It wants to simulate a scenario in which it requires 30,000 hours of small press time, 15,000 hours of mid-sized press time, and 5,000 hours of large press time. Exhibit 8.3 illustrates the structure of a schedule that will serve to determine whether those hours can actually be attained under the assumptions being made in the model.

Exhibit 8.3 Capacity Screen: Scenario 1

CAPACITY SCREEN
Scenario #1

Calendar hours per shift: 2,920

	Large Presses	Mid-Sized Presses	Small Presses
Number of presses	2	5	10
Equivalent 8-hour shifts in operation	2.0	2.0	2.0
Press hours available	11,680	29,200	58,400
Nonproduction-time-percentages:			
Weekend shutdown	28.6%	28.6%	28.6%
Setup	2.0%	4.0%	4.0%
Maintenance	5.0%	4.0%	3.0%
Holidays	3.0%	3.0%	3.0%
Breaktime	4.3%	4.3%	4.3%
Planned excess capacity	0.0%	10.0%	10.0%
Total nonproduction-time-percentages	42.9%	53.9%	52.9%
Press hours not available	5,011	15,739	30,894
Press hours available	6,669	13,461	27,506
Press hours required	5,000	15,000	30,000
Cushion (Shortage)	1,669	(1,539)	(2,494)
Cushion (Shortage) per press	835	(308)	(249)

The molder's capacity screen starts with an assumed number of calendar hours per shift. In this case, the assumed number of calendar hours represents 8 hours per day, 7 days per week (365 days × 8 hours = 2,920 hours). The screen did not have to start with 2,920 hours; it could have assumed 8 hours per day, 5 days per week, 10 hours a day, 6 days per week, or any other combination. The important point is that once this base is set, the rest of the information developed in the screen must be based on this same assumption.

The first step in developing the screen is to determine the number of press hours that are theoretically available, based on the number of presses owned, the number of shifts in operation, and the number of hours available per shift. Because the calendar hours per shift was based on an 8-hour shift, the shifts must be in terms of equivalent 8-hour shifts. For example, two 8-hour shifts would be 2.0 shifts, but two 10-hour shifts would be 2.5 shifts (2 × 10 hours/8 hours per shift) and one 12-hour shift would be 1.5 shifts (1 × 12 hours/8 hours per shift). In the case of the molder, they will begin testing their model by assuming two 8-hour shifts.

The molder owns two large presses, five mid-sized presses and ten small presses. Assuming each is available for two 8-hour shifts, 7 days per week, the large presses would have 11,680 hours available (2,920 hours × 2 presses × 2.0 shifts), the mid-sized presses would have 29,200 hours available (2,920 hours × 5 presses × 2.0 shifts), and the small presses would have 58,400 hours available (2,920 hours × 10 presses × 2.0 shifts). It would be impossible, however, to actually operate the presses for all of these hours. Time must be provided for weekend and holiday time when the plant is closed. Time must also be provided for periods when the press is being setup or maintained or when it is sitting idle while press operators are on breaks (unless relief operators continue operations during breaks). Finally, some time may represent a built-in excess capacity that is necessary for the company to meet seasonal surges in demand. Although it may be possible to "bank" products made during periods of less-than-peak demand, it is not always economically prudent to do so and the press hours themselves are not bankable. When such a situation exists, theoretical available hours must be reduced by these planned excess capacity hours.

These nonproduction-time hours must be subtracted from the gross or theoretical hours available before the molder can determine whether enough hours are available to meet demand. This is done by determining the percentage of available hours that will be eliminated by each of the items. In Exhibit 8.3, our molder assumes that it will not be working weekends, so two of the seven days, or 28.6% of the available hours, must be eliminated. The estimated time for setups and maintenance must also be eliminated. Elsewhere within the model, the molder determined that 234 setup hours would be required for the large presses, 1,168 required for the mid-sized presses, and 2,336 required for the small presses. Converted to percentages of press hours available, these represented 2.0%, 4.0%, and 4.0% of the hours respectively. Maintenance records indicated that large presses are down for maintenance 7 minutes for every hour of uptime, mid-sized presses are down 4.7 minutes for every uptime hour, and small presses are down 3.5 minutes for each hour of uptime. Based on the demand for press hours, this means that 5.0% of large press time will be lost to maintenance [(7 minutes/60 minutes × 5,000 press hours)/11,680 press hours)], 4.0% of mid-sized press hours will be lost [(4.7 minutes/60 minutes × 15,000 press hours)/29,200 press hours)], and 4.0% of small press time will also be lost to maintenance [(3.5 minutes/60 minutes × 30,000 press hours)/58,400 press hours)]. The molder has 11 paid holidays per year. These represent 3.0% of the facility's total calendar hours (11 holidays × 8 hours/2,920 calendar hours) and, as a result, 3.0% of the press hours available.

There are also two 15-minute paid breaks each day during which production stops. The 30 minutes per day for breaks applies regardless of the length of the shift. Downtime for breaks is probably the most complicated calculation in the screen because it is dependent on other input to the schedule—namely, weekend shutdown and holidays. This is, of course, because breaks happen only on those days when the plant is operating. As a result, one-half hour must be eliminated only on those days that the plant is actually in operation. By starting with the calendar hours per shift, eliminating the weekend shutdown and holiday time, then dividing by eight, the molder can determine how may days the facility is in operation. Multiplying the days in operation by the number of shifts determines the number of shift/days in operation; the number of shift/days multiplied by one-half hour calculates the total number of breaktime hours. Breaktime hours divided by press hours available will determine the downtime percentage caused by breaktime. In Exhibit 8.3, the breaktime percentage is 4.3% [2,920 calendar hours × (1 – weekend shutdown percentage – holiday percentage)/(8 hours per day × .5 hour break per day/2,920 press hours available)]. The final deduction from press hours available is planned excess capacity. As mentioned earlier, this represents the extra capacity required so that the molder can economically meet demand during its peak periods.

Once these deductions from available press hours are made, we find that the molder has 6,669 hours available on large presses, 13,461 available on mid-sized presses, and 27,506 available on small presses. Although this provides plenty of cushion on the large presses, it indicates that by working two shifts, eight hours per day, five days per week, the number of hours required on mid-sized and small presses will not be available. As a result, if the model is developed on the assumption that the plant will be in operation only two 8-hour shifts, five days per week, it will not be providing a realistic picture of the costs required to manufacture the amount of product assumed in the model. The molder cannot provide the press time based on the model's assumptions.

Exhibits 8.4 and 8.5 show two of the alternative ways that the molder can provide the number of press hours required. Exhibit 8.4 shows the impact of working Saturdays in the mid-sized and small press areas. This would enable the molder to provide the required press hours without adding additional presses, outsourcing any press operations, or working more than eight hours per day. Exhibit 8.5 shows the impact of working two 10-hour shifts per day in the mid-sized and small press areas. This would enable the molder to provide the required press hours without adding additional presses, outsourcing any press operations, or working any weekends. Other alternatives, such as adding presses or outsourcing work, could also

Exhibit 8.4 Capacity Screen: Scenario 2

CAPACITY SCREEN
Scenario #2

Calendar hours per shift: 2,920

	Large Presses	Mid-Sized Presses	Small Presses
Number of presses	2	5	10
Equivalent 8-hour shifts in operation	2.0	2.0	2.0
Press hours available	11,680	29,200	58,400
Nonproduction-time-percentages:			
Weekend shutdown	28.6%	14.3%	14.3%
Setup	2.0%	4.0%	4.0%
Maintenance	5.0%	4.0%	3.0%
Holidays	3.0%	3.0%	3.0%
Breaktime	4.3%	5.2%	5.2%
Planned excess capacity	0.0%	10.0%	10.0%
Total nonproduction-time-percentages	42.9%	40.5%	39.5%
Press hours not available	5,011	11,826	23,068
Press hours available	6,669	17,374	35,332
Press hours required	5,000	15,000	30,000
Cushion (Shortage)	1,669	2,374	5,332
Cushion (Shortage) per press	835	475	533

Exhibit 8.5 Capacity Screen: Scenario 3

CAPACITY SCREEN
Scenario #3

Calendar hours per shift: 2,920

	Large Presses	Mid-Sized Presses	Small Presses
Number of presses	2	5	10
Equivalent 8-hour shifts in operation	2.0	2.5	2.5
Press hours available	11,680	36,500	73,000
Nonproduction-time-percentages:			
Weekend shutdown	28.6%	28.6%	28.6%
Setup	2.0%	4.0%	4.0%
Maintenance	5.0%	4.0%	3.0%
Holidays	3.0%	3.0%	3.0%
Breaktime	4.3%	3.4%	3.4%
Planned excess capacity	0.0%	10.0%	10.0%
Total nonproduction-time-percentages	42.9%	53.0%	52.0%
Press hours not available	5,011	19,345	37,960
Press hours available	6,669	17,155	35,040
Press hours required	5,000	15,000	30,000
Cushion (shortage)	1,669	2,155	5,040
Cushion (Shortage) per press	835	431	504

be tested as could combinations of these actions. The point is that the means of providing the required press hours must pass through this "screen of realism," and the assumptions in the rest of the model must reflect the decisions made to provide the necessary hours. Failure to pass through the screen means a model's costs are inaccurate.

The mechanics for developing a screen shown here is just one of many ways in which a model developer can structure these screens. The important point is that if the model is to reflect reality, an appropriate screening mechanism should be established for any significant capacity constrained resource, be it machine time, warehousing space, hotel rooms, hospital beds, or delivery vehicles.

THE ABC PERSPECTIVE

The ABC perspective is not a mechanical tool like most other items in this toolbox; it is a conceptual tool. I have seen many theoretically valid implementations of ABC falter because the company did not define its ABC perspective. Simply stated, a company's ABC perspective is the cost breakdown level at which the individual concerned with accurate cost information views the company. The higher the cost breakdown level, the less detailed ABC must be at the lower levels. The lower the cost breakdown level, the more detailed it must be at those levels.

ABC perspective is easiest to explain using the cost breakdown diagram in Exhibit 8.6. This diagram shows the breakdown of an organization's costs at four levels of detail. At the first level, all the company knows is that 100% of its costs are attributable to the company (surprisingly, not all companies know even this). At the second level, those costs have been attributed to five groups of activities. At the third level, each of those five groups have been further attributed to two or more general activities. At the fourth level, many of those general activities have been attributed to detail activities. The result is that there are 25 activity centers that will be assigning their costs to cost objectives, 6 from the general activity level, and 19 from the detail activity level.

Consider the line of cost breakdown that results in activity centers 15 through 17. To make the discussion easier, let us assume that this represents costs related to throughput or material support activities. According to the diagram, 15% of the company's costs can be attributed to planning, controlling, purchasing, receiving, inspecting, handling, and storing direct materials, purchased parts, and direct outside services. At level three, these costs are broken down into two general activity groupings: one that relates to direct outside services accounts for 10% of the costs and one representing direct material and purchased parts accounts for 5% of the costs. At level four, the 5% general group is further broken down into two more activities: one accounting for direct materials, which represents 3% of the costs and one relating to purchased parts which accounts for 2% of the costs. Regardless of perspective, we now know that 10% of the company's costs relate to direct outside services (activity 15), 3% relate to direct materials (activity 16), and 2% relate to purchased parts (activity 17).

Activity-based costing perspective comes into play when the company must decide how it is going to assign the cost of these activities to the individual cost objectives that require them. If the ABC perspective is at the first level (the company president), it is not critical that a theoretically sound way be selected for assigning these activity costs to individual cost objectives. It is enough to know that costs attributable to supporting the company's outside processes is attributed to those outside processes, that

Exhibit 8.6 Four Levels of an Organization's Cost Breakdown

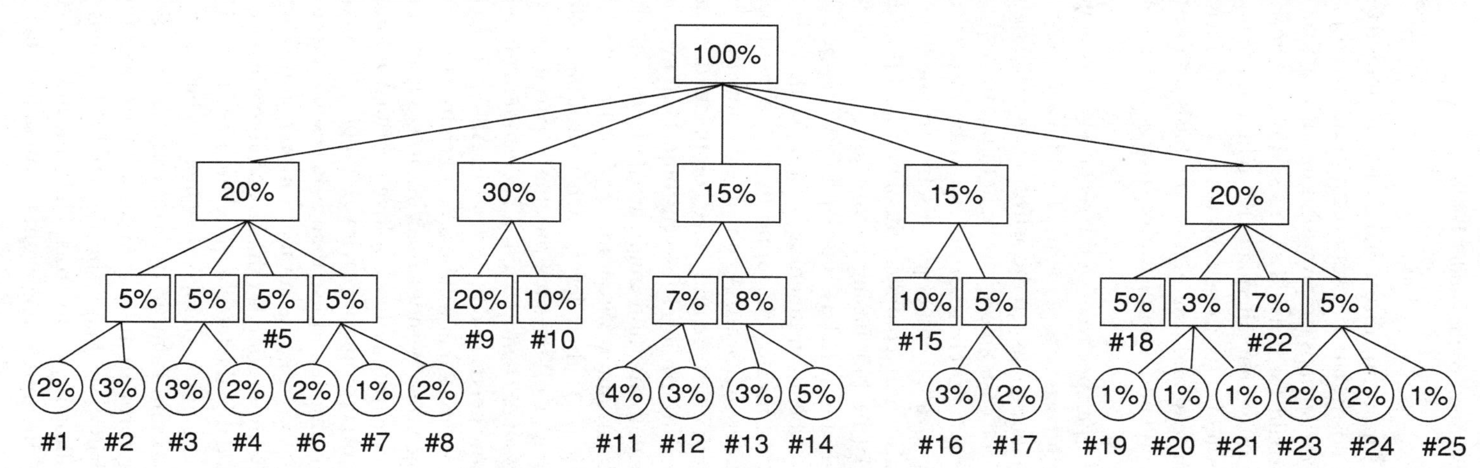

cost related to supporting direct materials is attributed to those direct materials, and that cost related to supporting purchased parts is attributed to purchased parts. Perhaps simply assigning these activity costs as a percentage of dollars paid for outside services, direct materials, and purchased parts would be more than adequate. Keep in mind that prior to the activity-based breakdown of costs, these costs were probably included in either manufacturing overhead and assigned on the basis of direct labor or machine time or in general and administrative (G&A) cost and added as a percentage of total cost.

If the ABC perspective is at the second level (the materials manager), simply assigning costs as a percentage of dollars spent may not be acceptable. Although it might assign the activity costs to the right things, it may not be assigning those costs among the right things the right way. Perhaps a cost per release or per purchase order would be more accurate in directing these costs to individual cost objectives. In addition to being more accurate, however, it is also more complicated. Similarly, if the ABC perspective is at the third level (the purchasing agent), assigning the cost of purchasing direct materials and purchase parts using a cost per release or purchase order might not be accurate enough, because there is a significant difference in the effort involved in supporting purchased parts than there is in supporting direct materials. Again, in addition to being more accurate, these assignment bases are also more complicated. Finally, if the ABC perspective is at the fourth level (the customer), an even more detailed (and more complicated) method might be desired. This is especially true in industries with customers who want (and get) detailed cost breakdowns in support of prices. At their level, each individual charge needs to make sense, and a simple, off-the-shelf purchased part does not require the same amount of support as a more complex, custom-made one.

A company needs to decide what its ABC perspective is before determining the mechanics that will be used to charge these activity costs to individual cost objectives. Without realizing it, companies implementing ABC often treat every activity as they would at the third or fourth level of ABC perspective. They overcomplicate their version of ABC and make it much more difficult to implement and use than is necessary. It must always be kept in mind that the objective is accuracy, not precision. The mechanics of ABC should never be more complex than is absolutely necessary. The more strategic the intended use, the less complex they need to be. The more tactical the intended use, the more complex they need to be.

One important factor in determining ABC perspective is the amount of cost flowing through the organization. If activity 17 represents 2% of $2 million in activity costs the perspective will be different than if it represents 2% of $200 million in activity costs. The value in having five bases for assigning the cost of one purchasing agent to cost objectives is far less than having five bases for assigning the cost of a 10-person purchasing department. In general, the smaller the company, the higher the level of ABC perspective should be.

The importance of size, however, can sometimes be overshadowed by another factor: diversity. If the company in Exhibit 8.6 is a manufacturer of one or two lines of products, ABC perspective can usually be placed at the higher levels. If, however, Exhibit 8.6 represents a marketing services organization that provides a variety of services to a wide array of customers, the situation may be quite different. For example, if activities 1 through 8 represent fulfillment services, activities 9 and 10 represent inbound telemarketing, activities 11 through 14 represent outbound telemarketing, activities 15 through 17 represent printing services, and activities 18 through 25 represent show management, the importance of accurately assigning such a diverse line of services would place the ABC perspective at level three or four.

Activity-based costing perspective is an important conceptual tool that should be used to ensure that a company's ABC structure and mechanics are at a level commensurate with the level of detail required to meet the organization's cost information needs. Perspective from a level too high can result in cost information that is still too generalized to adequately support management decisions whereas perspective from a level too low will generate information that is too detailed to be relevant and too complex to be maintained over the long haul.

WEIGHTED EVENTS AND TRANSACTIONS

Often, the cost of an order, a line item, a purchase order, or other such event or transaction is not always the same each time the event or transaction takes place. For example, a long-term care facility finds that the effort involved in sending an invoice varies considerably depending on who is paying the bill. Medicare invoices are fairly easy since a single invoice covering all insured residents is sent electronically each month using a standardized procedure. Medicaid, commercial insurance, and private pay invoices are all much more difficult, but to different degrees. In order to account for these differences, the facility can create four separate activity centers to accumulate the cost of preparing, sending, and collecting from each type of payor. It can then divide each activity's cost by the number of invoices issued to determine a cost per invoice.

A simpler method, which can still result in an accurate cost for each type of invoice is to use *weighted events or transactions.* Under this method, the cost of all related activities, regardless of payor, are accumulated in a single activity center. Before determining the cost per invoice, however, the invoices are weighted, based on the relative level of difficulty. In the case of the long-term care facility, Medicaid invoices require the least effort, so they can be given a weight of 1.0. The amount of effort required for invoices to the other payor types would then be given a weight in relation to the amount of effort required for a Medicaid invoice. For example, if Medicare invoices require three times the effort, they would be given a weight of 3.0. If commercial insurance requires four times the effort, they can be given a weight of 4.0. If private pay invoices require only two and one-half times the effort, they can be given a weight of 2.5. By accumulating the total cost of preparing, sending, and collecting all invoices in a single activity center and then weighing the different types of invoices, a cost per invoice can be calculated, as shown in Exhibit 8.7.

In the exhibit, $200,000 has been accumulated in an activity center that included those activities involved in the invoicing process. During the year, 2,880 invoices were processed—1,440 were to Medicaid, 240 to Medicare, 480 to commercial insurance organizations, and 720 to individuals. The weights assigned to each type of invoice are then used to calculate weighted invoices, an amount that actually represents the relative amount of effort spent in processing each invoice type. Weighted invoices for Medicare calculate to 720, half of the number of weighted invoices for Medicaid. This would indicate that twice as much time was spent processing all of the Medicaid invoices as was spent processing all of the Medicare invoices. Similarly, private pay extended to 1,800 weighted invoices, 25% more than Medicaid's total. This would indicate that 25% more time was spent processing all of the private pay invoices than was spent processing all of Medicaid's.

Using these weighted invoice amounts, the long-term care facility can calculate the percentage of the activity center's efforts that relate to each type of invoice. Commercial invoices represent 1,920 of the 5,880 total weighted invoices, so 32.7% of the activity center's effort relates to commercial invoices. Medicare invoices, however, represent only 720 of the 5,880 weighted invoices, so they account for only 12.2% of its efforts. Using these percentages, the facility can then distribute the $200,000 activity center cost among the four different invoice types. The resulting costs can then be divided by the number of unweighted invoices in each category to arrive at a separate cost per invoice for each invoice type.

This weighted event or transaction device can be used to significantly simplify model design. It reduces the number of activity centers that need to be established (one instead of four in the case of the long-term care facility) while still making it possible to assign different event or transaction amounts to cost objectives. This is also the case when events are used as surrogates for direct or value-adding activities. By weighing events that are used as surrogates, the model developer expands the number of areas in which this model simplifying device can be used.

Exhibit 8.7 Use of Weighted Events and Transactions

	Invoices	Weight	Weighted Invoices	Percentage	Activity Cost	Cost per Invoice
Medicaid	1,440	1.0	1,440	24.5%	$49,000	$34.03
Medicare	240	3.0	720	12.2%	$24,400	$101.67
Commercial	480	4.0	1,920	32.7%	$65,400	$136.25
Private pay	720	2.5	1,800	30.6%	$61,200	$85.00
Totals			5,880	100.0%	$200,000	

For years, one manufacturer included setup costs as part of its overhead. Instead of charging setup costs to the job or product being setup, it was included in the costs being charged to the job or product while it was being manufactured. Obviously, short-running jobs benefited from this costing practice because the fixed cost of a setup was diluted by all of the operating hours of the other, long-running jobs. Long-running jobs, however, suffered from this practice as the hourly rate charged while they were in production was bloated by the setup costs of these short-running jobs. In developing an activity-based approach to costing at this manufacturer, it was obvious that the cost of setup activities needed to be assigned to the jobs or products that would be run at the setup's completion. The critical issue was to remove setup cost from run cost. It was imperative that a job that took an hour to setup and an hour to run did not appear to have the same per hour cost as a job that took an hour to set up and 10 hours to run. The method of removing setup time from overhead was a secondary issue.

The most straightforward way to charge setup time to a job is to have setup personnel keep track of their time and charge an amount to each job being setup based on the number of labor hours involved. Although simple conceptually, this method requires the existence of a detailed time-keeping system and also requires that the number of setup hours be estimated when a job is quoted. This may add more complexity to the accounting and estimating system than the company can handle. Yet, it is still important that setups be charged directly to jobs and not buried in their run time. The solution is to treat setup as an event. Instead of charging setup to individual jobs, setup costs are accumulated in a single activity center. From that point on, setups receive the same handling as an invoice, an incoming order, or a purchase order. They can be assigned to cost objectives as a cost per event or a weighted cost per event.

If the effort required for setups does not vary greatly from job to job, as shown in the fairly steep bell curve in Exhibit 8.8, a simple cost per setup should suffice. Although not very good theoretically, it eliminates the most critical setup related costing problem. It removes setups from overhead and assigns them directly to cost objectives. If, however, the effort required for setups does vary significantly from job to job, as shown in the flatter bell curve in Exhibit 8.9, weighted setups can be established to account for this variability without detailed timekeeping procedures and having to estimate setup hours for each individual job estimated. Setup costs would be accumulated in a single activity center and assigned to cost objectives as a cost per weighted event. Although this method still does not get high marks for theoretical purity, it gets the job done. The two major costing problems with setups are solved. They are no longer buried in overhead but charged directly to cost

Exhibit 8.8 Setup with Little Variance from Job to Job

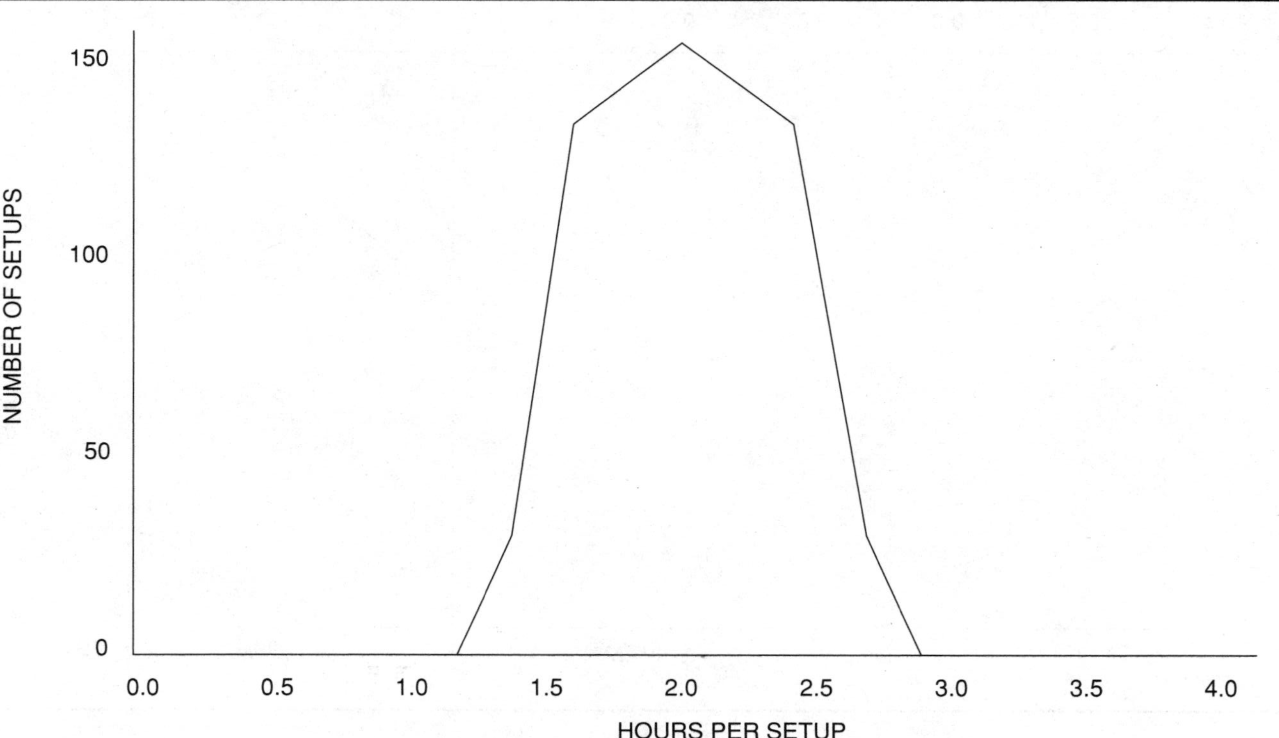

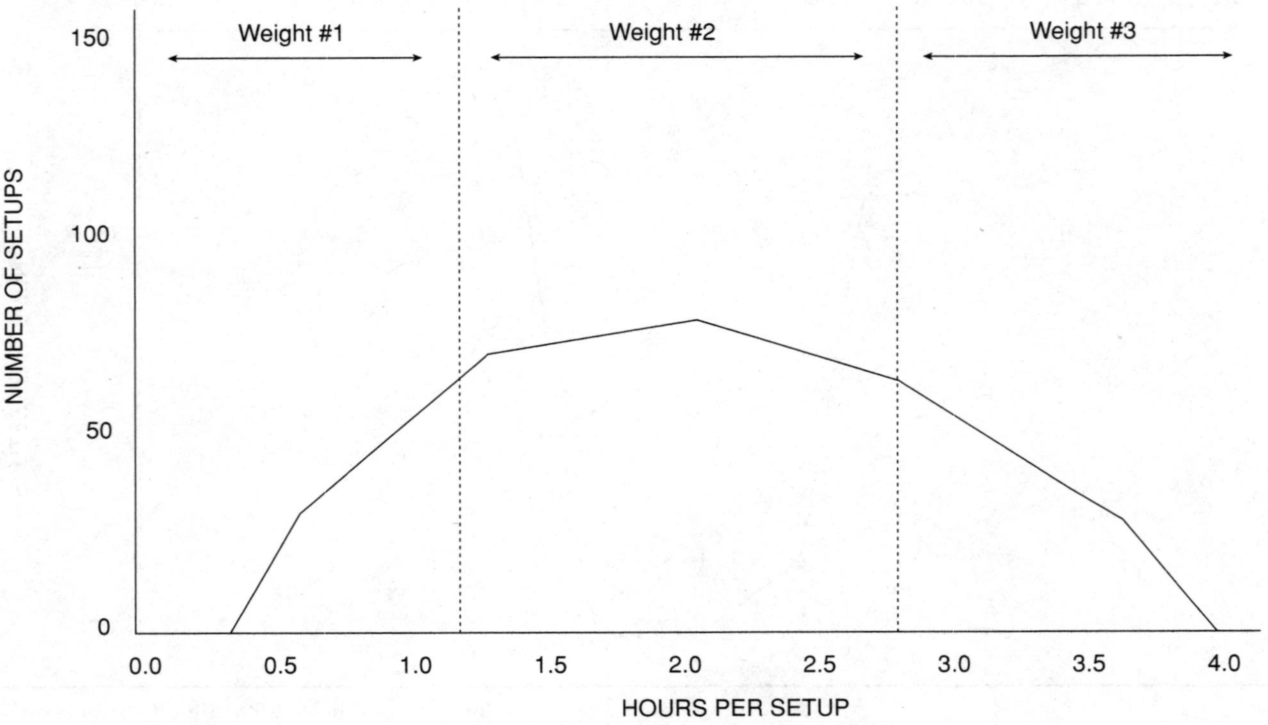

Exhibit 8.9 Setup with Significant Variance from Job to Job

objectives and the amount charged to each cost objective is determined by the relative amount of effort required in performing the setup.

This is only one area in which weighted transactions have proven to be a cost effective modeling tool in the transformation of activities that have historically been treated as indirect into direct activities. In-process material handling is another. The cost of activities involved in moving products from one operation to another have historically been buried in a company's overhead. At manufacturers for which these activities represent only 1% to 2% of total activity costs, this is not generally a problem. At many companies, however, the cost of in-process material handling and storage comprises a much greater percentage of activity costs. This is especially true at companies that manufacture large, heavy products, such as forging or stamping companies. In some of these companies, handling and storage costs for activities that take place between the first and last manufacturing operation comprise 10 percent to 15 percent of total activity cost. When this is the case, the cost of these activities cannot be safely buried in overhead.

Assume that a forging facility has a number of identical presses, each with a press rate of $90 per hour. Product A requires only one forging operation. When manufacturing Product A, the press can produce 20 products per hour. Product B requires three different forging operations. When manufacturing Product B, however, each press can perform its work on 60 products per hour. Following conventional practices, each product would be assigned $4.50 of manufacturing cost. Product A would receive 1/20th of the $90-per-hour press cost, whereas Product B would receive 1/60th of the $90-per-hour press cost at each of three different operations. Intuitively, it should be obvious that more work is required in the production of Product B because it must be removed from the press, moved to another press, and loaded onto a press two more times than Product A. Since loading and unloading the press is performed by the press operator, that is most likely covered in the three-minute (for Product A) and one-minute (Product B) cycle times. The extra movement required for Product B, however, is not covered. In companies in which material handling is 10 to 15% of activity cost, significant cost distortions can result.

As was the case with setups, in which the original issue was not that setups were incorrectly charged to jobs but that they were buried in overhead, the issue here is not that in-process movement is incorrectly charged to products but that it is buried in overhead. The most critical action required is to remove the cost of in-process handling from overhead and relate it to the actual in-process handling of products—even if the method used to effect that action is less than perfect. The simplest way of accomplishing this is to accumulate the cost of in-process handling in a single activity center, calculate the number of moves represented by those costs, and develop a "cost per move." Of course, some moves will cost more than others, but that is a secondary issue. The fact that moves will be directly assigned to products in proportion to the number of moves required solves the most critical costing problem.

Going back to the forging example, assume that by removing the cost of in-process movement from the press rates, those rates drop to $81 per hour. Further assume that the accumulation of in-process handling costs amounts to $240,000 and that 100,000 moves (which includes the movement of a finished product to storage) are made. This results in a cost of $2.40 per move. To calculate the cost of Products A and B, we now need to determine the forging costs, which will now be $4.05 each (substitute $81 per press hour for the $90 cost in the earlier calculation) and then add the cost of in-process movement. To do this, we need to know the number of operations and the number of parts that are included in a move. Both Products A and B are fairly large and only 10 can be put into a bin. As a result, 10 parts can be moved at a time. Each part will be assigned $.24 ($2.40 cost per move/10 parts) each time it is moved. This means that Product A, which is moved only once (from its one operation to storage), costs $4.29 [$4.05 + (1 move × $.24)]. The cost of Product B, which moved three times, increases to $4.77 [$4.05 + (3 moves × $.24)]. A significant improvement in costing through the use the simple cost-per-event technique.

There may be cases, however, in which the cost of certain moves may be so much greater than others that a simple cost per move will not suffice. For example, the forging facility has all but one of its forging presses located in a 100′-by-100′ area in the plant. The one press not in this area is located 600 feet away in a remote corner of the facility. Obviously, moves to and from this press will be more costly than moves within the major forging area. To accommodate this difference, the company can assign weights to the two different types of moves just as weights were assigned to the types of invoices at the long-term care facility. Assuming that 10,000 of the 100,000 moves are to or from this distant press and that the effort required is three times that of a move within the press area, we can establish a separate cost per short move and per long move. Using weights of 1.0 for short moves and 3.0 for long moves, 75% of the activity cost would be attributed to short moves [(90,000 moves × 1.0)/((90,000 moves × 1.0) + (10,000 moves × 3.0))]. This would result in a cost per short move of $2.00 ($240,000 × 75%/90,000 moves). The remaining 25% of activity cost would be attributed to long moves and would result in a cost of $6.00 per move ($240,000 × 25%/10,000 moves).

The impact on product cost could be substantial. If the second operation on Product B takes place at this remote press, its cost will increase to $5.45 [($4.05 + (2 moves × $6.00/10) + (1 move × $2.00/10)]. The cost of Product A will decrease to $4.25 [$4.05 + (1 move × $2.00/10)].

Weighted events and transactions are very cost-effective tools for directly assigning the cost of many activities that have traditionally been treated as indirect to cost objectives. They make it possible to effectively measure the impact of these activities on cost objectives without adding a substantial amount of complexity to the ABC model. In addition, they also highlight the cost of performing the activities in question. The cost per move, per invoice, or per order can be reduced through process analysis, reengineering, or simply by intuition once those costs are known. While they are buried in overhead, however, they lie hidden and unmeasured and provide no guidance for directing continuous improvement efforts or measuring the impact of those efforts once completed.

CONSUMPTION UNITS

In developing ABC models, it is useful to divide the category of cost normally termed *variable* into two separate categories: variable costs that change automatically with changes in volume and those that change only if some action is taken by management.

For example, a change in production volume will not result in a change in the size of the labor force unless action is taken to increase or decrease the number of employees. Workers must be hired or laid off by management. They do not automatically report or volunteer to go home. However, once this action is taken, a change in fringe benefit costs will be automatic. A change in volume will automatically result in a change in operating supplies or power consumption. If there is less welding, less welding rod and argon will be consumed. If there are more machine hours in the machine centers, more electricity will be required.

Activity-based cost accumulation models should be so structured that costs which vary automatically with changes in the volume or mix of the activities that cause them to be incurred do, indeed, vary when changes take place within those activities. This is accomplished by using the appropriate measures to drive these automatically variable costs. A simple tool for building this feature into a model is the consumption unit. A consumption unit should be established for each type of automatically variable cost. In some cases, a consumption unit can be an actual unit of measure, such as pounds, kilowatt hours, or number of employees. At other times, "phantom" consumption units must be devised. In the case of fringe benefits, measures such as headcounts, gross payroll, and hours worked are readily available means of driving costs. For many other major categories of automatic costs—major supplies and utilities—the driver is not easily converted into units of consumption.

The first difficulty comes when the cost driver for a particular element of cost is the same for all activity centers, but the amount that it affects each activity center varies. Office supplies are a common example of this situation. A driver frequently used to project the consumption of office supplies is headcount. If a company has many individuals working in a particular activity center, that activity center will usually experience greater consumption of office supplies than if it had fewer individuals. The problem arises in answering the question, "How much more consumption?" The use of *driver multipliers* to convert the cost drivers to consumption units is an effective way to answer this question. For example, in Exhibit 8.10, general/administration is selected as the activity center that represents the base consumption unit. This means that one general/administration employee will consume one unit of office supplies. The cost of one consumption unit (budgeted or historical general/administration office supply cost divided by headcount) is then determined. In the example, this unit cost is $500. This provides the base against which to compare all other activity centers.

Each activity center's consumption of office supplies can then be expressed in relation to general/administration, the base unit. According to the example, each individual in accounting, engineering, and production control requires twice as many office supplies as an individual in general/administration; whereas individuals in data processing require five times as many; in the tool room and maintenance, the same amount; in purchasing, 150% of the amount; and in all production departments, 20% of the base amount.

This information can be modeled in worksheet form, as shown in Exhibit 8.10. In this worksheet, the headcount for each activity center is multiplied by the driver multiplier (the relationship of each activity center's consumption to the base's consumption) to arrive at the consumption units. The result is multiplied by the consumption unit cost to arrive at total office supply cost for each activity center. Any change in employee headcount causes a change in office supply consumption. The amount of the change depends on the activity center in which the headcount change occurs. If engineering is reduced by two employees and two employees are added to data processing, there will be a net increase of $3,000 in office supply use (a reduction of $2,000 in engineering and an increase of $5,000 in data processing), although total employment remains the same. This is the result of the driver multiplier. However, when the general level of office supply cost changes, it is not necessary to change any factor in determining consumption units—the consumption of office supplies does not change. What would change is the cost per consumption unit. A general decrease in the cost of office supplies of 4% would reduce the cost per consumption unit to $480 and the overall office supply cost to $44,880.

Exhibit 8.10 Use of Consumption Units/Common Drivers with Different Impacts

	Driver Headcount	Driver Multiplier	Consumption Units	Cost @ $500.00 per Unit
General/administration	8	1.0	8.0	$4,000
Accounting	5	2.0	10.0	$5,000
Data processing	4	5.0	20.0	$10,000
Engineering	8	2.0	16.0	$8,000
Purchasing	3	1.5	4.5	$2,250
Production control	3	2.0	6.0	$3,000
Maintenance	6	1.0	6.0	$3,000
Tool room	8	1.0	8.0	$4,000
Production Dept. A	20	0.2	4.0	$2,000
Production Dept. B	10	0.2	2.0	$1,000
Production Dept. C	15	0.2	3.0	$1,500
Production Dept. D	30	0.2	6.0	$3,000
Total	120			$46,750

A second difficulty occurs when a particular element of cost is driven by different types of cost drivers. This is often the case in determining variable utility costs. In most cases, variable utility costs are concentrated in the direct or value-adding activities. This is particularly true in manufacturing settings, in which a variety of different cost drivers can exist. For example, one organization may have direct labor hours, cycle time, machine hours, and line time as drivers of its production activities. In these cases, the difficulty of having different impacts of the same driver is compounded by having multiple drivers for the same cost. Again, the use of driver multipliers can solve this problem.

Exhibit 8.11 shows such a situation. In this example, the manufacturing facility has four different drivers for its five production activities. The challenge is to develop a set of driver multipliers that will turn the drivers into the appropriate consumption units. If the cost element is electricity, the drivers can be converted into kilowatt hours (KWH). Water can be converted into gallons and gas into hundreds of cubic feet. In the early stages of model development, the drivers might simply be converted into a phantom consumption unit that can be redefined later.

Because there are a variety of cost drivers, one activity center cannot be selected as a base with the other multipliers measured in relation to this base as was done when there was a common driver with different impacts. Instead, each activity center must be considered individually and an independent driver multiplier developed for each.

An analysis of the relationship between historical consumption and the volume of activity as measured by the various drivers enables the organization to arrive at driver multipliers that will change the drivers into an approximation of KWH consumed. This last sentence might imply that the job is simple, but in most cases it is not. It is unusual for an organization to have the type of detailed driver and KWH consumption information necessary to make precise calculations of these multipliers. Keep in mind, however, that the goal is accuracy, not precision. By interviewing engineering or maintenance personnel and using other analytical techniques, reasonably accurate multipliers can be developed for the initial model. Although initial multipliers may contain a great many assumptions and estimates, they will be reasoned-out statistics and more preferable to arbitrary allocations. Subsequent experience and the accumulation of previously uncollected consumption information will make future refinement possible.

Once developed, these multipliers can be applied to the various cost drivers to develop the estimated KWH consumption. The kilowatt hours can then be extended by the unit cost to obtain variable electrical cost by activity center. Changes to the drivers will then result in the appropriate changes in the electrical costs depending on the activity center in which the changes take place. For example, a 500-hour increase in hot form will result in a $5,000

Exhibit 8.11 Use of Consumption Units/Different Drivers with Different Impacts

Activity Center	Driver		Multiplier	Units/KWH	Cost @ $0.125 per KWH
	Type	Measure			
Press	Direct labor hours	40,000	10.00	400,000	$ 50,000
Fabricate	Direct labor hours	80,000	2.50	200,000	$ 25,000
Hot form	Cycle time	6,000	80.00	480,000	$ 60,000
CNC machine	Machine hours	8,000	15.00	120,000	$ 15,000
Assembly	Line hours	4,000	12.00	48,000	$ 6,000
				1,248,000	$ 156,000

increase in electric cost (500 hours × 80.00 multiplier × $1.25), whereas the same increase in Computer Numeric Controlled (CNC) machine will result in only a $938 increase (500 hours × 15.00 multiplier × $.125).

LABOR-BASED COST ACCUMULATION AND DISTRIBUTION

The most common and well-known method of distributing indirect costs is direct labor. This practice is only part of a larger concept that can be used for both the accumulation and distribution of activity-based costs. The larger concept is total labor-based cost distribution.

Exhibit 8.12 provides an example of both accumulating and distributing costs using a labor-based approach. The category of costs in this case is fringe benefits. The organization in Exhibit 8.12 found three different measures of labor that serve as drivers for the incurrence of fringe benefit costs: headcount, labor dollars, and labor hours (cost accumulation). One of these drivers, labor hours, was also found to be the most appropriate driver for charging fringe benefits to other activity centers and cost objectives (cost distribution).

In developing the cost of fringe benefits, headcount is the preferred driver for costs that are basically the same for each employee, regardless of how much they earn. Labor dollars are preferred for benefits that depend on the level of earnings. Labor hours are best used for benefits based directly on hours worked, as is the case with some pension plans and supplemental employment benefit plans.

In Exhibit 8.12, three of the benefits were deemed to be headcount driven: health insurance, state unemployment, and federal unemployment. One issue to keep in mind when considering health insurance is whether the organization views insurance as providing coverage for the employee or paying health care costs for the employee. Self-insured organizations are often tempted to become more precise and charge the actual cost of benefits paid to the activity centers in which the applicable employees work. Although this approach might be useful in gathering information for cost-containment efforts, it is inappropriate for cost accumulation. For purposes of cost accumulation, a company should consider health insurance a payment of health care coverage, not the payment of health care costs for the employee. As a result, health insurance, as well as any similar coverage, should be treated as a cost per employee just as if it were an insurance premium. In the case at hand, health insurance is treated as a cost per employee and multiplied by the organization's headcount to arrive at the annual cost.

Initially, it might seem more logical to treat state and federal unemployment taxes as being driven by payroll dollars because they are calculated

Exhibit 8.12 Labor-Based Approach to Accumulating and Distributing Costs

Benefit	Dollars per Employee	Percent of Payroll $	Dollars per Labor/Hour	Driver	Benefit Cost
Health insurance	$4,200			100	$420,000
Workers' compensation		5.00%		$2,200,000	$110,000
State unemployment	$380			100	$38,000
Federal unemployment	$60			100	$6,000
Employer FICA		6.20%		$2,200,000	$136,400
Employer Medicare		1.45%		$2,200,000	$31,900
Pension			$0.15	208,000	$31,200
Total purchased fringe benefits					$773,500
Vacation pay					$84,600
Holiday pay					$101,500
Paid breaks					$152,900
Total paid time-off benefits					$339,000
Total fringe benefits					$1,112,500
Base hours worked					178,000
Fringe benefits per hour worked					$6.25

as a percentage of payroll. However, the maximum individual earnings on which the taxes are based is usually at a level low enough that all full-time employees exceed that level during the year. As a result, both of these elements of cost become a fixed amount for each employee as opposed to a fixed percentage of payroll costs. Their treatment in the cost accumulation process is, therefore, based on headcount.

Labor dollars are chosen as the driver for three of the cost elements in Exhibit 8.12: workers' compensation, employer FICA, and employer Medicare. Workers' compensation premiums are usually based on payroll dollars. As a result, the selection of this basis seems obvious. Like state and federal unemployment, employer FICA and Medicare are also a percentage of earnings, but unlike the other two, the FICA maximum is greater than the gross earnings of most employees and there is no maximum for employer Medicare. As a result, they can remain a labor dollar-driven cost element.

Some care must be taken in considering workers' compensation. If the activities taking place within the organization result in a group of widely varying workers' compensation rates, and the distribution of labor among those activities is such that the use of an average rate (e.g., the one used in Exhibit 8.12) would materially distort the distribution of the cost to the activities, an alternative treatment should be sought. One such alternative would be to handle workers' compensation as an automatically variable cost in a manner similar to that given to supplies in the discussion of consumption units earlier in this chapter.

In this example, it is assumed that pension cost is based on labor hours. As a result, labor hours are the most appropriate driver for determining the organization's total pension cost.

Holiday and vacation pay, as well as paid breaks, are also driven by labor-related factors, but the analysis of this area is a subject in itself and is discussed fully in Chapter 12. For the time being, these categories are included in Exhibit 8.12 as given amounts.

In looking at the possible drivers for distributing fringe benefit costs, labor hours was chosen. Although headcount is a practical means of distributing fringe benefits to activity centers, it is impractical for charging to the multitude of cost objectives. That leaves either labor dollars or hours. In most instances, the selection of labor dollars or hours is one of preference. Both have good arguments for their use. If the circumstances of the specific organization do not give the advantage to one or the other, either will work effectively.

One final note is the difference between the labor hours used in calculating the pension cost and the labor hours used as a base for distributing fringe benefit costs. The 208,000 hours used for determining pension cost includes all hours for which the employee was compensated, including holiday, vacation, and paid break hours. In distributing the costs, only hours actually worked receive fringe benefit charges, so holiday, vacation, and paid break hours are excluded from the labor distribution bases. The cost of paid time off is one of the benefits being distributed so it should logically be excluded from the base.

PIECE-RATE COST ACCUMULATION AND DISTRIBUTION

One general rule to follow in developing any cost system is to charge everything directly that can possibly be measured as direct. An area in which this rule is often overlooked is indirect materials. Although many indirect materials do not vary with operating time, they are often included as costs in a direct or value-adding activity center and charged to cost objectives as part of a cost per labor hour, machine hour, press hour, cell hour, or other time-based measure. Those indirect materials that do not vary with time often vary with the number and type of products being manufactured.

One example of this type of cost is coating material. In many forging or extruding operations, each part must be coated before it is processed. These coating materials are usually treated as indirect materials and included in the overhead costs of the activity center in which the coating takes place. Where the cost is material and the effort involved is within reason, it is preferable to treat these coating materials as if they were direct material. Exhibit 8.13 shows the development of piece-rate cost information for this type of indirect material.

Exhibit 8.13 Development of Piece-Rate Cost

	Surface Area (sq in)	Units per Square Inch	Units of Coating Material	Cost @ $0.115 per Unit
Part 001	24.0	3.0	8.00	$0.920
Part 002	32.5	3.0	10.83	$1.245
Part 003	27.6	3.0	9.20	$1.058
Part 004	18.2	3.0	6.07	$0.698
Part 005	21.1	3.0	7.03	$0.808
Part 006	42.0	3.0	14.00	$1.610
Part 007	11.6	3.0	3.87	$0.445
Part 008	9.2	3.0	3.07	$0.353
Part 009	36.5	3.0	12.17	$1.400
Part 010	21.2	3.0	7.07	$0.813
Part 011	29.5	3.0	9.83	$1.130

In this example, it was determined that a definite relationship existed between the surface area of a part and the amount of coating material required to coat the part. For each three square inches of surface area, one unit of coating material is required. By establishing the surface area of each part, the cost of the coating material directly attributable to each part can be determined. As a result of this analysis, coating materials can be treated as a direct cost, charged directly to the products on which they are used and excluded from the activity cost accumulation process.

There are other instances in which an engineered consumption can be used to convert indirect costs into direct costs. Perishable tools are a frequent candidate. The life of the tool can be determined and a consumption base and rate established. This information can then be used to effectively assign perishable tooling cost to individual cost objectives.

For example, one contract machining company works with items made from a wide variety of metals. Perishable tooling cost, when included as an indirect cost, accounted for over 10% of the company's total activity cost. The company knew that the consumption of tools was a factor of metal hardness and the amount of metal removed, not the amount of time it took to machine the product. As a result, it developed a tool consumption matrix that estimated the amount of tooling consumed based on the type of metal being machined and the amount of metal that was removed. This measured consumption of tooling was then charged directly to each cost objective based on these two factors.

The use of piece-rate cost distribution is intended to enable the organization to charge the cost of high-dollar indirect materials directly to the cost objectives that use them. If used, the concept should be restricted to those indirect materials that would not be fairly distributed if they were simply accumulated in an activity center and charged as part of that activity center's cost rate. Keeping in mind the goal of accuracy, not precision, most organizations will have only a few, if any, indirect materials that require such treatment.

MACHINE HOUR/CYCLE TIME DISTRIBUTION

Machine hour/cycle time cost distribution is a method of charging costs to cost objectives based on the amount of time the objective is processed on a particular piece of equipment. It is particularly useful in manufacturing activity centers that can be characterized as machines using workers as opposed to workers using machines.

In using this concept, an average hourly cost of operating all pieces of equipment in the activity center should be established and then applied to all products produced on any one of those pieces of equipment. Some organizations calculate an hourly cost for each individual machine. This approach is not recommended. Equipment should be grouped into activity centers by appropriate characteristics and average rates established. At times, an activity center may contain only one piece of equipment due to its unique characteristics, but this should be the exception, not the rule.

The costs included in activity centers to be distributed using a machine hour or cycle time rate should only be those costs related to the ownership and maintenance of the equipment itself or that vary in direct relationship with the hours the equipment operates at its most basic level of use. Costs related to the ownership and maintenance of the equipment itself would include depreciation or lease cost (better yet, some substitute for depreciation), insurance, fixed utilities, and outside maintenance, as well as distributions from operations support activities that assign the costs of building and grounds (for the space occupied by the equipment), maintenance, manufacturing engineering, and other support not directly related to the operation of the equipment. Costs that vary in direct relationship with the hours the equipment operates would include items such as variable utilities and manufacturing supplies. The labor required to operate the equipment would be included only if the equipment's crew size is fixed; if the number of individuals (or fraction thereof) required to operate the equipment is always the same. Only then would labor costs vary directly with the number of hours the equipment operates. Finally, all of these costs must be related to the use of the equipment whenever it is operated. If some costs only apply when the equipment is used for certain purposes, they should be excluded.

For example, one company has a hot form press that can be used for two different types of operations: hot forming and super plastic forming. Its most basic use is for hot forming. All of the costs incurred in hot forming are also incurred during super plastic forming. As a result, all costs involved in hot forming belong in the basic machine/cycle time rate for the press. Super plastic forming involves the temporary addition of another piece of capital equipment and the introduction of argon atmosphere. These costs should not be included in the basic rate. Instead, they should be accumulated in a separate activity center and form the basis of a supplemental or surcharge rate that is added to the basic machine hour/cycle time rate when the equipment is used for super plastic forming.

The operating labor issue is also important. If the equipment has the same manpower requirement whenever it is in operation, it is safe to include the cost of labor in the hourly rate. If, however, the nature of the product or the length of the operating cycle makes it necessary that different crew sizes attend the equipment at various times, labor should be left out of the rate and treated independently. This concept is discussed in detail in the Production Manpower Pool section of this chapter.

Exhibit 8.14 shows the development of machine hour/cycle time rates for two categories of equipment: hot forming activities and CNC machining activities. As discussed above, the hot forming equipment can also be used for super plastic forming. In the example, there are 8,000 press hours annually in hot forming and 10,000 machine hours annually in CNC machining. Of the 8,000 annual press hours in hot forming, 1,000 represent time when the press is actually doing super plastic forming.

The basic costs relating to the ownership, maintenance, and operation of the presses and machines are included in hot forming and CNC machining activity centers. Note that production labor is included. This implies that the operator/machine ratio is fixed—the crew size does not vary over time. If it did, production labor would have been excluded. The only costs included in the super plastic forming activity center are those additional costs that result from using a hot forming press for this more complex process. The additional depreciation belongs to the piece of capital that must be added when super plastic forming takes place. The utility and manufacturing supply costs represent the extra $10 and $4 per hour that are incurred when the presses are used for super plastic forming. There is no purchased maintenance involved in super plastic forming, no additional operators are necessary, and no more space is occupied. As a result, no costs are included in these areas. The extra equipment does, however, require a small amount of work by the company's maintenance department, and the process requires a more intensive level of effort from the manufacturing engineering staff.

The results are rates of $30 and $31 per hour for hot forming and CNC machining, respectively. When hot forming presses are used for super plastic forming, however, the super plastic forming rate of $22 per hour must be added to the basic hot forming rate of $30 for a combined rate of $52 per hour.

One important characteristic of machine hour/cycle time cost distribution is that each piece of equipment charges costs to cost objectives individually. Each product receives a charge from each piece of equipment that processes it. This characteristic differentiates the machine hour/cycle time method from line/cell time cost distribution, discussed next.

LINE/CELL TIME COST DISTRIBUTION

Several pieces of equipment are sometimes arranged in such a manner that they are regularly used to perform the same series of operations, either on one product or on a group of similar products, with little or no build up of work in process between operations. Individual pieces of equipment are not used in isolation but always in connection with the group as a whole. In

Exhibit 8.14 Development of Machine Hour/Cycle Time Rates for Hot Forming Activities and CNC Machining Activities

	Hot Forming	Super Plastic Forming	CNC Machining
Directly assigned costs:			
Depreciation	$40,000	$2,000	$50,000
Utilities	$60,000	$10,000	$20,000
Manufacturing supplies	$20,000	$4,000	$50,000
Purchased maintenance	$20,000		$10,000
Production labor	$30,000		$75,000
Subtotal	$170,000	$16,000	$205,000
Distributions:			
Building and grounds	$10,000		$20,000
Maintenance	$40,000	$1,000	$50,000
Manufacturing engineering	$20,000	$5,000	$35,000
Subtotal	$70,000	$6,000	$105,000
Total costs	$240,000	$22,000	$310,000
Annual operating hours	8,000	1,000	10,000
Cost per machine/cycle hour	$30.00	$22.00	$31.00

such cases, line/cell time cost distribution is usually the best method of assigning costs to cost objectives.

This distribution is best even if all the equipment is not used on all products. For example, a manufacturing line is established for producing Products A and B. This line is made up of machines 1 through 4, which are used in a specified sequence. If Product A is produced by using machines 1 through 4 in sequence, but Product B is produced without using machine 3, the cell/line concept nevertheless applies to both products. By grouping the machines together to be used as a continuous process, the organization has dedicated those resources to all products that go through the line or cell. As a result, all products being produced by the line must bear the cost of the entire line.

The cell/line concept develops an hourly cost for using one resource—the cell or line—instead of a cost for each piece of equipment on that line or in that cell. That rate is then applied to each product produced by the line based on the product's hourly production rate.

The costs included in an activity center for a cell or line are basically the same type of costs that were described for activity centers with machine hour or cycle time rates. The costs of ownership, maintenance, and operation of the cell or line should be included. Like the machine hour/cycle time situation, the labor to operate the line would be included only if the cell's/line's crew size is fixed (i.e., the number of individuals required to operate the cell or line is always the same). If the crew size varies from product to product, labor should be left out of the rate and treated independently. This concept is discussed further in the Production Manpower Pool section of this chapter.

Exhibit 8.15 shows the calculation of the hourly cost of a finishing line. Although this calculation is for a single line or cell, not multiple pieces of equipment, the calculation mirrors that in Exhibit 8.14 for machine/cycle time activities. The organization can finish 100 units of Product X per hour, 150 units of Product Y per hour, and 75 units of Product Z per hour. Regardless of whether X, Y, and Z use all individual operations available, each product has the entire line or cell dedicated to its manufacture while it is being processed through the line or cell. As a result, finishing costs for the three products are calculated as follows:

Product X: $150/100 per hour = $1.50 per unit
Product Y: $150/150 per hour = $1.00 per unit
Product Z: $150/75 per hour = $2.00 per unit

Care must be taken in using the line/cell concept. In some cells or lines, variable costs may be so great that two rates would be appropriate: one line/cell rate to cover the dedication of the entire line to the product's

Exhibit 8.15 Calculation of the Hourly Cost of a Finishing Line

		Finishing Line
Directly assigned costs:		
Depreciation		$100,000
Utilities		$60,000
Manufacturing supplies		$60,000
Purchased maintenance		$20,000
Production labor		$120,000
	Subtotal	$360,000
Distributions:		
Building and grounds		$20,000
Maintenance		$60,000
Manufacturing engineering		$40,000
	Subtotal	$120,000
	Total costs	$480,000
Annual operating hours		3,200
	Cost per cell/line hour	$ 150.00

manufacture, and a second machine hour rate to cover the variable costs driven by the operation of each piece of equipment in the cell or line.

Inappropriate costing practices often cause a great deal of confusion at companies in the process of cellularizing their manufacturing processes. One company, for example, had a product that went through three manufacturing steps during its manufacture. The first operation had a machine rate of $40 per hour and was able to complete its operation on 250 parts per hour. The second operation had a rate of $50 per hour but could complete only 200 parts in an hour. The third operation's rate was $36 per hour and completed 240 parts per hour. This resulted in a manufacturing cost attributable to the product of $.56 each [($40.00 per hour/250 parts) + ($50 per hour/200 parts) + ($36 per hour/240 parts)].

After cellularizing these three operations, the company recalculated a cell cost of $120 per hour, only $6 less than the sum of the individual activity rates. The rate at which it could produce products in this cell was, however, limited by the slowest machine, the one that formerly performed the second operation. With production at 200 units per hour, the postcellularization manufacturing cost per unit was $.60 ($120 per hour/200 parts), over 7% higher than it was before. The company knew intellectually about all of the benefits of cells. They could not, however, see any improvement in their cost calculations. As a matter of fact, their cost system said that the product now cost more than it did before.

A big part of the problem was that, although the postcellularization costing methodology was appropriate, their precellularization costing did not accurately measure the cost of the product. One of the costs eliminated by cellularization is the cost of moving product from one operation to the next, or from one operation to storage to the next. Under their costing practices, the cost of those moves was buried in the hourly rates for the machines.

When in-process material movement costs were removed from the old machine rates, those machine rates were reduced by 5% to $38 per hour for the first operation, $47.50 per hour for the second, and $34.20 per hour for the third. After accumulating all of these in-process movement costs in a separate activity center and dividing by the number of in-process moves, they learned that each move cost $1.50. Prior to cellullarizing the process, the company moved 50 parts at a time from each operation to in-process storage and then on to the next operation. As a result, it cost $.03 ($1.50 per move/50 parts) every time a part was moved. In recosting the previous manufacturing process, the company found that, despite the 5% reduction in rates which reduced manufacturing costs from $.56 to $.532, the actual cost per part had been $.652 [$.532 manufacturing + (4 moves × $.03 per move)]. The cellular rate actually represents an 8% reduction in cost. This did not even include the benefits of lower inventories, quicker throughput time, and additional available floor space.

Inappropriate accounting practices did not keep this company from realizing the benefits of cellularization, even though they could not prove the benefits using their cost system. Such methods have, unfortunately, proven to be an obstacle at many other organizations in which a failure in the ability to measure potential benefits has kept management from adopting this and other operating improvement techniques.

It is important to note the difference between machine/cycle time cost distribution and cell/line time cost distribution. These similar, but not identical, concepts both have places in the development of an effective cost system.

PRODUCTION MANPOWER POOL

A concept already touched on several times in this text is the production manpower pool. Although the concept can prove to be a use useful tool in a wide variety of situations, its use is almost mandatory if accurate costs are to be obtained in situations in which the number of workers required to operate a production resource (machine, cell, line, etc.) varies from product to product. For example, a machine center in one company requires two operators for half the products produced in the center but only one operator for the other half. If they include the average one and one-half operators in a machine hour rate and use it to cost products produced on the machine, one half of the products will be undercosted by the cost of one-half person and the other half will be overcosted by the cost of one-half person. However, if they included the cost of the machine's operation in the operators' direct labor rate, the products requiring two operators will receive twice the amount of machine operating cost every hour they are produced than the products requiring only one operator receive. Neither one of these approaches is acceptable.

The use of a production manpower pool is a convenient solution to this problem. Exhibit 8.16 shows how such a pool operates. This organization has many presses that have been grouped into three activity centers based on their size and other operating characteristics. All personnel-related costs applicable to employees working as press operators have been accumulated in an activity center called press manpower. Costs involved in the ownership, maintenance, and operation of the presses have been accumulated in the activity center for the applicable presses.

In the press manpower activity center, the personnel-related costs include fringe benefits, indirect labor worked by these primarily direct personnel, and overtime and shift premiums. It also includes distributions from other activity centers. In the example, these include human resources and general supervision. Each of the three press activity centers accumulates the costs directly assignable to the presses such as depreciation, utilities, purchased maintenance, and manufacturing supplies. They also receive distributions from other activity centers. In the example, these include building and grounds, maintenance, and engineering.

Once these costs have been accumulated by activity center, they can be divided by the appropriate number of hours (labor hours for production manpower and press hours for the press groups) to determine the individual costing rates. The result is one rate for the individuals involved in operating the presses and separate rates for the presses themselves. If a medium press operates with one operator, the cost would be $81 per hour ($21 for labor + $60 for the press). If, however, a medium press produces a part that

Exhibit 8.16 Operation of a Production Manpower Pool

	Press Manpower	Small Press Group	Medium Press Group	Large Press Group
Direct labor	$240,000			
Indirect labor	$75,000			
Fringe benefits	$50,000			
Overtime premium	$15,000			
Shift premium	$5,000			
Depreciation		$75,000	$50,000	$100,000
Utilities		$35,000	$30,000	$80,000
Purchased maintenance		$20,000	$30,000	$50,000
Manufacturing supplies		$45,000	$65,000	$95,000
Subtotal	$385,000	$175,000	$175,000	$325,000
Building and grounds		$10,000	$5,000	$8,000
Human resources	$10,000			
Maintenance		$15,000	$10,000	$37,000
Supervision	$25,000			
Engineering		$10,000	$20,000	$30,000
Total	$420,000	$210,000	$210,000	$400,000
Direct labor hours	20,000			
Press hours		7,000	3,500	5,000
Cost per hour	$21.00	$30.00	$60.00	$80.00

requires two operators, the cost would be $102 per hour [(2 operators × $21 per hour) + $60 per press hour].

Using a production manpower pool eliminates the cost distortions caused by combining the cost of equipment operators and the cost of owning, maintaining, and operating equipment into a single activity center and producing a single, composite rate.

INTERNAL COSTS

There are some activity centers that neither support other activity centers nor relate to specific cost objectives. These types of activity centers are generally those categorized as customer/market support activities, product/product-line support activities, and G&A activities. Instead of supporting other activity centers or being attributable to specific cost objectives, these activity centers support subsets of the company's business: a specific product line, a specific market, or a particular customer. In the case of G&A, the activity center supports the organization as a whole. The nature of these activities makes it difficult to find a theoretically sound basis for distributing their accumulated costs to specific products or services. Despite this difficulty, the costs of supporting a market must be attributed only to the products and services sold in that market, the cost of supporting a product line must be attributed only to the products and services that make up that product line, and G&A costs must be equitably distributed among all of the organization's products and services.

For example, one company manufactures products that are sold in two markets, Market A and Market B. The following is a summary of its pertinent operating information:

	Market A	*Market B*	*Total*
Direct material costs	$ 4,000,000	$ 6,000,000	$10,000,000
Manufacturing costs	6,000,000	4,000,000	10,000,000
Market support costs	480,000	520,000	1,000,000
Cost attributable to markets	$10,480,000	$10,520,000	$21,000,000
G&A			1,000,000
Total costs			$22,000,000

Direct materials can easily be attributed to the individual products within each market using standard material costing practices. Manufacturing costs can also be assigned to individual products within a market, using the appropriate manufacturing rates and bases (direct labor hours, machine hours, cell hours, etc.). How can the market support costs themselves be assigned to individual products within each market? One answer would be to leave them undistributed and use them only when evaluating the profitability of the entire market. The same answer could be given for G&A costs. Leave them undistributed, but make sure gross margins are adequate to cover them as well as the desired profit. There is, however, no such thing as not distributing these costs. By not distributing the costs, they are, in effect, being distributed on the basis of total costs without the undistributed activities.

For example, a company calculates the total manufactured cost of a product and then adds a 20% margin. This margin is intended to cover all market support and G&A costs as well as a profit. If the 20% is added on to the total manufactured cost, then market support and G&A cost is being distributed on the basis of total manufactured cost. There is no such thing as not distributing these costs.

The next question that then suggests itself is, "Does total manufactured cost represent a logical way to distribute market support and G&A costs?" Let us explore that question.

Suppose there are two products included in Market A that cost $10 to manufacture. Product 1 has $8 of direct material cost and $2 of manufacturing cost, whereas Product 2 has $2 of direct material cost and $8 of manufacturing cost. Which one generated more activity for the company? Product 1, which requires that the company perform $2 of work, or Product 2, which requires the company perform $8 worth of work? Of course, Product 2 generated more activity—four times more activity than Product 1. Product 1 generated four times more activity for the supplier of the company's direct materials. Perhaps manufacturing cost is a more appropriate basis for distributing our market support costs since it more closely measures the amount of activity generated by the marketing effort.

The picture becomes even clearer when we look at G&A costs. Which of the two products required the company to do more G&A work? Again, Product 2 required that the company perform four times more work. As a result, it is not illogical to assume that it also required four times more of the company's G&A efforts. The vendor G&As the production of the direct material, the company G&As only the work it does.

Using this rationale, we can develop rates based on internal costs; the cost of the activities performed by the company. In our example, the company has $12 million of internal costs. Of this, however, $2 million represents the costs that need to be distributed; $480,000 Market A support, $520,000 Market B support, and $1 million G&A. The first order of business is to develop rates for the two market support activities.

Support costs for Market A total \$480,000. Six million dollars of the \$10 million internal costs that occur before market support is addressed can be attributed to products sold to this market. By calculating a market support rate as a percentage of internal costs, we arrive at a Market A support rate of 8%. Market B support totals \$520,000. Internal cost attributable to Market B amount to \$4,000,000. The rate resulting from this relationship is 13% of internal costs. Using Market A's rate to add market support costs to Products 1 and 2, we arrive at costs of \$10.16 [(\$2 + (.08 × \$2) + \$8.00)] and \$10.64 [(\$8 + (.08 × \$2) + \$8)] respectively. Had these two products been part of Market B, Product 1's cost would have been \$10.26 [(\$2 + (.13 × \$2.00) + \$8)] and Product 2's cost \$11.04 [(\$8 + (.13 × \$8) + \$2)].

The G&A rate would include market support costs in its base since those activities are part of what is being G&A'd. As a result, the \$1 million of G&A costs would be divided by \$21 million in internal costs to arrive at a "G&A" rate of 5.7%. Applied to Products 1 and 2 (still part of Market A), this would generate a fully absorbed (G&A is the last cost added) cost of \$10.28 [\$10.16 + (.057 × \$2.16)] for Product 1 and \$11.13 [\$10.64 + (.057 × \$8.64)] for Product 2. Although not perfect, using internal costs as a base does provide a rational basis for assigning the cost of various types of support activities to cost objectives.

SUMMARY

The ABC modeling tools described in this chapter are some of those used most often in the development of ABC models. All of them are simply mathematical representations of an organization's actual cost behavior. It is seldom necessary to revert to any higher mathematics to reach the level of accuracy needed for developing cost information for management decisions. It should always be kept in mind that the objective is accuracy not precision. Computational virtuosity does not get any points from the judges. Simple mechanics that parallel the reality of an organization's actual costs receive the high marks.

9

Developing Cost Flow-Down Structures: Case Studies

I once read that the way to master a concept is to apply it over and over again in unlike circumstances. In this way, an individual becomes more and more cognizant of the principles involved and how they apply universally, not the mechanics of a specific type of application of the principles. Those who apply it time and again in similar circumstances never really master the concept. Instead, they master the mechanics of applying it under specific circumstances.

In my travels, I have seen evidence of this in many areas, particularly in the cost systems that existed at many of our clients at the time of our engagement. I have encountered excellent standard cost systems where job cost systems should have existed. I have also seen the opposite—job cost systems where standard cost systems should have been. I have seen manufacturing cost mechanics applied at distributors and batch costing in process industries. There have been beautifully designed and implemented labor-driven systems where machine rates were appropriate and machine rate–driven systems where labor rates were appropriate. Companies have had 50 different costing rates where 5 would have been adequate and 5 rates where 50 would not have been enough.

In almost all of these situations, the system in existence was developed by an accounting executive who came from an industry in which the inappropriate system was appropriate. The accountant from a company making tens of thousands of steel wheels annually takes the system to another company that makes 20 custom jobs each year. The accountant from an iron foundry imports his or her system to a metal fabricator. The accountant from a $500 million company imports the system to his or her new $10 million employer. In most of these cases, these systems were expertly implemented and ran efficiently and under control. The only problem was that they generated either insufficient or overabundant cost information that was inaccurate and irrelevant. These accountants were expert at a specific application of cost accounting principles, not at cost accounting principles themselves. They had not applied them in unlike circumstances. To these individuals, the mechanics of implementation were viewed as the principles themselves.

To help reinforce the principles of activity-based costing (ABC), this chapter will discuss their application at two completely different types of organizations. Because the detail case used to actually develop an activity-based model in Chapters 11 through 13 is a manufacturing company, neither of the two cases will be manufacturers. We will investigate a repackager and distributor of cut flowers and a company that designs and tours the country with trade show exhibits. Both cases are simplified versions of actual projects on which my firm has worked. In discussing these cases, I will first present the factual situation and then a narrative describing how the logic of ABC can be used to guide the thought processes necessary to develop an effective cost flow-down structure for the organization.

It should be kept in mind that there can be more than one "right answer" that will adequately model an organization's cost flow-down structure. The purpose of these case studies is to provide examples of how the thought process works, not to provide the only theoretically correct solution.

SUNSHINE FLOWERS, INC.

Sunshine Flowers, Inc., is an importer, repackager, and distributor of fresh cut flowers. The company is located near a major international airport. Flowers are flown in daily from a variety of farms in South America (primarily Ecuador and Colombia). Contracts with these farms are long term and require that a specific quantity of flowers be shipped each day. The contracts do, however, allow some flexibility in the daily mix of flowers due to the short-term uncertainties that are part of growing and shipping a perishable product. Over the long term, however, the mix of flowers is fixed. Although the amount of effort required to procure different types of flowers and process flowers from different points of origin through customs varies, the company does not believe that these factors should be considered in developing an activity-based cost flow. Management reasons that all procurement and customs efforts are necessary to provide the total inventory of flowers that is required to provide their overall portfolio of products.

Once they clear customs, the flowers are delivered by refrigerated truck to Sunshine Flowers' refrigerated warehouse (known as the cooler), where they can be kept for 7 to 10 days. The perishability of the various types of flowers is a function of their popularity as well as their expected life.

In addition to flowers, the company must also purchase decorative and packaging materials, such as baskets, vases, boxes, wrapping paper, and the like. Although most of these items are general purposes and can be used any time during the year, a significant number are seasonal and can be used only "in season" (Easter, Valentine's Day, Christmas, etc.). The inventory of general-purpose items turns fairly quickly and suffers very little obsolescence or shrinkage. Seasonal items, however, are sometimes carried in inventory for a number of years, which leads to much higher obsolescence and shrinkage than is the case with general-purpose items. These materials are purchased from domestic suppliers and are stored in a small warehouse that is not climate controlled.

Distribution of the flowers takes place through a variety of channels. Bulk sales of flowers are made to a small number of major "bouquet manufacturers" located throughout the United States. These sales involve no repackaging of the flowers. They are simply shipped to the customer in the container in which they were received after the container has been relabeled. This relabeling takes place inside the cooler. Orders are received two to three weeks before shipment is required and must be shipped during a two- to three-day window. Since shipment occurs soon after receipt, few flowers perish while waiting to go out as bulk sales. Sunshine Flowers puts very little sales or marketing effort into bulk sales. The small group of potential customers in this category are already identified and are contacted via telephone by a sales representative every week. This line of business exists primarily to give the company the volume to have enough leverage over the farms to negotiate favorable price breaks. This line of business results in a small number of high-dollar transactions.

Repack sales of flowers are made to a variety of small bouquet manufacturers. The volumes handled by these manufacturers are not great enough to require the quantities of each type of flower needed to make bulk purchases worthwhile but are too high to economically buy flowers on the open market. As a result, Sunshine Flowers repacks bulk items for these customers to provide them with a high-volume mix of flowers that makes it possible for the customer to receive some benefit from their volume and Sunshine Flowers to receive both benefits of higher volume and income from their value-adding repackaging services. Repackaging activities take place within the cooler. Like bulk sales, shipment occurs soon after receipt, so few flowers perish while waiting to go out as repack sales. Although greater than those for bulk customers, sales and marketing efforts for repack sales are not high. Customers are identified and contacted via telephone on a regular basis. This line of business also results in a small number of high-volume transactions, although the fact that some value is added by Sunshine Flowers personnel results in a slightly higher number of transactions than is the case with bulk sales. Both the relabeling of bulk sales and the repackaging of repack sales are performed by individuals working in the warehouse.

Quantity bouquets are high-volume, fairly standard bouquets that are sold in quantity to a variety of retailers, from grocery stores to department stores. They are also sold to retailer cooperatives that, in turn, sell them to their members. These bouquets are "assembled" and packaged on assembly lines in a special climate-controlled room at Sunshine Flowers' facility, known as "the chiller," and are comprised of a variety of seasonal flowers. The number of individuals working on the assembly lines varies from one bouquet type to another. Although there is great flexibility in the overall content of these bouquets, the core flowers are specified as to type and number in each customer's agreement. The fill-in flowers are selected from those available at the time of the bouquet's assembly, providing, of course, that they result in an attractive product. To meet contractual requirements when the supply of a core flower is low, Sunshine Flowers must often purchase the needed flowers on the open market at inflated prices. Much of Sunshine Flowers' sales and marketing efforts go into this line of products. Field sales representatives regularly visit customers, and marketing materials are provided to encourage sales at the customer's outlets. This line of business demands a much greater amount of planning, logistics, and transactions than either bulk or repack sales.

Fulfillment sales are individual bouquets, selected from a catalog and shipped directly to the final customer. Through partnership arrangements with several catalog retailers, Sunshine Flowers' bouquets are made available to customers on a next-day-delivery basis. Customers order the bouquets from the catalog just as they would any other type of merchandise. The catalog companies then electronically transmit orders to Sunshine Flowers three times each day: first thing in the morning, midday, and late afternoon. From these transmissions, Sunshine is able to generate assembly and packing instructions for the shop floor, labels for the packages, and shipping documents for the overnight air delivery service. Packaging of the orders takes place at stations located in the chiller. A worker packages one order at a time from a stock of flowers and materials kept within reach at the station. All orders are filled on the day they are received. Marketing efforts for this line of business consist of recruiting catalog retailers and providing pictures and copy for inclusion in their catalogs. Although this line of business generates the greatest amount of shop activity per order, the "high-tech" transaction processing and the fact that all shipments are paid for by the catalog companies, makes the administrative effort much less than it is for quantity bouquets. The same pool of laborers is used for both assembling quantity bouquets and fulfillment orders.

DISCUSSION

Sunshine Flowers' four distinct product lines are the most obvious features that should be taken into account in developing its cost flow-down structure. Although many of the activities that take place within those product lines will end up as separate activity centers, there appears to be enough general product-line activity, such as the varying levels of sales and marketing effort, to warrant activity centers that accumulate these product-line–related costs. As a result, activity centers for bulk sales support, repack sales support, quantity bouquet support, and fulfillment sales support should be established.

After making the obvious product-line designations, we can take a more orderly look at Sunshine Flowers' costing issues by going step-by-step through our cost and activity categories. The first category is direct or throughput costs. Direct or throughput costs themselves do not generally suggest any ABC issues. In Sunshine Flowers' case, however, there are several issues that must be addressed. The first of these is the open-market premium that must sometimes be paid for the core flowers required in quantity bouquets. Although it may be incurred due to a particular order, this premium is a cost of being in the quantity bouquet business and should not be charged to the specific jobs for which the premium is paid. Instead, it should be accumulated as part of quantity bouquet support and charged to products on whatever basis is chosen for that activity center.

A second issue that arises with regard to direct or throughput costs is the fact that some flowers will spoil before they can be sold. There are two ways that this issue can be handled. One way impacts the cost flow-down structure and the other does not. The cost of spoiled flowers could be accumulated in one or more cost pools and applied to good flowers as they are charged to jobs. This would impact the cost flow-down structure. As an alternative, flowers charged directly to jobs could simply be grossed up for spoilage, thereby charging a job for more than one flower for each flower that winds up in the product. Both approaches will work.

There are several issues related to spoilage that must be kept in mind when deciding how to handle the problem. First, perishability of the various types of flowers is a function of their popularity as well as their expected life. A popular flower will spend less time in inventory and, therefore, be less subject to spoilage. Similarly, a flower with a longer cooler life will also be less likely to spoil before used in a product. Second, perishability applies primarily to quantity bouquet and fulfillment sales. Flowers for bulk sales and repack sales are in and out so fast that there is little time for spoilage. As a result, the cost flow-down structure must result in spoilage costs' being directed toward quantity bouquet and fulfillment sales according to the volumes of high-spoilage and low-spoilage flowers they sell. (There could be more than two levels of perishability; for simplicity, we will assume that there are only two.) This could be accomplished by separated all flowers into two categories: high spoilage and low spoilage. The cost of spoiled flowers would then be charged to either a "high flower spoilage" cost pool or a "low flower spoilage" cost pool depending on the flower's category. The costs accumulated in the high flower spoilage cost pool would follow the high spoilage category flowers to jobs in quantity bouquets and fulfillment sales as either a cost per flower or a percentage of flower cost. The costs accumulated in the low flower spoilage cost pool would follow the low spoilage category flowers in the same manner.

Grossing up flower requirements for jobs in quantity bouquets and fulfillment sales would reach the same objective. After separating flowers into high-spoilage and low-spoilage categories, the ratio of each category's spoiled flowers to good flowers used in quantity bouquets and fulfillment sales could be calculated. This ratio would then be used to gross up flower requirements. For example, if 200,000 high-spoilage flowers and 50,000 low-spoilage flowers are discarded while 1 million of each category of flower are sold through quantity bouquets and fulfillment sales, the ratios would be 1.20 for high-spoilage flowers and 1.05 for low-spoilage flowers. As a result, for every high-spoilage flower sold in either of these two product lines, 1.20 flowers would be charged to the product, and for each low-spoilage flower, 1.05 flowers would be charged to the product. Either method would effectively charge the cost of spoiled flowers to the correct cost objectives. As this discussion continues, assume that the first method, creating and using cost pools, will be used.

The third issue relating to direct or throughput costs is the obsolescence and spoilage of decorative and packing materials. The problems presented here are similar to those involved in the spoilage of flowers. Decorative and packaging materials are used only in quantity bouquets and fulfillment sales. There are two categories of these materials, each with a different level of obsolescence or spoilage: general purpose and seasonal. Seasonal items suffer a much greater level of obsolescence and spoilage than do general items. The two possible solutions to these problems parallel those used for flower spoilage. Cost pools can be established for general material obsolescence and seasonal material obsolescence and the cost of obsolete or spoiled merchandise charged to these pools. Costs accumulated in the general material obsolescence cost pool would follow general materials to jobs in quantity bouquets and fulfillment sales as a percentage of merchandise cost and the costs accumulated in the seasonal material obsolescence cost pool would follow seasonal materials in the same manner. Because a common unit of measurement, similar to the cost-per-flower option available for flower spoilage, is not available in materials, applying the cost pools as a percentage of material cost is the most practical means available.

The grossing-up option is also available, although it would have to be done in terms of dollars instead of units. Ratios could be established to gross up materials required on a product and the resulting higher requirement of material used in charging direct or throughput costs to the product. As this discussion continues, again assume that the first method, creating and using cost pools, will be used.

The next category to address is throughput or material support activities. Although the amount of effort required to procure different types of flowers and process flowers from different points of origin through customs varies, management does not believe that these factors should be considered in developing an activity-based cost flow. Management reasons that all procurement and customs efforts are necessary to provide the total inventory of flowers that is required to provide their overall portfolio of products. As a result, a single flower support activity center can be established to accumulate all of the cost related to the procurement, handling, and storage of flowers prior to their being used in a product. The costs accumulated in this activity center would then follow flowers to their product or job using a volume related measure: either a cost per flower or a percentage of flower cost.

Procurement, handling, and storage costs for materials are different from those relating to flowers. As a result, throughput or material support activities for materials must be separated from those related to flowers. Although it is not specifically stated in the case, it is reasonable to assume that seasonal materials are purchased in much lower volumes than general materials and, because they tend to stay in inventory longer, they take up a disproportionate amount of space in the warehouse. This would suggest that separate activity centers should be established to accumulate the procurement, handling, and storage costs of seasonal material support and general material support. These activity costs could then be applied to materials as they are used on a job, using a volume related basis. For reasons mentioned earlier, using a percentage of material cost is the most practical basis.

Market and product-line issues have already been addressed, so the next area to be addressed is direct or value-adding activities. The only value-adding activity that takes place in bulk sales is relabeling. Otherwise, Sunshine Flowers simply reships the flowers in the containers in which they were received. Repack sales require a little more value-adding activity. Flowers must be resorted among the containers in which they arrived before being shipped. All of these value-adding activities, which are performed by warehouse personnel, takes place in the cooler itself.

The cost of these direct or value-adding activities can be accumulated in a relabeling and a repacking activity center, respectively. The costs of personnel, indirect materials, and occupancy would be included in the activity center. Because the activities related to each bulk sales item will be about the same, we can use a transaction or event as a surrogate driver (instead of measuring the actual amount of labor time involved) to charge this activity to individual jobs or products. This concept was discussed in Chapter 8. A cost per relabeled container should suffice. Repack sales, however, might vary slightly from container to container. If five different types of flowers are repacked into a single container, the effort is probably greater than if just two types of flowers are repacked. The variability and cost involved are probably not enough to warrant actually measuring the labor effort required on each job or product; however, this variability should be taken into account. To accomplish this, the weighted events and transactions concept can be used (also discussed in Chapter 8). A cost per container and a cost per flower type in the container can be established. That way, a repack box with five flower types will reflect a higher cost than one with two flower types, but the effort required to measure the cost of these differences will be minimal. This approach is similar to the use of a cost per order and cost per line item in the Acme Distributors example discussed in Chapter 6.

A different situation exists in quantity bouquets. Direct or value-adding activities in this area are much more like those of a manufacturing firm. In the chiller, another climate-controlled area outside of the cooler, assembly lines have been established on which the bouquets are "manufactured." Depending on the bouquet to be assembled, the appropriate types and quantities of flowers must be delivered to the line and an appropriate number of assemblers assigned to work the line. This suggests that there are three elements involved in quantity bouquet assembly: the setup, the line cost, and the production worker cost.

There is no physical line setup required, but the flowers to be used in assembling the bouquet must be delivered to the line before assembly can take place. These flowers are delivered to the line by individuals who work in the warehouse, not by production workers. Three factors determine the amount of effort required for this type of setup: the quantity of flowers to be pulled from the chiller and delivered to the line, the number of different types of flowers that must be pulled and delivered, and the number of times the line must be replenished during a particular bouquet's assembly run. Again, weighted events and transactions can be used as an effective means of attributing these costs to a particular job. First, a line setup activity center would be established to accumulate the costs related to setting up the bouquet assembly lines. Using weighted events, these would then be turned into a cost per flower (or more practically per hundred or thousand flowers) and a cost per flower type. In this way, if 10,000 each of 10 flower types are delivered, the cost will be somewhat higher than if 20,000 each of 3 flower types and 10,000 each of 4 flower types are delivered. This would parallel the intuitively obvious fact that a warehouse worker would require less effort to pull 100,000 flowers from 7 different warehouse locations than to pull 100,000 flowers from 10 different locations. If a job requires that the line be replenished during its run, a multiple of these weighted events would be added to its cost.

The operation of the line itself would be handled in the manner described in the line/cell time cost distribution section of Chapter 8. The cost of owning, maintaining, and operating the line, excluding the production labor cost, would be accumulated in an assembly line activity center. Costs accumulated in this activity center would be turned into a cost per line hour and charged to jobs or products based on the number of bouquets that can be assembled in an hour.

The size of the crew working on an assembly line varies from bouquet to bouquet; therefore, production labor cost cannot be included in the line cost. Instead, it must be added as a separate cost element based on the size of the crew assigned. This is accomplished using the production manpower pool concept discussed in Chapter 8. An assembly worker activity center would be established in which all costs related to assembly worker activity would be accumulated. These would not only include the workers' wages, but their fringe benefits and distributions from support activities (e.g., human resources, supervision) relating to the workers. These costs would then be used to develop a cost per production labor hour and that rate used to assign costs to jobs and products based on the number of bouquets that can be assembled in an hour and the number of workers that must attend the line while assembly is taking place.

Fulfillment takes place at stations in the chiller that are permanently stocked with the required quantities and mix of flowers. One worker is required at each station. There are varying degrees of effort in packaging different types of orders, but because these represent a lot of small transactions, it is impractical to have time-based rates for packaging each order. Here again, however, weighted events and transactions, as discussed in Chapter 8, are useful. Products can be divided into easy-to-package, average-to-package, and difficult-to-package categories (or some other categories representing relative packaging difficulty) and weights assigned to each. A fulfillment packaging activity center would be established to accumulate the cost of packaging fulfillment orders. These costs would include occupancy costs in the chiller; the cost of workers, their benefits, and their support distributions; the cost of continuous restocking; and the cost of any indirect materials required. A cost per easy, average, and difficult package can then be determined to include as part of product cost.

Next to be considered are the event- or transaction-related activities. The administrative cost or order processing, which appears to vary considerably between product lines, is a clear candidate for this area. Activity centers would be established for bulk orders, repack orders, quantity bouquet orders, and fulfillment orders. Costs related to processing each type of order would then be accumulated in the appropriate activity center and a cost per order determined for each one.

Before addressing G&A, we need to return to the four product line activity centers. Although we have established activity centers for each product line, we need to complete our discussion of what costs are included and how to charge activity center costs to cost objectives. It appears that marketing costs would be properly included in each of these activity centers. For three of them, that is all that might properly be considered as general product-line costs. For one, however, an additional cost must be added. That one is quantity bouquet support. The open-market premium cost discussed in direct or throughput costs must also be included in this activity center.

In bulk sales, repack sales, and fulfillment sales, Sunshine Flowers has only a few large customers. (Remember, their fulfillment sales customers are the catalog companies, not the individuals to whom they ship the flowers.) Marketing efforts do not relate to the volume of sales as much as it does the number of customers. As a result, these costs might best be assigned as a cost per customer. Quantity bouquet sales efforts, however, more closely mirror the volume of business. As a result, a basis that follows volume, such as using a percentage of flower cost, might be more appropriate.

Finally, the general costs of operating the business would be accumulated in a G&A activity center and charged to cost objectives, using internal costs, as discussed in Chapter 8, as a basis.

Exhibit 9.1 summarizes the proposed cost flow-down structure for Sunshine Flowers, Inc. Keep in mind that this is only a suggested solution. There could be other solutions that are just as valid.

ROAD SHOWS, INC.

Road Shows, Inc., is in the business of creating and managing trade show exhibits for industrial organizations. When an organization wishes to develop an exhibit for use at industry trade shows, it will request proposals from several firms like Road Shows. Each firm will develop a concept for the exhibit, prepare renderings, models, or other vehicles for making the concept appealing to the potential client, and prepare a proposal that not only

Exhibit 9.1 Sunshine Flowers, Inc., Proposed Cost Flow-Down Structure

Activity Center	Cost Contents	Distribution Basis
Direct or throughput support:		
Flower support	Procurement, handling, storage	$ per flower
High flower spoilage	High-Spoilage flower cost	$ per high spoilage flower charged to QB or Fulfillment
Low flower spoilage	Low-spoilage flower cost	$ per low spoilage flower charged to QB or Fulfillment
Seasonal material support	Procurement, handling, storage	% of seasonal material cost
General material support	Procurement, handling, storage	% of general material cost
Seasonal material support	Obsolete seasonal material cost	% of seasonal material support
General material obsolescence	Obsolete general material cost	% of general material cost
Product/market support:		
Bulk sales support	Bulk sales marketing costs	$ per bulk sales customer
Repack sales support	Repack sales marketing costs	$ per repack sales customer
Quantity bouquet support	Quantity bouquet sales costs and open-market premiums	% of quantity bouquet flower cost
Fulfillment Sales Support	Fulfillment sales marketing costs	$ per fulfillment customer
Direct/Value-Adding Activities:		
Relabel	Occupancy, labor, support	$ per container
Repack	Occupancy, labor, support	$ per flower and $ per flower type
QB: setup	Labor, support	$ per flower and $ per flower type
QB: assembly line	Occupancy, support	$ per line hour
QB: assembly workers	Labor, support	$ per labor hour
Fulfillment packaging	Occupancy, labor, support	$ per easy package
		$ per average package
		$ per difficult package
Event/transaction activities:		
Bulk orders	Administrative distributions	$ per bulk order
Repack orders	Administrative distributions	$ per repack order
Quality bouquet orders	Administrative distributions	$ per quantity bouquet order
Fulfillment order	Administrative distributions	$ per fulfillment order
General and administration:		
G&A	Administrative distributions	% of internal costs

covers the exhibit's construction, maintenance, and storage, but also its transportation to and from shows, its setup before each show, and its teardown and recrating at each show's conclusion.

Over the years, Road Shows has worked on contracts ranging from a single exhibit for a single show to multiple copies of the same exhibit that follow lengthy show tours. Revenue from these contracts has ranged from $10,000 to 1 million each. Road Shows does not perform the actual construction of the exhibits or the crates in which they are stored and transported. Exhibit construction is contracted out to a variety of shops, depending on the size and level of mechanization required by the exhibit. Crate construction is contracted out to a couple of nearby shops.

Road Shows' sales representatives develop client leads through a variety of means. In addition to ongoing contact with past and current clients, they visit with participants at industry trade shows, make cold calls, and generally "leave no stone unturned." The job of these sales representatives is to generate opportunities to submit proposals.

Once a request for proposal is received, Road Shows' creative design staff moves into action. Although these requests seldom provide guidelines as to cost, Road Shows' sales staff can usually provide designers with a cost range that would be appropriate for the prospective client's budget. The designers then attempt to develop the concept for an exhibit that would appeal to the client and cause it to contract with Road Shows for its construction and management. The design is forwarded to estimators who, after consulting with the company's engineers, purchasing personnel and potential contractors, develop the economic portion of the proposal.

Historically, Road Shows has been awarded between 30 and 40% of the "low-end" and "high-end" projects on which it submits proposals. "Mid-range" projects, however, have proven to be more difficult to win, with their award rate being in the 20 to 30% range.

Once a contract is awarded, Road Shows' engineers prepare detailed blueprints of the exhibit and its crates. Depending on its size and complexity, an exhibit can have anywhere from one crate to two dozen crates in which it is stored and moved. Purchasing and engineering then work together to identify the most qualified contractors for building the exhibit and its crates, solicit bids from these contractors, select the most appropriate contractor, and then monitor the construction process. Purchasing's role in this process can be characterized as administrative while engineering's is technical. The amount of effort required to select, support, and administer vendors for constructing the exhibits varies considerably. The major factors are the size of the exhibit and the amount of mechanization it entails.

Each exhibit also requires custom-built crates in which it is both stored and transported. Compared to exhibits, the level of effort involved in supporting the construction of crates and the variability of that effort from crate to crate are relatively small.

Once built, exhibits fall under the direction of Road Shows' show management team. These individuals control the storage of the exhibit when it is not in use and take care of all of the logistics for getting the exhibit to the show venue, setting it up before the event and tearing it down after the event. Show coordinators do all of the logistics work. Small and mid-sized exhibits can be delivered to local shows by Road Shows' own truck. Common carriers are used in all other cases. Although a "roadie" (an employee of the company) always accompanies the exhibit to take care of any day-to-day maintenance that might be required while it is on tour, the show coordinators must also arrange for any local contractor services that must be obtained at each venue. For example, electricians are usually required for setting up the exhibit, many exhibits will require that fresh flowers be delivered several times during the course of the show, carpet cleaners are often needed to keep the exhibit in good condition, and other "locals" will be needed for other such purposes. Roadies are usually carpenters who take care of most of the damage that may occur while the exhibit is being transported. They also ensure that the special crates that have been designed to safely move the exhibit remain in good shape and continue to protect it. Although these roadies are the exhibit's full-time "shepherds" while it is in use, many of the services it requires are either beyond the roadies capabilities or must be performed by local licensed personnel due to local restrictions or the venue's union rules. As noted earlier, the show coordinators arrange for and manage these on-site contractors.

When not in use, Road Shows stores the client's crated exhibit in its warehouse. Each exhibit has its own reserved area in the warehouse facility. Some of the crates are stackable (no more than three crates high) and some are not. When they are returned from tour and before they go back on tour, each exhibit is uncrated and inspected, any necessary repairs are made, and it is then recrated.

The price of the exhibit itself is invoiced after the client has approved the completed exhibit. Storage costs are billed annually. Fees for tour management are invoiced monthly during the time the exhibit is on tour.

DISCUSSION

Perhaps the most striking characteristic of Road Shows, Inc., is the amount of money that must be spent on speculation. Although the case does not specify dollar amounts, consider the amount of activity that goes into a proposal. The company's designers must develop a concept for the exhibit that will be more appealing to the prospective client than those of other exhibit firms. Road Shows must then develop physical representations of the exhibit in the form of drawings, models, or other mock-ups. The cost of constructing the exhibit must be estimated as well as the cost of managing the exhibit during its projected annual tour. Once this has all been completed, only 20 to 40% of the proposals actually become revenue-generating contracts for the company. Sixty to 80% of the work, most of which is performed by highly paid, creative individuals, goes for naught.

To effectively manage these substantial expenditures, a means must be developed for measuring the effectiveness of the company's proposal development efforts. To do this, proposal development costs must be matched against the amount of profit they generate for the company. Currently, Road Shows can only compare the total proposal development cost to the total profit generated. It cannot determine whether the combination of proposal cost and contract award rate is covered by the margins generated by any particular segment of the business. As a result, the first order of business would be to divide the company's business into logical segments (either product lines or markets) so that these costs can be matched against the margins generated in these segments.

Although there may be other ways to segment Road Shows' business, the case suggests that it can be divided into high-end, mid-range, and low-end projects. As a result, activity centers can be established for high-end support, mid-range support, and low-end support. Proposal development costs can be accumulated in these activity centers and applied to the contracts won as a percentage of internal costs.

The four major types of direct or throughput costs at Road Show, Inc., are the construction cost of exhibits, the construction cost of storage/transportation crates, common carrier transportation costs, and the cost of on-site contractors. Two of these are one-time costs for each exhibit: the cost of the exhibit and the cost of its crate(s). The other two are ongoing costs: the common carrier cost of transporting the exhibit from venue to venue and the cost of the on-site contractors required at each show. Unlike most organizations, procurement activities at Road Shows are not concentrated in the purchasing function. Purchasing and engineering both play major roles in placing and managing contracts for the construction of exhibits and storage/transportation crates. Transportation services and on-site contractors are managed by show coordinators. As a result, the cost flow-down structure for direct and throughput support activities will be different than at most organizations.

The amount of effort required to select, support, and administer vendors for constructing the exhibits varies considerably. The major factors are the size of the exhibit and the amount of mechanization it entails. A small exhibit with little or no mechanization requires very little support. A large exhibit that includes a turntable on which an automobile will rotate while being illuminated by a computer-controlled light show will demand a great deal more support. To provide accurate cost information, this variability needs to be taken into account.

The nature of the purchasing and engineering efforts while managing the construction of exhibits makes it impractical to directly charge the project on a cost-per-hour basis. Both functions can work on several projects simultaneously. Purchasing can check on the status of several jobs placed at one vendor at the same time. They can prepare quotation request forms, purchase orders, or process invoices relating to a myriad of contracts in one sitting. If they had to charge jobs directly, procurement personnel would have to charge two hours each day to a category called recording time. Similar circumstances exist in engineering. They can be performing work relating to many jobs at the same time, or at such small intervals of time to make timekeeping a bureaucratic burden. Therefore, another means must be established.

A simple, yet accurate, method would be to establish a single activity center for exhibit construction management to which purchasing and engineering personnel would charge the time spent in exhibit construction management activities for any project. Exhibit types could then be divided into several categories that represent differing levels of effort. Four logical categories would be large/high mechanization, small/high mechanization, large/low mechanization, and small/low mechanization. The weighted events or transactions concept discussed in Chapter 8 could then be used to charge different amounts of this activity center's cost to exhibits based on the exhibit's category.

The table below provides an example of how weighted transactions or events could be used in this situation:

	Exhibits	*Weight*	*Weighted Exhibits*	*Percentage*
Large/high mech	20	10	200	33%
Large/low mech	30	4	120	20%
Small/high mech	40	7	180	30%
Small/low mech	100	1	100	17%
Totals			600	100%

If the total cost accumulated in the activity center was $240,000 the cost per exhibit for large/high mechanization exhibits would be $4,000 ($240,000 × 33%/20 exhibits). For large/low mechanization exhibits, it would be $1,600 ($240,000 × 20%/30 exhibits). Small/high mechanization exhibits would be assigned \$2,400 (\$240,000 × 30%/40 exhibits), and small/low mechanization exhibits would be charged \$400 (\$240,000 × 17%/100 exhibits).

In this manner, an accurate (remember accuracy, not precision, is our objective) measure of the cost of selecting, supporting, and administering vendors used in constructing the exhibits can be assigned to each exhibit.

The cost of selecting, supporting, and administering the purchase of crates is much simpler than is the case with exhibits. Although their design is more complex than one would anticipate (they must effectively protect the exhibit during its frequent moves), their construction is fairly simple. The same engineers and purchasing personnel support these expenditures as support the construction of exhibits. Although the level of effort required to support different crates might vary, the total cost required to support all crates will be substantially less than is the case with exhibits, and the variability of effort among crates will also be less than in the case of the exhibits. As a result, we can accurately assign the cost of supporting the construction of crates by establishing a single activity center for crate construction management, to which purchasing and engineering personnel would charge the time spent in crate construction management activities for any project. Road Shows can then use the events or transactions concept, this time unweighted, to develop a cost per crate for these activities. In this way, an exhibit with only one crate would get one tenth the crate management cost as one that requires 10 crates, taking Road Shows one step closer to accuracy without adding much complexity.

Activities relating to the procurement and control of transportation services can be handled in much the same manner as was developed for crates. A single activity center for common carrier support can be established to collect the cost of all activities having to do with the procurement and control of common carrier services for transporting exhibits from one location to another. Road Shows can again use the *unweighted* events or transactions concept to establish a cost per trip. In this way, an exhibit used at only one show would be assigned the cost of two moves (warehouse to show to warehouse), whereas one being used at five shows would be assigned the cost of six moves. Again, Road Shows would be taking one step closer to accuracy without adding much complexity to its cost calculations.

Support for the final major type of direct or throughput cost, on-site contractors, can be handled in a similar manner. The effort to support on-site contractors would seem to have more to do with the number of contractors being managed than the amount being paid to the contractors. As a result, a single activity center can again be established, this time for on-site contractor support, that would accumulate the cost of all activities relating to the procurement and control of on-site contractor services. Road Shows can then develop an unweighted cost per contractor/event. A contractor/event would be one contractor working at one event. For example, an exhibit requiring three contractors (e.g., a florist, an electrician, and a carpet cleaner) would represent three contractor/events. If that exhibit was on a tour of three shows, it would require nine contractor/events (3 contractors × 3 shows). In this way, the cost of managing on-site contractors would be equitably assigned to projects without a great deal of complexity.

The next category to address would be the direct or value-adding activities. The first direct activity that takes place once a contract is awarded is the preparation of detailed blueprints by the engineering staff. Unlike their activities in managing the construction of exhibits and crates, where they can be working on multiple projects at the same time, engineers will generally prepare detailed blueprints in a continuous effort, or at least in large blocks of time, over a number of hours, days, or weeks. This situation makes it reasonable for them to "keep time" while performing this direct activity. As a result, engineering costs can be accumulated in an engineering support activity center and a cost per hour established to assign engineering costs that are not distributed to other activities directly to contracts based on the number of engineering hours required.

Once completed, exhibits must be stored until they are transported to a show. The exhibit's required storage space is permanently assigned to it. When it is being used at a show, that space is not used to store another exhibit. As a result, the exhibit must "rent" that space from Road Shows 365 days each year. The warehouse space required is a function of the exhibit's size and stackability. No more than three exhibits, however, are ever stacked. This stackability factor makes it impossible to use a simple cost per square foot for assigning warehousing costs to exhibits.

After establishing a storage activity center to accumulate the cost related to warehousing client exhibits, there are several ways to incorporate stackability into the assignment of warehousing cost to exhibits. One way would involve the use of cubic feet instead of square feet. A simpler way would be to use the consumption unit concept discussed in Chapter 1 to develop a common *annual storage unit* (ASU). Using the fact that crates can be stacked up to three high, an ASU could be one third of a square foot of floor space. An exhibit stored in a stackable crate that could be included in a three-high stack would be assigned the cost of one ASU for each square foot of its "footprint." For example, if the crate were 5′–by-6′, the exhibit would be charged the cost of 30 ASUs (5′ × by 6′ × 1 ASU). If it were 4′-by-10′, it would be charged the cost of 40 ASUs (4′ × 10′ × 1 ASU). If, however, the exhibit could only be included in a two-high stack, it would be assigned one and one-half ASUs for each square foot of its footprint. A 5′-by-6′ crate would be assigned 45 units (5′ × 6′ × 1.5 ASUs) and a 4′-by-10′ crate would be assigned 60 ASUs (4′ × 10′ × 1.5 ASUs). Assuming a cost per ASU of $1.50

was determined, annual storage costs for an exhibit with four unlike crates would be calculated as follows (the stacking factor represents the maximum stack size in which the crate can be stored):

	Dimensions	*Footprint*	*Stacking Factor*	*ASUs*	*Cost @ $1.50/ASU*
Crate 1	10′ × 6′	60 sq ft	3	20	$ 30.00
Crate 2	16′ × 10′	160 sq ft	2	80	$120.00
Crate 3	12′ × 15′	180 sq ft	2	90	$135.00
Crate 4	15′ × 30′	450 sq ft	1	450	$675.00
Total annual storage cost					$960.00

Using the consumption unit concept in this way simplifies the method of assigning annual storage costs to specific exhibits without sacrificing accuracy.

Show management personnel, in addition to their efforts in arranging of transportation and on-site contractors, must manage each exhibit's participation in each show. Although the special procedures we have developed for directing the cost of managing transportation and on-site contractors takes care of two significant causes of the variability in management effort among exhibits, intuition tells us that there still may be show-related differences that should be taken into account. It may simply be a case of some shows being run by "sweethearts" and some being run by "jerks." It may be that multishow tours require less effort per show than is the case when an exhibit makes only one show appearance and returns to be warehoused. Whatever the reason, variability must be provided for in the assignment of show management costs if our cost flow-down is to be accurate. In this case, we will split shows into two categories: those that are part of a multishow tour and those that are a one-stop show.

This can be accomplished by using a single activity center and the weighted events or transactions concept one more time. An activity center can be established for show management that accumulates the costs related to managing exhibits while being used at a show (except, of course, for the transportation and on-site contractor support activities). Shows can then be divided into appropriate categories and weights assigned to each category representing the relative levels of effort involved in their management. Mechanics identical to those described for exhibit construction management can then be used to arrive at a cost per show for each show category. Again, this will enable Road Shows to account for the variability in managing various categories of shows without adding a great deal of complexity to the cost flow-down structure.

Roadies are assigned to exhibits for clearly measurable periods of time. As a result, assignment of their costs to cost objectives can be accomplished using a simple cost-per-day (or cost-per-hour) rate. An activity center for roadie labor would be established in which all costs related to these employees, including fringe benefits and distributions from the appropriate support activities, would be accumulated. These accumulated costs would then be converted into a cost per day (or per hour) that would be used to assign roadie costs to cost objectives.

The only remaining direct or value-adding activity would be deliveries in Road Shows' own truck. Although more elaborate methods are possible, the total cost involved in local deliveries would probably not be significant enough to warrant a complex method of assigning costs to jobs. It is important to assign local delivery costs only to those contracts which use Road Shows' trucks, but it is not important that those costs be very precise. As a result, we would establish a delivery activity center to accumulate the cost related to the operation of the company's truck and assign it to cost objectives as a cost per delivery (unweighted).

Although we have used events or transactions (both weighted and unweighted) as surrogate cost drivers in our direct or value-adding activities, the case suggests one area in which they truly represent a transaction—billing. Road Shows has three types of billings: billings for exhibit construction, billings for exhibit storage, and billings for touring services. Each exhibit is billed only once; at its completion and acceptance by the client. Each exhibit's storage fees are billed annually. Services for managing the exhibit while it is on tour are billed once per month during the tour. If the effort required to generate each billing were equal, all billing-related costs could be accumulated in a single activity center and a cost per invoice developed. It is more likely, however, that the effort involved in the various types of billings differs, but that total billing costs are not great enough to warrant three separate activity centers. For one last time, Road Shows can use the weighted events or transactions concept to develop a cost per invoice for each type of invoice. A billing activity center can be established and weighted per invoice costs developed for exhibit billings, storage billings, and show tour billings.

Finally, the general costs of operating the business would be accumulated in a (G&A) activity center and charged to cost objectives, using internal costs, as discussed in Chapter 8 as a basis.

Exhibit 9.2 summarizes the proposed cost flow-down structure for Road Shows, Inc. Again, keep in mind that this is only a suggested solution. There could be other solutions that are just as valid.

Exhibit 9.2 Road Shows, Inc., Proposed Cost Flow-Down Structure

Activity Center	Cost Contents		Distribution Basis
Direct or throughput support:			
Exhibit construction management	Purchasing, engineering	$	per large/high-mech exhibit
		$	per large/low-mech exhibit
		$	per small/high-mech exhibit
		$	per small/low-mech exhibit
Crate construction management	Purchasing, engineering	$	per crate
Common carrier support	Show management, coordinators	$	per trip
On-site contractor support	Show management, coordinators	$	per contractor/event
Product/market support:			
High-end support	Proposal development costs	%	of high-end internal costs
Mid-range support	Proposal development costs	%	of mid-range internal costs
Low-end support	Proposal development costs	%	of low-end internal costs
Direct/value-adding activities:			
Engineering	Occupancy, labor, support	$	per engineering labor hour
Storage	Occupancy, labor, support	$	per annual storage unit
Show management	Occupancy, labor, support	$	per show/single-stop tour
		$	per show/multistop tour
Roadie labor	Labor, support	$	per day (or hour)
Delivery	Truck costs, labor, support	$	per delivery
Event/transaction activities:			
Billing	Administrative distributions	$	per exhibit billing
		$	per storage billing
		$	per show tour billing
General and administration:			
G&A	Administrative distributions	%	of internal costs

SUMMARY

The cases of Sunshine Flowers, Inc., and Road Shows, Inc. provide examples of how an organization can be viewed through the lens of ABC. The issues identified and the answers developed to accurately handle those issues may have been different, but the thought processes were the same. How do the company's various products and/or services require that activities be performed, and what costs are incurred as a result of those activities? What is the best way to then direct costs to the activities that made them necessary and from there to the products or services that made the activities necessary. There is no "one size fits all" solution. Cost flow-down structures are unique to each organization. Once a sound cost flow-down structure is established, it can be used to develop valuable activity-based decision support tools for the company. These will be explored in the chapters that follow.

10

Building a Cost Accumulation and Distribution Model

The process of developing a cost flow-down structure that mirrors the actual operation of its business is the most important part of an organization's implementation of activity-based costing (ABC). Although having new, activity-based numbers to use in supporting management decisions proves to be valuable, the *paradigm shift* that occurs during the intellectual process of designing the cost flow-down proves to be even more valuable.

For example, several years ago, we worked with a client who manufactured and distributed a line of molded rubber plumbing products. The products were manufactured to stock and shipped from two warehouses as orders were received. The cost system used by this client was typical of a manufacturer; overhead was charged to products as they were manufactured as either a cost per direct labor hour or a cost per machine hour. During the intellectual process of developing the cost flow-down structure, we pointed out that the company was made up to two very distinct businesses. The first was a manufacturer, that sold all of its output to a single customer. The second was a distributor that bought almost all of its products from a single source and then sold them to a wide variety of customers. Under the existing system, all of the costs related to the distributed business, which had nothing to do with manufacturing, were included in manufacturing overhead and charged to products as they were produced.

During the project, we helped the client come up with better methods of measuring that cost of manufacturing activities and an entirely new set of concepts for measuring the cost of distribution activities. At the conclusion of the project, however, the chief executive officer's parting words were, "All of these new costing methods and rates will be very informative and help us to make better decisions, but the most valuable benefit we received from the project is that we will never look at ourselves the same way again." The paradigm shift was the biggest benefit received; accurate and relevant cost information was a way of effectively exploiting management's new view of the company.

Once management's mindset has been changed to view costs through the lens of ABC, it must develop the tools to put that new mindset to use. The most cost-effective means of providing these tools is through the development of a cost accumulation and distribution model.

A cost accumulation and distribution model is a model that begins with the volume and mix of products or services provided by an organization, accumulates the cost of activities involved in providing that volume and mix of products or services, and then turns that cost into a set of rates that can be used to cost individual processes as well as the products or services. It reflects the "bottom-up" and then "top-down" flow of costs described in Chapter 5:

- Products and services drive the activities they make necessary.
- Activities drive the costs they make necessary.
- Costs are assigned to the activities that made them necessary.
- Accumulated activity costs are assigned to the products and services that made them necessary.

Exhibit 10.1 shows this accumulation and then distribution of costs. Following this general outline, a company can develop a model that can provide the accurate and relevant cost information necessary to support sound business decisions of all types.

Exhibit 10.1 Accumulation and Distribution of Costs

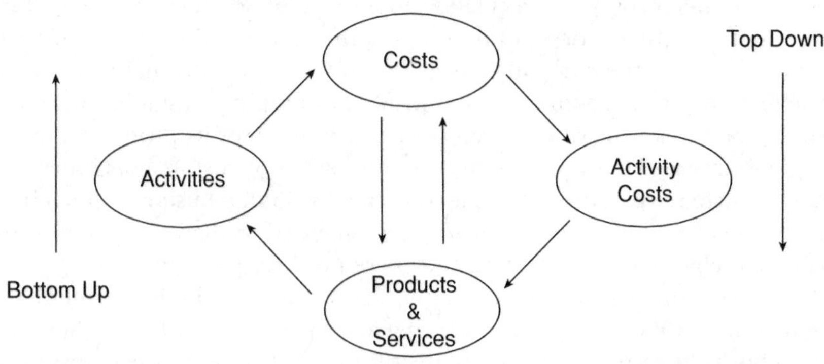

There are commercial ABC software packages on the market. Some are complex, integrated systems that support the incorporation of ABC into an organizations day-to-day activities. Others are designed to develop activity-based models of the company. Some incorporate elements of both. In the discussion that follows, I will pretend that such software does not exist. My emphasis will be on the things a small to mid-sized organization's ABC accumulation and distribution model should be able to do if it is to effectively support management decisions. If the reader chooses to use commercial software in building a model, it can use this narrative as a checklist to see how the software measures up. One word of warning, however: It has been my observation that a strange phenomenon occurs when ABC software is purchased; the purchase of ABC software causes all brain cells involved in analytical thinking to go dormant. Once software is purchased, the emphases moves to implementing the software and away from developing relevant and accurate cost information. If a commercial software package is to be used, it should be done only after all of the intellectual work required to develop the company's cost flow-down structure has been completed.

COST MODEL STRUCTURE—GENERAL

The structure of a cost accumulation and distribution model should follow the bottom-up and then top-down approach outlined in Chapter 5. It should begin with the volume and mix of products or services that the model is intended to represent. That volume and mix of products or services should then be converted into the volume and mix of measurable activities that are required. The volume and mix of measurable activities should then be used to generate the cost of providing that volume and mix of measurable activities. This completes the bottom-up cost accumulation portion of the model.

Once the model has determined the total cost required, it can then begin the top-down distribution of costs that will result in the cost of activities and processes and rates to attach costs to the company's products and services. Accumulated costs are first distributed to the activities that made them necessary. The accumulated cost of the various activities are then turned into rates so that they can be attributed to the products and services that were used to drive the model in the first place.

It needs to be understood at the outset that there is a difference between the model and the data in the model. The model is the machine that "crunches the data" entered as input. A company can have numerous editions of its model, each containing different sets of input. One edition might contain data representing the current year's volume and mix of business.

Another edition might contain data representing the company's volume and mix of business at its practical capacity or at the "real" volume and mix of business as discussed in Chapter 4. Still another edition might contain data representing next year's volume and mix of business or some hypothetical volume and mix of business that is anticipated if the company moves forward with a particular decision. The model represents the relationships between activities, costs, and products or services. The data represents the measure of those activities, costs, and products or services.

The remainder of this chapter will provide a conceptual overview of the structure of a cost accumulation and distribution model. It is intended to provide a "big picture" view of an entire model before we begin worrying about a model's details. In all likelihood, reading this chapter will not make the structure of a cost accumulation and distribution model perfectly clear. This structure should, however, become clearer in the chapters that follow, as we use it as a map for actually constructing a model of our sample company, Small Time Manufacturing.

COST MODEL STRUCTURE—BOTTOM UP

Operating Information and Resource Requirements

The model must start with the volume and mix of products or services. Remember, the concept of ABC starts by stating that products and services cause activities. With this as the starting point, the model can be built to reflect any volume and mix of activities, providing, of course, that the basic structure of the organization does not change as a result of that volume and mix of business. Since products and services cause activities, the model must then proceed to determine what volume and mix of activities are required to provide that volume and mix of products and services. How much of what does the company need to do? This volume and mix of activity must be measured in terms of the drivers that have been established to assign costs to final cost objectives.

For example, a model built for Acme Distributors example in Chapter 6 would have its volume and mix of activities defined by (1) the dollar volume of merchandise that is quick turning, (2) the dollar volume of merchandise that is slow turning, (3) the dollar volume of merchandise that is sold to big chains, (4) the dollar volume of merchandise that is sold to little retailers, (5) the number of orders processed, and (6) the number of line items on those orders.

Similarly, a manufacturer's volume and mix of activity might be defined by the required number of direct labor hours, machine or cycle hours, cell or line hours, dollars of material purchased, shipments to outside processors, shipments to customers, setups, or in-process material moves. A long-term care facility's volume and mix might be defined by resident days, resident days by resident acuity level, nursing visits, meals served, shopping trips, billing by payor, or therapy units.

The first step in model development is shown in Exhibit 10.2. "Operating Information and Resource Requirements" represents all of the activity measures, defined in terms of the drivers used to attach costs to final cost objectives, and the direct or throughput costs that are associated with those cost objectives. Direct and throughput costs are not subject to cost flow-down; they are assigned directly to specific products and services. As a result, they flow immediately to "Total Accumulated Costs." The activity measures must begin the cost accumulation process so that the cost of those activities can also make its way to "Total Accumulated Costs."

Activity measures can be divided into two types; those that will actually *drive* costs and those that will serve only as *divisors* to establish cost rates. Those that actually drive costs are those measures that result in a significant amount of variable cost. For example, a machine hour will result in operator costs, utility costs, tooling costs, and supply costs. More machine hours will result in higher costs and less machine hours will result in lower costs. A resident day will result in nursing costs, meal costs, and cleaning costs—more resident days, more costs; less resident days, less costs. Tour days at Road Shows, Inc. (see Chapter 9) will result in labor costs for the roadies as well as lodging and meal costs—more tour days, more costs; less tour days; less costs. These types of activity measures have a direct impact on the amount of cost incurred by the organization.

Exhibit 10.2 Model Development: Step One

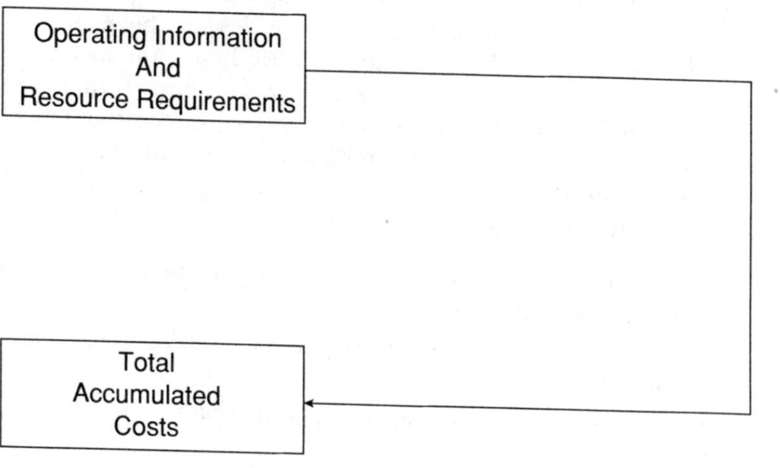

Those activity measures that serve only as divisors do not have the kind of direct impact on costs. Suppose, for example, that a staff of two order-entry personnel can handle between 1,000 and 1,500 orders annually. In such a case, the total cost of processing 1,100 orders will not be materially difference from the cost of processing 1,400 orders. At some point, it may be necessary to add a third individual to process orders, but the relationship between orders processed and the total cost of processing orders is not linear. Similarly, if a group of 10 "order pickers" can pick anywhere between 120,000 and 150,000 line items annually, a linear relationship will not exist between orders picked and the total cost of picking orders. In these cases, the activity measure will be used to establish a cost per order or cost per line item, but it will not be used to directly drive the accumulation of costs.

Resource Conversion

To begin the accumulation of activity costs, many of the activity measures that will actually drive costs must be stated in terms of operating time (chronological time), especially those that will drive labor costs, utility costs, and other costs that are incurred when the activity is "on," but not when it is "off." Some will already be stated in terms of operating time. Machine hours, resident days, labor hours, cell hours, and tour days are examples of activity measures that are already stated as operating time. Others, like the number of setups or the number of delivery stops, are not. To begin accumulating the cost of these type of measures, they must first be converted to some form of operating time. How may labor hours, machine hours, line hours, or cell hours does a setup take? How long in terms of labor hours does each delivery stop require? Once converted, the cost accumulation process can begin.

Exhibit 10.3 shows the entry of this "Resource Conversion" process into the model. If, for example, line set-up activities have been measured by the number of setups, and each setup takes two hours, the process would begin by multiplying the number of setups by two hours. If there are 500 setups, he model will know that 1,000 line hours are required. Once converted, a chain of cost calculations can begin. If each setup requires a crew of four workers and setup supplies average $1 per set-up labor hour, the chain of cost calculations would go as follows:

- 1,000 line hours are not available for production (500 setups × 2 hours per setup.)
- 4,000 set-up labor hours will be required (1,000 line hours × 4 person set-up crew).
- $4,000 of set-up supplies will be required (4,000 set-up labor hours × $1.00 of supplies).

Exhibit 10.3 Model Development: Step Two

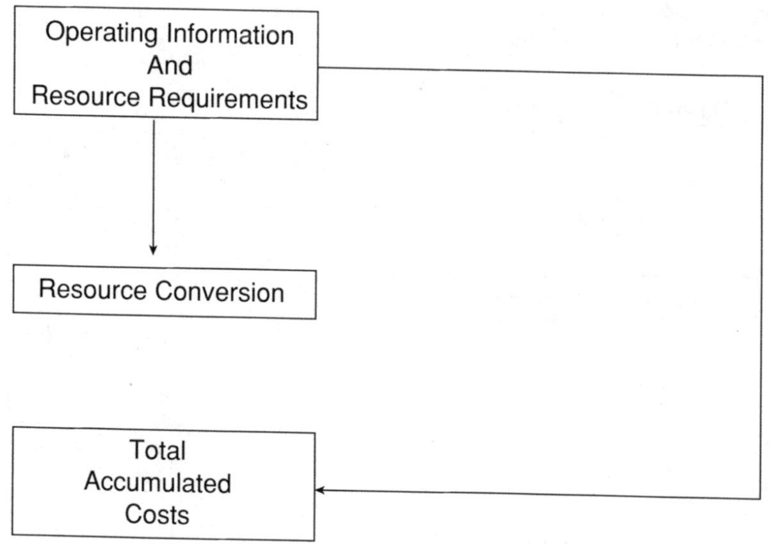

The beginning activity measure, number of setups, does not provide sufficient information to begin this process, making this conversion process necessary.

Screens

Once the necessary conversions are completed, it is advisable to make sure that there is enough capacity under existing model assumptions to actually provide the amount of resources that are required. This is accomplished by including "capacity screens" in the model (see the "Screens" section of Chapter 8). The resource requirements arrive at the screens either directly as entered at the beginning of the model or after being translated into operating time through the resource conversion process. Exhibit 10.4 shows the addition of screens to the model structure.

If 4,500 machine hours are required, the model must make sure that 4,500 machine hours are available. If the data being entered into the model assumes that there are two machines and that the facility will operate 8 hours per day, 5 days per week, 50 weeks per year, it will be impossible to provide the 4,500 hours (2 machines × 5 days × 52 = 4,000 hours). Whatever costs are accumulated under these assumptions will be incorrect. The facility must work another shift, longer shifts, some weekend days, or obtain

Exhibit 10.4 Model Development: Step Three

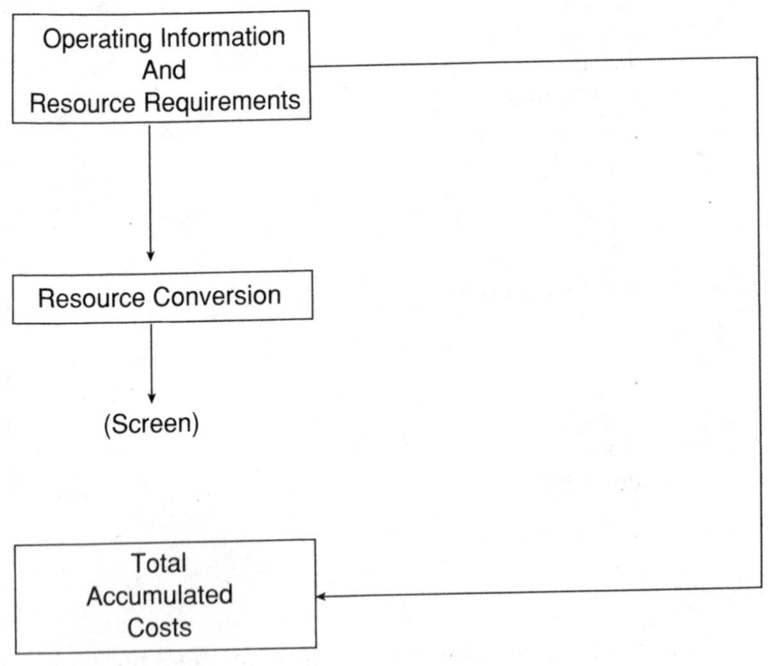

another machine. All of these actions will change the cost of operating the facility. Without putting resources with a physical constraint through such screens, the company will not know whether it is "violating the laws of physics" in accumulating its costs.

Operating Manpower—Demand

After clearing the screens, the model can proceed to determine the demand for variable labor resulting from the activity measures entered at the beginning of the model (see the "Operating Labor Demand/Supply Equation" section of Chapter 8). As detailed in Chapter 8, operating time can be multiplied by the required crew size to determine the "perfect world" number of labor hours that are required and the perfect world labor hours further increased by the indirect activity allowance to determine the actual labor hours required to provide the level of activity entered at the beginning of the model.

Exhibit 10.5 shows the inclusion of the "Operating Manpower" demand calculation in the model's structure. The operating time requirements that

Exhibit 10.5 Model Development: Step Four

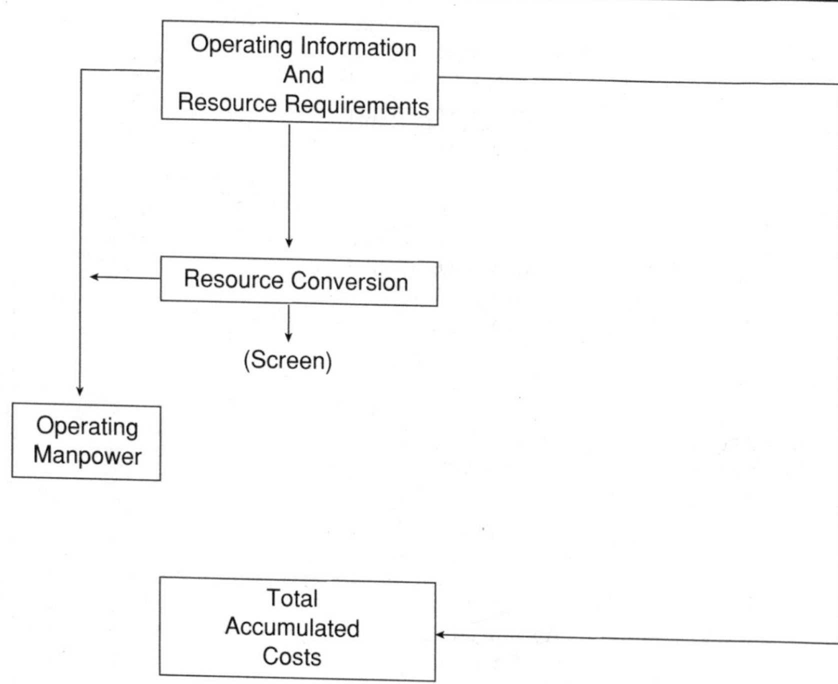

begin the calculation of labor demand come either directly as entered at the beginning of the model or after being translated into operating time through the resource conversion process. Although the computations done in these areas are critical for accumulating the appropriate amount of costs, they have not yet generated any additional costs. At this point, the costs accumulated in "Total Accumulated Costs" are only the direct and throughput costs.

Automatically Variable Costs

After ensuring that all operating hours pass through the model's screens and that the demand for variable labor is known, the model can move forward and begin calculating costs again. There will usually be several nonlabor variable costs that have a linear relationship with an activity center's operating time or with its unconverted activity measures. At a manufacturer, operating hours might drive such *automatically variable* costs are variable utility costs, perishable tooling costs, and manufacturing supplies. At a long-term care facility, resident days might drive food costs. As mentioned earlier, at Road Shows, Inc., tour days will drive such nonlabor costs as roadie

Exhibit 10.6 Model Development: Step Five

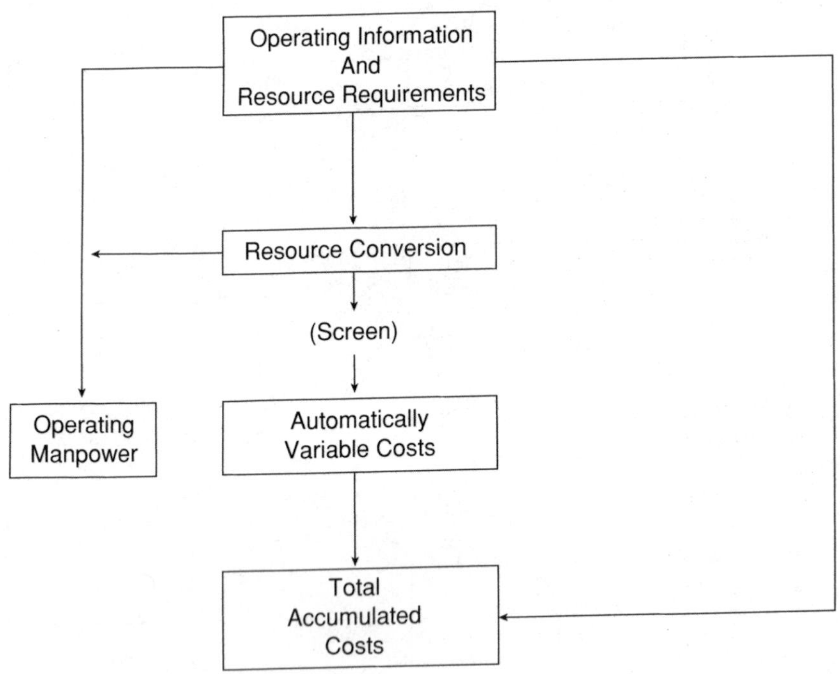

meal and lodging costs. As shown in Exhibit 10.6, the model can bring the operating time or other resource information forward, use them to calculate these "Automatically Variable Costs," and add them to "Total Accumulated Costs." The "Consumption Units" section of Chapter 8 described methods for including such calculations in the model.

Operating Manpower—Supply

Having determined the demand for variable labor, the model can now be structured to complete the balancing act required to provide that labor in a manner consistent with reality. The "Operating Labor Demand/Supply Equation" section of Chapter 8 describes this process in detail. Once the combination of headcount and overtime has been determined, the model can then go on to calculate the straight-time labor, overtime premium, and shift premium (if any) costs. This addition of labor cost to "Total Accumulated Costs" is shown in Exhibit 10.7.

Exhibit 10.7 Model Development: Step Six

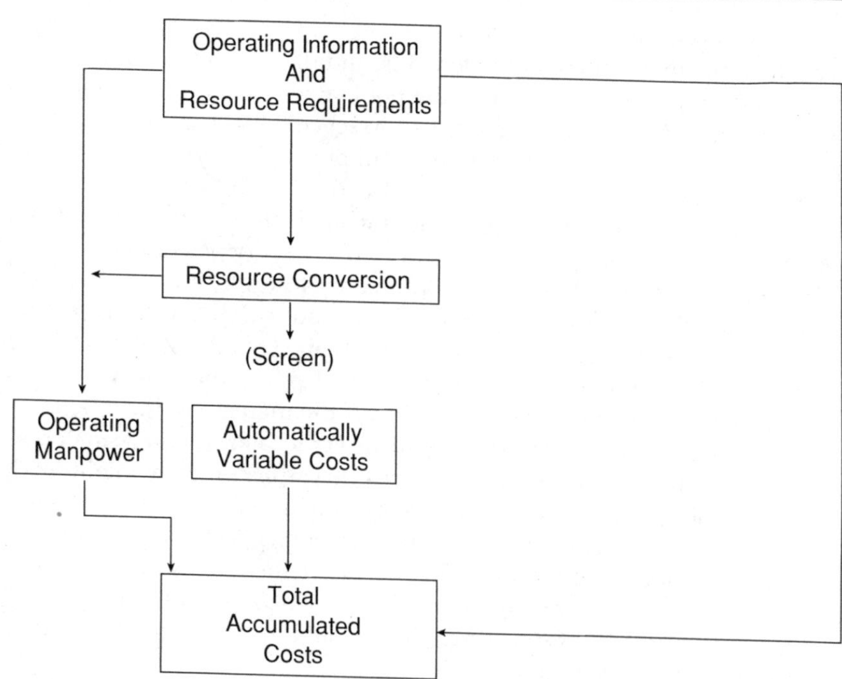

Nonvariable Costs

At this point, the model requires the input of costs and other data that are not directly connected with the model's volume and mix of activities. These are the items whose relationship with activity measures are not linear. They are better described as either *step variable, budgeted,* or *fixed.*

Step Variable Costs—Support Staff

Step variable items are those that remain fixed for a fairly wide range of activity measurement, but then will increase or decrease significantly when the level of activity moves out of that range. The staff of two order-entry personnel mentioned earlier in this chapter is an example. They can handle between 1,000 and 1,500 orders annually. If volume increases from 1,200 to 1,440 orders, an increase of 20%, the total cost of processing orders will not increase much at all. If, however, volume increases to 1,620 orders, an increase of 35%, the addition of another individual in order processing could increase the cost by 50% or more.

At a small or mid-sized organization, it is critical that these step variable items not be treated as either variable or fixed. If they are treated as either variable or fixed, the model will not be very useful for "what if" analyses. The variability of these items depends, and the things that they depend on are situation specific. Earlier in the book, it was stated that "the definition of fixed and variable costs are situation specific." It is in this area where this concept is of particular importance. Simple mathematics is insufficient to determine the behavior of these types of costs.

For example, the general statement made with regard to order-entry personnel may be fundamentally true; two order-entry personnel can handle between 1,000 and 1,500 orders annually. However, if orders increase from 1,200 per year to 1,620 per year, this does not automatically mean that the order-entry staff increases to three individuals. The means of processing the additional 420 orders, particularly the 120 that take the activity above its two person maximum, is situation specific. If the increase is due to a large, one-time event, someone in another activity center may spend a small portion of his or her time assisting in order entry, the company might work order-entry personnel overtime, or a "temp" might be brought in for a few months to help with the overload. In these situations, costs will not increase a significant amount. If, however, the 420-order increase is due to an ongoing increase in the company's volume of business, it would probably be wise to actually add the third person. This would increase the total cost of order processing substantially.

As might be expected, step variable costs are most prevalent in the service and operations support activities. These types of activities might vary generally with changes in the volume and mix of activities, but they seldom vary directly with those changes. Once the staffing of service and operations support activities is determined, however, the model can continue on with its automatic costs accumulation calculations.

Fringe Benefits/Other Headcount-Driven Costs

With both the operating manpower and support staff information now in the model, it is possible to move forward to the calculation of fringe benefit costs and any headcount-driven variable costs. Fringe benefits are usually driven by headcount, hours worked, or dollars of wages, all of which have already been included in the model or can be calculated using data already in the model. The "Labor-Based Cost Distribution" section of Chapter 8 details the mechanics for accumulating fringe benefit costs and developing a rate for distributing them inside the model. Mechanics for accumulating headcount driven costs are covered in the "Consumption Units" section of the same chapter. The addition of support staff to the model and the resulting accumulation of payroll, fringe benefit, and other headcount-driven costs in "Total Accumulated Costs" is shown in Exhibit 10.8.

Exhibit 10.8 Model Development: Step Seven

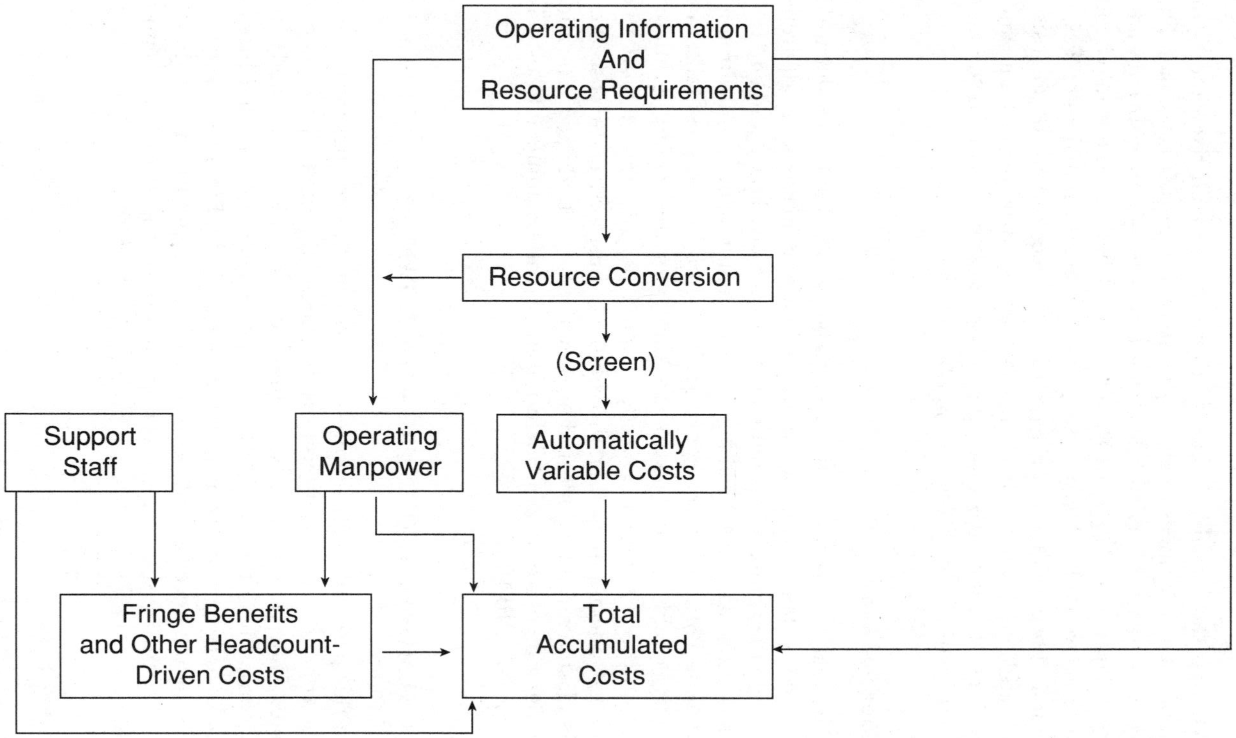

Operating Information And Resource Requirements

Resource Conversion

(Screen)

Support Staff

Operating Manpower

Automatically Variable Costs

Fringe Benefits and Other Headcount-Driven Costs

Total Accumulated Costs

Fixed Costs

Whereas step variable items are those that remain fixed for a *fairly* wide range of activity measurement, *fixed* items are those that remain fixed for a *very* wide range of activity measures. If you choose to ignore my advice and treat depreciation expenses as a cost (see Chapter 4), it would be included here. So would long-term leases, property taxes, annual audit fees, registration and license fees, many types of insurance, and any other costs that are not affected by moderate changes in the organization's volume and mix of business. Exhibit 10.9 shows the addition of fixed costs to the model and their inclusion in "Total Accumulated Costs."

Budgeted Costs

The final group of costs that need to be included in the model are the *budgeted* costs. These costs have more to do with management's discretion than they do the company's volume or mix of activity. Travel and entertainment, marketing materials, legal fees, outside maintenance, consulting fees, and training fall into this category. If the volume of business falls, marketing efforts could be cut back to save money or they could be intensified to regain the lost volume. Outside maintenance might have more to do with the age of equipment than the volume of business. These costs are neither fixed, step variable, nor variable; they are simply budgeted. The addition of budgeted costs and their inclusion in "Total Accumulated Costs" is shown on Exhibit 10.10.

COST MODEL STRUCTURE—TOP DOWN

At this point, all costs required to perform the activities necessary to meet the volume and mix of business that began the model have been accumulated. The bottom-up cost accumulation feature of the model has been accomplished. Products and services have generated the activities that they make necessary and those activities have resulted in the costs that the activities make necessary. What remains is the top-down distribution of costs and their translation into costing rates that can be used to assign them to the organization's individual products and services.

Other Data

Some of the frequently used bases for distributing costs have already been entered into the model or can be calculated from data in the model. For example, if headcount is to be used as a distribution basis, the percentages

Exhibit 10.9 Model Development: Step Eight

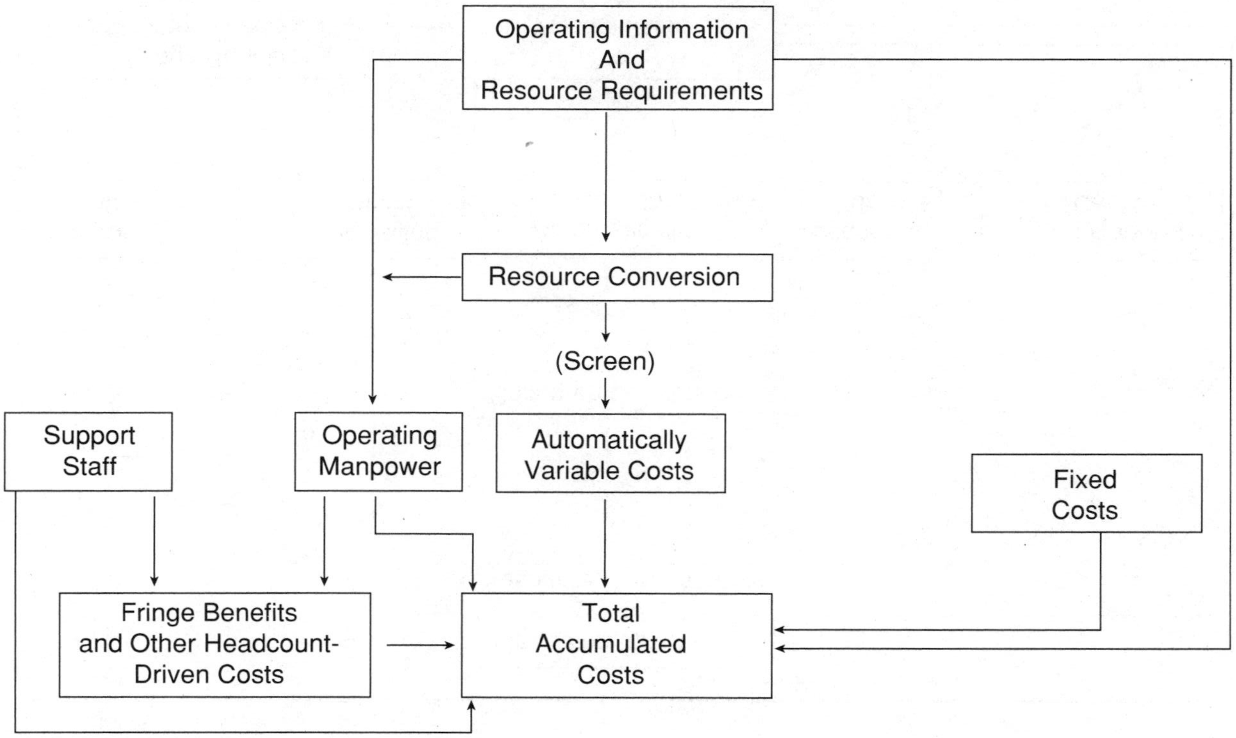

Exhibit 10.10 Model Development: Step Nine

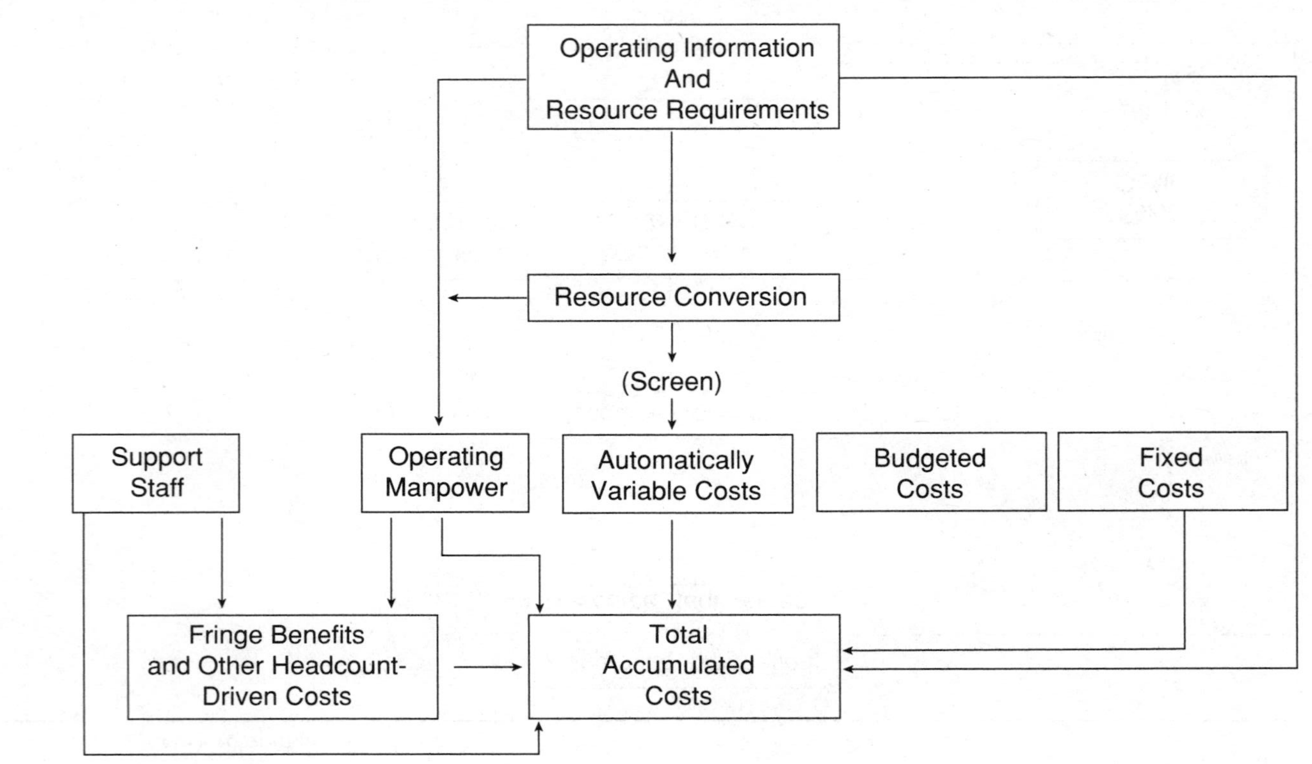

can be derived from headcount information already entered into the model. Similarly, if machine hours are to be used as a distribution base, those percentages can be derived from already existing model data. Other distributions will be based on statistical information that was not needed to accumulate cost. This data will need to be added to the model. Most of the distribution information, however, will be based on an analysis of the activity center being distributed.

For example, Sunshine Flowers' (see Chapter 9) purchasing personnel support three activity centers: flower support, general material support, and seasonal material support. If a statistical base, such as a number of purchase orders, is to be used to distribute the cost of purchasing's efforts, the number of purchase orders (POs) applicable to flowers, general material, and seasonal material must be entered. Assuming purchasing costs are $100,000 and 1,300 POs are for flowers, 500 are for general merchandise, and 200 are for seasonal merchandise, they can then be used to calculate percentages for distributing the purchasing activity's costs as follows:

	Number of POs	*Percentage of POs*	*Purchasing Costs*
Total purchasing costs			$100,000
Flower support	1,300	65%	$ 65,000
General material support	500	25%	$ 25,000
Seasonal material support	200	10%	$ 10,000
Total	2,000	100%	$100,000

If, as is likely the case, all POs are not created equal, weights can be assigned to each category of PO that represent the relative level of effort required for each type of purchase. For example, if there is four times more effort in placing a general merchandise PO as there is for a flower order and ten times the effort in a seasonal material order, the distribution of the purchasing activities cost would be modified as follows:

	Number of POs	*Wt*	*Weighted of POs*	*Percentage of POs*	*Purchasing Costs*
Total purchasing costs					$100,000
Flower support	1,300	1	1,300	24%	$ 24,000
General material support	500	4	2,000	38%	$ 38,000
Seasonal material support	200	10	2,000	38%	$ 38,000
Total	2,000		5,300	100%	$100,000

Exhibit 10.11 Model Development: Step Ten

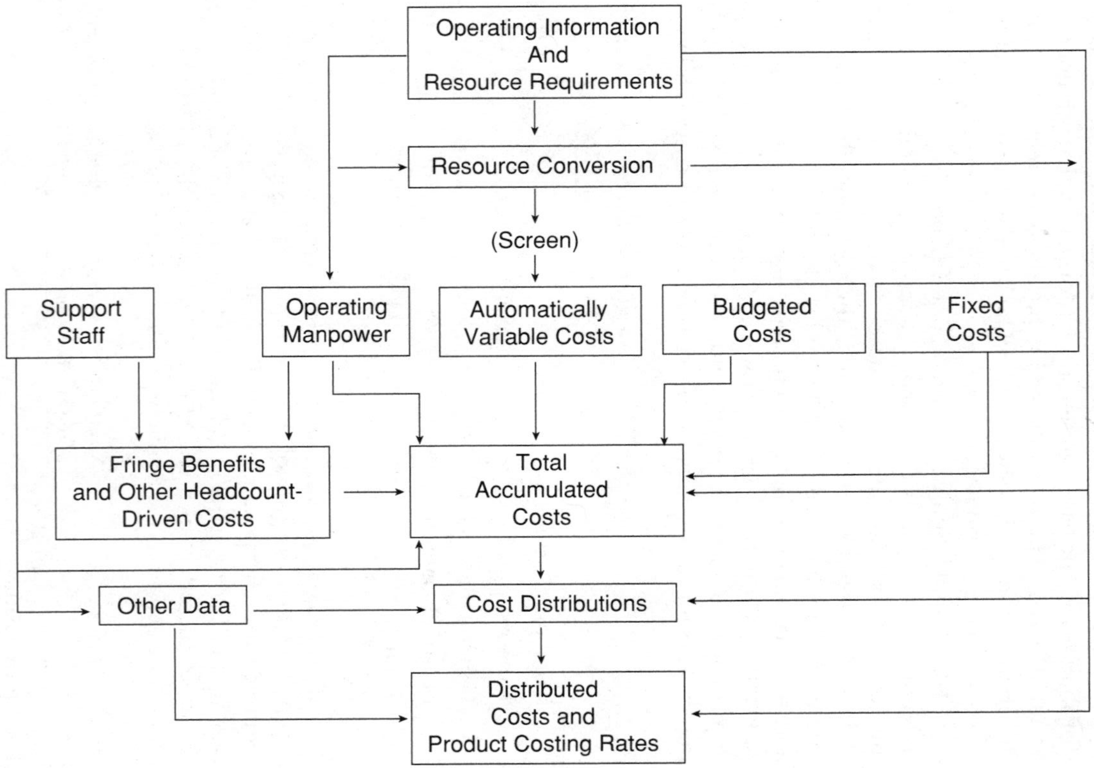

Operating Information And Resource Requirements

Resource Conversion

(Screen)

Support Staff

Operating Manpower

Automatically Variable Costs

Budgeted Costs

Fixed Costs

Fringe Benefits and Other Headcount-Driven Costs

Total Accumulated Costs

Other Data

Cost Distributions

Distributed Costs and Product Costing Rates

In a majority of cases, however, interviews with the individuals involved in performing the activity being distributed will be more than adequate for arriving at an accurate distribution of their activity center's costs. They can simply estimate the percentages that they spend supporting each of the three direct or throughput support activity centers. The entry of this distribution information is represented by the "Other Data" section of Exhibit 10.11.

Cost Distribution/Distributed Costs/Costing Rates

The balance of Exhibit 10.11 represents the use of the distribution information to complete the cost flow-down process and turn the resulting activity center costs into rates for assigning costs to products and services. This cost distribution is a *zero sum* process. The total costs accumulated in "Total Accumulated Costs" will be the same as the "Distributed Costs" that are translated into "Product Costing Rates."

Bases for calculating the rates for applying activity costs to cost objectives will come from the data entered at the beginning of the model, with data entered as part of the "Other Data," or from calculations made by the model itself. This process completes the top-down portion of the model. The total costs accumulated by the model are assigned to the activities that made them necessary and the accumulated activity costs have been translated into a form that allows them to be assigned to the products and services that made the activities necessary.

SUMMARY

There are a variety of ways to develop a model that follows the general structure outlined in this chapter. The means depends on the complexity of the organization being modeled and the inclination of the model builder. Regardless of the method, the issues addressed in the structure outlined must be covered if the model is to reflect reality and be useful in supporting management decisions of all types.

11

Small-Time Manufacturing: Developing the Conceptual Model

Small-Time Manufacturing is a small contract manufacturer with sales between $2.5 and $3.0 million annually. The company is primarily a machining operation, but in recent years, it has also begun adding value to its customers' products by performing various assembly operations. All contracts require that the company purchase basic raw materials and purchased components. Historically, the cost of purchased components for any contract has been less than that of raw materials. In recent years, however, as assembly activities have grown in importance, the cost of purchased components has increased to the point that they sometime exceed the raw material cost on an individual contract. In addition, the company must contract out certain manufacturing activities (primarily heat treating) on 30 to 40% of its contracts.

Since it began operations over a decade ago, Small-Time Manufacturing has costed its contracts using a shop-wide rate based on direct labor hours. General and administrative (G&A) costs are then added to the contract as a percentage of the direct costs (raw material, purchased components, outside manufacturing services) and shop costs that have been charged to the job. They refer to this direct cost/shop cost base as *total cost input.* Currently, the company's shop-wide costing rate is $40.45 per actual direct labor hour, and the G&A rate is 14.2% of total cost input. The traditional costing summary in Exhibit 11.1 details the calculation of these two rates.

Exhibit 11.1 Traditional Costing Summary

TRADITIONAL COSTING SUMMARY

Small-Time Manufacturing

	Shop Costs	G&A Costs	Total
Support—Base	$253,277	$177,116	$430,394
Manufacturing - Straight time/Over-time	$26,676		$26,676
Fringe benefits	$200,939	$67,130	$268,070
Overtime premium	$13,338		$13,338
Utilities	$80,000		$80,000
Tooling	$60,000		$60,000
Mfg supplies	$79,000		$79,000
Admin supplies	$10,000	$15,000	$25,000
Fixed/budget expenses	$243,800	$56,200	$300,000
Total indirect costs	$967,031	$315,447	$1,282,477
Direct labor	$250,204		$250,204
Direct material			$1,000,000
Total operating costs	$1,217,235	$315,447	$2,532,681
Base	30,000	$2,217,235	
	$40.57 per direct labor hour	14.2% of total cost input	

VENTURING INTO ACTIVITY-BASED COSTING

Small-Time Manufacturing's management realized that their business was not as simple as it once was. Whereas at one time their contracts only required them to perform machining operations on purchased raw materials, they must now also perform assembly operations as well as qualify vendors and contract for the purchase of component parts and outside manufacturing services. This increase in complexity and variety caused them to begin to doubt whether the simple method they had been using for both cost accounting and cost estimating purposes was giving them a true picture of cost.

As a result of these concerns, the company's management decided to perform an activity-based analysis of its operations and develop a method of costing their contracts that more closely followed activity-based costing's

(ABC's) "cost to activity to contract" principle. After spending a day rationalizing their business with an ABC consultant, they arrived at the following conceptual design.

THROUGHPUT OR DIRECT COSTS

Small-Time Manufacturing has $1 million of costs that fall into the *throughput or direct costs* category. These include $500,000 of raw materials, $300,000 of purchased components, and $200,000 of purchased manufacturing services. All of these costs are directly related to and easily traceable to specific jobs, products, or contracts. Removing this $1 million from the company's total costs of $2,532,681 leaves $1,532,681 that represents the cost of activities performed by Small-Time Manufacturing in the operation of its business.

SERVICE AND OPERATIONS SUPPORT ACTIVITIES

A group of 14 individuals perform the service and support functions required for the business to operate. These include employees who maintain the building and grounds; supervise the shop workforce; plan and schedule production; purchase materials, components, and outside manufacturing services; maintain equipment; check incoming materials; develop and execute quality plans and practices; explore and implement cost reduction opportunities; transport products to and from outside processors; respond to quotation requests; develop marketing materials; perform accounting and human resource functions; participate in trade organizations; and perform the many other support activities necessary for the company to function.

The company decided to create five service or operations support activity centers to collect the cost of these activities. These five activity centers and their contents are as follows:

1. *Building and grounds*, which will represent the cost of owning, operating, and maintaining the physical facility in which manufacturing and administrative activities take place.
2. *Supervision*, which will represent the cost of providing supervision for the shop workforce.
3. *Procurement*, which will represent the cost of administrative activities relating to the purchase of direct or throughput items and supplies.
4. *Manufacturing support*, which will represent the cost of support activities relating to the shop floor itself, such as maintenance, scheduling, receiving, inspection, transportation, and material handling.

5. *Management and Administration,* which will represent the cost of management and administrative support activities that not only relate to the general operation of the business but can also be related to other activity centers. These would include activities such as accounting, engineering, human resources, and general management.

THROUGHPUT OR MATERIAL SUPPORT ACTIVITIES

In rationalizing the categories of throughput or direct costs incurred by the company and the amount of effort involved in making sure the various items were at the right place at the right time, Small-Time Manufacturing's management noted that a greater effort was involved in supporting purchased parts than in supporting raw materials. Raw materials are purchased off the shelf from a small group of service centers. Purchased components, however, require that bids be solicited, the selected vendor qualified and supported through first part approval, and extra inspection be performed on incoming parts.

During the rationalization, management also noted that the primary use of the company's stake truck is to move products to and from those vendors who provide outside manufacturing services. Although other activities supporting these outside processors are similar to those for purchased components, the only throughput or direct cost receiving transportation support is outside manufacturing services.

As a result of these observations, the company's management decided to establish throughput/material support activity centers for raw materials, purchased components, and outside services.

MARKET OR CUSTOMER SUPPORT ACTIVITIES AND PRODUCT OR PRODUCT-LINE SUPPORT ACTIVITIES

In reviewing its support activities, the company's management did not identify any market or customer that required a disproportionate amount of effort, nor did it find any relevant way to divide its work into product lines. As a result, it was not deemed necessary to establish any activity centers in these two categories.

VALUE-ADDING OR DIRECT ACTIVITIES

The general flow of manufacturing operations at Small-Time Manufacturing is as follows:

- The machining of raw stock into a component part

- The performance, when necessary, of outside manufacturing processes
- The assembly of purchased components and the machined part(s)
- The inspection, packaging, and shipment of the product

There are two components to machining. Machine set-up requires the effort of two set-up workers for two to four hours. Once the machine is setup, it can operate as long as needed for the part(s) being machined without the need for a full-time machine attendant. In recent years, the machine hour/operator hour ratio has averaged 5:3. The machining time required varies considerably from product to product.

Assembly operations are fundamentally manual operations. Assemblers are assisted by small hand tools, but the equipment required to perform assembly operations is inexpensive to both purchase and operate. The assembly time required varies considerably from product to product.

The inspection, packaging, and processing of a shipment requires between one and three labor hours. Usually, one individual performs the entire process, but there are times when two individuals work together to get an order ready for shipment. When this occurs, it takes only one half of the chronological time for the shipment to be processed. These activities are manual in nature and do not require the assistance of any significant capital equipment.

In considering the nature of these shop activities, management decided that four value-adding or direct activity centers are required. These are machine/setup, machine/operate, assembly, and inspect/pack/ship.

As noted, there is only a minor amount of variability in machine/setup and inspect/pack/ship activities from job to job. As a result, management decided that it would be able to keep the eventual ABC process simpler without sacrificing accuracy if they assumed that each setup took the same amount of time and each shipment took the same amount of inspect, pack, and ship time. Management did not, however, decide on the basis for assigning these costs to individual jobs until it considered possible event or transaction activities (which are discussed later).

Machine/operate and assembly operations, on the other hand, vary considerably from job to job. As a result, management determined that it would be necessary to specifically measure the amount of machining and assembly time each job requires. Because machines can operate without a full-time attendant, it was determined that machine hours would be the appropriate basis for charging machine/operate activity costs to individual jobs. The cost of the machine operators would be part of the cost included in the machine hour rate. Assembly, however, is a strictly manual operation.

As a result, direct labor hours were determined to be the most appropriate basis for assigning its costs to individual jobs.

EVENT OR TRANSACTION ACTIVITIES

Small-Time Manufacturing's management did not find any administrative event or transaction activities that it thought significant enough to segregate from the other activities. It did, however, decide that the cost-per-event or cost-per-transaction concept would be useful in assigning the cost of machine/setup and inspect/pack/ship activities to jobs. The cost of machine/setup would be calculated as a cost per setup, and the cost of inspect/pack/ship would be calculated as a cost per shipment.

GENERAL & ADMINISTRATIVE ACTIVITIES

The balance of the company's activity costs relate to the general operation of the business. The company does not spend a significant amount of time or resources in formal activities designed to facilitate the company's growth. As a result, it did not believe it needed to segregate any of these costs so that they would not be assigned to current business.

A G&A activity center was established to accumulate these costs. Management decided that these costs should be assigned to individual jobs as a percentage of internal activity costs. It rationalized that these costs were incurred to support the other activities taking place within the organization. They were not incurred to actually support the production of raw materials or purchased components or the performance of outside manufacturing services. As a result, these throughput or direct costs would not be included in the base for assigning G&A's costs to individual contracts.

OTHER CONSIDERATIONS

Under its traditional costing methods, the company included all work performed by production workers classified as *direct labor* as direct labor hours. In reality, a portion of the work performed by these personnel was of an indirect nature. When assemblers gathered the parts they require to perform their assembly activities, they charged their labor to the job as direct even though they were not performing assembly operations. When machine operators were waiting for the setup to be complete, they also charged their labor to the job as direct even though they were not performing machining operations.

A study performed of the 30,000 direct labor hours included in the traditional costing summary shown. Exhibit 11.1 revealed that only 24,600 of the hours were truly direct. The result of this study is summarized below:

Activity Center	*Reported Direct Hours*	*Actual Direct Hours*	*Indirect Activity Add-On (%)*
Machine set/up	2,880	2,400	20%
Machine operate	6,240	4,800	30%
Assemble	18,000	15,000	20%
Inspect/pack/ship	2,880	2,400	20%
Totals	30,000	24,600	22%

Management decided that, in the future, it would express hours relating to shop operating activities in terms of these *actual* direct hours and would treat the additional hours as indirect activities performed by direct personnel. With this conceptual design established, management proceeded to Cost Flow-Down Step 1.

COST FLOW-DOWN STEP 1: ASSIGNING COSTS TO ACTIVITIES

Once activity centers are identified and the structure of the ABC flow of costs is established, the cost flow-down process can begin. The first step in the process is to assign all costs that cannot be assigned directly to a cost objective to the activity centers that made them necessary. These costs include items such as salaries, wages, and fringes; utilities; tooling; supplies; depreciation; leases and rentals; legal and accounting costs; real and personal property taxes; purchased maintenance; and employee training. This assignment of costs to activities at Small-Time Manufacturing is summarized in Exhibit 11.2.

At the conclusion of this step, the company has assigned all of its nonthroughput or direct costs to the activities that made them necessary. It is not, however, in a position to assign costs to jobs, products, or contracts. Before that can be done, it must first distribute the cost of service and operations support activity centers to those other activity centers that require their support. This takes place in Cost Flow-Down Step 2.

Exhibit 11.2 Assignment of Costs to Activities

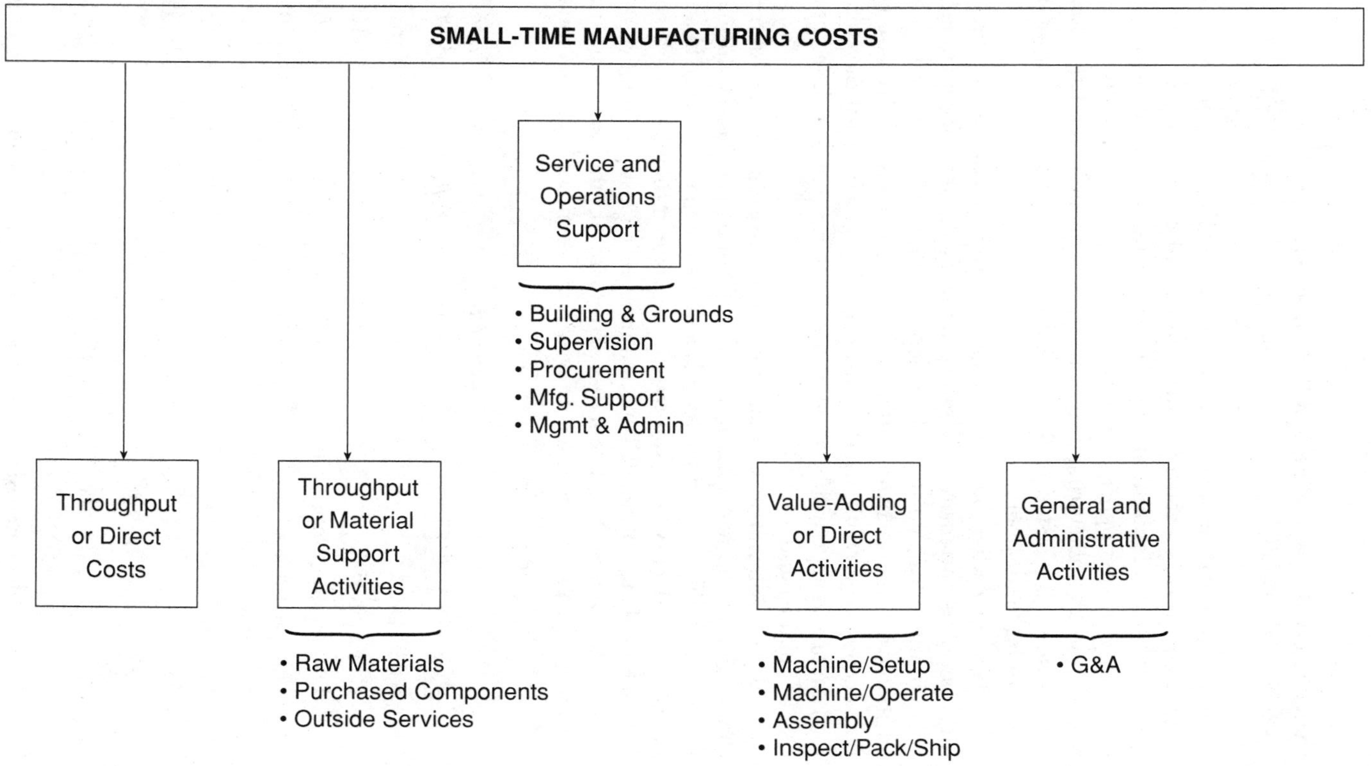

SMALL-TIME MANUFACTURING COSTS

Throughput or Direct Costs

Throughput or Material Support Activities
- Raw Materials
- Purchased Components
- Outside Services

Service and Operations Support
- Building & Grounds
- Supervision
- Procurement
- Mfg. Support
- Mgmt & Admin

Value-Adding or Direct Activities
- Machine/Setup
- Machine/Operate
- Assembly
- Inspect/Pack/Ship

General and Administrative Activities
- G&A

COST FLOW-DOWN STEP 2: ASSIGNING COSTS AMONG ACTIVITIES

In Step 2 of the flow-down process, service and support activity costs are distributed to other activity centers using either (1) a relevant statistical base (automatic distributions) or (2) an analysis of the activities performed by the service or support activity center (activity analysis distributions). In Small-Time Manufacturing's case, two activity centers lend themselves to distribution using a statistical base. Those two activity centers are building and grounds and supervision.

As noted earlier, building and grounds will accumulate the cost of owning, operating, and maintaining the physical facility in which manufacturing and administrative activities take place. The demand for this service can be attributed to other activity centers based on the amount of square footage they occupy. As a result, each activity center's percentage of the company's total square footage will be used as the statistical basis for distributing the cost of building and grounds.

Supervision will accumulate the cost of providing supervision for the shop workforce. One common way of distributing activities of this nature is to use each activity center's percentage of the company's overall headcount. Management decided that this was appropriate in their case.

The balance of Small-Time Manufacturing's support activity centers must be distributed after an analysis of the activities they perform. After performing such an analysis, the company's management arrived at the following distribution percentages:

Activity Center	*Procure-ment*	*Mfg Support*	*Mgmt & Admin*
Sales, G&A	10%	10%	50%
Raw materials	20%	5%	10%
Purchased components	40%	5%	10%
Outside services	30%	10%	10%
Machine/setup		5%	5%
Machine/operate		40%	5%
Assembly		15%	5%
Inspect/pack/ship		10%	5%
Totals	100%	100%	100%

The performance of the Step 2 distributions is summarized in Exhibit 11.3. At the conclusion of this step, the company knows the cost of the

Exhibit 11.3 Assigning Costs Among Activities

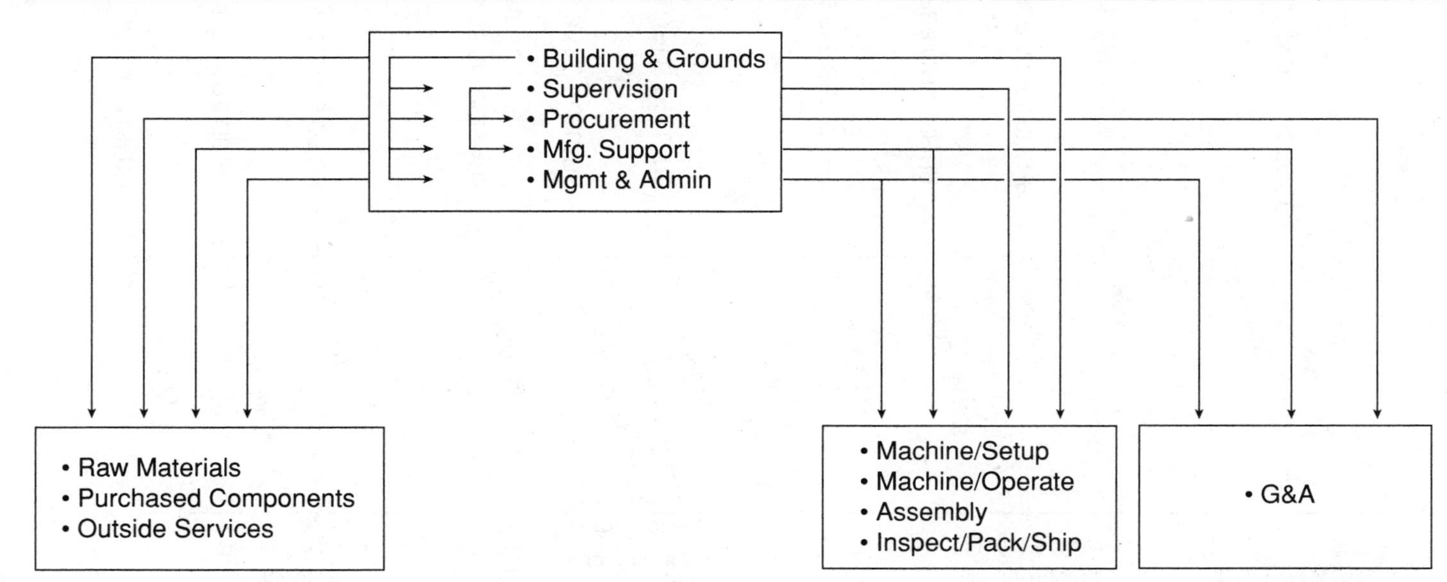

Exhibit 11.4 Assigning Activity Cost to Jobs/Products

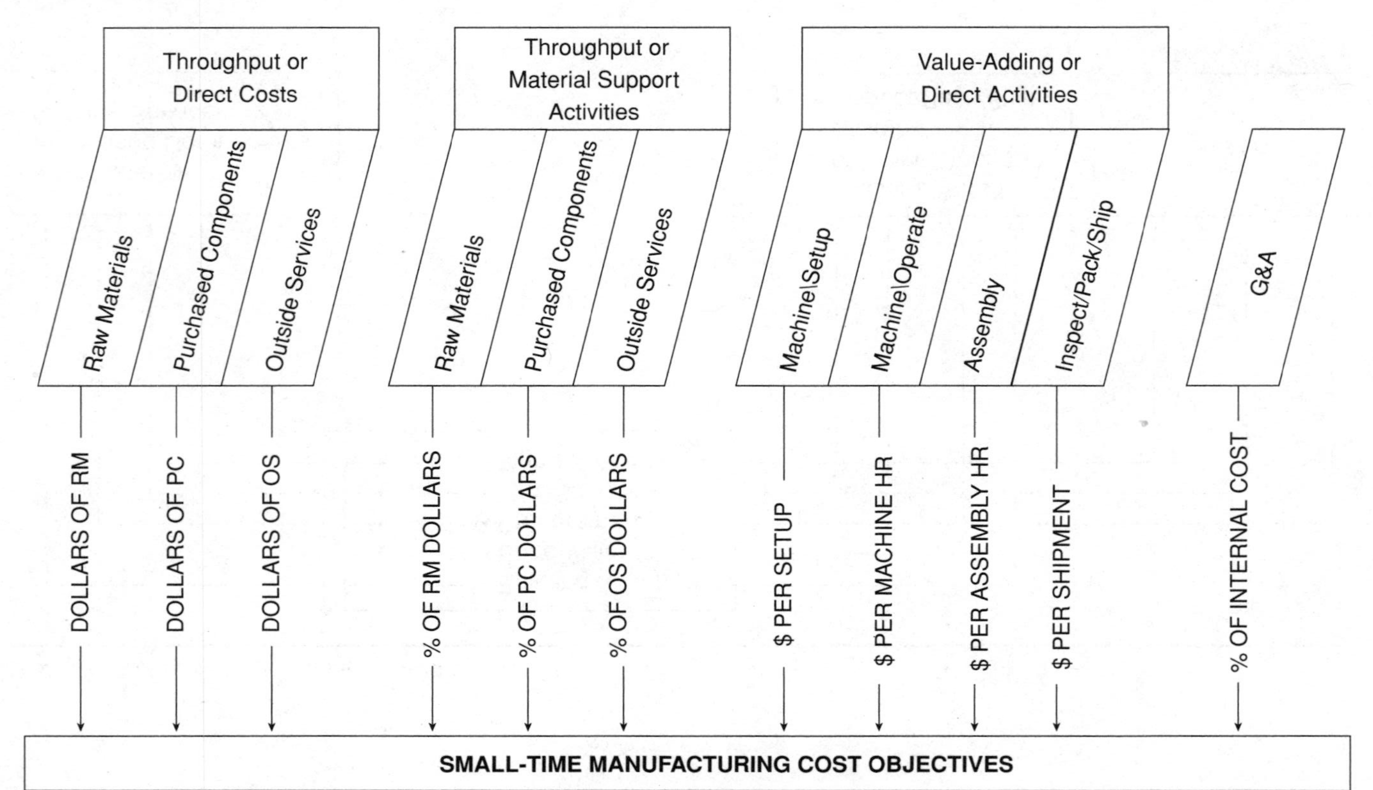

activities it performs for its customers (as defined during the conceptual stages of the analysis).

COST FLOW-DOWN STEP 3: ASSIGNING ACTIVITY COSTS TO JOBS/PRODUCTS

Statistical bases for the assignment of manufacturing and G&A costs were determined earlier in the ABC process. Recall that machine/setup and inspect/pack/ship will be event-driven activities and will be assigned to jobs as a cost per setup and as a cost per shipment, respectively. Machine/operate will be assigned as a cost per machine hour, and assembly will be assigned as a cost per direct labor hour. General and administrative will be charged to jobs as a percentage of internal activity costs.

To keep the process as simple as possible, management decided to attach throughput overhead costs to jobs as a percentage of throughput dollars. Although some other basis might be more precise, applying the cost on dollars does not require collecting any new information (e.g., pounds, pieces, trips) while still applying throughput-related overhead to the throughput, not to the manufacturing operations that used to carry these costs. Exhibit 11.4 shows Step 3 in the cost flow-down process.

SUMMARY

After completing the design of the company's activity-based cost flow-down structure, Small-Time Manufacturing's management was ready to take the next step—the development of a cost accumulation and distribution model that will accurately represent the company's cost structure and behavior.

12

Small-Time Manufacturing: Building the Cost Accumulation and Distribution Model

Part I—Cost Accumulation

Now that Small-Time Manufacturing's management has decided on a cost flow-down structure that they believe reflects the actual cost behavior of their company, they can develop a cost accumulation and distribution model that can be used to quantify that behavior. As outlined in Chapter 10, this model must have a bottom-up and then top-down structure. It must be able to accumulate the cost of providing the activities required to support a particular volume and mix of business and then develop rates to assign those costs to the individual products or services that make up that volume and mix of business.

I suggest that you boot up your computer and build the model along with the book. You need not be a spreadsheet-building expert to do so. By building the model, you will not only see how uncomplicated such a model really is, but you will be able to replicate the "what if" and other analyses that the model will be used for in Chapters 15 and 16. The model will be constructed as a single, two-dimensional worksheet and will follow the structure described in Chapter 11. The worksheet will be composed of a series of individual schedules that will interact with each other. You can visualize the model as a series of multicolumn "green sheet" schedules with the top of each schedule attached to the bottom of the schedule immediately preceding it. Although you can dress up your model to meet your personal tastes, the book's model will be presented in a plain vanilla format. There will be nothing included that you could not have done with spreadsheet software in the late 1980s.

None of the schedules in Small-Time Manufacturing's cost accumulation and distribution model will require more than 40 worksheet lines. As a result, we will start a new schedule at intervals of 40 lines (lines 41, 81, 121, 161, etc.). The widest schedule will be 18 columns wide, reaching to column "R." All columns will be set at a 12-character width. Finally, in the model exhibits, input data will be distinguished from the model itself by being presented in boxes. The boxes represent unprotected cells where the data required to drive the model is entered. The unboxed areas represent the protected cells where the formulae and text that comprise the model itself reside.

As we construct Small-Time Manufacturing's cost accumulation and distribution model, we will be entering data that represents its most recent year's actual operating information. The purpose of using this historical information is twofold: (1) to learn the relationships between drivers and the costs they drive and (2) to show that the model can actually recreate the total cost of operating the company using its products to activities to costs rationale.

Before being used for supporting management decisions, the model will need to be updated with more forward-looking information. After all, Small-Time Manufacturing will not be producing any more products last year, so costs and rates based on last year's information will not be of value. The value of last year's information is that it enables the model builder to gather the information necessary for the model to reflect economic realities.

In using a prior period's information, the model builder must make sure that *real* costs are used. Any distortions caused by the "deadly virus of GAAP" (generally accepted accounting principles) (see Chapter 4) should be corrected. Only then will historical costs be useful in projecting future cost behavior.

OPERATING INFORMATION AND RESOURCE REQUIREMENTS

As noted in Chapter 11, the model begins with the volume and mix of products or services for which costs are to be accumulated and distributed. The resource and activity requirements that result from this volume and mix of products will drive the organization's costs. As a result, we begin with a schedule that enables us to enter that information.

SCHEDULE #01: CONTRACT ACTIVITY SUMMARY

This schedule begins on line 41 of the worksheet. The first 40 lines will be reserved for a directory that we will create after the balance of the model is completed. As outlined in the previous chapter, there are seven items that drive Small-Time Manufacturing's costs; three are measures of direct or throughput costs and four drive the company's activities. The three direct or throughput cost measures are raw material, purchased components, and outside service dollars. The four activity drivers are the number of setups, machine hours, assembly labor hours, and shipments.

As shown in Exhibit 12.1, Schedule #01 provides for the entry of this information in a variety of ways. In the exhibit, data from the 10 contracts on which Small-Time Manufacturing worked during the previous year are entered. That is the volume and mix of business at which our example will be set. In the future, however, it will not be necessary for input data to represent actual contracts. A single line on this schedule could be used to simply enter amounts representing *practical capacity* or the *real* volume and mix of business as discussed in Chapter 4. Several lines could be used for booked business and other lines used to represent anticipated bookings. It is always advisable, however, to reserve several lines that can be used for "what if" scenarios. These will make it simpler to use the model to measure the impact on costs of incremental changes in the company's volume and mix of business that would be the result of various decision situations. In Exhibit 12.1, the three Scenario categories are set aside for this purpose.

The mathematics involved on this schedule are simply the summation of each column's amounts to arrive at the company's cost or activity measure in each of the seven categories. These totals are carried forward to Schedule #02.

SCHEDULE #02: OPERATING INFORMATION AND RESOURCE REQUIREMENTS

Schedule #02, shown in Exhibit 12.2, begins on line 81. It is included to provide a summary of the seven activity measures (brought forward from Schedule #01) and a place to enter activity center abbreviations for use in the model. Because the model's columns are 12 characters wide, abbreviations are developed for all activity centers that are 11 characters or less. These abbreviations will be carried forward automatically by the model to identify any column or row relating to the activity center. Once these abbreviations are established, we are ready to move forward and begin the cost accumulation process.

Exhibit 12.1 Contract Activity Summary

CONTRACT ACTIVITY SUMMARY

Schedule #01

Small-Time Manufacturing

	Raw Materials	Purchased Components	Outside Services	Number of Set-Ups	Machine Hours	Assembly Labor Hrs	Number of Shipments
Contract #01	$50,000	$20,000		20	800	1,000	25
Contract #02	$25,000	$10,000		40	800	500	100
Contract #03	$100,000	$40,000	$25,000	60	1,600	2,000	200
Contract #04	$50,000	$10,000		40	1,600	500	200
Contract #05	$50,000	$20,000	$75,000	20	400	1,000	50
Contract #06	$25,000	$40,000		40	400	2,000	50
Contract #07	$75,000	$20,000		60	600	1,000	150
Contract #08	$50,000	$60,000	$50,000	40	600	3,000	200
Contract #09	$50,000	$40,000		60	800	2,000	75
Contract #10	$25,000	$40,000	$50,000	20	400	2,000	150
Future Use							
Future Use							
Future Use							
Future Use							
Future Use							
Scenario #01							
Scenario #02							
Scenario #03							
Totals	$500,000	$300,000	$200,000	400	8,000	15,000	1,200

Exhibit 12.2 Operating Information and Resource Requirements

OPERATING INFORMATION AND RESOURCE REQUIREMENTS ==================================== Schedule #02

Small-Time Manufacturing

Description	Model Abbrev.	Cost or Activity Measure	Unit of Measure
Raw materials	Raw Mat'ls	$500,000	Dollars of throughput
Purchased components	Purch Comp	$300,000	Dollars of throughput
Outside services	OSServices	$200,000	Dollars of throughput
Machine/setup	Machine-SUp	400	Setups
Machining/operate	Machine-Opr	8,000	Machine hours
Assembly	Assembly	15,000	Direct labor hours
Inspect/pack/ship	Ins/Pak/Shp	1,200	Shipments
Service and operations			
Support activities:			
Building and grounds	Bldg & Grnd		
Supervision	Supervision		
Procurement	Procurement		
Manufacturing	Mfg Support		
Management/Admin	Mgmt & Admn		
G&A	Gen & Admin		

RESOURCE CONVERSION

To begin the accumulation of activity costs, activity measures for those activity centers that actually drive costs must be stated in terms of chronological operating time. Two of Small-Time Manufacturing's four activity drivers are already stated in those terms. Machine/operate and assembly are measured in machine hours and direct labor hours, respectively. Machine/setup and inspect/pack/ship are measured in terms of events, the number of setups for machine/setup and the number of shipments for inspect/pack/ship. These two must be translated into some form of operating time.

SCHEDULE #03: RESOURCE CONVERSION

Schedule #03, which begins on line 121, performs this resource conversion. As shown in Exhibit 12.3, the number of setups and shipments are brought forward from Schedule #02. The hours per setup and hours per shipment are entered as input data. The number of events is multiplied by the hours per event to arrive at the hours required: 1,200 machine hours for machine/setup and 2,400 direct labor hours for assembly. It is important to note that setups are being converted into machine hours, not direct labor hours. These hours represent the amount of time the machine is not available due to its being setup for the next job. Shipments are being translated into direct labor hours. As long as the selected time measure is appropriate for the activity, it does not matter what type of chronological time is used.

At this point, all cost-driving activity measures have been converted into some form of operating time. The next step in the model building structure is to provide any necessary screens to serve as macro capacity tests.

SCREENS

Screens are included in the model to ensure that there is enough capacity under existing model conditions to actually provide the amount of resources that are required. At Small-Time Manufacturing, assembly and inspect/pack/ship are not physically constrained by capacity within any relevant range of operations. If more activity is required, more workers can be hired. Machining, however, does represent a significant capacity constraint. The number of available machines cannot be increased or decreased in the same way that the number of workers can be adjusted. As a result, a screen is developed for the machine/operate activity center.

Exhibit 12.3 Resource Conversion

RESOURCE CONVERSION
====================
Small-Time Manufacturing

Schedule #03

Activity Center	Activity Measure	Activity Description	Hours per Measure	Operating Hours Required Quantity	Operating Hours Required Description
Machine-SUp	400	Setups	3.0	1,200	Machine hours
Ins/Pak/Shp	1,200	Shipments	2.0	2,400	Direct labor hours

SCHEDULE #04: SCREEN

Schedule #04, which begins on line 161, provides the screen for machining activities. As shown in Exhibit 12.4, certain data must be entered to arrive at the maximum hours that would be available. This data includes the number of machine centers that are available (MC), the number of shifts the company will be in operation each day (SH), the number of hours worked in a shift (HR), and the number of days the plant will operate in a year (DY). The product of these four items (MC × SH × HR × DY) calculates the maximum hours of machine time available per year. In our example, the total is 10,100 machine hours (5 machines × 1 shift × 8 hours × 252.5 days). As you will learn later, Small-Time Manufacturing's employees are allowed 30 minutes of paid breaktime daily. If the machines were shut down during this break period, only 9,394 machine hours would be available (5 machines × 1 shift × 7.5 hours × 252.5 days), because they would be in operation only seven and one-half hours per day. It is Small-Time Manufacturing's practice, however, to stagger the breaks of machine operators so that the equipment can remain in operation a full eight hours per shift.

Having calculated the maximum hours available for machining operations, the company must now deduct the amount of machine time that will be consumed by nonproduction activities. One of these nonproduction activities has already been measured elsewhere in the model. On Schedule #03, the model determined that 1,200 machine hours would be lost while the machine was being setup (remember that setups were converted into machine hours, not direct labor hours). These hours are brought forward and deducted from the maximum hours available.

In addition to setup, there are other causes of machine downtime, the major one being maintenance. To account for this, the model provides for the input of an additional downtime percentage to cover the additional production hours lost. On Schedule #04, the percentage is entered as a percentage of maximum hours available. This percentage goes on to calculate the additional lost hours and subtract them, along with the setup hours, from the maximum hours available. The result is the number of machine hours that are actually available for production.

Schedule #04 then brings forward the machine hours required from Schedule #02, compares them to the net hours available, and determines whether the amount of production required can actually be provided under the model's assumptions. If a cushion exists, as is the case in our example, the balance of the model's input can be based on the assumed number of machines, shifts, hours per shift, days per year, and downtime percentage included on the schedule. If the screen shows that not enough hours are available, the schedule's assumptions must be modified until a cushion exists and the balance of the model's input based on the revised assumptions.

Exhibit 12.4 Screen for Machining Activities

```
SCREEN FOR MACHINING ACTIVITIES                          Schedule #04
=====================
Small-Time Manufacturing


Machine centers available                                          5

Shifts in operation                            1.0
Hours per shift                                8.0
Days per year                                252.5             2,020
                                                             -------
Maximum hours available                                       10,100
Set-up hours                                                 (1,200)
Maintenance and other downtime                  5%             (505)
                                                             -------
Net hours available                                            8,395
Hours required                                                 8,000
                                                             -------

Hours over (short)                                               395
                                                             =======
```

OPERATING MANPOWER DEMAND

Now that all cost-driving activity measures are stated in terms of operating hours and the required machine hours have cleared the screen, the model can proceed to calculate the amount of variable labor that results from the volume and mix of activities entered on Schedule #01. This is accomplished by multiplying each activity center's operating hours by the crew size required during each operating hour. This determines the minimum or net production labor hours required. This amount is then increased by an *indirect activity allowance* to "gross up" production labor hours to the amount that history has shown will actually be required. A detailed discussion of this process is included in Chapter 8.

SCHEDULE #05: OPERATING MANPOWER/DEMAND

Schedule #05, shown in Exhibit 12.5, begins on line 201. It begins by bringing forward the operating hours from Schedule #02 (for machine/operate

Exhibit 12.5 Operating Manpower/Demand

OPERATING MANPOWER / DEMAND

Schedule #05

Small-Time Manufacturing

	Operating Hours	Crew Size	Net Production Labor Hrs	Indirect Activity Allowance	Gross Production Labor Hrs
Machine-SUp	1,200	2.0	2,400	20%	2,880
Machine-Opr	8,000	0.6	4,800	30%	6,240
Assembly	15,000	1.0	15,000	20%	18,000
Ins/Pak/Shp	2,400	1.0	2,400	20%	2,880
Totals			24,600		30,000

and assembly) or Schedule #03 (for machine/setup and inspect/pack/ship). The average crew size for each activity center is entered and the net production labor hours calculated.

At this point, Small-Time Manufacturing's model builder compares these hours, which represent the "perfect world" number of hours that are required, with the actual number of hours worked in these areas. The actual hours were:

Machine/setup	2,880 hours
Machine/operate	6,240 hours
Assembly	18,000 hours
Inspect/pack/ship	2,880 hours

In order for the model to arrive at these hours, an indirect activity allowance of 20% must be entered for machine/setup, assembly, and inspect/pack/ship and a 30% allowance entered for machine/operate.

This is the first instance in developing the model in which historical information is used to "solve for B." As you may have already noted, the model is filled with A × B = C calculations. A is either an input or a number calculated by the model. In order to arrive at C, which is a function of A, the relationship between A and C must be determined. The measure of that relationship is B.

Earlier in the model, B was determined by a direct method—either observation, interview, or analysis of detailed records. For example, on Schedule #03, the machine hours per setup and the direct labor hours per shipment could be determined by one of these direct methods. Similarly, the crew sizes that are entered on this schedule could also be determined by direct means. The indirect activity allowance, however, is not something that can usually be measured directly, especially by a smaller organization whose time-keeping records do not break down production labor activity in fine detail. As a result, the indirect activity allowance must be backed into by solving for B.

Returning to our equation, as we construct the model, A is known and C is known from computation or historical information. Because we know that A × B = C, the model builder can solve the equation for B and enter the answer as a model input. We do not want the model to solve for B. It must be calculated outside of the model. The model must use A and B to determine C as it projects cost behavior. Although it is always preferable to calculate B by some direct method, solving for B provides an accurate estimate in cases in which direct methods are either unavailable or impractical.

At some companies, the breakdown of actual operating labor by activity center might not be available. Only total operating labor hours are known.

This should not be an obstacle to completing this schedule. If Small-Time Manufacturing knew only that it paid for 30,000 gross production labor hours, it could have done one of two things: It could simply have developed an overall indirect activity allowance of 22% by comparing the 24,600 net hours to the 30,000 gross hours, or it could have had the most appropriate individuals in management estimate a breakdown of the 30,000 hours among the four activity centers. Either way, it would have been developing an accurate (not precise) estimate of input that is essential for the effective functioning of its model. As is always the case, it is better to estimate the input data that is needed than to ignore it because precise data is not available.

AUTOMATICALLY VARIABLE COSTS

Because the volume and mix of business entered at the beginning of the model has cleared the model's screen, the model can proceed to calculate the automatically variable costs that are being driven by Schedule #02's activity measures. The only major expense item that fits the *automatically variable* definition in machine/setup, assembly, and inspect/pack/ship is manufacturing supplies. Last year's manufacturing supply costs associated with these areas were $16,000, $45,000, and $18,000 respectively. Two expense items fit the automatically variable definition in machine/operate. These are utilities and tooling. Utility costs relating to machining operations were $80,000 and tooling costs were $60,000.

SCHEDULE #06: AUTOMATICALLY VARIABLE COSTS

Schedule #06, shown in Exhibit 12.6 starts on line 241. It begins by bringing forward the driver measures from Schedule #02. By solving for B, Small-Time's model builder develops a manufacturing supply cost per setup for machine/setup, per direct labor hour for assembly, and per shipment for inspect/pack/ship. A utility cost and a tooling cost per machine hour are developed for machine/operate by again solving for B. Once these five input items are determined, they can be entered into the model where they are multiplied by the appropriate driver measures to arrive at total automatically variable costs for each activity center.

OPERATING MANPOWER SUPPLY

The next step in accumulating costs is to determine how the company will supply the demand for production labor hours calculated on Schedule #05.

Exhibit 12.6 Automatically Variable Costs

AUTOMATICALLY VARIABLE COSTS — Schedule #06

Small-Time Manufacturing

	Activity				
	Measure	Description	Variable Expense	Cost/Unit	Cost
Machine-SUp	400	Setups	Mfg Supply	$40.00	$16,000
Machine-Opr	8,000	machine hours	Utilities	$10.00	$80,000
			Tooling	$7.50	$60,000
Assembly	15,000	direct labor hours	Mfg Supply	$3.00	$45,000
Ins/Pak/Shp	1,200	shipments	Mfg Supply	$15.00	$18,000
				Total	$219,000

As discussed in Chapter 8, there are various combinations of headcount and overtime that will provide the required labor hours, each resulting in a different cost. The model must provide for the balancing act that must take place to ensure that the headcount/overtime combination is reasonable.

SCHEDULE #07: OPERATING MANPOWER/HOURS AVAILABLE

Before beginning the operating labor demand/supply balancing act, the net annual straight-time hours available for each full-time equivalent (FTE) employee must be determined. Schedule #07, which starts on line 281 and is shown in Exhibit 12.7, is included for this purpose. To arrive at net annual straight-time hours per FTE, the model needs to subtract all paid time off hours as well as absent hours from the gross straight-time hours per FTE. Although not technically time off, paid time off hours also includes time that is not available for production due to training sessions, quality meetings, and the like.

The schedule first requires the input of gross straight-time hours per FTE. At most companies, this is assumed to be 2,080 hours (8 hours per day × 5 days per week × 52 weeks per year). From that total, any paid time off hours must be subtracted. At Small-Time Manufacturing, these include vacations, holidays, and paid breaks. The average hourly employee receives 60 hours of paid vacation, the company has 7.5 paid vacation days, and there are two 15-minute breaks each day. In addition, the average employee is absent (without pay) 80 hours annually. The hours of paid vacation and holiday time can be entered directly into the model, as can the hours of absenteeism. The total hours of paid break time, however, are dependent not only on the daily break minutes, but also on the paid vacation and holiday time as well as the time absent. The breaktime should not be included for days the employee is not on the job.

This results in one of the few "tricky" cell formulae in the model (it is not really that tricky, just trickier than A × B = C). Hours absent for vacation (VH), holiday (HH), and absences (AH) must be subtracted from gross hours (GH) to arrive at the number of hours on the job annually. Of that time, a percentage of time determined by dividing break minutes (BM) by minutes per day (DM) represents the portion of annual on the job hours that the employees are on breaks. The cell formula would, therefore, be as follows: (GH – VH – HH – AH)/(BM/DM). In the model, the answer is rounded to the nearest whole hour.

After entering the 30 daily break minutes, Small-Time Manufacturing's model performs the calculation as follows: (2,080 hours – 60 hours – 60 hours – 80 hours)/(30 minutes/480 minutes) = 117.5 hours. When rounded to the nearest whole hour, annual break time is 118 hours.

Exhibit 12.7 Operating Manpower/Hours Available

OPERATING MANPOWER / HOURS AVAILABLE				Schedule #07
Small-Time Manufacturing				
Gross straight-time hours/employee			2,080	100.0%
Paid time off hours:				
Vacation		60		
Holidays		60		
Breaks	30 mins/day =	118		
Paid time off hours			238	11.4%
Absenteeism			80	3.8%
Net straight-time hours/employee			1,762	84.7%
Annual straight-time hours paid/employee			2,000	96.2%

The schedule then goes on to calculate the net straight-time hours per FTE (2,080 hours – 238 paid time off hours – 80 absent hours = 1,762 hours) and annual straight-time hours paid per FTE (2,080 hours – 80 absent hours = 2,000 hours). Both of these amounts are also calculated as a percentage of gross straight-time hours.

SCHEDULE #08: OPERATING MANPOWER/SUPPLY

On Schedule #05, the model calculated the demand for production labor. On Schedule #07, it calculated the straight-time hours available per FTE. With this information, it is now possible to determine how the company supplies the necessary production labor hours. Schedule #08, which starts on line 321 and is shown in Exhibit 12.8, is included for this purpose. The straight-time hours per FTE are brought forward from Schedule #07. The gross production labor hours are brought forward from Schedule #05.

Straight-time hours available are calculated by multiplying the FTE headcounts (which are input on this schedule) by the straight-time hours per FTE. Available hours are then subtracted from gross production labor hours and the difference, if positive, treated as overtime hours required. If the difference is negative, overtime is assumed to be zero (the model assumes that there is no *undertime*, only *idle* time). This is accomplished with a simple "If" formula that instructs the model to enter the difference if it is equal to or greater than zero and enter a zero if the difference is less than zero. The overtime percentages are then calculated for each activity center by dividing the overtime hours by the straight-time hours available.

The balancing act takes place by entering FTE headcounts for each activity center until the overtime percentage is reasonable. At Small-Time Manufacturing, employees cannot be transferred among the four production activity centers. Setup personnel perform only setups. Assemblers do only assembly work. As a result, fractions of FTE are only possible if the company has full-time employees for part of the year. They cannot be used to split an individual employee's time among the activity centers.

As you will recall from Schedule #05, a two-person crew is required in machine/setup. This means that Small-Time Manufacturing cannot have less than two FTEs assigned to this activity center. As can be seen from the schedule, this results in underutilization of setup personnel. Only 2,880 hours are required while 3,542 hours will be available and must be paid for.

Machine/operate and assembly have no such minimum headcount requirement. Various FTEs can be tried until an appropriate level of overtime is reached. In the exhibit, three machine operators and nine assemblers will generate a reasonable amount of overtime. One less machine operator would have resulted in an overtime percentage of over 75%, not

Exhibit 12.8 Operating Manpower/Supply

OPERATING MANPOWER / SUPPLY Schedule #08

Small-Time Manufacturing

	FTE Headcount	St-Time Hours per Employee	Total St-Time Hours Available	Gross Production Labor Hrs Required	Overtime Hours Required	Percentage Overtime Required
Machine-SUp	2.0	1,762	3,524	2,880	0	0.0%
Machine-Opr	3.0	1,762	5,286	6,240	954	15.3%
Assembly	9.0	1,762	15,858	18,000	2,142	11.9%
Ins/Pak/Shp	2.0	1,762	3,524	2,880	0	0.0%
Totals	16.0			30,000	3,096	10.3%

a reasonable amount. One more operator would have provided over 800 more hours than required. Therefore, three operators seems to be the most reasonable number. In assembly, 10 operators would have been fully utilized and still have required about 2% overtime. Eight operators would have required overtime in excess of 25%. Management decided that the 11.9% overtime level required with nine employees was the most appropriate scenario.

Inspect/pack/ship has no minimum employment level like machine/setup, but it does pose another problem. The level of activity in inspect/pack/ship is fairly stable during the year. There are no unusually high levels of activity that are offset by unusually low levels of activity. As a result, the company must have a stable level of resources available in this activity center all year long. The most logical way for Small-Time Manufacturing to do this is to have two employees assigned to inspect/pack/ship. This does result, however, in the same situation that existed in machine/setup, an underutilization of the workforce.

At the conclusion of this balancing act, Small-Time has determined the combination of headcount and overtime that best meets its gross production labor requirements.

SCHEDULE #09: OPERATING MANPOWER/COST

Now that the model has not only determined the amount of production labor required to produce the volume and mix of products entered on Schedule #01, but how much of each activity center's production labor will be at straight time and at overtime, it can proceed to calculate production labor cost. Full-time equivalent headcounts are brought forward from Schedule #08. The average straight-time hours paid per FTE are brought forward from Schedule #07. After entering the hourly pay rate for each activity center, as shown on Schedule #09 in Exhibit 12.9, gross straight-time pay can be calculated by multiplying the FTE headcount by the average straight-time hours paid and then multiplying that product by the average hourly pay rate. In assembly, for example, nine employees are each paid for 2,000 straight-time hours at $8 per hour. The result (9 employees × 2,000 hours × $8) is $144,000.

Part of this gross straight-time pay is not for production efforts; it is payment for time not worked. On Schedule #07, it was determined that each of Small-Time Manufacturing's employees was paid for 238 hours of holiday, vacation, and breaktime. As a result, the model can determine what portion of the gross straight-time pay is properly classified as a paid time off benefit by bringing forward total paid time off hours from Schedule #07, multiplying it by each activity center's FTE headcount, and multiplying that

Exhibit 12.9 Operating Manpower/Cost

OPERATING MANPOWER / COST　　　　Schedule #09

Small-Time Manufacturing

	FTE Headcount	Average Hourly Pay Rate	Average St-Time Hours Paid	Gross St-Time Pay	Paid Time Off Benefits	Paid St-Time Worked
Machine-SUp	2.0	$12.00	2,000	$48,000	$5,712	$42,288
Machine-Opr	3.0	$10.00	2,000	$60,000	$7,140	$52,860
Assembly	9.0	$8.00	2,000	$144,000	$17,136	$126,864
Ins/Pak/Shp	2.0	$8.00	2,000	$32,000	$3,808	$28,192
Totals	16.0			$284,000	$33,796	$250,204

	Overtime Hours	Average Hourly Pay Rate	St-Time Overtime Paid	Overtime Premium @ 50%	Total St-Time Paid	Total Paid
Machine-SUp	0	$12.00	$0	$0	$42,288	$42,288
Machine-Opr	954	$10.00	$9,540	$4,770	$62,400	$67,170
Assembly	2,142	$8.00	$17,136	$8,568	$144,000	$152,568
Ins/Pak/Shp	0	$8.00	$0	$0	$28,192	$28,192
Totals	3,096		$26,676	$13,338	$276,880	$290,218

product by the center's average hourly pay rate. Again using assembly as an example, 238 hours of time off would be paid to nine employees at $8 per hour. The result (238 hours × 9 employees × $8) is $17,136. This amount is then subtracted from gross straight-time pay to determine straight-time pay for production hours worked.

Schedule #08 calculated the number of overtime hours worked by production personnel in each activity center. These hours are brought forward and multiplied by the hourly rates to calculate additional straight-time pay resulting from this overtime. Since Small-Time Manufacturing pays a 50% premium for all overtime worked, the schedule proceeds to multiply the straight-time overtime paid by 50% to determine the resulting overtime premium. The two straight-time categories, regular straight-time and straight-time overtime, are combined to arrive at the total straight-time wages paid for production activities and then overtime premium is added to arrive at total wages paid for production activities.

STEP VARIABLE COSTS—SUPPORT STAFF

At this point in the model, all of the variable costs that are directly impacted by the volume and mix of business entered on Schedule #01 have been accumulated. What remains to be accumulated are the nonvariable costs. The first group to be addressed are the step variable costs.

The majority of step variable costs relate to the company's service and operations support activities. The amount of support activity will generally rise and fall as the volume and mix of business changes, but there is no simple method of directly linking the effort required of each support activity to volume and mix. Note that there is no *simple* method. There are complicated methods. An algorithm might be devised to link the number of purchasing personnel to the volume and mix of direct and throughput costs. Another might be devised to link the number of manufacturing support personnel to the number of contracts, setups, and shipments. At small and mid-sized firms this is seldom worth the effort. After all, we are talking about relatively small staffs and relatively indirect linkages.

SCHEDULE #10: SUPPORT STAFF

Schedule #10, which begins on line 401 and is shown in Exhibit 12.10, provides for the entry of support staff information. The FTE headcounts and average salary (stated in terms of pay per hour) are entered for each activity center. Because salary personnel are not docked for absenteeism, the gross straight-time hours paid are brought forward from Schedule #07.

Exhibit 12.10 Support Staff

SUPPORT STAFF
=============

Small-Time Manufacturing

Schedule #10

	FTE Headcount	Average Hourly Pay Rate	Average St-Time Hours Paid	Gross St-Time Pay	Paid Time Off Benefits	Paid St-Time Worked
Bldg & Grnd	1.0	$11.54	2,080	$24,000	$2,747	$21,253
Supervision	2.0	$17.31	2,080	$72,000	$8,240	$63,760
Procurement	1.0	$19.23	2,080	$40,000	$4,577	$35,423
Mfg Support	5.0	$14.42	2,080	$150,000	$17,160	$132,840
Mgmt & Admn	5.0	$19.23	2,080	$200,000	$22,884	$177,116
Gen & Admin	xxxx	xxxx	xxxx	xxxx	xxxx	xxxx
Totals	14.0			$486,000	$55,606	$430,394

Gross straight-time pay is calculated by multiplying the FTE headcount by the average straight-time hours paid and that product multiplied by the average hourly pay rate. On Schedule #10, this calculation is rounded to the nearest $100. As was the case with production workers, the paid time off benefits are separated from paid time worked. On Schedule #10, the paid time off benefits are calculated by multiplying gross straight-time pay by the paid time off benefit percentage on Schedule #07. Subtracting this amount from gross straight-time pay determines the salaries paid for time worked.

You will note that the model does not allow for entering any personnel information directly to the sales/general/administrative activity center. As a general rule, it is advisable to never let anyone attribute their work directly to G&A. It is too easy for managers to cavalierly attribute all of their effort as G&A when, in reality, there is not much activity that cannot be attributed to some other activity center. By not allowing any personnel to be directly assigned to a G&A category, they are forced to at least consider the distribution of their work to other activity centers. At Small-Time Manufacturing, those personnel normally considered as G&A are included in management/administration and their efforts must be distributed later in the model.

FRINGE BENEFITS AND OTHER HEADCOUNT-DRIVEN COSTS

With all of the company's personnel and their wages accumulated in the model, it is possible to determine certain costs that are automatically variable once the step variable elements of cost are known. These are fringe benefits and other headcount-driven costs.

SCHEDULE #11: FRINGE BENEFITS

There are two types of fringe benefits: payments made to employees for time not worked and payments to outside parties on behalf of the employees. Those payments made to outside parties on behalf of the employees can usually be reduced to a cost per employee, a cost per dollar paid, or a cost per hour worked. Small-Time Manufacturing has no benefits that relate to hours worked, but employer FICA/Medicare and pension/profit sharing are driven by gross wages and health insurance and unemployment taxes are driven by headcount. Payments made to employees for time not worked have already been calculated on Schedules #09 and #10.

Schedule #11, which begins on line 441 and is shown in Exhibit 12.11, provides for the calculation of fringe benefit costs and development of a fringe benefit rate for distributing fringe benefits among the activity centers.

Exhibit 12.11 Fringe Benefits

FRINGE BENEFITS
Small-Time Manufacturing

Schedule #11

	Headcount	Gross Wages	Cost per Head/$	Fringe Benefit Expense
Health insurance	30.0		$3,000	$90,000
Employer FICA/Medicare		$776,218	7.65%	$59,381
Fed/state unemployment	30.0		$200	$6,000
Pension/profit sharing		$776,218	3.00%	$23,287
Total purchased fringe benefits				$178,667
Hourly paid time off				$33,796
Salary paid time off				$55,606
Total fringe benefits				$268,070
Straight-time hourly wages				$276,880
Straight-time salary wages				$430,394
Total fringe benefit base wages				$707,274
Fringe rate				37.9%

Headcount and gross wage information is brought forward from Schedules #08, #09, and #10. The cost per head or cost per dollar of wages is entered for each benefit category. The model proceeds to multiply each benefit's driver by its cost per unit of driver to determine the cost of each fringe benefit paid to an outside party. The paid time off benefits from Schedules #09 and #10 are added to the total fringe benefits paid to outside parties to arrive at the company's total fringe benefit cost.

Small-Time Manufacturing selected straight-time wages as a base for distributing fringe benefit costs among the activity centers. Total straight-time wages were brought forward from Schedules #09 and #10 and added together to provide the fringe benefit base. Dividing total fringe benefits by the fringe benefit base wages establishes a fringe benefit rate calculated as a percentage of straight-time wages.

In this model, hourly and salary fringes were combined for a rate. This was done to keep the model relatively simple. In most companies, separate salary and hourly rates would be established. The mechanics for each calculation would be similar to those included in Small-Time's model.

SCHEDULE #12: OTHER HEADCOUNT-DRIVEN COSTS

Schedule #12, which begins on line 481 and is shown in Exhibit 12.12, provides for the calculation of other headcount driven costs. At Small-Time Manufacturing, the other headcount-driven costs are administrative supplies attributable to service and operations support activities. Headcounts are brought forward from Schedule #10 and a cost per head for administrative supplies entered. This is another area where the cost per head can be determined by solving for B. The headcounts are multiplied by the per head costs to calculate administrative supply cost.

FIXED COSTS AND BUDGETED COSTS

The only costs that must still be addressed are the fixed and budgeted costs. These costs are either fixed over a wide range of operating activity or are influenced more by management's discretion than by any change in the volume and mix of business.

SCHEDULE #13: FIXED AND BUDGETED COSTS

Schedule #13, which begins on line 521 and is shown in Exhibits 12.13 and 12.14, provides a matrix for entering fixed and budgeted costs. The company's activity centers comprise the matrix's rows and various types of costs

Exhibit 12.12 Other Headcount-Driven Costs

OTHER HEADCOUNT-DRIVEN COSTS — Schedule #12

Small-Time Manufacturing

	Activity		Variable		
	Measure	Description	Expense	Cost/Unit	Cost
Bldg & Grnd	1.0	Headcount	Adm Supply	$1,000	$1,000
Supervision	2.0	Headcount	Adm Supply	$500	$1,000
Procurement	1.0	Headcount	Adm Supply	$3,000	$3,000
Mfg Support	5.0	Headcount	Adm Supply	$1,000	$5,000
Mgmt & Admn	5.0	Headcount	Adm Supply	$3,000	$15,000
Gen & Admin	xxxx				
				Total	$25,000

Exhibit 12.13 Fixed and Budgeted Costs

FIXED AND BUDGETED COSTS
========================
Small-Time Manufacturing

Schedule #13
Page 1 of 2

	Deprecia-tion	Leases	Telephone	Property Taxes/Ins	Travel & Entertain
Bldg & Grnd	$5,000	$50,000	$600	$30,000	
Supervision	$500		$1,200		$1,000
Procurement	$500		$3,200		$4,000
Mfg Support	$1,000		$1,800		$1,000
Mgmt & Admn	$1,000		$3,200		$25,000
Gen & Admin					
Raw Mat'ls	$4,000			$3,000	
Purch Comp	$2,000			$5,000	
OSServices	$1,000				
Machine-SUp					
Machine-Opr	$50,000			$10,000	
Assembly	$8,000			$1,000	
Ins/Pak/Shp	$7,000			$1,000	
Totals	$80,000	$50,000	$10,000	$50,000	$31,000

Exhibit 12.14 Fixed and Budgeted Costs

FIXED AND BUDGETED COSTS
========================
Small-Time Manufacturing

Schedule #13
Page 2 of 2

	Describe	$	Total
Bldg & Grnd	Pur Maint	$10,000	$95,600
Supervision	Training	$9,000	$11,700
Procurement	Training	$3,000	$10,700
Mfg Support	Training	$5,000	$8,800
Mgmt & Admn	Training	$12,000	$41,200
Gen & Admin	Legal/Acct	$15,000	$15,000
Raw Mat'ls	Describe		$7,000
Purch Comp	Describe		$7,000
OSServices	Describe		$7,000
Machine-SUp	Describe		$0
Machine-Opr	Pur Maint	$25,000	$85,000
Assembly	Describe		$9,000
Ins/Pak/Shp	Describe		$8,000
Totals		$79,000	$300,000

its columns. Two columns are set aside for entering types of costs not covered in the column headings: one column to describe the cost and the other to enter the amount. Once the cost information is entered, totals are determined by activity center and by cost type.

Once this schedule is completed, all costs required to operate Small-Time Manufacturing at the volume and mix of business entered on Schedule #01 have been accumulated.

TOTAL COST ACCUMULATION

Schedules #03 through #13 have been used to calculate the cost of supporting the volume and mix of business entered on Schedule #01 using a methodical step-by-step process. Each step addressed a particular issue or element of cost that needed to be resolved before future steps could be taken. Upon completion of Schedule #13, enough information is available to not only determine the company's total cost, but to assign those costs to the activity centers in which they would belong at the completion of Cost Flow-Down Step 1, the assignment of costs to activities.

SCHEDULE #14: COST ACCUMULATION

Schedule #14, which begins on line 561 and is shown in Exhibits 12.15 through 12.17, provides a summary of all cost accumulation activity and the assignment of costs through the first cost flow-down step. Except for its final two columns, the schedule's columns represent each of the activity centers or, in the case of fringe benefits, a cost pool. The final two columns summarize the company's direct or throughput costs and each cost category's total cost. No data needs to be entered on this schedule. All information is brought forward from earlier schedules.

Costs relating to the three throughput cost categories (raw materials, purchased components, and outside services) are brought forward from Schedule #02. These costs can be assigned directly to cost objectives so they are not included in any activity center.

"Support—Base" wages are brought forward from Schedule #10 and are entered in the appropriate activity center's column. "Manufacturing—Base" and "Manufacturing—ST-OT" (ST-OT is shorthand for straight-time overtime) and brought forward to the appropriate activity centers from Schedule #09. This sum of these amounts determines the total straight-time wages applicable to each activity center.

"Fringe benefits" are brought forward to the Fringe Benefits column from Schedule #11. The model then proceeds to use the fringe rate calculated on Schedule #11 to distribute fringe benefit costs among the activity centers as a percentage of straight-time wages. For example, the $35,423 in straight-time wages accumulated in procurement is multiplied by the 37.9% fringe rate from Schedule #11 to arrive at the $13,426 fringe cost attributable to procurement. The total of these fringe applications is subtracted from total fringe benefit costs in the Fringe Benefits column to assure that all of the costs have been distributed. The fact that both the Fringe Benefits column and the Applied Fringe Benefit row "zero out" attests to the distribution of all fringe costs.

After the fringe benefits have been applied, "Overtime premium" is brought forward from Schedule #09 to complete the accumulation of wage and fringe costs attributable to each activity center.

"Utilities," "tooling," and "mfg supplies" are all brought forward from Schedule #06 and included in the appropriate activity center. In like

Exhibit 12.15 Cost Accumulation

COST ACCUMULATION
Small-Time Manufacturing

Schedule #14
Page 1 of 3

	Fringe Benefits	Bldg & Grnd	Supervision	Procurement	Mfg Support	Mgmt & Admn
Throughput Costs:						
Raw materials						
Purchased components						
Outside services						
Wages & Fringes:						
Support–Base		$21,253	$63,760	$35,423	$132,840	$177,116
Manufacturing–Base						
Manufacturing–ST/OT						
Total S-time wages		$21,253	$63,760	$35,423	$132,840	$177,116
Fringe benefits	$268,070					
Applied fringes	($268,070)	$8,055	$24,166	$13,426	$50,349	$67,130
Overtime premium						
Total wages & fringes	$0	$29,309	$87,927	$48,849	$183,189	$244,247
Costs & Expenses:						
Utilities						
Tooling						
Mfg supplies						
Admin supplies		$1,000	$1,000	$3,000	$5,000	$15,000
Fixed/budget expenses		$95,600	$11,700	$10,700	$8,800	$41,200
Total Accumulated Costs:	$0	$125,909	$100,627	$62,549	$196,989	$300,447

Exhibit 12.16 Cost Accumulation

COST ACCUMULATION
Small-Time Manufacturing

Schedule #14
Page 2 of 3

	Gen & Admin	Raw Mat'ls	Purch Comp	OSServices
Throughput costs:				
Raw materials				
Purchased components				
Outside services				
Wages & fringes:				
Support–Base				
Manufacturing–Base				
Manufacturing–ST/OT				
Total S-time wages				
Fringe benefits				
Applied fringes				
Overtime premium				
Total wages & fringes				
Costs & expenses:				
Utilities				
Tooling				
Mfg supplies				
Admin supplies				
Fixed/budget expenses	$15,000	$7,000	$7,000	$1,000
Total accumulated costs:	$15,000	$7,000	$7,000	$1,000

Exhibit 12.17 Cost Accumulation

COST ACCUMULATION
Small-Time Manufacturing

Schedule #14
Page 3 of 3

	Machine-SUp	Machine-Opr	Assembly	Ins/Pak/Shp	Throughput Costs	Total
Throughput costs:						
Raw materials					$500,000	$500,000
Purchased components					$300,000	$300,000
Outside services					$200,000	$200,000
Wages & fringes:						
Support–Base						$430,394
Manufacturing–Base	$42,288	$52,860	$126,864	$28,192		$250,204
Manufacturing–ST/OT	$0	$9,540	$17,136	$0		$26,676
Total S-time wages	$42,288	$62,400	$144,000	$28,192		$707,274
Fringe benefits						$0
Applied fringes	$16,028	$23,651	$54,579	$10,685		$104,943
Overtime premium	$0	$4,770	$8,568	$0		$13,338
Total wages & fringes	$58,316	$90,821	$207,147	$38,877		$988,681
Costs & expenses:						
Utilities		$80,000				$80,000
Tooling		$60,000				$60,000
Mfg supplies	$16,000		$45,000	$18,000		$79,000
Admin supplies						$25,000
Fixed/budget expenses	$0	$85,000	$9,000	$8,000		$300,000
Total accumulated costs:	$74,316	$315,821	$261,147	$64,877	$1,000,000	$2,532,681

manner, "admin supplies" are brought forward from Schedule #12 and "fixed/budget expenses" are brought forward from Schedule #13.

The total of each activity center's costs are calculated (the column totals), as are the total of each type of cost (the row totals).

SUMMARY

At this point, all costs have been accumulated and distributed to the activity centers to which they are directly related. What remains is to complete the cost distribution process and develop rates for assigning activity costs to Small-Time Manufacturing's cost objectives.

13

Small-Time Manufacturing: Building the Cost Accumulation and Distribution Model

Part II—Cost Distribution

At this point in its development, Small-Time Manufacturing's model can start with a given volume and mix of business and accumulate the costs required to support that volume and mix of business. Due to the step-by-step mechanics of the model, those costs are not just known in total, but have been accumulated in those activity centers where they would properly be assigned after Cost Flow-down Step 1. What remains is to proceed with Cost Flow-down Step 2, which performs any necessary interactivity center cost distributions and Cost Flow-down Step 3, which develops rates for assigning activity costs to cost objectives.

Small-Time Manufacturing's model contains five service and support activity centers whose accumulated costs need to be distributed to other activity centers. These five activity centers are building & grounds, supervision, procurement, manufacturing support, and management/administration. Building & grounds and supervision are to be distributed using measurable statistical bases. Building & grounds is to be distributed using square footage, and supervision using headcount. Procurement, manufacturing support, and management/administration are to be distributed using percentages obtained through an analysis of each activity center's activities.

OTHER DATA AND COST DISTRIBUTION

Although the basic headcount information needed to distribute supervision is already in the model, the square footage information required to distribute building & grounds is not. As a result, provision must be made for the entry of this information into the model. Similarly, the model must also provide for the entry of the distribution percentages developed for procurement, manufacturing support, and management/administration.

SCHEDULE #15: SQUARE FOOTAGE

Schedule #15, which begins on line 601 and is shown in Exhibit 13.1, provides for entry of the square footage amounts assigned to each activity center. As can be seen in the exhibit, there are three activity centers in which the model prevents the entry of square footage information: Building & Grounds, General & Administration (G&A), and machine setup. Square footage cannot be assigned to building & grounds because building & grounds is the activity being distributed by square footage. An activity center cannot distribute costs to itself. If some of Small-Time Manufacturing's facility is used for activities included in building & grounds, the square footage occupied by those activities should be ignored. For example, from Schedule #10 we know that one individual works in building & grounds. If that person has an office, that office space occupies some of the available square footage. Similarly, if there is a storage area for building maintenance supplies and equipment, that also occupies some of the company's available square footage. Both of these should be excluded from Schedule #15. This means that the total square footage shown on the schedule may not equal the company's total square footage. The difference will be any square footage that would have been assigned to building & grounds.

General & Administration does not take up any space. This activity center was created to accumulate costs in two ways. First, to accumulate distributions from other activity centers for that portion of their activities that are G&A in nature. Second, to accumulate fixed and budgeted expenses that are also G&A in nature. As you will recall from the discussion of Schedule #10, no one works directly in G&A. It does not occupy any specific area within the facility, so no square footage can be assigned to it.

The activities that comprise machine/setup occur in the same area in which machine/operate takes place. Last year's volume and mix of business (which is the data being entered into the model as we build it) required 1,200 machine hours for set-up activities versus 8,000 machine hours for machining activities. To be theoretically correct, we might enter the 5,000

Exhibit 13.1 Square Footage

```
SQUARE FOOTAGE                                      Schedule #15
===============
Small-Time Manufacturing
                                            Square
                                             Feet          %
                                          ----------  ----------

Bldg & Grnd                                   xxxxx         0.0%
Supervision                                     500         2.5%
Procurement                                     500         2.5%
Mfg Support                                   2,000        10.0%
Mgmt & Admn                                   2,000        10.0%
Gen & Admin                                   xxxxx         0.0%

Raw Mat'ls                                    1,000         5.0%
Purch Comp                                    1,500         7.5%
OSServices                                      500         2.5%

Machine-SUp                                   xxxxx         0.0%
Machine-Opr                                   5,000        25.0%
Assembly                                      4,000        20.0%
Ins/Pak/Shp                                   3,000        15.0%
                                          ----------  ----------

                                 Totals      20,000       100.0%
                                          ==========  ==========
```

square feet that relate to machining operations on this schedule, bring forward the set-up and operate hours from Schedule #02, and split the 5,000 square feet in the setup/operate proportions. This would result in 652 square feet assigned to machine/setup and 4,348 square feet to machine/operate. This, in turn, would cause 3.3% of building & grounds' cost to be assigned to machine/setup and 21.7% to machine/operate. Is it worth this extra effort to be more theoretically correct?

Keeping in mind that the goal is accuracy, not precision, Small-Time Manufacturing reasoned that since 87% of the machining area's use is related to machine/operate and only 13% is related to machine/setup, it was hardly worth the effort and added complexity to split the square footage between them. As a result, they determined that all of the square footage would be assigned to machine/operate.

Once the square footage information is entered, the model calculates the percentage each activity center's square footage represents of the total. These percentages are carried forward to Schedule #16 for use in distributing building & grounds' accumulated costs.

SCHEDULE #16: AUTOMATIC DISTRIBUTIONS

Schedule #16, which begins on line 641 and is shown in Exhibit 13.2, performs the distributions for the two support activities distributed using measurable statistical bases; namely, building & grounds and supervision. The distribution percentages for building & grounds were calculated on Schedule #15 where the square footage information was entered into the model. The distribution percentages for Supervision are calculated on this schedule.

Distribution of the cost of supervision is to be based on the headcounts of activity centers that supervision supervises. At Small-Time Manufacturing, this includes all employees except for those included in management/ administration and, of course, those in supervision itself. As a result, the model brings forward procurement and manufacturing support headcounts from Schedule #10 and production employee headcounts from Schedule #09. These are then used to calculate the distribution percentages based on the percentage each activity center represents of the total supervised employee.

The $125,909 of costs to distribute for building & grounds are brought forward from Schedule #14. The square footage percentages are then used to distribute this cost among the activity centers. An extra step is required, however, in determining the costs to be distributed for supervision. $100,627 of costs are brought forward from Schedule #14, but before they are distributed, any distribution that Supervision might have received from building & grounds must be added. Since $3,148 was distributed to supervision from building & grounds, this is added to the $100,627 of costs directly related to supervision to arrive at the total cost to be distributed of $103,775. The distribution of this total among the activity centers is then made using the percentages that were derived from headcounts.

SCHEDULE #17: ACTIVITY ANALYSIS DISTRIBUTIONS

Schedule #17, which begins on line 681 and is shown in Exhibit 13.3, provides for the distribution of those support activity centers whose distributions are based on an analysis of the activity center's activities. These activity centers are procurement, manufacturing support, and management/administration.

Based on the activities they perform, these support activity centers can only distribute their costs to certain other activity centers. For example, the model precludes Procurement from assigning its costs to any activity centers except G&A, raw materials, purchased components, and outside services. The distribution percentages entered are those that were developed during analyses of each activity center's activities.

Exhibit 13.2 Automatic Distributions

AUTOMATIC DISTRIBUTIONS Schedule #16

Small-Time Manufacturing

	Act Center:	Bldg & Grnd	Act Center:		Supervision
	%	$	Headcount	%	$
Costs to distribute		$125,909			$103,775
Supervision	2.5%	$3,148	xxxxx	xxxxx	xxxxx
Procurement	2.5%	$3,148	1.0	4.5%	$4,717
Mfg Support	10.0%	$12,591	5.0	22.7%	$23,585
Mgmt & Admn	10.0%	$12,591	xxxxx	xxxxx	xxxxx
Gen & Admin	0.0%	$0	xxxxx	xxxxx	xxxxx
Raw Mat'ls	5.0%	$6,295	xxxxx	xxxxx	xxxxx
Purch Comp	7.5%	$9,443	xxxxx	xxxxx	xxxxx
OSServices	2.5%	$3,148	xxxxx	xxxxx	xxxxx
Machine-SUp	0.0%	$0	2.0	9.1%	$9,434
Machine-Opr	25.0%	$31,477	3.0	13.6%	$14,151
Assembly	20.0%	$25,182	9.0	40.9%	$42,453
Ins/Pak/Shp	15.0%	$18,886	2.0	9.1%	$9,434
Totals	100.0%	$125,909	22.0	100.0%	$103,775

Exhibit 13.3 Activity Analysis Distributions

ACTIVITY ANALYSIS DISTRIBUTIONS

Small-Time Manufacturing

Schedule #17

	Act Center: Procurement		Act Center: Mfg Support		Act Center: Mgmt & Admn	
	%	$	%	$	%	$
		$70,414		$233,165		$313,037
Supervision	xxxxx	xxxxx	xxxxx	xxxxx	xxxxx	xxxxx
Procurement	xxxxx	xxxxx	xxxxx	xxxxx	xxxxx	xxxxx
Mfg Support	xxxxx	xxxxx	xxxxx	xxxxx	xxxxx	xxxxx
Mgmt & Admn	xxxxx	xxxxx	xxxxx	xxxxx	xxxxx	xxxxx
Gen & Admin	10.0%	$7,041	10.0%	$23,317	50.0%	$156,519
Raw Mat'ls	20.0%	$14,083	5.0%	$11,658	10.0%	$31,304
Purch Comp	40.0%	$28,166	5.0%	$11,658	10.0%	$31,304
OSServices	30.0%	$21,214	10.0%	$23,317	10.0%	$31,304
Machine-SUp	xxxxx	xxxxx	5.0%	$11,658	5.0%	$15,652
Machine-Opr	xxxxx	xxxxx	40.0%	$93,266	5.0%	$15,652
Assembly	xxxxx	xxxxx	15.0%	$34,975	5.0%	$15,652
Ins/Pak/Shp	xxxxx	xxxxx	10.0%	$23,317	5.0%	$15,652
	100.0%	$70,414	100.0%	$233,165	100.0%	$313,037

The costs to distribute include those costs directly attributable to each activity center from Schedule #14 plus any distributions that have been made to the activity center from any "upstream" support activity. In the cases of these three activity centers, the costs to distribute were determined as follows:

	Procurement	*Mfg Support*	*Mgmt & Admn*
From Schedule #14	$62,549	$196,989	$300,447
From Schedule #16			
Bldg & grnd	3,148	12,591	12,591
Supervision	4,717	23,585	
Total costs to distribute	$70,414	$233,165	$313,037

Management/administration totals $313,037 instead of $313,038 due to rounding that occurs when the amounts are presented in the model.

The distribution of these totals among the activity centers is then made using the percentages that were determined by activity analysis.

SCHEDULE #18: COST DISTRIBUTION

Schedule #18, which begins on line 721 and is shown in Exhibits 13.4 through 13.6, provides a summary of all cost distribution activity. This schedule should be viewed as a continuation of Schedule #14: Cost Accumulation. Its columns are identical to those on that schedule and it begins by bringing forward each activity center's total costs as accumulated on the schedule.

The portion of Schedule #18 included in Exhibit 13.4 documents the distribution activity taking place in Small-Time Manufacturing's support activities. Fringe benefits were already distributed on Schedule #14, so none of that cost pool's costs remain to distribute on Schedule #18. Building & grounds and supervision distribution information is brought forward from Schedule #16. procurement, manufacturing support, and management/ administration information is brought forward from Schedule #17. As is clearly shown in Exhibit 13.4, all costs in these support activities have been accumulated and then distributed to other activity centers.

The portion of Schedule #18 included in Exhibit 13.5 documents the distribution activity taking place in Small-Time Manufacturing's G&A activity center and in the throughput or material support activity centers and the calculation of these activity centers' cost assignment rates. These include G&A, raw materials, purchased components, and outside services. The distribution

Exhibit 13.4 Cost Distribution

COST DISTRIBUTION

Small-Time Manufacturing

Schedule #18
Page 1 of 3

	Fringe Benefits	Bldg & Grnd	Supervision	Procurement	Mfg Support	Mgmt & Admn
Costs brought forward	$0	$125,909	$100,627	$62,549	$196,989	$300,447
Distributions:						
Bldg & Grnd		($125,909)	$3,148	$3,148	$12,591	$12,591
Supervision			($103,775)	$4,717	$23,585	
Procurement				($70,414)		
Mfg Support					($233,165)	
Mgmt & Admn						($313,037)
Total costs	$0	$0	$0	$0	$0	$0
Base						
Cost assignment rate						

Exhibit 13.5 Cost Distribution

COST DISTRIBUTION
Small-Time Manufacturing

Schedule #18
Page 2 of 3

	Gen & Admin	Raw Mat'ls	Purch Comp	OSServices
Costs brought forward	$15,000	$7,000	$7,000	$1,000
Distributions				
Bldg & Grnd	$0	$6,295	$9,443	$3,148
Supervision				
Procurement	$7,041	$14,083	$28,166	$21,124
Mfg Support	$23,317	$11,658	$11,658	$23,317
Mgmt & Admn	$156,519	$31,304	$31,304	$31,304
Total costs	$201,877	$70,340	$87,571	$79,892
Base	$1,330,805	$500,000	$300,000	$200,000
Cost assignment rate	15.2%	14.1%	29.2%	39.9%
	of internal costs	of purchase cost	of purchase cost	of purchase cost

Exhibit 13.6 Cost Distribution

COST DISTRIBUTION

Small-Time Manufacturing

Schedule #18
Page 3 of 3

	Machine-SUp	Machine-Opr	Assembly	Ins/Pak/Shp	Throughput Costs	Total
Costs brought forward	$74,316	$315,821	$261,147	$64,877	$1,000,000	$2,532,681
Distributions						
Bldg & Grnd	$0	$31,477	$25,182	$18,886		$0
Supervision	$9,434	$14,151	$42,453	$9,434		($0)
Procurement						$0
Mfg Support	$11,658	$93,266	$34,975	$23,317		$0
Mgmt & Admn	$15,652	$15,652	$15,652	$15,652		$0
Total costs	$111,060	$470,367	$379,408	$132,166	$1,000,000	$2,532,681
Base	400	8,000	15,000	1,200		
Cost assignment rate	$277.65	$58.80	$25.29	$110.14		
	per set-up	per machine hour	per direct labor hour	per shipment		

amounts on this schedule are brought forward from Schedules #16 and #17 and the each activity center's total costs determined.

The bases for raw materials, purchased components, and outside services cost assignment rates (purchase dollars) are brought forward from Schedule #02. The "internal costs" that comprise G&A's base are calculated within the cell by subtracting G&A's total cost as well as all throughput costs from total accumulated costs as determined on Schedule #14 ($2,532,681 total costs less $201,877 G&A cost less $1,000,000 throughput cost = $1,330,805 internal costs). Rounding again causes the calculation to appear to be off by $1.

These bases are then used to calculate percentage cost assignment rates for these nonproduction activities. General and administration as a percentage of internal costs and raw materials, purchased components, and outside services as a percentage of purchase cost.

The portion of Schedule #18 included in Exhibit 13.6, documents the distribution activity taking place in Small-Time Manufacturing's direct or value-adding activity centers and the calculation of these activity centers' cost assignment rates. These include machine/setup, machine/operate, assembly, and inspect/pack/ship. Distribution information is again brought forward from Schedules #16 and #17 and the total cost of each activity center determined.

The bases for all four activity centers' cost assignment rates are brought forward from Schedule #02. These bases represent the number of set-ups (for machine/setup), the number of machine hours (for machine/operate), the number of direct labor hours (for assembly) and the number of shipments (for inspect/pack/ship). Total costs are then divided by the bases to arrive at each activity center's cost assignment rate.

SCHEDULE #19: COST/RATE RECONCILIATION

Schedule #18 completes the cost accumulation and distribution process. The model began with a volume and mix of products, proceeded to accumulate the cost necessary to produce and sell that volume and mix of products and then converted those costs into a set of costing rates that can be used to assign the model's costs to the individual jobs, products, services, or contracts that comprise the volume and mix of business which drove the model.

It is advisable to add one final schedule as a test to make sure that no costs have "fallen through the cracks" or that none have been inadvertently included more than once. In other words, if we multiply all of the bases by all of the rates, will we arrive at the total cost of operating the company? Schedule #19, which begins on line 761 and is shown in Exhibit 13.7, documents that test.

Exhibit 13.7 Cost/Rate Reconciliation

COST/RATE RECONCILIATION — Schedule #19

Small-Time Manufacturing

	Rate	Base		Total Cost
Throughput costs:				
Raw materials				$500,000
Purchased components				$300,000
Outside services				$200,000
Total throughput costs				$1,000,000
Throughput overhead:				
Raw Mat'ls	14.1%	$500,000	Dollars of throughput	$70,340
Purch Comp	29.2%	$300,000	Dollars of throughput	$87,571
OSServices	39.9%	$200,000	Dollars of throughput	$79,892
Manufacturing overhead:				
Machine-SUp	$277.65	400	Setups	$111,060
Machine-Opr	$58.80	8,000	Machine hours	$470,367
Assembly	$25.29	15,000	Direct labor hours	$379,408
Ins/Pak/Shp	$110.14	1,200	Shipments	$132,166
Total Internal Costs				$1,330,805
General & Administration:				
G&A	15.2%	$1,330,805	Internal costs	$201,877
Total costs				$2,532,681

The schedule begins by bringing forward the throughput costs from Schedule #02. It then brings forward the seven bases from Schedule #02 and the eight cost assignment rates from Schedule #18. The base for G&A costs is calculated on the schedule itself. The three throughput or material support bases are multiplied by the applicable percentages and the four direct or value-adding activity bases are multiplied by their time or event based rates to arrive at Small-Time Manufacturing's total internal costs. These total internal costs then become the base for applying the general and administrative cost assignment percentage.

If all has gone well in constructing the model, the sum of these costs will be the same as Small-Time Manufacturing's total accumulated costs as they appear on Schedules #14 and #18. If you have done any rounding in the model, the total could be off by a dollar or two. This is not a problem. If, however, the total is different from the totals on Schedules #14 and #18 by more than a few dollars, there is either a logic or computational problem in the model that needs to be located and corrected.

MODEL DIRECTORY

Once all schedules are completed, the model builder should create a directory that will make it possible to "goto" various schedules in the model efficiently. A simple directory, which can be placed at the very beginning of the model, is shown in Exhibit 13.8. It provides a "goto" cell reference together with the schedule number and title. The "goto" cell reference is the cell a user needs to "goto" for the upper left hand corner of the desired schedule to appear in the upper left hand corner of the computer screen.

MODEL COMPLETION

With the completion of the model, Small-Time Manufacturing has a tool that can be used in a variety of decision costing situations. Because it accumulates costs, it can be used in the myriad of decision situations where incremental costs are those needed to support a decision. Because it distributes costs, it can also be used where *fully absorbed* costs are relevant for the decision at hand. The accumulation of activity costs has also focused the former "blob" of overhead costs into logical groups, based on work being performed, making the identification of cost reduction opportunities much easier. The model structure provides a blueprint for a day-to-day cost accounting system that would accurately reflect the company's cost behavior. These and many other benefits have been gained from the model design and development process.

Exhibit 13.8 Model Directory

MODEL DIRECTORY
===============
Small-Time Manufacturing

Location	Schedule Number	Schedule Title
A41	Schedule #01	CONTRACT ACTIVITY SUMMARY
A81	Schedule #02	OPERATING INFORMATION AND RESOURCE REQUIREMENTS
A121	Schedule #03	RESOURCE CONVERSION
A161	Schedule #04	SCREEN
A201	Schedule #05	OPERATING MANPOWER—DEMAND
A241	Schedule #06	AUTOMATICALLY VARIABLE COSTS
A281	Schedule #07	OPERATING MANPOWER—HOURS AVAILABLE
A321	Schedule #08	OPERATING MANPOWER—SUPPLY
A361	Schedule #09	OPERATING MANPOWER—COST
A401	Schedule #10	SUPPORT STAFF
A441	Schedule #11	FRINGE BENEFITS
A481	Schedule #12	OTHER HEADCOUNT DRIVEN COSTS
A521	Schedule #13	FIXED AND BUDGETED COSTS
A561	Schedule #14	COST ACCUMULATION
A601	Schedule #15	SQUARE FOOTAGE
A641	Schedule #16	AUTOMATIC DISTRIBUTIONS
A681	Schedule #17	ACTIVITY ANALYSIS DISTRIBUTIONS
A721	Schedule #18	COST DISTRIBUTION
A761	Schedule #19	COST/RATE RECONCILIATION

Keep in mind that the numbers currently in Small-Time Manufacturing's model represent its cost structure during the year just ended. Two things have been accomplished by including this historical data: the model builder has (1) validated the model by using it to recreate the previous year and (2) developed the variable costs per unit of measure (remember solving for B?) necessary to drive the model in the future.

SUMMARY

Developing and building the model was an interesting intellectual exercise, but intellectual exercises do not usually benefit the company. The model must be put to use in making Small-Time Manufacturing a more profitable organization. In the chapters that follow, we will demonstrate ways in which Small-Time will be able to use the model to improve the quality of its decisions and, as a result, improve its performance.

14

Small-Time Manufacturing: Product Costing

Once the activity-based cost accumulation and distribution model was completed, Small-Time Manufacturing's management wanted to compare the costs of its current contracts using traditional methods (which were used when the contracts were won) with those using the new activity-based costing (ABC) activity-based rates. Before that could be done, however, the company needed to develop a bridge to match the old direct labor hour measures for attaching costs to jobs with the new ABC measures (setups, shipments, machine hours, assembly hours). The bridge developed to link old and new measures is summarized in Exhibit 14.1.

As discussed in the "Other Considerations" section of this case (Chapter 12), the company's old costing methodology treated as a direct cost all labor performed by personnel classified as direct; even when they were performing indirect activities. In revising its methodology to incorporate ABC concepts, the company decided to change its definition so that only actual direct work is treated as direct. Indirect activities performed by personnel classified as direct would now be treated as indirect. This change in classification is part of the bridge between the old and new measures.

Small-Time Manufacturing's activity-based approach will use the number of setups to assign the cost of machine/set-up. The average setup takes three hours and is performed by a team of two set-up workers. This calculates to six direct labor hours per setup. However, the records show that 2,880 direct labor hours were charged to jobs to accomplish 400 setups, an average of 7.2 hours per setup. The difference is the 20% add-on that was calculated in the "Other Considerations" section of this case to account for

Exhibit 14.1 Traditional/ABC Activity Bridge

TRADITIONAL/ABC ACTIVITY BRIDGE
======================
Small-Time Manufacturing

Activity Center	ABC Activity Measure	Hours per Event	Crew Size	Indirect Add-On Percentage	Traditional Direct Labor Hrs.	Labor Hrs. per ABC Measure
Machine/setup	400	3.0	2.0	20%	2,880	7.20
Machine/operate	8,000		0.6	30%	6,240	.78
Assembly	15,000		1.0	20%	18,880	1.20
Inspect/pack/ship	1,200	2.0	1.0	20%	2,880	2.40
Total					30,000	

the indirect activities performed by these set-up workers. As a result, a 20% indirect add-on percentage needs to be included in the bridge.

In a like manner, any ABC activity measure that is expressed in terms of events must be multiplied by the number of chronological hours required per event. Activities that are already measured in terms of hours need no such conversion. Each activity's hours are then multiplied by the crew size required during that chronological period. Finally, the resulting hours must be increased by the indirect activity add-on percentage to gross them up to the direct labor measure as defined using the old methodology. In the contract costing comparisons that follow, ABC measures can be converted to the traditional cost measures using the mechanics outlined earlier.

CONTRACT COSTING COMPARISONS

The base of business on which Small-Time Manufacturing's cost calculations have been built consists of 10 contracts. These 10 contracts and the throughput cost and activity measures attributable to each were entered on Schedule #01 of the model (see Exhibit 12.1). Calculations of the traditional costing rates originally used to estimate the cost of these contracts was shown in Exhibit 11.1. The costing of each contract using traditional and ABC methods is documented in Exhibits 14.2 through 14.11. Of the 10 contracts, we will explore three of them in detail to contrast the traditional and ABC results. The three we will explore are Contracts #04, #06, and #07.

When calculated using ABC rates, Contract #04 costs $42,881 more than it did using traditional rates. This amounts to a 22.6% difference in total cost. This percentage, however, is not really representative of the swing between the ABC and traditional costs. Since throughput or direct material costs are charged directly to the contract in either case, the better measure would be the cost difference divided by internal activity costs. This differential amounts to 33.1%.

Does this difference make sense? A look at the details of the calculation reveals that Contract #04 requires a great deal of machining (20% of the company's total annual machine hours) and very little assembly (less than 3.5% of the company's total annual assembly hours). The traditional methodology used a shop-wide hourly rate based on direct labor. As a result, the higher hourly cost of operating a machine was averaged with the lower hourly cost of manual assembly operations resulting in a rate that understated the hourly machine cost (Contract #04 has a lot of machine hours) and overstated the hourly assembly cost (Contract #04 has very few assembly hours). Compounding this shortcoming is the fact that a machine does not require a full-time operator. This results in only six tenths of a direct labor

Exhibit 14.2 Contract Cost Estimate-Contract #01

CONTRACT COST ESTIMATE — Contract # 01

Small-Time Manufacturing

			Internal Costs	Total Costs
TRADITIONAL COSTING				
Raw materials				$50,000
Purchased components				$20,000
Outside services				$0
Direct labor hours @	$40.57			
Setup		144	$5,842	$5,842
Machining		624	$25,316	$25,316
Assembly		1,200	$48,684	$48,684
Inspect/pack/ship		60	$2,434	$2,434
Subtotal			$82,276	$152,276
General & Administration @		14.2%	$21,623	$21,623
Total contract cost			$103,899	$173,899
ACTIVITY-BASED COSTING				
Direct materials:				
Raw materials	$50,000	14.1%	$7,050	$57,050
Purchased components	$20,000	29.2%	$5,840	$25,840
Outside services	$0	39.9%	$0	$0
Operating activities:				
Machining:				
Setups	20	$277.65	$5,553	$5,553
Machine hours	800	$58.80	$47,040	$47,040
Assembly:				
Assembly hours	1,000	$25.29	$25,290	$25,290
Inspect/pack/ship:				
Shipments	25	$110.14	$2,754	$2,754
Subtotal			$93,527	$163,527
General & Administration @		15.2%	$14,216	$14,216
Total contract cost			$107,743	$177,743
Cost differential			3.7%	2.2%

Exhibit 14.3 Contract Cost Estimate-Contract #02

CONTRACT COST ESTIMATE
Small-Time Manufacturing

Contract # 02

			Internal Costs	Total Costs
	TRADITIONAL COSTING			
Raw materials				$25,000
Purchased components				$10,000
Outside services				$0
Direct labor hours @	$40.57			
Setup		288	$11,684	$11,684
Machining		624	$25,316	$25,316
Assembly		600	$24,342	$24,342
Inspect/pack/ship		240	$9,737	$9,737
Subtotal			$71,079	$106,079
General & Administration @		14.2%	$15,063	$15,063
Total contract cost			$86,142	$121,142
	ACTIVITY-BASED COSTING			
Direct materials:				
Raw materials	$25,000	14.1%	$3,525	$28,525
Purchased components	$10,000	29.2%	$2,920	$12,920
Outside services	$0	39.9%	$0	$0
Operating activities:				
Machining:				
Setups	40	$277.65	$11,106	$11,106
Machine hours	800	$58.80	$47,040	$47,040
Assembly:				
Assembly hours	500	$25.29	$12,645	$12,645
Inspect/pack/ship:				
Shipments	100	$110.14	$11,014	$11,014
Subtotal			$88,250	$123,250
General & Administration @		15.2%	$13,414	$13,414
Total contract cost			$101,664	$136,664
Cost differential			18.0%	12.8%

Exhibit 14.4 Contract Cost Estimate-Contract #03

CONTRACT COST ESTIMATE
Small-Time Manufacturing

Contract # 03

			Internal Costs	Total Costs
TRADITIONAL COSTING				
Raw materials				$100,000
Purchased components				$40,000
Outside services				$25,000
Direct labor hours @	$40.57			
Setup		432	$17,526	$17,526
Machining		1,248	$50,631	$50,631
Assembly		2,400	$97,368	$97,368
Inspect/pack/ship		480	$19,474	$19,474
Subtotal			$184,999	$349,999
General & Administration @		14.2%	$49,700	$49,700
Total contract cost			$234,699	$399,699
ACTIVITY-BASED COSTING				
Direct materials:				
Raw materials	$100,000	14.1%	$14,100	$114,100
Purchased components	$40,000	29.2%	$11,680	$51,680
Outside services	$25,000	39.9%	$9.975	$34,975
Operating activities:				
Machining:				
Setups	60	$277.65	$16,659	$16,659
Machine hours	1,600	$58.80	$94,080	$94,080
Assembly:				
Assembly hours	2,000	$25.29	$50,580	$50,580
Inspect/pack/ship:				
Shipments	200	$110.14	$22,028	$22,028
Subtotal			$219,102	$384,102
General & Administration @		15.2%	$33,304	$33,304
Total contract cost			$252,406	$417,406
Cost differential			7.5%	4.4%

Exhibit 14.5 Contract Cost Estimate-Contract #04

CONTRACT COST ESTIMATE
Small-Time Manufacturing

Contract # 04

			Internal Costs	Total Costs
	TRADITIONAL COSTING			
Raw materials				$50,000
Purchased components				$10,000
Outside services				$0
Direct labor hours @	$40.57			
Setup		288	$11,684	$11,684
Machining		1,248	$50,631	$50,631
Assembly		600	$24,342	$24,342
Inspect/pack/ship		480	$19,474	$19,474
Subtotal			$106,131	$166,131
General & Administration @		14.2%	$23,591	$23,591
Total contract cost			$129,722	$189,722
	ACTIVITY-BASED COSTING			
Direct materials:				
Raw materials	$50,000	14.1%	$7,050	$57,050
Purchased components	$10,000	29.2%	$2,920	$12,920
Outside services	$0	39.9%	$0	$0
Operating activities:				
Machining:				
Setups	40	$277.65	$11,106	$11,106
Machine hours	1,600	$58.80	$94,080	$94,080
Assembly:				
Assembly hours	500	$25.29	$12,645	$12,645
Inspect/pack/ship:				
Shipments	200	$110.14	$22,028	$22,028
Subtotal			$149,829	$209,829
General & Administration @		15.2%	$22,774	$22,774
Total contract cost			$172,603	$232,603
Cost differential			33.1%	22.6%

Exhibit 14.6 Contract Cost Estimate-Contract #05

CONTRACT COST ESTIMATE — Contract # 05
Small-Time Manufacturing

			Internal Costs	Total Costs
TRADITIONAL COSTING				
Raw materials				$50,000
Purchased components				$20,000
Outside services				$75,000
Direct labor hours @	$40.57			
Setup		144	$5,842	$5,842
Machining		312	$12,658	$12,658
Assembly		1,200	$48,684	$48,684
Inspect/pack/ship		120	$4,868	$4,868
Subtotal			$75,052	$217,052
General & Administration @		14.2%	$30,821	$30,821
Total contract cost			$102,874	$247,874
ACTIVITY-BASED COSTING				
Direct materials:				
Raw materials	$50,000	14.1%	$7,050	$57,050
Purchased components	$20,000	29.2%	$5,840	$25,840
Outside services	$75,000	39.9%	$29,925	$104,925
Operating activities:				
Machining:				
Setups	20	$277.65	$5,553	$5,553
Machine hours	400	$58.80	$23,520	$23,520
Assembly:				
Assembly hours	1,000	$25.29	$25,290	$25,290
Inspect/pack/ship:				
Shipments	50	$110.14	$5,507	$5,507
Subtotal			$102,685	$247,685
General & Administration @		15.2%	$15,608	$15,608
Total contract cost			$118,293	$263,293
Cost differential			15.0%	6.2%

Exhibit 14.7 Contract Cost Estimate-Contract #06

CONTRACT COST ESTIMATE
Small-Time Manufacturing

Contract # 06

			Internal Costs	Total Costs
TRADITIONAL COSTING				
Raw materials				$25,000
Purchased components				$40,000
Outside services				$0
Direct labor hours @	$40.57			
Setup		288	$11,684	$11,684
Machining		312	$12,658	$12,658
Assembly		2,400	$97,368	$97,368
Inspect/pack/ship		120	$4,868	$4,868
Subtotal			$126,578	$191,578
General & Administration @		14.2%	$27,204	$27,204
Total contract cost			$153,783	$218,783
ACTIVITY-BASED COSTING				
Direct materials:				
Raw materials	$25,000	14.1%	$3,525	$28,525
Purchased components	$40,000	29.2%	$11,680	$51,680
Outside services	$0	39.9%	$0	$0
Operating activities:				
Machining:				
Setups	40	$277.65	$11,106	$11,106
Machine hours	400	$58.80	$23,520	$23,520
Assembly:				
Assembly hours	2,000	$25.29	$50,580	$50,580
Inspect/pack/ship:				
Shipments	50	$110.14	$5,507	$5,507
Subtotal			$105,918	$170,918
General & Administration @		15.2%	$16,100	$16,100
Total contract cost			$122,018	$187,018
Cost differential			-20.7%	-14.5%

Exhibit 14.8 Contract Cost Estimate-Contract #07

CONTRACT COST ESTIMATE — Contract # 07
Small-Time Manufacturing

			Internal Costs	Total Costs
TRADITIONAL COSTING				
Raw materials				$75,000
Purchased components				$20,000
Outside services				$0
Direct labor hours @	$40.57			
Setup		432	$17,526	$17,526
Machining		468	$18,987	$18,987
Assembly		1,200	$48,684	$48,684
Inspect/pack/ship		360	$14,605	$14,605
Subtotal			$99,802	$194,802
General & Administration @		14.2%	$27,662	$27,662
Total contract cost			$127,464	$222,464
ACTIVITY-BASED COSTING				
Direct materials:				
Raw materials	$75,000	14.1%	$10,575	$85,575
Purchased components	$20,000	29.2%	$5,840	$25,840
Outside services	$0	39.9%	$0	$0
Operating activities:				
Machining:				
Setups	60	$277.65	$16,659	$16,659
Machine hours	600	$58.80	$35,280	$35,280
Assembly:				
Assembly hours	1,000	$25.29	$25,290	$25,290
Inspect/pack/ship:				
Shipments	150	$110.14	$16,521	$16,521
Subtotal			$110,165	$205,165
General & Administration @		15.2%	$16,745	$16,745
Total contract cost			$126,910	$221,910
Cost differential			-0.4%	-0.2%

Exhibit 14.9 Contract Cost Estimate-Contract #08

CONTRACT COST ESTIMATE
Small-Time Manufacturing

Contract # 08

			Internal Costs	Total Costs
TRADITIONAL COSTING				
Raw materials				$50,000
Purchased components				$60,000
Outside services				$50,000
Direct labor hours @	$40.57			
Setup		288	$11,684	$11,684
Machining		468	$18,987	$18,987
Assembly		3,600	$146,052	$146,052
Inspect/pack/ship		480	$19,474	$19,474
Subtotal			$196,197	$356,197
General & Administration @		14.2%	$50,580	$50,580
Total contract cost			$246,776	$406,776
ACTIVITY-BASED COSTING				
Direct materials:				
Raw materials	$50,000	14.1%	$7,050	$57,050
Purchased components	$60,000	29.2%	$17,520	$77,520
Outside services	$50,000	39.9%	$19,950	$69,950
Operating activities:				
Machining:				
Setups	40	$277.65	$11,106	$11,106
Machine hours	600	$58.80	$35,280	$35,280
Assembly:				
Assembly hours	3,000	$25.29	$75,870	$75,870
Inspect/pack/ship:				
Shipments	200	$110.14	$22,028	$22,028
Subtotal			$188,804	$348,804
General & Administration @		15.2%	$28,698	$28,698
Total contract cost			$217,502	$377,502
Cost differential			-11.9%	-7.2%

Exhibit 14.10 Contract Cost Estimate-Contract #09

CONTRACT COST ESTIMATE — Contract # 09

Small-Time Manufacturing

			Internal Costs	Total Costs
TRADITIONAL COSTING				
Raw materials				$50,000
Purchased components				$40,000
Outside services				$0
Direct labor hours @	$40.57			
Setup		432	$17,526	$17,526
Machining		624	$25,316	$25,316
Assembly		2,400	$97,368	$97,368
Inspect/pack/ship		180	$7,303	$7,303
Subtotal			$147,513	$237,513
General & Administration @		14.2%	$33,727	$33,727
Total contract cost			$181,239	$271,239
ACTIVITY-BASED COSTING				
Direct materials:				
Raw materials	$50,000	14.1%	$7,050	$57,050
Purchased components	$40,000	29.2%	$11,680	$51,680
Outside services	$0	39.9%	$0	$0
Operating activities:				
Machining:				
Setups	60	$277.65	$16,659	$16,659
Machine hours	800	$58.80	$47,040	$47,040
Assembly:				
Assembly hours	2,000	$25.29	$50,580	$50,580
Inspect/pack/ship:				
Shipments	75	$110.14	$8,261	$8,261
Subtotal			$141,270	$231,270
General & Administration @		15.2%	$21,473	$21,473
Total contract cost			$162,742	$252,742
Cost differential			-10.2%	-6.8%

Exhibit 14.11 Contract Cost Estimate-Contract #10

CONTRACT COST ESTIMATE
Small-Time Manufacturing

Contract # 10

			Internal Costs	Total Costs
	TRADITIONAL COSTING			
Raw materials				$25,000
Purchased components				$40,000
Outside services				$50,000
Direct labor hours @	$40.57			
Setup		144	$5,842	$5,842
Machining		312	$12,658	$12,658
Assembly		2,400	$97,368	$97,368
Inspect/pack/ship		360	$14,605	$14,605
Subtotal			$130,473	$245,473
General & Administration @		14.2%	$34,857	$34,857
Total Contract Cost			$165,330	$280,330
	ACTIVITY-BASED COSTING			
Direct materials:				
Raw materials	$25,000	14.1%	$3,525	$28,525
Purchased components	$40,000	29.2%	$11,680	$51,680
Outside services	$50,000	39.9%	$19,950	$69,950
Operating activities:				
Machining:				
Setups	20	$277.65	$5,553	$5,553
Machine hours	400	$58.80	$23,520	$23,520
Assembly:				
Assembly hours	2,000	$25.29	$50,580	$50,580
Inspect/Pack/Ship:				
Shipments	150	$110.14	$16,521	$16,521
Subtotal			$131,329	$246,329
General & Administration @		15.2%	$19,962	$19,962
Total contract cost			$151,291	$266,291
Cost differential			-8.5%	-5.0%

hour being charged for each hour a machine runs. No wonder a contract that emphasizes machining operations was severely undercosted using traditional methods.

Contract #06, on the other hand, ends up costing $31,765 less when costed using ABC rates. This is a 14.5% difference in total cost and a 20.7% difference in internal activity costs. A look at the details reveals why this result makes perfect sense for this contract. This contract emphasizes assembly operations and has a minimal amount of machining. Assembly hours are over 13% of the company's total annual assembly time while machine hours are only 5% of its annual machine hours. The impact of this situation is the opposite of that experienced on Contract #04. The contract's emphasis on assembly hours, which were overcosted using the traditional methodology's average rate, caused the contract to be severely overcosted.

Contract #07 shows that even an overgeneralized approach to costing, such as the one that had been used by Small-Time Manufacturing, will develop accurate costs for an *average* contract. In this case machine hours amounted to 7.5% of the company's total while assembly hours were about 6.7% of its total. Contracts with such an average mix of the company's resources will arrive at a contract cost that is reasonably accurate despite overgeneralized costing methods. There are, however, very few average jobs or products at most companies. The nature of business is such that different contracts will usually demand different proportions of the company's resources. A summary of the cost differentials of all 10 contracts is included in Exhibit 14.12. The $1,244 difference in total contract costs is due to the rounding of costing rates to the nearest .1% for percentage rates and to the nearest $.01 for dollar rates. This .05% difference is irrelevant. Had Small-Time carried rates out to more decimals, the difference would have been zero. Remember, however, our goal is accuracy, not precision.

CONTRACT PROFITABILITY COMPARISONS

Having seen the cost differences among the 10 contracts, Small-Time's management wanted to see how this impacted each contract's profitability. In its very competitive marketplace, Small-Time has been quoting jobs at 5% above its fully absorbed cost estimate. For example, when it quoted Contract #1, it estimated the fully absorbed cost as $173,899 (see Exhibit 14.2) and added 5% for a price of $182,594. All contracts won (as well as those not won) had been quoted following this procedure. By comparing the ABC cost to each contract's sales price and then ranking the contracts by profit generated, the company came up with the contract profitability analysis shown in Exhibit 14.13.

Exhibit 14.12 Traditional/ABC Contract Cost Comparison

TRADITIONAL/ABC CONTRACT COST COMPARISON

Small-Time Manufacturing

	Traditional	ABC	Difference	Total Cost (%)	Internal Costs (%)
Contract #01	$173,899	$177,743	$3,844	2.2%	3.7%
Contract #02	$121,142	$136,664	$15,522	12.8%	18.0%
Contract #03	$399,699	$417,406	$17,707	4.4%	7.5%
Contract #04	$189,722	$232,603	$42,881	22.6%	33.1%
Contract #05	$247,874	$263,293	$15,419	6.2%	15.0%
Contract #06	$218,783	$187,018	($31,765)	-14.5%	-20.7%
Contract #07	$222,464	$221,910	($554)	-0.2%	-0.4%
Contract #08	$406,776	$377,502	($29,274)	-7.2%	-11.9%
Contract #09	$271,239	$252,742	($18,497)	-6.8%	-10.2%
Contract #10	$280,330	$266,291	($14,039)	-5.0%	-8.5%
	$2,531,928	$2,533,172	$1,244		

Exhibit 14.13 Contract Profitability Analysis

CONTRACT PROFITABILITY ANALYSIS

Small-Time Manufacturing

	Sales Price	ABC Cost	Contract Profit	Profit of Sales (%)	Cumulative Profit
Contract #08	$427,115	$377,502	$49,613	11.6%	$49,613
Contract #06	$229,722	$187,018	$42,704	18.6%	$92,317
Contract #09	$284,801	$252,742	$32,059	11.3%	$124,376
Contract #10	$294,347	$266,291	$28,056	9.5%	$152,431
Contract #07	$233,587	$221,910	$11,677	5.0%	$164,109
Contract #01	$182,594	$177,743	$4,851	2.7%	$168,960
Contract #03	$419,684	$417,406	$2,278	0.5%	$171,237
Contract #05	$260,268	$263,293	($3,025)	-1.2%	$168,212
Contract #02	$127,199	$136,664	($9,465)	-7.4%	$158,747
Contract #04	$199,208	$232,603	($33,395)	-16.8%	$125,352
	$2,658,524	$2,533,172	$125,352	4.7%	

As can be seen in the exhibit, the contract generating the largest amount of profit was Contract #08 ($49,613), and the one generating the largest profit as a percentage of sales was Contract #06 (18.6%). Three contracts generated losses. The worst was Contract #04, which generated a loss of $33,395 and a –16.8% profit as a percentage of sales. The company then used this information to develop the "fishing pole" diagram shown in Exhibit 14.14. In a fishing pole diagram, a company first sorts its jobs, products, services, or contracts (its profit units) by profitability as Small-Time Manufacturing did in Exhibit 14.13. It then determines the cumulative profit after the addition of each profit unit. After the least profitable profit unit is added, cumulative profit will equal the company's annual profit. The graph of the cumulative profits forms the fishing pole diagram. From the shape these diagrams always take, you can see how they get their name.

From Exhibit 14.14 you can see that seven of Small-Time Manufacturing's contracts generated profits of approximately $171 thousand, which the three unprofitable contracts reduced to its overall profit of $125 thousand. Of that $46 thousand drop in profitability, $33 thousand was caused by Contract #04.

Small-Time's management believed that they might be able to take some action that would enable Contracts #05 and #02 to become profitable. Contract #04, however, seemed like a lost cause. A price increase was out of the question, at least according to the vice president of sales, and reducing the cost by over $30 thousand seemed to be an impossible task. The task seemed even more impossible when it was pointed out that total internal costs on Contract #04 were only $173 thousand, which would make it necessary to reduce internal costs by almost 20% for the contract to break even.

Some members of management suggested that Contract #04 be dumped. The company could not afford to carry such a loser in its portfolio of business. Other members of management were not so sure. They thought it might still be somehow contributing to the company's overall profit despite the substantial loss. Then someone came up with a bright idea. Why not use the cost accumulation and distribution model to see what would happen if Contract #04 was dropped?

CONTRACT CONTRIBUTION ANALYSIS: ELIMINATE CONTRACT #04

The cost accumulation and distribution model can be used to determine the total cost of operating Small-Time Manufacturing without Contract #04. The steps are fairly simple.

Exhibit 14.14 "Fishing Pole" Diagram of Cumulative Profits

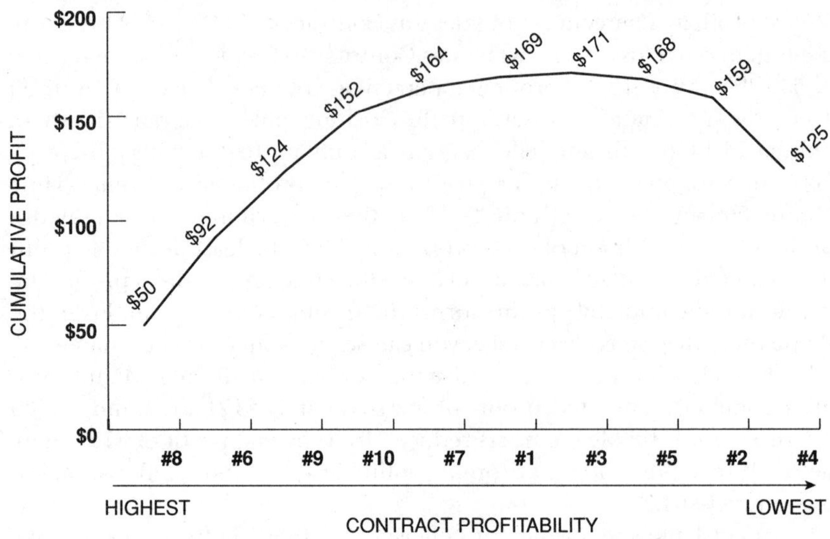

The first step is to eliminate Contract #04's throughput costs and activity measures on Schedule #01: Contract Activity Summary. Without the contract, $50,000 of raw materials and $10,000 of components will not need to be purchased. There will also be 40 less setups, 1,600 less machine hours, 500 less assembly hours, and 200 less shipments. The model automatically updates all calculations driven by these activity measures.

The second step is to make sure the manpower supply is appropriate for the revised manpower demand. This is accomplished by reviewing Schedule #08: Operating Manpower/Supply. With Contract #04, 16 production employees were required: two in machine/setup, three in machine/operate, nine in assembly, and two in inspect/pack/ship. At this level of employment, 15.3% overtime was required in machine/operate and 11.9% overtime was necessary in assembly. As can be seen in the updated Schedule #08, shown in Exhibit 14.15, the elimination of Contract #04 will result in an increase in the underutilization of employees in machine/setup and inspect/pack/ship, will eliminate the need for overtime in machine/ operate and put that activity center in a position of underutilization, and will reduce assembly's required overtime to 8.9%.

Since crew sizes cannot be less than two in machine/setup and inspect/pack/ship, Small-Time would have to live with the additional underutilization of these employees. The underutilization in machine/operate would be so

Exhibit 14.15 Operating Manpower/Supply

OPERATING MANPOWER / SUPPLY — Without Contract #04 — Schedule #08

Small-Time Manufacturing

	FTE Headcount	St-Time Hours per Employee	Total St-Time Hours Available	Gross Production Labor Hrs Required	Overtime Hours Required	Percentage Overtime Required
Machine/setup	2.0	1,762	3,524	2,592	0	0.0%
Machine/operator	3.0	1,762	5,286	4,992	0	0.0%
Assembly	9.0	1,762	15,858	17,400	1,542	8.9%
Ins/pak/shp	2.0	1,762	3,524	2,400	0	0.0%
Totals	16.0			27,384	1,542	5.6%

slight that a headcount reduction would not be possible (reducing headcount to two would result in over 40% overtime). Finally, the nine individuals in assembly would still be the correct headcount for that activity center. As a result, the employment of all 16 production workers would still be necessary.

The third step is to evaluate the headcounts on Schedule #10: Support Staff. Management does not believe that the elimination of Contract #04 would reduce the administrative or support workload enough to make it possible to operate with less than the 14 employees currently on the job. As a result, no change would be made in support staff if Contract #04 was eliminated.

The final step would be to review Schedule #12: Fixed and Budgeted Expense to see if any of those items might change. Again, management does not believe that any of the fixed or budgeted expenses would be reduced by the elimination of Contract #04, so no change would be required on this schedule.

The revised total accumulated cost on Schedule #14: Cost Accumulation now represents Small-Time Manufacturing's total cost without Contract #04. The reduction in cost, which is summarized in Exhibit 14.16, can be compared to the reduction in revenue to determine Small-Time's profit without the contract. The revised amounts are as follows:

	Before	*Eliminate Contr #04*	*After*
Total revenues	$2,659,314	$199,208	$2,460,106
Total costs	2,532,681	117,901	2,414,780
Total profit	$ 126,633	$(81,307)	$ 45,326

Somewhat surprisingly, eliminating a contract that generates a $33,000 loss would decrease profits by $81,000.

How can this be? In this instance, Small-Time Manufacturing is better off with Contract #04 than without it because the definition of fixed and variable costs are situation specific. The model measured the impact of eliminating Contract #04 under a specific set of circumstances. Some of the current major conditions that allow this loser contract to contribute so much to the company's bottom line are:

- Machine/setup and inspect/pack/ship are already underutilized at their minimum staffing levels with all ten contracts. The elimination of this one contract would not reduce the labor cost of these two activities.

Exhibit 14.16 Accumulated Cost Comparisons

ACCUMULATED COST COMPARISONS — Without Contract #04

Small-Time Manufacturing

	Costs Before "What If?"	Costs After "What If?"	Change
Throughput costs:			
Raw materials	$500,000	$450,000	($50,000)
Purchased components	$300,000	$290,000	($10,000)
Outside services	$200,000	$200,000	$0
Wages & fringes			
Support–Base	$430,394	$430,394	$0
Manufacturing–Base	$250,204	$250,204	$0
Manufacturing–ST/OT	$26,676	$12,336	($14,340)
Total s-time wages	$707,274	$692,934	($14,340)
Fringe benefits	$268,070	$265,779	($2,291)
Applied fringes			
Overtime premium	$13,338	$6,168	($7,170)
Total wages & fringes	$988,681	$964,880	($23,801)
Costs & expenses			
Utilities	$80,000	$64,000	($16,000)
Tooling	$60,000	$48,000	($12,000)
Mfg supplies	$79,000	$72,900	($6,100)
Admin supplies	$25,000	$25,000	$0
Fixed/budget expenses	$300,000	$300,000	$0
Total accumulated costs	$2,532,681	$2,414,780	($117,901)

- Although reduced labor costs would be realized in machine/operate, the supply would not be reduced by as much as the reduction in demand. Demand would fall from 6,240 to 4,992, a decline of 1,248 hours. Supply, however, would fall from 6,240 to 5,286, a decline of only 954 hours. This occurs because demand falls enough to put production labor in machine/operate in a underutilized position.
- The elimination of Contract #04 would not reduce administrative and management activities to the extent that the support staff could be reduced from its current level of fourteen employees.
- None of the fixed or budgeted expenses could be reduced as a result of the lower volume of business.

Under this decision situation, only $117,901 of the $232,532 total costs attributable to Contract #04 are actually variable. The contract's $199,269 revenue more than covers these costs. Had the situation been different, the results would have been different. It may even have indicated that Contract #04 should go.

CONTRACT CONTRIBUTION ANALYSIS: ADD ANOTHER CONTRACT #10

Small-Time Manufacturing did not deliberately quote Contract #04 at a loss, knowing it would still contribute to the company's profits. The company quoted the contract under the assumption that it would generate a 5% profit. What if the company had avoided this mistake? What if it had not been awarded Contract #04 but instead had won another contract identical to Contract #10? How would that have impacted Small-Time's profit picture? Small-Time can again use the model to find out.

Using the revised model (without Contract #04) as a base, the company would return to Schedule #01: Contract Activity Summary and add the throughput and activity measures required to complete another contract identical to Contract #10. With such a contract, an additional $25,000 of raw materials, $40,000 of components, and $50,000 of outside services would need to be purchased. There would also be 20 more setups, 400 more machine hours, 2,000 more assembly hours, and 160 more shipments. The model automatically updates all calculations driven by these activity measures.

Because it is adding to the volume and mix of business, the company's next stop would be to review Schedule #04: Screen. The company must make sure that the additional business does not cause it to exceed its capacity under its current operating structure. A quick review will indicate that the one screened activity, machine/operate, still has a cushion of over 1,600 hours.

Next to be addressed would be Schedule #08: Operating Manpower/Supply. With the additional contract, the 16 production workers may need to be changed. The additional volume reduces the underutilization in machine/setup and inspect/pack/ship. It also eliminates the underutilization in machine/operate and even makes a nominal amount of overtime (0.3%) necessary. To meet the demand for assembly with the existing 9 workers, however, would require 25% overtime at a time when no other activity centers require any significant amount of overtime. The company decides that, under these circumstances, it will level off the overtime and add two more workers in assembly. This would reduce the need for overtime to just over 2%. The result of this change in manpower can be seen on the updated Schedule #08 shown in Exhibit 14.17.

Exhibit 14.17 Operating Manpower/Supply

OPERATING MANPOWER/SUPPLY — Add Another Contract #10 — Schedule #08

Small Time Manufacturing

	FTE Headcount	St-Time Hours per Employee	Total St-Time Hours Available	Gross Production Labor Hrs Required	Overtime Hours Required	Percentage Overtime Required
Machine/setup	2.0	1,762	3,524	2,736	0	0.0%
Machine/operator	3.0	1,762	5,286	5,304	18	0.3%
Assembly	11.0	1,762	19,382	19,800	418	2.1%
Ins/pak/shp	2.0	1,762	3,524	2,760	0	0.0%
Totals	18.0			30,600	436	1.4%

The next step is to evaluate the headcounts on Schedule #10: Support Staff. Management does not believe that the substitution of another Contract #10 for Contract #04 would increase the administrative or support workload enough to make it necessary to increase the workforce above the 14 current employees. As a result, no change would be made in support staff if the additional contract were included. A review of Schedule #12: Fixed and Budgeted Expense also indicates that no additional fixed or budgeted costs would result from the additional business.

The revised total accumulated cost on Schedule #14: Cost Accumulation now represents Small-Time Manufacturing's total cost with another contract identical to Contract #10 instead of Contract #04. The net change in cost, which is summarized in Exhibit 14.18, can be compared to the net

Exhibit 14.18 Accumulated Cost Comparisons

ACCUMULATED COST COMPARISONS — Add Another Contract #10

Small-Time Manufacturing

	Costs Before "What If?"	Costs After "What If?"	Change
Throughput costs			
Raw materials	$500,000	$475,000	($25,000)
Purchased components	$300,000	$330,000	$30,000
Outside services	$200,000	$250,000	$50,000
Wages & fringes			
Support–Base	$430,394	$430,394	$0
Manufacturing–Base	$250,204	$278,396	$28,192
Manufacturing–ST-OT	$26,676	$3,524	($23,152)
Total s-time wages	$707,274	$712,314	$5,040
Fringe benefits	$268,070	$277,581	$9,512
Applied fringes			
Overtime premium	$13,338	$1,762	($11,576)
Total wages & fringes	$988,681	$991,657	$2,976
Costs & expenses:			
Utilities	$80,000	$68,000	($12,000)
Tooling	$60,000	$51,000	($9,000)
Mfg supplies	$79,000	$81,950	$2,950
Admin supplies	$25,000	$25,000	$0
Fixed/budget expenses	$300,000	$300,000	$0
Total accumulated costs	$2,532,681	$2,572,607	$39,926

change in revenue to determine the impact on Small-Time Manufacturing's profit. The revised amounts are as follows:

	Revenues	*Costs*	*Profit*
Original model	$2,659,314	$2,532,681	$126,633
Less: Contract #04	(199,208)	(117,901)	(81,307)
Plus: new contract	294,347	157,827	136,520
Revised model	$2,754,453	$2,572,607	$181,846

The impact is considerable. Had Small-Time Manufacturing's quoting practices enabled it to win one more job like Contract #10 instead of Contract #04 (which it would never have quoted at the artificially low price that won the contract), its mix of business would have generated 44% more profit at the same volume of business (total internal costs differ by less than 1%). Consider what would have happened if all of the contracts won had been quoted with an accurate knowledge of each contract's potential profitability.

SUMMARY

As can be seen from this case, a great deal of improvement in product costing can be achieved without a tremendous investment in time and money. A thoughtful, activity-based analysis of a company, such as that outlined in this case, will provide the information necessary to significantly improve profitability. Contracts such as Contract #04 will no longer be awarded simply because the company's costing practices caused it to underestimate its cost. Instead, the company will now become more competitive on contracts similar to Contract #06, which it frequently lost because its costing practices caused contract costs to be overestimated. Simply by substituting one profitable contract that was previously lost due to overestimated costs for an unprofitable one that was previously won because underestimated costs can have a substantial impact on a company's bottom line.

In addition, the activity-based cost accumulation and distribution also provides the company with a tool for evaluating those incremental jobs that, under certain circumstances, might enhance its profitability overall despite their apparent undesirability.

Small-Time Manufacturing did not have to convert its existing day-to-day cost accounting system to accomplish this. It did not have to buy special software. What it did need to do is:

- Make the intellectual investment necessary to begin viewing its business through the lens of ABC.

- Develop a cost flow-down structure that accurately (not precisely) reflects the company's actual cost behavior.
- Build a model that can simulate that cost behavior.
- Develop the decision costing skills that can turn the accurate and relevant information developed through ABC into higher profits through better informed management decisions.

Product costing is not the only area in which ABC and an activity-based cost accumulation and distribution model will improve decision making. In the next few chapters, we will carry the Small-Time Manufacturing case further and show how it can be used in a variety of other decision costing situations.

15

Small-Time Manufacturing: Discrete Event Simulation or "What If" Analysis

In the previous chapter, we looked at the impact of activity-based costing (ABC) on Small-Time Manufacturing's understanding of its contract costs and profitability. We also saw how fully absorbed contract profitability was not an accurate indicator of an individual contract's contribution to the company's performance. To do that, we needed to use the model to simulate the impact on costs of dropping and/or adding a contract. The latter was an example of discrete event simulation, or as most of us call it, "what if?" analysis.

Because a major portion of a small or mid-sized business' costs can be characterized as step variable, the ability to accurately simulate cost behavior under a wide variety of circumstances is one of the most powerful benefits of an activity-based cost accumulation and distribution model. When using the model for "what if" analyses, the company is taking into account the fact that the definitions of fixed and variable costs are situation specific, especially at a small or mid-sized organization. As a result, decision makers will get both accurate and relevant cost information to support all types of management decisions.

In this chapter, we will explore a variety of decision situations in which Small-Time Manufacturing will use its cost accumulation and distribution model to support the decision-making process. To keep things simple, we will continue to use the previous year's data that was entered while building the model as a base. In the real world, the model would have been reset at some future (this or next year) or theoretical (practical capacity) volume and mix of business. Remember, Small-Time will not be making any more products last year. None of the decisions being made are retroactive—they will all impact future costs.

SCENARIO 1

A potential new customer approaches Small-Time Manufacturing with a proposal. It seems that the company is unhappy with a current supplier and would like to transfer all of that supplier's business to Small-Time. The transfer would result in a 50% increase in all of Small-Time's activities. The additional revenue that would be generated from this transfer of business is $1.1 million.

In evaluating this decision, Small-Time estimated that it would have to purchase and handle an additional $250,000 of raw materials, $150,000 of purchased components, and $100,000 of outside services. In addition, it would have to perform 200 more setups, run its machines for an additional 4,000 hours, perform 7,500 more hours of assembly work, and prepare 600 more shipments. After developing this data, the company entered it into its contract costing template and came up with the results shown in Exhibit 15.1.

The resulting $1,266,586 contract cost exceeded the contract's revenue by $166,586. According to this calculation, the contract would have generate a 15% loss as a percentage of sales. Although the company had been quite excited at the prospect of increasing its volume by 50% in "one fell swoop," this activity-based information had most managers convinced that this would be a bad contract to add to its portfolio of business. Fortunately, not all managers were so convinced. A few suggested that perhaps the company was not looking at this decision properly.

These managers questioned whether this contract should be looked at in the same way as the company's core business. Fully absorbed cost information, such as was used in the calculation, is relevant only for core business pricing decisions. The company's core business consisted of $100,000 to $400,000 contracts bid under competitive conditions. This was a take-it-or-leave-it decision for a contract two and one-half times bigger than the company's largest current contract. Were the costs determined by using the company's core business costing mechanics the relevant and accurate costs needed in support of this decision?

The determination was made that this was a decision situation that should be looked at incrementally. How much would Small-Time's total cost increase if it took on this contract? To determine this increment in cost,

Exhibit 15.1 Contract Cost Estimates

CONTRACT COST ESTIMATE

Small-Time Manufacturing

Special Order

ACTIVITY-BASED COSTING

			Internal Costs	Total Costs
Direct materials:				
Raw materials	$250,000	14.1%	$35,250	$285,250
Purchased components	$150,000	29.2%	$43,800	$193,800
Outside services	$100,000	39.9%	$39,900	$139,900
Operating activities:				
Machining:				
Setups	200	$277.65	$55,530	$55,530
Machine hours	4,000	$58.80	$235,200	$235,200
Assembly:				
Assembly hours	7,500	$25.29	$189,675	$189,675
Inspect/pack/ship:				
Shipments	600	$110.14	$66,084	$66,084
Subtotal			$665,439	$1,165,439
G&A @		15.2%	$101,147	$101,147
Total contract cost			$766,586	$1,266,586

the company began with the base model (total cost of $2,532,681) and performed the following steps:

- The additional throughput costs and activity measures were added to Schedule #01: Contract Activity Summary.
- The screen on Schedule #04: Screen was checked and found to be 4,205 hours short of the hours needed with the new contract added. After reviewing its options for adding machining capacity, the company decided to add a second shift in the machining area. The addition of the shift changed the 4,205 hour shortage to a 5,390 hour cushion.
- The labor situation was checked on Schedule #08: Operating Manpower/Supply. At current manpower levels, overtime requirements would be 18.4% for machine/setup, 43.5% for machine/operate, 41.3% for assembly, and 18.4% for inspect/pack/ship. Although overtime for machine/setup and inspect/pack/ship were acceptable, overtime levels in excess of 40% would not be acceptable. As a result, it was decided that an additional two individuals would be needed in machine/operate and an additional four needed in assembly, resulting in overtime requirements of 5.9% and 15.2%, respectively. Adding only one new employee in machine/setup would have resulted in an overtime requirement of 24.7%, which would have still been unacceptable.
- Required support staff additions were then added on Schedule #10: Support Staff. As a result of the additional shift, it was estimated that headcounts in Supervision and manufacturing support would have to increase by one each. As a result of the additional volume, it was decided that a second addition would be needed in manufacturing support as well as one more individual in management/administration. These four additional employees were added to the schedule.
- After reviewing Schedule #13: Fixed and Budgeted Costs, management decided that no cost changes would result in either of the two categories.

These changes being made to the model's input data, the model was recalculated and a total accumulated cost of operation determined.

This cost, as summarized on Exhibit 15.2, totaled $3,489,560. By comparing this result to the $2,532,681 total cost without the contract, the company can see that the incremental cost that would be incurred by accepting the new contract is approximately $957,000. By examining the Change column, we can test this result for reasonableness.

Throughput costs increase by 50%. This is as should be expected. Providing the mix of business remains constant, which it does in this scenario,

Exhibit 15.2 Accumulated Cost Comparisons

ACCUMULATED COST COMPARISONS — Scenario 1

Small-Time Manufacturing

	Costs Before "What if?"	Costs After "What if?"	Change
Throughput costs:			
Raw materials	$500,000	$750,000	$250,000
Purchased components	$300,000	$450,000	$150,000
Outside services	$200,000	$300,000	$100,000
Wages & fringes			
Support–Base	$430,394	$550,833	$120,440
Manufacturing–Base	$250,204	$341,828	$91,624
Manufacturing–ST-OT	$26,676	$54,172	$27,496
Total S-Time Wages	$707,274	$946,833	$239,560
Fringe benefits	$268,070	$356,640	$88,571
Applied fringes			
Overtime premium	$13,338	$27,086	$13,748
Total wages & fringes	$988,681	$1,330,560	$341,878
Costs & Expenses			
Utilities	$80,000	$120,000	$40,000
Tooling	$60,000	$90,000	$30,000
Mfg supplies	$79,000	$118,500	$39,500
Admin supplies	$25,000	$30,500	$5,500
Fixed/budget expenses	$300,000	$300,000	$0
Total accumulated costs	$2,532,681	$3,489,560	$956,878

throughput costs have linear variability. Support wages increase by 28%. Since the support staff increased by 29%, from 14 employees to 18 employees, this change appears reasonable.

Straight-time manufacturing wages increase only 43% [($91,624 + $27,496)/$250,204 + $26,676)] despite a 50% increase in volume. This disparity relates to machine/setup and inspect/pack/ship in which workers go from an underutilized situation to one in which they are required to work overtime. In both activity centers, the first 644 hours of additional work is free, resulting in a much smaller increase in labor supply than the increase in labor demand. Similarly, fringe benefit costs rise only 33% as the total labor force rises by only one third [(4 support employees + 6 production employees)/(14 support employees + 16 production employees)].

Directly variable cost categories, utilities, tooling, and manufacturing supplies, all rise 50% as would be expected, whereas administrative supplies rise only 22%, in line with the 29% increase in support employees. The overall projected change in costs does appear to be reasonable.

The $957,000 increase in costs means an additional profit of $143 thousand would be realized by the company. The change to the company's overall profitability would be as follows:

	Before	*Change*	*After*
Revenues	$2,659.314	$1,110,000	$3,759,314
Total costs	2,532,682	956,878	3,489,560
Profit	$ 126,632	$ 143,122	$ 269,754
Profit % to sales	4.8%	13.0%	7.2%

It appears as if Small-Time Manufacturing would be better off if it accepted the potential new customer's proposal. By using the activity-based cost accumulation and distribution model effectively, the company was able to accurately determine the relevant information for this decision. The cost information did not, however, tell Small-Time management what decision to make; it only provided support information. There may be other issues to consider. What is the potential customer's reputation? Once in the door, will they demand price decreases?

Assuming the model's distribution information does not change, this new contract will still generate a loss on a fully-absorbed basis even at the higher volume of business. The rate structure that would exist with the new contract is summarized on the revised model's Schedule #19: Cost/Rate Reconciliation. This schedule is shown in Exhibit 15.3. Using those rates to recost the new contract results in a total contract cost of $1,163,327 as shown in Exhibit 15.4. This fully absorbed cost of $1,163,327 generates a loss of $63,327 or .6% of the contract's revenues. If word of the new customer's prices get out in the marketplace, will existing customers begin pressuring the company for similar prices? Could the company aggressively price four or five smaller jobs that would also increase its volume by 50% but do it more profitably?

All these types of issues should be considered when making a decision such as this one. Activity-based cost information alone does not provide management with the answers. It does, however, supply management with critical facts—accurate and relevant cost information on which its decision can be based.

Exhibit 15.3 Cost/Rate Reconciliation

COST/RATE RECONCILIATION ========================
Scenario 1
Schedule #19

Small-Time Manufacturing

	Rate	Base		Total Cost
Throughput costs:				
Raw materials				$750,000
Purchased components				$450,000
Outside services				$300,000
Total throughput costs				$1,500,000
Throughput overhead:				
Raw Mat'ls	10.6%	$750,000	Dollars of throughput	$79,788
Purch Comp	21.6%	$450,000	Dollars of throughput	$97,044
OSServices	31.2%	$300,000	Dollars of throughput	$93,643
Manufacturing overhead:				
Machine/setup	$240.29	600	Setups	$144,176
Machine/operator	$52.38	12,000	Machine hours	$628,538
Assembly	$24.25	22,500	Direct labor hours	$545,608
Ins/pak/shp	$91.46	1,800	Shipments	$164,622
Total internal costs				$1,753,419
General & Administration				
Gen & Admin	13.5%	$1,753,419	Internal costs	$236,141
Total costs				$3,489,560

Exhibit 15.4 Contract Cost Estimate

```
CONTRACT COST ESTIMATE                        Special Order/Scenario #1 Rates
======================
Small-Time Manufacturing
```

			Internal Costs	Total Costs
	ACTIVITY-BASED COSTING			
Direct materials:				
Raw materials	$250,000	10.6%	$26,500	$276,500
Purchased components	$150,000	21.6%	$32,400	$182,400
Outside services	$100,000	31.2%	$31,200	$131,200
Operating activities:				
Machining:				
Setups	200	$240.29	$48,058	$48,058
Machine hours	4,000	$52.38	$209,520	$209,520
Assembly:				
Assembly hours	7,500	$24.25	$181,875	$181,875
Inspect/pack/ship:				
Shipments	600	$91.46	$54,876	$54,876
Subtotal			$584,429	$1,084,429
G&A @		13.5%	$78,898	$78,898
Total contract cost			$663,327	$1,163,327

SCENARIO 2

Small-Time Manufacturing's manufacturing support personnel have found new machine center controls that would make it possible to reduce machining time by 10%. These controls would cost $7,000 for each of the company's machine centers. To evaluate the economics of this potential investment, the company's management needs to know the cash savings that the investment would provide at its current volume and mix of business.

Management recognizes the cost accumulation and distribution model as an efficient and accurate way to measure these savings. To calculate this decrease in cost, the company began with the base model (total cost $2,532,681) and performed the following steps:

- The 10% reduction in machining hours (800 hours) was subtracted on Schedule #01: Contract Activity Summary.

- The labor situation was checked on Schedule #08: Operating Manpower/Supply. At current manpower levels, overtime requirements would fall to 5.9% for machine/operate. No reduction in headcount would be possible, but overtime requirements would be reduced significantly.

Because this savings was from a decrease in one activity center's level of activity, it was not necessary to check the screen of Schedule #04 or the support staff on Schedule #10.

These changes being made to the model's input data, the model was recalculated and a total accumulated cost of operation determined. This cost, as summarized on Exhibit 15.5, totaled $2,508,324 representing a savings of

Exhibit 15.5 Accumulated Cost Comparisons

ACCUMULATED COST COMPARISONS — Scenario #2

Small-Time Manufacturing

	Costs Before "What if?"	Costs After "What if?"	Change
Throughput costs:			
Raw materials	$500,000	$500,000	$0
Purchased components	$300,000	$300,000	$0
Outside services	$200,000	$200,000	$0
Wages & fringes:			
Support–Base	$430,394	$430,394	$0
Manufacturing–Base	$250,204	$250,204	$0
Manufacturing–ST-OT	$26,676	$20,436	($6,240)
Total s-time wages	$707,274	$701,034	($6,240)
Fringe benefits	$268,070	$267,073	($997)
Applied fringes			
Overtime premium	$13,338	$10,218	($3,120)
Total wages & fringes	$988,681	$978,324	($10,357)
Costs & expenses:			
Utilities	$80,000	$72,000	($8,000)
Tooling	$60,000	$54,000	($6,000)
Mfg supplies	$79,000	$79,000	$0
Admin supplies	$25,000	$25,000	$0
Fixed/budget expenses	$300,000	$300,000	$0
Total accumulated costs	$2,532,681	$2,508,324	($24,357)

$24,357 annually. When compared to the required investment of $35,000 (5 machines × $7,000 each), this capital expenditure would generate a simple return on investment of 70% and a payback period of 1.4 years. In addition, it would improve profitability at the company's current volume and mix of business from $126,633 to $150,990, an increase of 19%.

Does this $24,357 savings make sense? In the base model, personnel in machine/operate are required to work 6,240 hours of which 954 hours are overtime. By reducing the labor requirements by 10%, 624 hours of labor will not be necessary. Because 954 hours of overtime are included in the base model, the 624-hour savings would comprise a 624-hour decrease in overtime hours. At $10 per hour, that would be a $6,240 straight-time savings and an additional 50%, or $3,120, savings in overtime premium.

Two fringe benefits are driven by labor dollars: employer FICA/Medicare (7.65% of labor dollars) and pension/profit sharing (3.00% of labor dollars). Applying the combined rate of 10.65% to the labor savings of $9,360 ($6,240 straight time + $3,120 overtime premium) results in a $997 fringe benefit savings. Headcounts remain the same, so no fringes driven by that factor will change.

Finally, the 10% reduction in machine hours will reduce the two machine hour driven variable costs, utilities and tooling, by 10%. Utilities will drop from $80,000 to $70,000 and tooling from $60,000 to $54,000—a total of $14,000.

Combining the labor cost savings of $9,360, the fringe cost savings of $997, and the machine hour–driven variable cost savings of $14,000, results in our overall savings of $24,357. No other costs will change significantly. In this decision situation, the amount of savings does make sense. Had the decision situation been different, the savings would have been different. For example, if the reduction in hours reduced only straight-time labor, the savings would have been $3,452 less [($3,120 overtime premium + $332 fringe benefits (10.65% rate × $3,120 savings)]. The model effectively determined the impact of the new controls under the specific decision.

SCENARIO 3

Development of the activity-based cost accumulation and distribution model heightened management's awareness of the amount of time production workers spend on non-production activities. They realized that some indirect activities by these individuals were unavoidable, but the 20%–30% indicated by the activity-based analysis was unacceptable.

At management's request, a manufacturing consultant submitted a proposal to study production activities and develop ways of reducing the nonproductive hours worked by production personnel. Both the consultant and management believed that the four production activity centers' indirect activity allowances could be reduced by at least one half. The consultant's fee for services was projected as $45,000.

To evaluate this expenditure, management needed to know the cash savings that would be provided by such a reduction in the indirect activity allowances. The cost accumulation and distribution model was again used to measure this potential savings.

The company began with the base model (total cost of $2,532,681) and performed the following steps:

- Indirect activity allowances were cut in half on Schedule #05: Operating Manpower/Demand. Allowances of 10% remained for machine/setup, assembly, and inspect/pack/ship and an allowance of 15% remained for machine/operate.
- The labor situation was checked on Schedule #08: Operating Manpower/Supply. At current manpower levels, overtime requirements would fall to 4.2% for machine/operate and 3.9% for assembly. No labor savings would be realized in machine/setup or inspect/pack/ship, existing personnel would just be more underutilized. No reduction in headcount would be possible, but overall overtime requirements would be reduced significantly.

Since there is no change in any activity center's level of activity, it was not necessary to check the screen of Schedule #04 or the support staff on Schedule #10.

These changes being made to the model's input data, the model was recalculated and a total accumulated cost of operation determined. This cost, as summarized on Exhibit 15.6, totaled $2,500,814 representing a savings of $31,867 annually. When compared to the required investment of $45,000, this expenditure would also generate a simple return on investment of 70% and a payback period of 1.4 years. In addition, it would improve profitability at the company's current volume and mix of business from $126,633 to $158,500, an increase of 25%.

Again, does this savings make sense? Under the circumstances, this proposed action would result only in savings in the two value-adding activity centers that were not already being underutilized: machine/operate and assembly. The reduction in machine/operate would be 720 hours (.15/1.30 × 6,240) and in assembly it would be 1,500 hours (.1/1.2 × 18,000). At $10 per hour, a savings of $7,200 would be realized in machine/operate and at $8 per hour, a savings of $12,000 would occur in assembly. This combines to a $19,200 straight-time labor savings. In both cases, the savings would be reflected as reductions in overtime hours. As a result, an overtime premium savings of $9,600 (50% premium × $19,200) would be realized. Finally, a

Exhibit 15.6 Accumulated Cost Comparisons

ACCUMULATED COST COMPARISONS — Scenario #3

Small-Time Manufacturing

	Costs Before "What if?"	Costs After "What if?"	Change
Throughput costs:			
Raw materials	$500,000	$500,000	$0
Purchased components	$300,000	$300,000	$0
Outside services	$200,000	$200,000	$0
Wages & fringes:			
Support–Base	$430,394	$430,394	$0
Manufacturing–Base	$250,204	$250,204	$0
Manufacturing–ST-OT	$26,676	$7,476	($19,200)
Total s-time wages	$707,274	$688,074	($19,200)
Fringe benefits	$268,070	$265,002	($3,067)
Applied fringes			
Overtime premium	$13,338	$3,738	($9,600)
Total wages & fringes	$988,681	$956,814	($31,867)
Costs & expenses:			
Utilities	$80,000	$80,000	$0
Tooling	$60,000	$60,000	$0
Mfg supplies	$79,000	$79,000	$0
Admin supplies	$25,000	$25,000	$0
Fixed/budget expenses	$300,000	$300,000	$0
Total accumulated costs	$2,532,681	$2,500,814	($31,867)

$3,067 fringe benefit savings (10.65% × $28,800 payroll savings) would result from the decrease in payroll dollars. Combining these results in an overall savings of $31,867. Again, the model provided an accurate, situation-specific change in costs.

SCENARIO 4

Since both expenditures seemed to have good returns, management thought it might be worth doing both of them. Before moving forward, however, the company decided to run both projects through the model at the same time to reconfirm the $56,224 annual savings. To calculate the decrease in cost, the company again began with the base model (total cost $2,532,681) and performed the following steps:

- The 10% reduction in machining hours (800 hours) was subtracted on Schedule #01: Contract Activity Summary.
- Indirect activity allowances were cut in half on Schedule #05: Operating Manpower/Demand. Allowances of 10% remained for machine/setup, assembly, and inspect/pack/ship and an allowance of 15% remained for machine/operate.
- The labor situation was checked on Schedule #08: Operating Manpower/Supply. At current manpower levels, overtime would fall to 3.9% for assembly. In fact, the three workers in machine/operate would be underutilized by 318 hours. No reduction in headcount would be possible, but overtime requirements would be reduced significantly.

This savings was from a decrease in one activity center's level of activity; therefore, it was not necessary to check the screen of Schedule #04 or the support staff on Schedule #10.

After making these changes to the model's input data, the model was recalculated and a revised total accumulated cost of operation determined. This cost, as summarized on Exhibit 15.7, totaled $2,482,930 representing an annual savings of $49,751. Obviously $49,751 is not $56,224, not by $6,473. Small-Time Manufacturing's management became concerned. Something must be wrong with the model.

Actually, the fact that the sum of the savings from Scenario 2 and Scenario 3 did not equal the savings from Scenario 4 is not an indication that something is wrong with the model. It is, instead, an indication that something is right with the model. The design of Small-Time Manufacturing's activity-based cost accumulation and distribution model did not allow it to (1) save the same money twice, or (2) eliminate labor costs simply because the demand for labor declined.

Be reducing the number of machining hours from 8,000 to 7,200, the demand for machining labor was reduced by 624 hours (800 machine hours × 0.6 worker crew size × 1.30 indirect activity gross-up). As a result, 72 hours of savings in machine/operate from the 15 percentage point reduction in its indirect activity allowance [(624 hours/(.15/1.30)] were already realized when the 800 machine hours were eliminated. In addition, after eliminating 624 hours of production labor by adding new controls, only 330 overtime hours remained. As a result, the 648 hour savings resulting from the 15 percentage point reduction in indirect activity allowance on the balance of the machine/operate production labor hours

Exhibit 15.7 Accumulated Cost Comparisons

ACCUMULATED COST COMPARISONS — Scenario #4

Small-Time Manufacturing

	Costs Before "What If?"	Costs After "What If?"	Change
Throughput costs			
Raw materials	$500,000	$500,000	$0
Purchased components	$300,000	$300,000	$0
Outside services	$200,000	$200,000	$0
Wages & Fringes			
Support–Base	$430,394	$430,394	$0
Manufacturing–Base	$250,204	$250,204	$0
Manufacturing–ST-OT	$26,676	$5,136	($21,540)
Total s-time wages	$707,274	$685,734	($21,540)
Fringe benefits	$268,070	$264,629	($3,441)
Applied fringes			
Overtime premium	$13,338	$2,568	($10,770)
Total wages & fringes	$988,681	$952,930	($35,751)
Costs & expenses			
Utilities	$80,000	$72,000	($8,000)
Tooling	$60,000	$54,000	($6,000)
Mfg supplies	$79,000	$79,000	$0
Admin supplies	$25,000	$25,000	$0
Fixed/budget expenses	$300,000	$300,000	$0
Total accumulated costs	$2,532,681	$2,482,930	($49,751)

[5,616 hours/(.15/1.30] only resulted in 330 hours being eliminated; 318 hours of savings were not realized.

The duplicate savings represented by the combined 390 production labor hours (72 hours + 318 hours) accounts for the $6,473 difference. Individuals in machine/operate earn a straight-time rate of $10 per hour. All of the hours saved represented overtime hours. Fringe benefits driven by labor dollars are employer FICA/Medicare of 7.65% and pension/profit sharing of 3.00%. The 390 duplicated hours at $10 per hour total $3,900. The 50% overtime premium is another $1,950 hours for a total wage savings of $5,850. Adding another 10.65% (7.65% + 3.00%) to that total for fringe benefits brings the duplicate savings total to $6,473.

This reconciliation treated the reduction in indirect activity allowance percentages as occurring after the new controls are added. As a result, the savings are assumed to be duplicated in the indirect activity allowance reduction. The calculation can also be performed under the assumption that the new controls were added after the indirect activity allowance reduction and the savings are duplicated in the new controls amount. The details will be different but the final answer will be the same.

SUMMARY

In this chapter we have touched on only a few of the situations in which a well-designed and -constructed cost accumulation and distribution model can be used in discrete event simulations (or "what if" analyses). Other areas include strategic pricing analyses, make/buy decisions, and product line add/drop decisions. For the small and mid-sized business, it is imperative that the model perform this function well. The predominance of step variable activities and costs in such organizations make traditional views of costs as either fixed or variable useless at best and dangerous at worst. Remember that the definitions of fixed and variable costs are situation specific. Only through a customized model that actually parallels the behavior of a company's cost can the small or mid-sized business hope to have the accurate and relevant costs necessary to support sound business decisions.

In the next chapter, we will show how Small-Time Manufacturing can use its model and a special contract costing template to support one type of decision that has become more critical in recent years: a long-term pricing decision that requires percentage price reductions during the course of the contract.

16

Small Time Manufacturing: Multiyear Costing and Pricing

One challenge facing many organizations is the long-term pricing commitments increasingly required by their customers. This is especially true of the small and mid-sized organization that serves as a supplier to one or more major corporations. These customers often require multiyear fixed prices or even guaranteed annual price reductions from their suppliers as a means of controlling their own costs.

Although these customer demands create opportunities for small and mid-sized organizations, the long-term commitments involved can also make these opportunities dangerous. Decisions based on bad information today could lead to tremendous problems, if not total disaster, tomorrow. This is especially true when the organization is considering a single, long-term project that cannot be modified to any significant extent during its period of performance.

Activity-based costing (ABC) and the cost accumulation and distribution model can be valuable tools for evaluating and minimizing the risk of making long-term pricing commitments. The first step in the process is to use the cost accumulation and distribution model to develop "then year" cost structures and rates. The second step is to determine the year-by-year resource requirements of the contract under consideration. The third step is to apply the "then year" rates to the resource requirements to estimate the cost of executing the contract. The fourth and final step is to determine the price that will provide the company with its targeted profit objective *over the life of the contract.*

It is important to understand that normal financial reporting following generally accepted accounting principles and practices will not effectively measure the profitability of an organization with long-term contracts. Consider again our example from Chapter 4. A manufacturer had an opportunity to bid on a three-year, fixed price contract. The contract was for 30,000 units of a product with 10,000 units to be shipped during each year. The company estimated that its cost of manufacturing the product would be $10 in the first year, $9 in the second year, and $8 in the third year. Its total cost would be $270,000 [(10,000 units x $10) + (10,000 units × $9) + (10,000 units x $8)]. To realize its target margin of 10% over the life of the contract, it would need to earn a profit of $30,000. To attain that target, a fixed price of $10 per unit [($270,000 cost + $30,000 profit)/30,000 units] was bid. The company was awarded the contract.

The company's estimators were right on target with their cost estimates. During the first year, sales were $100,000 (10,000 units × $10 per unit) and costs were $100,000 (10,000 units × $10 per unit). The books showed that the company just broke even on this contract. Is that a fair representation of the company's performance? Did it really just break even?

I believe the company earned a profit of either $10,000 or $11,111 on this contract during the first year. The cost estimates on which the contract price was based assumed that during the first year of the contract, the product would cost $10, which it did. The contract was quoted at a 10% margin which works out to $1 per unit. Since costs are exactly as estimated, how can the company not be earning its targeted profit during the first year? If you look at the target as a $1 per unit profit, it earned $10,000. If you look at the target as a 10% markup, it earned $11,111. Either way, it did not simply break even.

The opposite would happen in the third year of the contract if costs end up exactly as estimated. The financial results will show revenues of $100,000 and costs of $80,000, a $20,000 profit. Was there really a $20,000 profit in the third year? Again, I would propose that the profit was either $10,000 or $8,889. $10,000 if you look at the target as $1 per unit and $8,889 if you view it as a 10% markup.

The point here is that, despite financial accounting rules, management cannot view results that include long-term pricing arrangements the same way it views results when all contracts are short-term. Each long-term contract with a long-term pricing commitment must be treated more like a large construction contract than like the month-to-month sale of individual products or services. The contract is the unit for measuring profitability, not the individual transactions or events that make up that contract. With this in mind, we can see how Small-Time Manufacturing uses ABC to respond to an opportunity to quote a multiyear contract that requires annual price reductions.

SMALL-TIME MANUFACTURING'S OPPORTUNITY

One of Small-Time Manufacturing's customers has asked it to bid on a contract to produce 150,000 units that would be manufactured and shipped during a four-year period: 20,000 units would be required during the first year with 50,000, 50,000, and 30,000 required in the three succeeding years. The price quoted would be effective for the first year only. In each succeeding year, a 3% price reduction would be required.

Small-Time's estimator determined that each unit would require $1.75 (current cost) of direct and throughput costs. Raw material cost would be $1.00, purchased components $.50, and outside services $.25. The units would be manufactured in lots of 1,000. The company would be able to machine 32 units per hour and assemble 65 units per hour. Shipments would be made in lots of 500.

At this point, the estimator stopped. He knew that simply loading this information into the company's normal activity-based cost estimating template would not provide the necessary information. That template assumes that all activities will be performed and costs incurred in the short term. This contract would be executed over a four-year period. Having never been asked to estimate costs over a such an extended period before, the estimator turned to management for direction.

ESTABLISHING "THEN YEAR" COSTING RATES

After building its activity-based cost accumulation and distribution model and loading it with the previous year's data, management had already begun to develop an edition of the model that would reflect the current year's forecast volume and mix of business. With the appearance of this multiyear contract opportunity, they decided that simply having an edition of the model representing the current year would not be enough. The company would need to develop a forecast of its volume and mix of business over the next four years and then use that forecast to develop a realistic set of costing rates for each year.

After reviewing market opportunities and strategies, management came up with the following four-year forecast of the company's seven cost driving activity measures:

	Year 1	*Year 2*	*Year 3*	*Year 4*
Raw materials	$550,000	$650,000	$725,000	$825,000
Purchased components	$350,000	$390,000	$470,000	$530,000
Outside services	$200,000	$225,000	$275,000	$275,000
Machine/setups	450	510	590	710
Machine/operating hours	9,000	10,600	11,800	14,600
Assembly hours	16,600	18,600	22,600	25,600
Shipments	1,400	1,600	1,825	2,175

While developing this forecast, management also took a look at other model variables and forecast future developments in those areas as well.

After developing the original edition of the cost accumulation and distribution model which contained the previous year's data, management decided that the time requirements for setups and shipments needed to be addressed. They quickly found a method that would make it possible to reduce setups from 3.0 hours to 2.5 hours. A quick and simple means of reducing the time required for shipments was not found. Management did, however, set a goal of reducing the time required for shipment by 20% during the next two years. As a result, it was decided that set-up hours would be reduced from 3.0 to 2.5 hours in Year 1 and that shipment time would be reduced from 2.0 to 1.6 hours in Year 3.

It was management's desire to avoid adding a second shift in machining for as long as possible. Reducing set-up time provided several hundred additional hours of machine capacity and management decided that it could extend the length of a shift in machining from eight to nine hours without any difficulty. Once the capacity available from a daily nine-hour shift was exhausted, however, management was willing to switch to two eight-hour shifts in machining.

The identification and measurement of indirect activity allowances that took place during model development caused management to focus more attention on this area as a source of cost reductions. It set targets for reducing the allowances in machine/setup, assembly, and inspect/pack/ship from 20% to 18% in Year 1, 16% in Year 2, and 14% in Year 4. It also set targets for reducing machine/operate's rates from 30% to 27% in Year 1, 24% in Year 2, and 20% in Year 4.

The cost of manufacturing supplies, utilities, and tooling were forecast to increase by 10% in Year 2 and another 10% in Year 4. Pay rates for all employees would increase at the rate of 3% per year. Administrative supply costs are expected to increase by 5%, 3%, 2%, and 3% in Years 1, 2, 3, and 4 respectively. If a second shift in becomes necessary, headcounts in supervision and manufacturing support would have to be increased by one. In addition, the increases in volume forecast for Years 3 and 4 would require an additional individual in management/administration during Year 3 and one additional head in procurement, manufacturing support, and management/administration in Year 4.

Health insurance costs are expected to increase by $200 per employee in Year 1, another $200 per employee in Year 2, and $300 per employee in Years 3 and 4. Lease cost and property taxes are both expected to increase by $1,500 in Year 1 and again in Year 3. No other costs were expected to change enough to warrant modifying the model.

Management did not believe that the changes in volume and mix would have any impact on the activity analysis distribution percentages. As a result, those percentages remained the same in all editions of the model.

Using the original edition of the model containing the previous year's data as a base, the company prepared an edition of the model representing the forecast information for each of the next four years. The input required to effect the year-to-year changes is summarized in Exhibit 16.1 and 16.2. The costing rates calculated in these four models are included on the copies of each model's Schedule #19: Cost/Rate Reconciliation that are shown in Exhibits 16.3 through 16.6.

MULTIYEAR COSTING/PRICING TEMPLATE

Once the "then year" rates were established, Small-Time Manufacturing needed to develop a template for estimating contract costs that would then be used to develop a price that could be reduced by 3% annually but still result in its targeted profit margin on the overall contract.

I again suggest that you boot up your computer and build the template along with the book. Like the model, it will be constructed as a single, two-dimensional worksheet and will be presented in a plain vanilla format. It will be nine columns wide, of which the first four columns will include text and the other five will contain annual and total contract data. All columns will be set at a 12-character width. As was the case with the model, input data will be distinguished from the template itself by being presented in boxes. The boxes represent unprotected cells where the data required to drive the template is entered. The unboxed areas represent the protected cells where the formulae and text that comprise the template itself reside.

PRODUCTION REQUIREMENTS

Page 1 of the template is shown in Exhibit 16.7. The first data that must be entered into the template are the unit production requirements by year.

Exhibit 16.1 Data Required for Forecast Information

Schedule	Description		Year #1	Year #2	Year #3	Year #4
Schedule #01	Raw materials		$550,000	$650,000	$725,000	$825,000
	Purchased components		$350,000	$390,000	$470,000	$530,000
	Outside services		$200,000	$225,000	$275,000	$275,000
	Setups		450	510	590	710
	Machine hours		9,000	10,600	11,800	14,600
	Assembly hours		16,600	18,600	22,600	25,600
	Shipments		1,400	1,600	1,825	2,175
Schedule #03	Hours per setup		2.5	2.5	2.5	2.5
	Hours per shipment		2.0	2.0	1.6	1.6
Schedule #04	Shifts in operation		1.0	2.0	2.0	2.0
	Hours per shift		9.0	8.0	8.0	8.0
Schedule #05	Machine/setup	Ind allow	18%	16%	16%	14%
	Machine/operate	Ind allow	27%	24%	24%	20%
	Assembly	Ind allow	18%	16%	16%	14%
	Ins/pak/shp	Ind allow	18%	16%	16%	14%
Schedule #06	Machine/setup	Mfg supply	$40.00	$44.00	$44.00	$48.40
	Machine/operate	Utilities	$10.00	$11.00	$11.00	$12.10
		Tooling	$7.50	$8.25	$8.25	$9.08
	Assembly	Mfg supply	$3.00	$3.30	$3.30	$3.63
	Ins/pak/shp	Mfg supply	$15.00	$16.50	$16.50	$18.15
Schedule #08	Machine/setup	Headcount	2.0	2.0	2.0	2.0
	Machine/operate	Headcount	3.0	4.0	4.5	5.0
	Assembly	Headcount	11.0	11.0	14.0	14.0
	Ins/pak/shp	Headcount	2.0	2.0	2.0	2.0
Schedule #09	Machine/setup	Pay rate	$12.36	$12.73	$13.11	$13.50
	Machine/operate	Pay rate	$10.30	$10.61	$10.93	$11.26
	Assembly	Pay rate	$8.24	$8.49	$8.74	$9.00
	Ins/pak/shp	Pay rate	$8.24	$8.49	$8.74	$9.00

Exhibit 16.2 Data Required for Forecast Information

Schedule	Description		Year #1	Year #2	Year #3	Year #4
Schedule #10	Bldg & grnd	Headcount	1.0	1.0	1.0	1.0
	Supervision	Headcount	2.0	3.0	3.0	3.0
	Procurement	Headcount	1.0	1.0	1.0	2.0
	Mfg support	Headcount	5.0	6.0	6.0	7.0
	Mgmt & admn	Headcount	5.0	5.0	6.0	7.0
	Bldg & grnd	Pay rate	$11.89	$12.25	$12.62	$13.00
	Supervision	Pay rate	$17.83	$18.36	$18.91	$19.48
	Procurement	Pay rate	$19.81	$20.40	$21.01	$21.64
	Mfg Support	Pay rate	$14.85	$15.30	$15.76	$16.23
	Mgmt & admn	Pay rate	$19.81	$20.40	$21.01	$21.64
Schedule #11	Health insurance		$3,200	$3,400	$3,700	$4,000
Schedule #12	Bldg & grnd	Adm supply	$1,050	$1,082	$1,104	$1,137
	Supervision	Adm supply	$525	$541	$552	$569
	Procurement	Adm supply	$3,150	$3,245	$3,310	$3,409
	Mfg support	Adm supply	$1,050	$1,082	$1,104	$1,137
	Mgmt & admn	Adm supply	$3,150	$3,245	$3,310	$3,409
Schedule #13	Bldg & grnd	Leases	$51,500	$51,500	$53,000	$53,000
	Bldg & grnd	Prop taxes	$30,900	$30,900	$31,830	$31,830
	Raw Mat'ls	Prop taxes	$3,090	$3,090	$3,180	$3,180
	Purch comp	Prop taxes	$5,150	$5,150	$5,300	$5,300
	Machine/operate	Prop taxes	$10,300	$10,300	$10,610	$10,610
	Assembly	Prop taxes	$1,030	$1,030	$1,060	$1,060
	Ins/pak/shp	Prop taxes	$1,030	$1,030	$1,060	$1,060

Exhibit 16.3 Cost/Rate Reconciliation

COST/RATE RECONCILIATION
Small-Time Manufacturing

Schedule #19
Year #1

	Rate	Base		Total Cost
Throughput costs:				
Raw materials				$550,000
Purchased components				$350,000
Outside services				$200,000
Total throughput costs				$1,100,000
Throughput overhead:				
Raw Mat'ls	13.2%	$550,000	Dollars of throughput	$72,327
Purch Comp	25.7%	$350,000	Dollars of throughput	$90,076
OSServices	41.1%	$200,000	Dollars of throughput	$82,196
Manufacturing overhead:				
Machine/setup	$256.93	450	Setups	$115,618
Machine/operate	$56.31	9,000	Machine hours	$506,764
Assembly	$24.77	16,600	Direct labor hours	$411,150
Ins/pak/shp	$98.47	1,400	Shipments	$137,855
Total internal costs				$1,415,985
General & Administration				
G&A	14.7%	$1,415,985	Internal costs	$207,878
Total costs				$2,723,863

Exhibit 16.4 Cost/Rate Reconciliation

COST/RATE RECONCILIATION — Schedule #19

Small-Time Manufacturing — Year #2

	Rate	Base		Total Cost
Throughput costs:				
Raw materials				$650,000
Purchased components				$390,000
Outside services				$225,000
Total throughput costs				$1,265,000
Throughput overhead:				
Raw Mat'ls	11.8%	$650,000	Dollars of throughput	$76,850
Purch Comp	24.4%	$390,000	Dollars of throughput	$95,261
OSServices	40.0%	$225,000	Dollars of throughput	$90,026
Manufacturing overhead:				
Machine/Setup	$251.91	510	Setups	$128,476
Machine/Operate	$56.92	10,600	Machine hours	$603,398
Assembly	$26.27	18,600	Direct labor hours	$488,615
Ins/Pak/Shp	$98.29	1,600	Shipments	$157,270
Total internal costs				$1,639,895
General & Administration				
G&A	13.3%	$1,639,895	Internal costs	$218,331
Total costs				$3,123,226

Exhibit 16.5 Cost/Rate Reconciliation

COST/RATE RECONCILIATION

Small-Time Manufacturing

Schedule #19

Year #3

	Rate	Base		Total Cost
Throughput costs:				
Raw materials				$725,000
Purchased components				$470,000
Outside services				$275,000
Total throughput costs				$1,470,000
Throughput overhead:				
Raw mat'ls	11.7%	$725,000	Dollars of throughput	$84,640
Purch comp	22.0%	$470,000	Dollars of throughput	$103,544
OSServices	35.7%	$275,000	Dollars of throughput	$98,140
Manufacturing overhead:				
Machine/setup	$232.43	590	Setups	$137,134
Machine/operate	$55.33	11,800	Machine hours	$652,915
Assembly	$25.75	22,600	Direct labor hours	$581,953
Ins/pak/shp	$89.41	1,825	Shipments	$163,176
Total internal costs				$1,821,502
General & Administration				
G&A	13.9%	$1,821,502	Internal costs	$253,389
Total costs				$3,544,891

Exhibit 16.6 Cost/Rate Reconciliation

COST/RATE RECONCILIATION — Schedule #19

Small-Time Manufacturing — Year #4

	Rate	Base		Total Cost
Throughput costs:				
Raw materials				$825,000
Purchased components				$530,000
Outside services				$275,000
Total throughput costs				$1,630,000
Throughput overhead:				
Raw mat'ls	13.0%	$825,000	Dollars of throughput	$107,179
Purch comp	26.3%	$530,000	Dollars of throughput	$139,184
OSServices	47.2%	$275,000	Dollars of throughput	$129,823
Manufacturing overhead:				
Machine/setup	$233.70	710	Setups	$165,924
Machine/operate	$54.55	14,600	Machine hours	$796,379
Assembly	$26.02	25,600	Direct labor hours	$666,170
Ins/pak/shp	$87.05	2,175	Shipments	$189,324
Total internal costs				$2,193,982
General & Administration				
G&A	13.6%	$2,193,982	Internal costs	$299,133
Total costs				$4,123,115

Exhibit 16.7 Multiyear Costing/Pricing Template

MULTIYEAR COSTING/PRICING TEMPLATE

Small-Time Manufacturing

Page 1

	Year 1	Year 2	Year 3	Year 4	Program
Production Requirements	20,000	50,000	50,000	30,000	150,000
Direct and throughput costs:					
Raw materials:					
Cost per unit	$1.000	$1.020	$1.040	$1.061	
Raw material economics		2.0%	2.0%	2.0%	
Material cost without improvement	$20,000	$51,000	$52,000	$31,830	
Cumulative improvement		1.5%	2.0%	2.5%	
Material cost with improvement	$20,000	$50,235	$50,960	$31,034	$152,229
Raw material support rate	13.2%	11.8%	11.7%	13.0%	
Raw material support costs	$2,640	$5,928	$5,962	$4,034	$18,564
Total raw material-related costs	$22,640	$56,163	$56,922	$35,068	$170,793
Purchased components:					
Cost per unit	$0.500	$0.505	$0.510	$0.515	
Component economics		1.0%	1.0%	1.0%	
Component cost without improvement	$10,000	$25,250	$25,500	$15,450	
Cumulative improvement		0.5%	1.0%	1.0%	
Component cost with improvement	$10,000	$25,124	$25,245	$15,296	$75,665
Component cost support rate	25.7%	24.4%	22.0%	26.3%	
Purchased component support costs	$2,570	$6,130	$5,554	$4,023	$18,277
Total purchased component-related costs	$12,570	$31,254	$30,799	$19,319	$93,942

Units produced in each year will be costed using that year's data set (rates, productivity measures, inflation, etc.). For the contract currently under consideration, annual requirements are 20,000 units in Year 1, 50,000 units in Years 2 and 3, and 30,000 units in Year 4. Once the units are entered, the template can begin addressing direct and throughput costs.

DIRECT AND THROUGHPUT COSTS

The first cost to be addressed is raw materials. Small-Time's cost estimator has determined that, at current costs, $1.00 of raw material will be required for each unit produced. That does not mean, of course, that the cost will remain at $1 per unit for the duration of the contract. Two forces will change that cost. One force is economics. The cost of the raw materials themselves will most likely change during the course of the contract. The other force is utilization. As it gains experience in manufacturing the product, the company may find ways to use less material. Both of these forces need to be factored into the determination of raw material costs.

Raw material economics represents each year's estimated change in basic raw material cost. Small-Time anticipates an increase of 2% during each year (after the first year) of the contract. Beginning with the initial raw material cost of $1.000, the template proceeds to project the raw material cost per unit during the three years that follow. In the template, the increase is stated as a percentage of the previous year's cost, not the base year's cost. For example, the 2% increase in Year 4 is 2% of Year 3's cost of $1.040, not Year 1's cost of $1.000. That is why the cost calculates to $1.061 instead of $1.060. Using these projected unit costs, the template calculates each year's total raw material costs by multiplying each year's production requirements by the projected cost per unit.

The result of this calculation is the raw material cost if no improvements are made to get a better yield from the raw materials purchased. Such improvements may be possible. If they are, they should be factored into the contract's cost estimate. These improvements might result from a decrease in the scrap rate as the company moves down the learning curve. They may result from a redesign of the form in which the raw material is received. They may result from developing material handling and storage practices that result if less spoilage. Regardless of the reason, if these improvements are expected to materialize during the course of the contract, the company needs to incorporate them if it is to base its pricing decision on accurate cost information.

To incorporate material usage improvements, the template provides for a cumulative improvement percentage for each of the contract's years. This improvement percentage is used to reduce the previously calculated raw material cost. In Year 3, for example, the $50,960 total raw material cost is determined by multiplying the 50,000 production units by the $1.040 cost per unit and then multiplying that product by one minus the 2.0% cumulative improvement [50,000 units × $1.04 × (1–.02)].

Once each year's total raw material cost has been estimated, the raw material support costs must be added. This is accomplished by entering the raw material support rates that were developed in each year's cost accumulation and distribution model in the applicable columns. Each year's total raw material costs are then multiplied by its support rate to calculate raw material support costs. Adding the support costs to the total raw material costs determines total raw material related costs.

In a similar fashion, purchased component and outside service costs are calculated for each contract year. First year costs are adjusted for economics and yield improvements before being applied to the subsequent year's production requirements. Each year's support rate is then applied to the total cost to determine support costs. These are then combined to arrive at total purchased component and outside service related costs. Details of the purchased component calculations are at the bottom of page 1 of the template. Outside service's details are included at the top of page 2, which is shown in Exhibit 16.8. Direct and throughput related costs are summarized at the bottom of page 2.

DIRECT/VALUE-ADDING COSTS

Page 3 of the template, as shown in Exhibit 16.9, calculates the cost of direct/value-adding activities during the contract. The first activity addressed is machine/setup. As noted earlier, the estimator determined that this product would be manufactured in lots of 1,000 units. By entering this average lot size, the template can calculate the number of setups that will be required each year. As currently structured, the template assumes that the lot size will not change during the course of the contract. If the average lot size might change as annual quantities change, it could be treated as a separate input item each year. The cost per setup as determined in each year's cost accumulation and distribution model is entered and the total setup cost for each year of the contract determined. Remember that the cost per setup as calculated in each year's model includes the expected reduction in set-up time from 3.0 hours to 2.5 hours as well as the anticipated reductions in the activity's indirect activity allowance.

The machine/operate activities are addressed next. The machine hour rates as determined in each year's model are entered as is the first year's production rate stated in terms of units produced per hour. The machine hour rates already include the anticipated reductions in machine/operate's

Exhibit 16.8 Multiyear Costing/Pricing Template

MULTIYEAR COSTING/PRICING TEMPLATE

Small-Time Manufacturing

Page 2

	Year 1	Year 2	Year 3	Year 4	Program
Production Requirements	20,000	50,000	50,000	30,000	150,000
Direct and throughput costs:					
Outside services:					
Cost per unit	$0.250	$0.258	$0.266	$0.274	
Outside service economics		3.0%	3.0%	3.0%	
Outside service cost without improvement	$5,000	$12,900	$13,300	$8,220	
Cumulative improvement	0.0%	0.0%	0.0%	0.0%	
Outside service cost with improvement	$5,000	$12,900	$13,300	$8,220	$39,420
Outside service support rate	41.1%	40.0%	35.7%	47.2%	
Outside service support cost	$2,055	$5,160	$4,748	$3,880	$15,843
Total outside service-related costs	$7,055	$18,060	$18,048	$12,100	$55,263
Summary:					
Raw materials	$20,000	$50,235	$50,960	$31,034	$152,229
Purchased components	$10,000	$25,124	$25,245	$15,296	$75,665
Outside services	$5,000	$12,900	$13,300	$8,220	$39,420
Total direct/throughput support	$7,265	$17,218	$16,264	$11,937	$52,684
Total direct/throughput-related costs	$42,265	$105,477	$105,769	$66,487	$319,998

Exhibit 16.9 Multiyear Costing/Pricing Template

MULTIYEAR COSTING/PRICING TEMPLATE

Small-Time Manufacturing

Page 3

	Year 1	Year 2	Year 3	Year 4	Program
Production requirements	20,000	50,000	50,000	30,000	150,000
Direct/value-adding costs:					
Machine/setup:					
Average lot size	1000	1,000	1,000	1,000	
Number of setups	20	50	50	30	
Cost per setup	$256.93	$251.91	$232.43	$233.70	
Total setup costs	$5,139	$12,596	$11,622	$7,011	$36,367
Machine/operate:					
Cost per machine hour	$56.31	$56.92	$55.33	$54.55	
Units per hour	32	33	33	34	
Cumulative improvement		2.0%	4.0%	6.0%	
Machine hours	625	1,515	1,515	882	
Total machining costs	$35,194	$86,242	$83,833	$48,132	$253,401
Assembly:					
Cost per assembly hour	$24.77	$26.27	$25.75	$26.02	
Units per hour	65	68	70	71	
Cumulative improvement		4.0%	7.0%	9.0%	
Assembly hours	308	735	714	423	
Total assembly costs	$7,622	$19,316	$18,393	$10,994	$56,325
Inspect/pack/ship:					
Units per shipment	500	500	500	500	
Number of shipments	40	100	100	60	
Cost per shipment	$98.47	$98.29	$89.41	$87.05	
Total setup costs	$3,939	$9,829	$8,941	$5,223	$27,932
Total direct/value-adding costs	$51,893	$127,983	$122,789	$71,360	$374,024

indirect activity allowance. That improvement has an impact on the activity's rate. Productivity improvements, however, must be included in the template itself. Just as experience can produce yield improvements in materials, it can improve the productivity of machining operations. As a result, percentages representing the cumulative improvement in productivity (the number of units that can produced per hour) must be entered for Years 2 through 4.

Before calculating machining costs, the template must determine the number of units that can be produced per hour during each year. This is done by dividing the first year's production rate (32 units per hour) by one minus the year's cumulative improvement percentage. In the template, production rates are stated in whole units per hour. For example, in Year 3, the production rate of 33 units per hour was calculated by dividing 32 by .96 (1 – .04 improvement). The 33.3 answer was rounded to 33, the nearest whole number. Once the units per hour are determined for each year, total machining costs can be calculated.

Machining hours are determined by dividing the annual production requirements by each year's production units per hour. The resulting number of hours is then multiplied by the year's machine hour costing rate to calculate the year's total machining costs. In Year 4, the 30,000 units required will be machined at a rate of 34 units per hour. As a result, 882.36 hours will be required. Multiplying those hours by the $54.54 rate will determine the $48,124 machining costs. The total machining costs that result from these calculations include both improvements to the process itself (which are reflected in the rates) and in the use of the process on this specific product (which is reflected in the units per hour).

Costing assembly activities follows the same rationale. The annual rates, which include improvements to the process, are entered as is the first year's units per hour. Cumulative improvement percentages are entered for Years 2 through 4. The required assembly hours are calculated and multiplied by the year's production requirements to determine total assembly costs. As was the case in machining, this methodology allows both anticipated process and productivity improvements to be included in the multiyear cost calculations.

The methodology for inspect/pack/ship parallels that used for setups. Units per shipment are entered as are the inspect/pack/ship rates from each year's model. The units per shipment are used to determine the number of shipments that will be required each year. Each year's cost per shipment is multiplied by the number of shipments to arrive at the total inspect/pack/ship costs.

At the bottom of Page 3, each year's direct and value-adding activity costs are totaled.

GENERAL AND ADMINISTRATIVE ACTIVITIES

The only costs that remain to be attached to the contract are general and administrative (G&A) costs. This is done on the top of page 4 of the Multiyear Costing/Pricing Template, which is shown in Exhibit 16.10. The base for applying these costs, total internal costs, is calculated by bringing forward total direct/throughput support costs from Page 2 and total direct/value-adding costs from Page 3. After the G&A cost rates that were developed in each year's model are entered, they are multiplied by each year's total internal costs to calculate the general and administrative costs attributable to the contract.

At this point, total contract costs can be determined by adding total direct/throughput–related cost from page 2, total direct/value-adding costs from page 3, and the G&A costs calculated on page 4. The total for this contract is $752,686. To earn its target margin of 10%, Small-Time Manufacturing needs approximately $836,300 in revenues [$752,000/(1 – .10)]. The template's last step is to determine the initial unit price that will lead to the generation of that amount of contract revenue.

MULTIYEAR PROGRAM PRICING

The last portion of the template provides for entering a proposed unit price, reducing it by a certain amount annually, and determining the total revenues that will be generated under those conditions. The unit price that generates a margin of 10% on the entire contract is the minimum price Small-Time Manufacturing can quote if it hopes to earn its target margin.

The template assumes that each year's price reduction is a percentage of the previous year's price, not the original price. The original price is then reduced year by year to establish the price that would be in effect during each year of the contract. Those prices are multiplied by each year's production requirements to determine annual revenues. The sum of those annual revenues is compared to the contract's total costs to determine the margin. For this contract, the template indicates that Small-Time Manufacturing must charge an initial price of $5.852 per unit. For all practical purposes, this means that the company should find a price between $5.80 and $5.90 per unit acceptable. Never forget, our costs calculations are accurate, they are not precise. The danger for Small-Time Manufacturing is not that they miss out on a few thousand dollars of profit over the four year period due to inappropriate pricing. The danger is that it will accept a price that will cause the contract to be a disaster or that it will miss out altogether on

Exhibit 16.10 Multiyear Costing/Pricing Template

MULTIYEAR COSTING/PRICING TEMPLATE Page 4

Small-Time Manufacturing

	Year 1	Year 2	Year 3	Year 4	Program
Production requirements	20,000	50,000	50,000	30,000	150,000
G&A costs:					
Total direct/throughput support	7,265	17,218	16,264	11,937	
Total direct/value-adding costs	$51,893	$127,983	$122,789	$71,360	
Total internal costs	$59,158	$145,201	$139,053	$83,297	
G&A rate	14.7%	13.3%	13.9%	13.6%	
Total G&A costs	$8,696	$19,312	$19,328	$11,328	$58,664
Total costs	$102,854	$252,772	$247,886	$149,175	$752,686
Revenue:					
Unit sales price	$5.852	$5.676	$5.506	$5.341	
Required price reduction		3.0%	3.0%	3.0%	
Total revenues	$117,040	$283,800	$275,300	$160,230	$836,370
Net profit contribution	$14,186	$31,029	$27,415	$11,055	$83,684
Profit percentage of sales	12.1%	10.9%	10.0%	6.9%	10.0%

a valuable contract because it charged a price that would have actually represented a margin far above one that they find acceptable.

The following table summarizes the margin percentages that Small-Time Manufacturing would actually be seeking over the course of the contract at various initial unit prices:

Price	*Margin*
$6.25	15.7%
$6.00	12.2%
$5.75	8.4%
$5.50	4.3%
$5.25	–0.3%

If the company believes the market will accept an initial price of $6.25 or $6, it should definitely bid that price. There is nothing wrong with earning a margin above the targeted amount. But it certainly would not want to bid the job at $6 and lose it to a competitor that bid $5.90 when a price of $5.85 would have enabled it to win the contract and earn its target margin. If, on the other hand, it knows the market will not accept a price over $5.50, it has to decide whether it is worth going after a contract whose profitability will be marginal at best. At least if it wins the contract at $5.50, it has made a conscious decision to accept the lower profit. It has not won the contract because it mistakenly believed that $5.50 would generate the margins it desires.

With the Multiyear Costing/Pricing Template, Small-Time Manufacturing also has a mechanism for measuring the impact of changes in volume and/or timing during the execution of the contract. Customers have a tendency to overstate their anticipated volume and understate the interval of time before shipments will begin. What if the contract's total units fall short of the 150,000 anticipated and shipments are pushed back into the contract's later years? The template can be used to estimate the impact of such occurrences.

For example, if Small-Time's customer only purchases 130,000 units during the four-year period and the timing of shipments is 10,000 in Year 1, 20,000 in Year 2, 40,000 in Year 3, and 60,000 in Year 4, an initial unit price of $5.852 will not result in the desired 10% margin. Using the template, Small-Time can determine that, under such circumstances, the contract's margin would be only 8.9%. It would take an initial unit price of $5.925 to earn 10% under those conditions. If it anticipated that the customer may be over optimistic in its projections, maybe Small-Time should base its price on its own estimates of the likely volume and timing, not the customer's estimates. "The numbers," however, do not make that decision; management makes that decision. The information generated by the template provide accurate and relevant information that needs to be used as part of the decision making process.

What Small-Time Manufacturing has gained by going through this exercise is an accurate measurement of the relevant costs for this pricing decision. It has included all of the relevant cost factors. Changes in the company's volume and mix of activities during the term of the contract have been considered. Wage increases have been considered. Increases in the cost of supplies, fringe benefits, and other operating costs have been considered. But not only cost increases have been considered. Anticipated improvements in operating processes have been considered as have anticipated productivity improvements. All of the relevant factors that could impact the cost of executing the contract have been taken into account.

Some individuals with whom I have discussed this process have objected, saying that it is impossible to look into the future and estimate the economic changes and productivity improvements. What these individuals fail to realize is that whenever they make a long-term pricing decision, *they are estimating all of these factors.* The difference is that, without using a rational approach similar to the one outlined in this chapter, they are estimating them subconsciously. Their guesses, intuitive hunches, or "back of the envelope" calculations try to include them all without addressing them individually or measuring the impact they have on each other. It would be a talented individual, indeed, who could accurately forecast the cost of multiyear contract on a regular basis without "doing the details." I would much rather base the future of my company on a rational analysis of its cost and activities than on a general massaging of an undefined "blob" of costs.

SUMMARY

The long-term pricing commitments that are an important part of today's multiyear contracts require that an organization be able to look into the future, make realistic estimates of future events, and then measure the impact of those future events on its cost structure. Only then will the company have a sound basis on which to base its pricing decisions. An inappropriately priced multiyear contract has led to the downfall of many organizations.

Although no one can predict the future with 100% certainty, a thoughtful, structured estimate of future events provides an organization with a mechanism for planning a successful contract and then monitoring its progress as the contract proceeds. When the company knows one of the factors that is critical to the contract's success is going off plan, it can measure the impact and take corrective action. Picking a price and then saying a prayer provides no such mechanism.

An activity-based cost accumulation and distribution model supports the process in two ways. First, the ABC process itself identifies the activities, transactions, and events that need to be forecast if a rational projection of contract cost is to be made. Second, it provides the machine for taking those forecasts and turning them into estimates of "then year" costs and costing rates. Incorporating these into a multiyear costing and pricing template gives the company a powerful tool for effectively pricing long-term contracts or programs and then monitoring their progress as the contract or program is executed.

17

Impediments to Adopting Activity-Based Costing at the Small and Mid-Sized Organization

In recent years, the Cost Management Group of the Institute of Management Accountants (IMA) has conducted an annual Survey on Cost Management Methods and Activity-Based Costing (ABC). The results of these surveys are published each year in the January issue of *Cost Management Update*, the Cost Management Group's monthly newsletter. A consistent finding of these surveys is that large organizations adopt ABC far more frequently than small organizations. The 1996 survey, for example, revealed that sales of adopting firms averaged $101 to $500 million, whereas non-adopters sales were in the $11 to $100 million range. No mention was made of organizations whose sales were below $11 million, but I imagine that adoption in that group was almost nil. The report also indicated that "several companies cited the lack of resources (people and dollars) as a reason for not adopting ABC." It concludes that "this issue is probably most prevalent in smaller companies."

In the 13 years that I have been working with small and mid-sized companies to effectively incorporate modern cost management concepts in their decision-making processes, I have encountered a wide variety of impediments to the effective implementation of ABC at smaller organizations. Some of these impediments keep the firm from attempting ABC altogether, whereas others are impediments to its being used effectively once it has been adopted.

IMPEDIMENTS TO ATTEMPTING ABC

As mentioned in Cost Management Update's report on the 1996 survey, the lack of resources is apparently a smaller organization's major reason for not adopting ABC. Our experience has been that it is not the lack of resources that keeps small firms from adopting ABC, it the *perceived* lack of resources. Three other major reasons have also appeared regularly: entrepreneurial ego, the lack of decision costing skills, and a desire to be a settler, not a pioneer.

PERCEIVED LACK OF RESOURCES

Since the concept was given a name in the late 1980s, an industry has grown up around ABC. Special software packages have been created and are marketed through seminars and full-page advertisements in accounting publications. In-depth, scholarly articles by educators, consultants, and practitioners appear regularly in business periodicals. Costly seminars and conferences are held throughout the country. Large and small consulting and accounting firms become instant ABC experts and form their own ABC/ABM (activity-based management)/ABB (activity-based budgeting) groups. Word gets around about six-figure consulting fees, hundreds of person-days of work, massive data collection efforts, and expensive system conversions. No wonder smaller organizations believe that they do not have the resources to undertake a project to implement ABC!

Fortunately, this perception is incorrect. Unfortunately, most small organizations have yet to find out. As outlined in this book, ABC is a simple concept that can be adopted in a wide variety of ways. The complex, integrated systems devised by consultants and software companies are seldom appropriate at a smaller organization. The goal of ABC is to develop cost information that accurately reflects the relationships between costs, activities, and products or services. Sometimes, all that is required is that managers change the way they think. At other times, modifications must be made in the way the existing cost system works. Most often, personal computer spreadsheets can be developed to provide accurate and relevant cost information "offline." Only in rare instances does a smaller organization need to implement an ABC system.

In the second portion of this book, I have used the simple example of Small-Time Manufacturing as an ongoing case study. It is an organization with only four major operating activities. It has only 30 employees and $1.5 million in operating costs. Yet by applying the basic concepts of ABC and developing simple spreadsheet model that parallels the actual cost behavior of the organization, it has gained an understanding of its costs far beyond that which existed at the beginning of the case. It also created a powerful tool that it can use to provide accurate and relevant cost information for the myriad of decisions that are supported by cost information.

Assume that Small-Time Manufacturing had invested as much as $20,000 in the development of its activity-based model, an amount 50% to 100% higher than would probably be the case. Further assume that by using the model to support its pricing decisions, it avoided another contract like Contract #04 and won another contract like Contract #10. As shown in Chapter 14, this would have increased its profits by over $55,000. Even if no further benefits were realized, the investment would have been nominal and the return phenomenal. Of course, other benefits will continue to accrue if the model is used effectively making the return on the modest investment even greater.

Until managers of small organizations realize that ABC is a concept that is adopted, not a system that is implemented, the perceived lack of resources will continue to be a major impediment to its use. Once that impediment is overcome, however, and an activity-based view of costs is obtained, the benefits will be immeasurable.

ENTREPRENEURIAL EGO

One of the key characteristics of successful entrepreneurs is the ability to use their intuition and knowledge of their product and marketplace to make quick and effective decisions without a lot of facts. At some point in the evolution of every growing organization, however, "flying by the seat of the pants" ceases to be an effective way to make decisions.

Unfortunately, too many entrepreneurs cannot tell when they reach this point or refuse to admit to a decline in the quality of their decisions when they reach it. Although many continue to be successful, the thrust of their efforts changes from growing profitably to hanging on. Their business moves into the category of underachiever. The wrong products or services are emphasized. Investment funds are not directed into those areas where they will generate the highest return. Quite often, these companies continue to grow while their profits dwindle, or profits grow while return on investment dwindles. All the while, the entrepreneur finds external reasons for the decline in his or her organization's performance. They fail to comprehend that much of the problem is due to the ongoing implementation of decisions based on information that does not reflect reality.

Those entrepreneurs who do recognize the need for more sophisticated accounting information usually acquire the services of a financial professional to assist them in developing the information needed for them to make more effective decisions. Too often, however, the skills of the financial professional selected do not include effective decision costing skills.

LACK OF DECISION COSTING SKILLS

Top financial personnel at small organizations tend to have a general accounting, financial accounting, or tax background. This includes both employees and the outside certified public accountants (CPAs) who advise them. For years, such individuals have operated under the mistaken assumption that the primary purpose of cost information is to support the financial or tax accounting system. To them, using resources to improve the quality of cost information that is already adequate for its primary purpose is a poor use of the organization's time and money. In their view, if the information is good enough to value inventory and calculate cost of sales, it must be good enough to use in supporting management decisions.

These individuals, whose skills are strong in many other areas, do not understand the ramifications of using overgeneralized cost information in supporting management decisions and they tend to use cost information from the accounting system in situations where it is irrelevant.

On more than one occasion, experienced financial professionals have told me things like, "We don't charge setups to jobs because the customer won't pay for them," or "We don't need accurate product costs because the market determines the product's price." I have even had some tell me that they sometimes use contract labor instead of an employee on a job "because you don't have to charge overhead to the job when a contract laborer does it." Think about these comments. Does a cost not exist when a customer refuses to pay for it? Is it prudent for a company to take on a job at the market price even if it has no idea what it costs? When a contract laborer stands next to an employee performing the same job, do the utility, supervision, occupancy, and supply costs relate only to the employee?

The organization whose decision costing skills are poor cannot see when the tool it is using to make important management decisions is ineffective.

DESIRE TO BE A SETTLER, NOT A PIONEER

I frequently have opportunities to speak to business owners and managers at trade association meetings. Whether the association represents a special group of manufacturers, distributors, printers, or health care providers, I can predict the reaction of a significant group of attendees. After my session, they will invariably say, "This is powerful stuff. I hope they have you back to speak in a couple of years after some of our members have implemented ABC. I'll be anxious to see how it worked out and the impact it had on their business."

It is human nature to want someone else to do the pioneering work. Let them take the chances. Once they have solved the problems and perfected the process, I might follow. It is also a part of human nature that separates the exceptional performer from the also ran. Unfortunately for these settlers, it is the pioneers who will be using the new tool to exploit the marketplace, winning the good contracts, investing in equipment and technology with the greatest return, and otherwise "skimming the cream" while leaving the scraps for the settlers.

What is the risk of being a pioneer? It is the same risk that motorists run when they decide to use headlights at night instead of driving in the dark. Instead of not knowing where they are, where they are going, or what dangers lie ahead, they can clearly see the road and surrounding areas, making it possible for them to make the appropriate driving decisions.

IMPEDIMENTS TO SUCCEEDING WITH ABC

Once the impediments to attempting ABC have been overcome, there are still more impediments in the way of it becoming a successful management tool. These include the desire to be taught, not to learn, the lack of decision costing skills, and employee turnover.

DESIRE TO BE TAUGHT, NOT TO LEARN

Activity-based costing is not a mechanical process that can be taught; it is a concept that must be learned. Too often, organizations that have recognized the inadequacies of their existing cost information and are willing to spend money and time to implement ABC, are unwilling to expend the intellectual energy required to learn it. They will enthusiastically participate in meetings, gather data, and learn the mechanics of the software or model, but they will not make the intellectual effort needed to gain the sound understanding of ABC's core principles that will enable them to look at all future cost issues through the lens of ABC. The result of this situation is usually an effective tool for using ABC that is underutilized at first and that eventually becomes ineffective through neglect.

The intellectual investment in ABC is many times more important than the physical investment. An organization that does not have an ABC system but understands ABC and looks at decisions through the lens of

ABC is much better off than one that has a sophisticated ABC system, but has not mastered the concept and its uses. Unfortunately, the sign Thomas A. Edison kept in his office is too true: "It is remarkable to what lengths people will go to avoid thought."

LACK OF DECISION COSTING SKILLS

The lack of decision costing skills can sometimes be overcome as an impediment to attempting ABC. Unfortunately, this impediment often reveals itself later, causing many of those firms implementing ABC to make the transition from a firm that did not know how to use bad cost information effectively to one that does not know how to use good cost information effectively.

Although these firms can accurately determine the fully absorbed cost of its core products and services and the incremental costs of various possible courses of action, they continue to lack the ability to determine what cost information is relevant for what decisions and how to merge that cost information with other relevant decision considerations to support the decision making process. For this reason, their powerful new tool is underutilized, misused, or both.

EMPLOYEE TURNOVER

Employee turnover occurs in all organizations, but its impact on the smaller organization is much greater because the percentage of a firm's required skills resident in one individual is much higher at the small firm that at the large one. For example, the loss of a controller who has mastered ABC at a small company will have a more serious impact on the continued effective use of the concept than the loss of a controller at a larger firm at which an assistant controller and cost manager have also mastered ABC. Similarly, the departure of a small firm's plant or sales manager who has learned how to use ABC information effectively will have a more serious impact than at a larger firm where "ABC" wise subordinates can continue its effective use even if the manager is replace by someone from outside the company.

The employee turnover problem has even become an impediment during the implementation process itself. During a 13 week implementation project, we have seen up to half of an implementation team (four of eight employees) leave the client company for higher-paying jobs elsewhere. At a plant of one multilocation manufacturer, the industrial engineer and controller (the two key players in implementing ABC at the plant) were promoted to positions at other facilities less that three weeks before the project's scheduled completion. The industrial engineer was replaced with a very capable one hired from outside of the organization who had never even heard of ABC, and the controller was replaced from outside the organization with one that had heard a little about ABC but had never before worked at a manufacturing firm. In another case, we had to conduct an ABC course for a client one year after a project was completed because of an 80% turnover in key management positions during the intervening period.

When key employees at smaller firms are replaced by individuals from outside the organization, they tend to bring the ideas that made them successful at their old company along with them. If they came from a non-ABC environment, the job of selling ABC begins all over again. In more than one instance, we have seen a controller who has mastered ABC replaced by one with no ABC background. Soon after the new controller's arrival, ABC costing practices have been replaced with out-of-date, inaccurate, and irrelevant practices used by the controller at his or her previous company.

SUMMARY

These are just some of the impediments to the successful adoption of ABC at the smaller firm. Those that are imaginary, such as the lack of resources, can be overcome by emphasizing the fact that ABC is not mechanical system but a concept that can be incorporated into a firm's decision-making process in a wide variety of ways. Those that are real must be addressed by increasing emphasis on *decision costing* skills in both academic and continuing education programs and by continually updating implementation methodologies to overcome the real world "people and personality" impediments that exist in the field.

18

Making Activity-Based Costing Work at the Small and Mid-Sized Business

"As part of modern industrial organization the importance of cost accounting can hardly be overestimated. At the same time there is perhaps no part regarding which so little is known." "Care must be exercised that the [cost] system installed is not too complex and that the cost of securing the detailed information is not greater than the gain that may result from its possession." "Complexity is no assurance of accuracy." All of these statements are as true today as they were when they were written over 80 years ago. They are taken from a work titled *Modern Business Texts—Vol. 12: Cost Finding* that was written by Dexter S. Kimball of Cornell University and published by the Alexander Hamilton Institute in 1915. The sad part is that they are true even after a decade of activity-based costing (ABC).

Great cost information will rarely make a company great, but inadequate cost information will certainly prevent an otherwise great organization from achieving superior results. It might even cause disaster by leading the company to take actions that are totally opposite those that it would have taken had its cost information been accurate and relevant. Accurate and relevant cost information is crucial to the quality of a company's decisions. Along with inadequate financing, the absence of accurate and relevant cost information is probably one of the leading reasons for the high turnover among small companies. In a highly competitive, complex world where every customer wants customized products and services, a company has to make sure that its portfolio of business covers its costs and provides the desired profit or return if it is to thrive and grow in the future.

There is a joke among auto industry suppliers that "the contract goes to the company that makes the biggest mistake." Unfortunately, it is not really a joke. During the past decade, I have seen numerous auto industry suppliers that were ecstatic to receive the contract that later drove them out of business. If you go back to Chapter 7 and look at Exhibit 7.3, you can picture those contracts at the far left-hand side of the graph: contracts with built-in losses. Now picture those contracts as being long term, with 4% annual price reductions. Pretty scary stuff isn't it?

Unfortunately, even after 10 years of ABC, business executives still seem to be more ignorant in the area of cost information and how to use it effectively than in any other area of their business' operation. Activity-based costing experts have emphasized software packages, process mapping, massive data collection efforts, integrated systems, and computational virtuosity, ignoring the fact that "complexity is no assurance of accuracy." Small business owners and managers have been wise enough to know that the cost of implementing an ABC system is probably "greater than the gain that may result from its possession," but instead of following another course and developing accurate and relevant cost information that has business utility, most have done nothing. They continue to "fly blind."

As outlined in this book, the accurate and relevant cost information that decision makers at small and mid-sized businesses need to make fact-based business decisions is more comprehensive, yet less complex, that one would think after 10 years of ABC propaganda. It is more comprehensive in that more must be changed than simply the way costs are allocated and then charged to products and services. It is less complex in that the way costs are allocated and then charged to products and services does not need to be as complicated as ABC experts imply, special software is not mandatory, and conversion of the day-to-day accounting system is seldom required.

The major investment required for the adoption of ABC at a small or mid-sized business is intellectual. Decision makers must be able to view the organization's costs through the lens of ABC, they must understand the difference between true economic costs and the costs recorded in the general ledger, and they must learn to use cost information appropriately. For very small companies, this might be all the investment required. Business decisions will be improved because the "brainware" of the company has improved. The thought processes followed by the company's decision makers parallel the actual cost behavior of the organization.

As an organization grows, improved "brainware" must be supplemented by improved "number crunching" capabilities. Decision makers understand cost behavior, but a tool is required to actually make the calculations. This is where a cost accumulation and distribution model becomes a necessity. A model that does not rely on general ledger costs and that is flexible enough to determine both incremental and fully absorbed costs becomes the tool for developing accurate cost information to support all types of business decisions.

Only when an organization becomes very large might an integrated ABC system prove valuable. An integrated system is, however, the portion of ABC that constitutes 80% of the cost but provides only 20% of the benefits. For a smaller organization, that 20% will seldom be enough to justify the expenditure.

In Exhibit 18.1, the cases of four companies are considered, one with sales of $5 million, one with sales of $10 million, one with sales of $50 million, and one with sales of $100 million. In these cases, we will assume that decisions and actions based on activity-based cost information will improve each company's bottom line by 1% of sales. We will further assume that 40% of this savings can be attained by the first 5% of the investment (the intellectual investment), 40% can be attained by the next 15% of investment (developing a cost accumulation and distribution model), and the final 20% by implementing a fully integrated ABC system. The assumed investments, which include consulting fees, software, and the company's internal resources, are based on proposals received by our clients from "Big 6" and other ABC consultants during the past decade. As can be seen in the exhibit, the returns for all four companies are tremendous for the first 20% of the investment. Only when company size gets very large do the benefits from an ABC system begin to justify the expenditure.

Consider example case of Small-Time Manufacturing. At the beginning of the case, it had a very rudimentary method of calculating costs.

Exhibit 18.1 Return from ABC Investments—Companies of Various Sizes

Company sales	$5,000,000	$10,000,000	$50,000,000	$100,000,000
1% Benefit	$50,000	$100,000	$500,000	$1,000,000
Investment	$150,000	$200,000	$250,000	$300,000
5% Investment	$7,500	$10,000	$12,500	$15,000
40% Benefit	$20,000	$40,000	$200,000	$400,000
Return on investment	266.7%	400.0%	1600.0%	2666.7%
15% Investment	$22,500	$30,000	$37,500	$45,000
40% Benefit	$20,000	$40,000	$200,000	$400,000
Return on investment	88.9%	133.3%	533.3%	888.9%
80% Investment	$120,000	$160,000	$200,000	$240,000
20% Benefit	$10,000	$20,000	$100,000	$200,000
Return on investment	8.3%	12.5%	50.0%	83.3%

Products were costed by rates based on direct labor and total cost input, and no tool existed for calculating incremental costs for decisions not supported by fully absorbed costing rates. Those decisions had to be supported by special analyses on an as-needed basis.

In adopting ABC, the company first made the required intellectual investment to develop a cost flow-down structure that was an accurate (not precise) representation of its actual cost behavior. It then created a simple, computer spreadsheet-based cost accumulation and distribution model that paralleled the intellectual model. No "brain surgery" or "rocket science" was involved. The model provided it with a tool to better understand contract profitability, making it possible to better manage its portfolio of contracts. The process and model highlighted areas where actions could be taken to increase capacity and reduce costs. The model gave it the capability to properly evaluate special orders, capital expenditure opportunities, make/buy decisions, and other decisions requiring accurate and relevant cost information. It made it possible to accurately measure future costs under different sets of assumptions. It provided the basis for a multiyear costing model that made it possible to better price and control multiyear contracts. In short, Small-Time Manufacturing developed the costing tools necessary for it to thrive and grow into the future. It will not be a company in which inadequate cost information will prevent an otherwise great organization from achieving superior results.

All this and it did not implement an ABC system. The accounting mechanics and spreadsheet techniques employed in the design and development of the model were not difficult to comprehend or implement. There was no mysterious "black box" that took data on one end and printed out an unexplained answer at the other end. No complex software was required. It simply analyzed its activities in a logical, structured way, organized those activities into a cost flow-down structure that reflected actual cost behavior, and built a model that paralleled that structure using basic computer spreadsheet techniques.

The theories, principles, and mechanics described in this book apply to all organizations, regardless of their purpose or size. They apply to manufacturers, trade associations, distributors, advertising agencies, auto dealerships, insurance companies, law firms, and hospitals. They apply to $100 thousand-per-year organizations and $100 billion-per-year organizations. The very smallest might find that intuition provides the answers without calculating actual cost data. The very largest might prefer more detailed information. The vast majority of businesses, however, fall into the small and mid-sized category. They are too large to be run by intuition and too small to create and handle masses of detailed information. The approach described in this book provides these organizations with an understandable and affordable method of gaining the relevant and accurate cost information that will be needed to prosper and grow in the next millennium without investing outrageous amounts of time and money for unneeded ABC systems.

Small-Time Manufacturing was able to capitalize on the improved cost information provided by ABC without spending a small fortune. So were Acme Distributors, Road Shows, Inc., Sunshine Flowers, and scores of other small and mid-sized companies. Now your company can too.

Index